GERMANIA

Also by Simon Winder

The Man Who Saved Britain

AS EDITOR
Night Thoughts
Sea Longing
The Feast
'My Name's Bond . . .'

Simon Winder

GERMANIA

A Personal History of Germans Ancient and Modern

PICADOR

First published 2010 by Picador

First published in paperback 2010 by Picador

This edition first published 2010 by Picador
an imprint of Pan Macmillan, a division of Macmillan Publishers Limited
Pan Macmillan, 20 New Wharf Road, London N1 9RR
Basingstoke and Oxford
Associated companies throughout the world
www.panmacmillan.com

ISBN 978-0-330-53628-8

For Felix

'What things there are to see, if we can only get away from our own fireside!'

Joseph von Eichendorff, *Life of a Good-for-Nothing*

'Watch out! Historical steps!'

Sign on a slightly uneven staircase at Luther's birthplace in Eisleben

Contents

Contents

Contents

Germany

North Sea

Kiel

Lübeck

Hamburg

Wilhelmshaven

Bremen

Lüneburg

R. Elbe

Oldenburg

NETHERLANDS

Amsterdam

R. Ems

R. Weser

Osnabrück

Hannover

Brandenburg

Hildesheim

Braunschweig

Münster

Wolfenbüttel

Magdeburg

Goslar

Halberstadt

Wittenberg

Quedlinburg

Dessau

Essen

Dortmund

Harz Mtns

Düsseldorf

Ruhr

Eisleben

Halle

Wuppertal

Kassel

Mühlhausen

Leipzig

Brussels

Cologne

Naumburg

BELGIUM

Aachen

Erfurt

Weimar

Altenburg

Bonn

Königswinter

Eisenach

Gotha

Jena

Gera

Koblenz

Marburg

Zwickau

Greiz

Franconia

Thuringian Woods

Coburg

R. Mosel

Wiesbaden

Frankfurt-am-Main

LUXEM-BOURG

Mainz

R. Main

Bamberg

Trier

Darmstadt

Würzburg

Worms

Weikersheim

Mannheim

Speyer

Heidelburg

Ansbach

Nuremberg

Karlsruhe

Schwäbisch Hall

Regensburg

Nancy

Schwäbisch Gmünd

R. Danube

Strasbourg

R. Rhine

Stuttgart

Ingolstadt

FRANCE

Swabia

Ulm

Augsburg

Freiburg

Munich

Dijon

R. Saône

Basel

Zürich

R. Inn

Bern

Innsbruck

A U

SWITZERLAND

ITALY

The sixteen Länder and their capital cities

Introduction

'Bound with chains of flowers'

I have spent many years chewing over German history and this book is an entirely personal response to it. Dozens of visits to Germany and Austria form the core of *Germania*. It is an attempt to tell the story of the Germans starting from their notional origins in the sort of forests enjoyed by gnomes and heroes and ending at the time of Hitler's seizure of power, by way of my own thoughts about what I have seen, read and found interesting. Of course people travel for different reasons and what I find bewitching someone else may well find stupefying. If, for some, travel is a chance to admire Counter-Reformation altarpieces and for others a chance for a one-on-one roughhouse with a Dortmund transsexual, then these are possibly irreconcilable priorities – although they could intersect in some of the less bustling regional museums. It is therefore built into this book that I will bore or alienate some readers – but I hope not too many. *Germania* is designed to be an entertainment – although I hope the implications of some of what I am saying are reasonably thought-provoking.

Germany is a sort of Dead Zone today. Its English-speaking visitors tend to be those with professional reasons for being there – soldiers, historians, builders. One of the amusements at Frankfurt airport is seeing baffled little clumps of British recent ex-students in special dark suits waiting for planes – given jobs by German banks purely because they are part of, in evolutionary terms, an alarmingly un-diverse band who had happened to study German at university, their career choice based on a facility with languages rather than being able to, say, count, flatter clients or take smart decisions.

Germany is shunned for a very good reason – the enormity of its actions in part of the last century. But is there perhaps a point when this quarantine becomes too mutilating to Europe's culture, when in effect it allows Hitler's estimation of his own country to prevail? This book is, of course, soaked in the disaster of the Third Reich, but by beginning in those ancient forests and ending when he seizes power in 1933, I want to get round the Führer and try to reclaim a bit of Europe which is in many ways Britain's weird twin, and which for almost all of its history has been no less attractive and no more or less admirable than many other countries. Germany is a place without which European culture makes no sense, and for over sixty years Germans have been working strenuously to rebuild that culture in a way that, while admitting the legacy of the Third Reich, allows that earlier past to shine again.

The book is in chronological order, although the Roman and medieval bits veer around alarmingly and are as much about why later Germans were so obsessed with these periods as they are about the periods themselves. Every attempt has been made to avoid a mere sequence of dreary dynastic events. The chronology is less oppressive than it might be because I take regular time-outs to talk about music, fairy tales, alcohol and so on. But where did this interest come from?

Some families relish action and adventure, others are perhaps more passive. Growing up, I – like all children – assumed that my own family was just like any other – that we in fact provided a benchmark by which other families were more rambunctious than ourselves or more snobbish or more gloomy. Looking back from the slightly more comparative heights of adulthood, my family (myself included) now strike me as almost crazily inert. Months would go by with effectively no form of activity whatsoever. We would engage in a restricted range of household chores, but otherwise my parents and my younger sisters and I lived, in our west Kent idyll, in a sort of enchanted castle of torpor. My mother disapproved of any form of exercise so we had no bicycles and, despite having a large garden, I had a clear sense that it was probably a mistake to go outside at all, with its lack of comfortable chairs and reading lamps. Occasionally my father would battle to mow the moss-clogged lawn, but I certainly never volunteered to help and the garden always won. Once a summer we would stir ourselves sufficiently to have lunch outside, but my sisters and I would take turns to be alarmed by wasps, something would always get spilled and the conversation would tend to veer acrimoniously in wrong directions. My hatred for all forms of sport – stemming of course from incompetence – put the final lid on. While we were busy in the usual ways during the school term, the weekends and holidays seemed to drift by in a genial slough of inaction. This background is necessary to understand the sheer drama and excitement of my first encounter with Germanness, the unintended pivot that changed the direction of my life.

Looking back I think my father was a little frustrated by the general housebound stasis. He liked to do DIY and had run and fenced at school. His one great surprise was that he was in the Royal Naval Reserve. This was a commitment he began shortly before meeting my mother and she always hated it as it meant that for two weeks of the year he would disappear with an irritating combination of nonchalance and patriotism, while she had to deal with a pile of needy if unvigorous children. How I loved his annual trip. He would go on nuclear submarines, minesweepers, aircraft carriers (the *Ark Royal!*), fly as a passenger in Phantom fighter-bombers. Clearly the whole thing was a laugh, and because the Cold War never went anywhere, it simply became a government-paid-for way to eat huge fatty breakfasts, wear a devastatingly lovely uniform, drink a lot and fire guns. He wound up with the James Bond rank of commander, with a gorgeous peaked cap and a jacket festooned at the cuff with the sort of gold-stitching that makes fighting wars almost worthwhile. He would send me occasional, curtly mysterious postcards with suitable pictures of jets and missiles and stuff, which gave me a cumulative, phony credibility at my boarding school.

So, as may be imagined, there was what could potentially be viewed as a creative tension in the household between the day-today cheerful somnolence and the secret two-week burst of apparent action and adventure enjoyed by my father. Our annual family holidays were always very happy events, almost always in France, every now and then (and much less happily) in Scotland or Wales, depending on how much money was around. In France we usually and sensibly went to the seaside, staying in little rented houses, and while the ferry journey was an epic of vomiting and distress, these trips to Brittany or Normandy were genuine idylls – sunshine, child-friendly food, just enough sightseeing and small museums to be tolerable, regular intakes of ice-cream.

But one year, when I was aged fourteen, this all changed. I have never quite dared confront my father with why he thought this was a good idea – at some level I can see why, of course, but it implied such an absolute failure to understand the weakness of the human materials at hand that it leaves me at a loss. In any event, he decided that we should go on a barge holiday to Alsace and Lorraine, taking a week to chunter along a canal to Strasbourg. Once there he would get a taxi back to our car and we would all go on to a holiday house in the Alsatian countryside.

The objections to this were considerable. The sheer lack of coast was a bit perplexing – holidays, by definition, were on the fringe of the land and Alsace and Lorraine were almost aggressively not. As a parent now myself I can see this as a wholly legitimate cry for help. Slumped on beach after beach, part of a colossal herd of bored adults, I will routinely fantasize about taking everyone off to Chad or Missouri for a holiday – a dream of inland, of an environment not shaped by the tyranny of the salty margin. But at the time we were all incredulously unable to deal with what might have been going through my father's head.

Of course the whole thing was not improved by my being in the middle of a grim, sulky, epicene sort of phase – an adolescent extension of my childhood inertia. Everything was too much trouble, too much fuss, but also everything was insufficiently glamorous or intellectually aspiring. Indeed it is, on reflection, quite possible that my parents gleefully conspired to come up with a holiday that would do most humiliating damage to my little fort of self-regard.

Burping along in a tiny boat down a reeking canal through an almost featureless bit of scarred eastern French landscape may have been a joke on a scale I have never managed to grasp.

The whole trip was a predictable disaster. My father stalked the bridge like a trainee version of the grizzled Captain McWhirr in Conrad's *Typhoon*, or a general sort of Conradian amalgam, grimly breasting aside Fate, thinking how nice it would be if only he could harbour some dark secret or had some hidden flaw which a crisis would fatally show up. He had the part down pat, but alas his crew, far from being the swarming, nimble lascars of his imagination, consisted of me and my younger sisters. I proved of limited value as the morning mist on the water turned out to give me a migraine, so I would lie below decks with multi-coloured thread-worms flowing through my eyes, listlessly reading an early Anita Brookner novel between bouts. My sisters were slightly more helpful but obsessed with keeping their gorgeously patterned holiday trousers from getting dirty. Each time we reached a lock we all leapt around, heaving on a variety of stanchions, nauseated by the filthy water, squealing as wet ropes slapped about. Memorably a dead rat bobbing in the lock water, inflated with gas like a bolster, burst as we incompetently crashed the barge into the concrete side wall. We were always letting go of the wrong ropes or heaving on the wrong side, my father once having to take emergency action (a Conrad-style life test that could not be failed!) as the ropes remained tied on one side of the lock and, as the water level rapidly went down, the boat threatened to be left hanging on its side from the top of the lock – presumably only for a few moments before the ropes snapped under the immense weight and we crashed to the lock's bottom, leaving nothing to remember us by but a sodden copy of Anita Brookner's *A Start in Life*.

The real sufferer in all this was, as ever, my mother. It is an odd feature of so many holidays that they are structured around having far worse facilities for cooking and cleaning than at home. So the expression of festive family special time becomes having a single little hot plate, or no washing machine. Every summer, the world fills with individuals huddled in houses, boats and caravans, cursing a tiny gas flame and battered pot, unable to express any of the creativity which was so often a key to our shared existence. Perversely, holidays therefore dull down the heart of family life and leave only tins of soup, spaghetti and pieces of ham. This was certainly the case in our ill-starred barge. My mother was an exuberant, complex chef, but here she was catastrophically reined in. Like some woefully uninvolving card game, each meal was played out within the same set of desperate, narrow variants. Aware of this, my mother was in a permanent rage – she had not asked to chug through grey countryside on a filthy, evil-smelling, dwarf, shunned, freshwater cousin of the Good Ship *Lollipop*.

Of course, the canal cutting through a haggardly agricultural landscape and in itself harbouring frequent stagnant patches, the stage set for our barge generated a constantly changing, but massive, chorus of insects. These came in every size – seemingly fitting neatly, like keys, through different sizes of crack in the boat. The evenings were intolerable, as we grimly munched through the usual spaghetti with bits of ham and an incredible, almost Pandoran pile of flying creatures filled the room, the air thick with the reek of useless anti-mosquito smoke and the desperate, if artful, screams of my sisters. It must have been an enjoyable sight for any passing Alsatian labourer at the end of a day of toil, to see the barge rocking at its moorings, glowing with insect-attracting light, smelling strangely of Italian cooking and giving off a rich blend of buzzes, shrieks and moans.

In any event as we steadily headed eastward I little realized that I was, very slowly, being injected into the Germanic lands which have now occupied me for more than a quarter of a century; through what at the time seemed a sodden, dull part of the world, but which had been fought over by the French and Germans for centuries and in which hardly a field had not been the arena for some awful war, with everyone from Louis XIV to Patton passing through. My ignorance shielded me as, in the trip's low point, we turned a bend in the canal, looking forward to reaching Strasbourg the next morning, only to find a tunnel, blocked up with mangy old planks clearly of great age and a massive sign proclaiming that the canal was closed – and must have been for some years. I never worked out the source of this spectacular failure of communication, but we returned to the nearest lock and abandoned the stupid barge. My father sheepishly tracked down a taxi via the lock-keeper; this took him the startlingly short distance back to the car and we then all drove on in comfort, style and speed. What happened to the barge I will never know – perhaps we were the last people poorly informed enough to use it. We stayed in a hotel for a night, resolved never to go on an action holiday again, and then moved on to our tiny house in the Alsatian countryside. I had arrived.

It would be good to imply that being in Alsace was a sort of instant revelation to me, but to be honest it was more just a puzzle. We had not asked for a holiday on some world-historical fault line, but just for the usual sort of jolly vacation cottage in France generally demanded by English families. On the first morning we capered down, as traditional, to get croissants only to find that there was only a sort of crusty roll available. The houses looked funny too. If English towns were my unthinking baseline and French towns the exotic variant, then these houses fitted with neither – their whole vocabulary was just subtly wrong. The village's name was also a little confusing: Wolfskirchen. Settling down the first morning while my father negotiated with the heavily whiskered old lady in a bulky house-coat who owned the house, there were further oddities. Her French was almost unintelligible and she clearly spoke something else to other people in her little shop. Her offer of a glass of schnapps to my father (this was about eight in the morning) also seemed to cross some sort of line – particularly when he, driven on as ever by the needs of politeness, drank three in quick succession, thereby putting the rest of the day on a rather odd footing.

As with almost all important events, the significance only becomes clear in retrospect – but I do remember throwing Anita aside and becoming immediately much more alert. Walking around the mournful tunnels of the Maginot Line with its empty gun emplacements and a long-deserted underground canteen painted with elaborate Mickey Mouse murals by bored French troops in the 1930s was perhaps goad enough for anyone with a potential curiosity about historical events: the expression in millions of tons of concrete that Alsace was eternally, if intermittently, French. An afternoon in Baden-Baden, the nearest German town, was another. My parents had never been to Germany before and were patently uneasy with the whole idea – not helped by my sisters and I wandering through the streets yelling 'Dummkopf!' and 'Achtung!' at each other and whistling the Great Escape music in a way that probably didn't promote post-war healing.

The real surprise was Strasbourg, which we at last visited, sensibly using the car. It really did seem something new to me. I was probably at a vulnerable age, but Strasbourg's grandeur and the sense it had of belonging to a culture I did not understand gave it a strange clarity in my mind. Like some acne-laden Kentish Goethe, I had arrived. Wandering around the extraordinary cathedral museum was the first occasion when I realized I had an aesthetic sense. There is a famous double sculpture there, brought down from the cathedral's facade, of a simpering maiden being offered an apple by a finely dressed and winning man. As you walk around the back of the male statue you can see that his cloak is decorated with toads and other loathsome creatures. I remember spending ages staring at this statue and being thrilled to be back in Strasbourg a couple of days later, allowing me to look at it again. This was also my first encounter with those late medieval paintings of Adam and Eve before and after the Fall – 'after' showing them as repulsive, tortured semi-corpses.

The cathedral itself again had a different atmosphere – Gothic but odd. For me its unbeatable centrepiece was the astronomical clock – a monstrous nineteenth-century confection clinging to one wall, featuring at midday a skeleton beating out the time on drums, a cock crowing in remembrance of Peter's denying Jesus and an unworkable jumble of mechanical pagan and Christian elements (Juno in a little chariot, various Apostles) cavorting around to Death's drum. And so my art sense was born: evil creatures lurking in a cloak, plague-derived Grand Guignol, dusty mechanical toys. This all now seems so long ago and yet thirty years on I cannot say I have progressed much, still clinging to a sort of ghost-train aesthetic, despite any number of failed attempts to haul myself onto the higher ground of Beauty.

Looking back, and knowing a little bit more, Strasbourg Cathedral is what you would expect to find – a hybrid German– French building, showing in itself Alsace's tragic inability to be clearly definable as belonging to one nationalism or another. I became more and more interested in the area and found myself reading more and more. So what started with rat-filled canal locks and an odd lack of croissants ended in an adult life reading voraciously around the subject, editing (my real job) many history books about Germany and having countless conversations with historians, an unmethodical but zealous immersion that has resulted in this book.

I come, though, with a tragic flaw. In the dystopic waiting room that is one's forties it is possible to be quite serene on the language issue. I am reconciled to being useless at languages in the same way that I am now reconciled to dying *still* unable to identify tree species or remember phone numbers. But for many years I charged at language after language in the manner of someone running up against some massively barred and studded fortress door: Italian, Latin, Spanish, French, Russian, Arabic (in a moment of lunatic lack of self-knowledge), German, Ancient Greek – a catalogue of complete pointlessness. On a conservative estimate I must have spent over a thousand hours of my childhood in Latin lessons – a magnificent grounding in that tongue and the sort of steady application that takes full advantage of the sponge-like absorbency of the young mind. In an adult spasm of masochism I recently bought *Teach Yourself Latin* which, to my total dismay, showed that eight years of Latin lessons had actually only got me about twenty-five pages into a three-hundred-page book. This hopelessness extended everywhere – Italian, Spanish and French were always doomed simply because they were taught at school. I have some vague memory of being castigated in a French lesson aged eleven or so for having spent much of the lesson trying to fill my pen cap with saliva. Spanish and Italian were exam subjects of which I now have no memory at all.

Russian, Arabic and German were different because they were actively self-motivated. Trying to learn Russian was stupid – a humiliation but a short-lived one. Arabic was more serious. I had spent some time in the Middle East selling books and became completely enamoured of cultural Islam, souks and sand – but above all the shape of the letters and their artistic use. Given that I had a clear block on all language learning I'm not sure really *what* I was thinking. I was living in New York at the time and it is possible I had erroneously felt a sense of opportunity in the air. I trooped into my evening class at New York University and happy hours curling, looping and dotting followed. Many in the group were Lebanese-American men who, in their twenties, were suffering a legitimate pang of anxiety about their loss of family roots. It was curious to see the difficulties they immediately crashed into – the sense that they had some genetic relationship with Arabic which would allow it naturally to flow with a little work, a relationship which in practice did not exist at all. They had no more of a leg-up on this fiendish language than I did, with my head fizzing with images of hookahs, divans and minarets. In any event, after a perfect term learning the wonderful script there was an awful awakening – Arabic beyond the alphabet turned out to be even worse than French. My attention wandered – I may even have toyed with seeing how quickly I could fill my pen cap with saliva. So another language bit the dust and I was left with the (very briefly) amusing trick of showing friends what their names looked like in rough Arabic transcription.

There was an unhappy sequel to this. I still vividly remember wandering around the abbey of St-Denis, north of Paris, where all the French kings were buried, and vowing to improve my knowledge of medieval monarchs. I had the sequence down from 1550 or so (everyone's called Louis, in order, with a handful of easily remembered, vivid exceptions) – but the huge accumulation of earlier people called Louis or Charles was a tangle. This was when I realized the limits of the human brain. I had always assumed

I could indefinitely add stuff – battles, capital cities, dynasties. As I loaded up those Merovingian and Capetian kings I felt my brain, like some desperately rubbish, home-assembled bathroom shelf, lurch suddenly to one side, and all the Arabic alphabet fall off the other end. Shortly after that the whole thing came off the wall, taking the pointless Merovingians with it too.

So I reeled into my adult life with a virtual language blank, beyond an ability to order beer or ask for train platform numbers. I can see in my mind all my teachers: stern, bland, desirable, desiccated, impatient, prim, fiery, resigned, bitter, bilious, despairing. It is an enjoyable exercise, in fact: faces, mannerisms, bodies all so clearly recalled by my brain's purring visual functions – a stark contrast to the crashed spaceship that is the bit dealing with languages.

It was then that I encountered German. By this point in my adult life even at my most delusive I could see that I had a problem with languages. I was resigned to always flunk Tlingit, say, or Miao – but perhaps through sheer effort I could land one mainstream European language and not remain trapped in the roomy but over-familiar cage of English. Ever since that teenage visit to Strasbourg my enthusiasm for German history and literature had grown and grown. Thomas Bernhard, Joseph Roth and Günter Grass were my heroes, and it was time to be serious at last about engaging with their work and the real version of the words they had written.

And so I embarked on the last great language adventure. Thinking about it now, intellectually it seemed to be the equivalent of one of those grizzled, independent-minded medieval German warlords who, pondering too long in his isolated castle, decides to go on one final raid, having already lost most of his best hounds, horses and sons on earlier outings, galloping down to the plains in a hopeless yet honourable bid to die, yet live on in story.

Galloping into New York University again I remember being oddly buoyant and cheerful about the whole business: a new exercise book, a new language, nicely sharpened pencils. Quite quickly I ran into the usual problems – like not really understanding anything. The individual words were as sonorous and magnificent as

I'd hoped and many hours were spent rolling them over my tongue and getting what I imagined to be a rather wonderful accent. However: they knocked on the door and they rang on the bell, but Mr Language was not at home. After a term the only real breakthrough was when there was a flurry at the door and Roland Gift, formerly of the Fine Young Cannibals, was ushered into the classroom through one door and then out the other – to avoid his fans: or, more plausibly by that point, to avoid imaginary fans. In any event, happy minutes were spent thinking, 'That *really* was Roland Gift,' while issues of sentence structure drifted along in the background.

There followed a fruitless few months with four other students and a Latvian dancer who was gamely attempting to use language lessons to construct a financial rope bridge between her free-form-dance-explosion income and her Village rental outgoing. These lessons were as futile as the rest, but on the subway each morning and evening I would practise by reading Heine's poems, with a crib, and became absolutely obsessed with the German language and its beauties even as my brain continued to be wrongly structured for any absorptive work. I do not know now why I chose Heine – probably just as a random find in a bookstore, in an edition that did not appear threateningly long. My head filled with Moorish princes, ivy-clad castles, sea-ghosts and roses. I would plunge along each day on the N train, unable even to manage the simplest German idioms but, with a faltering confidence, articulate enough to say that my lance and shield were stolen and my love had bound me up with chains of flowers. Once I started my wanderings around Germany I kept crossing Heine's path and he has since always stood for everything attractive and thoughtful – but I really think that my making him my mentor was an accident, and my view of Germany could equally have been shaped by other more malign, grandiloquent or stuffy figures. In any event, Heine may walk by my side, but we are unable to talk to each other.

Regensburg is a small German city on the upper Danube, tucked into a corner of eastern Bavaria and well on the way to Austria. It remains medieval in an almost cartoonish form, with its Gothic cathedral, its swaggering merchants' houses, narrow alleys with cute and obscure names and, above all, the great bridge. By building a fortified stone bridge over the Danube, by having a town at the only point where, thanks to an island, this was feasible, by defending it over the centuries against all comers and charging everyone for going over it or round it, the Regensburgers became rich, controlling the trade between Northern Europe and Venice. The simplicity of their cunning and good fortune gives their town a happy, daft quality.

The huge piers of the bridge cause chaos for the Danube's flow, which is sedately implacable on one side and a dangerous cauldron on the other. The pleasure of this sight is much enhanced by the surviving medieval watchtower and salt depot, and a tiny, ancient bratwurst restaurant, saturated inside by smoking grills and steaming sinks. I had been chatting by this restaurant to a cheerful couple from Rottweil who, after a few minutes, nudged each other and in some embarrassment asked: 'So: why are you *here*?' They were happy to visit Regensburg themselves but could not understand what someone English could be doing there – and it was true that over several days I had bumped into nobody English and only a couple of Americans, and these were retired veterans who had once been stationed in Germany. It was as though Regensburg's amazing cathedral, a shop selling potatoes made from marzipan, a Roman wall, the site of Napoleon's headquarters, the former assembly chamber of the Holy Roman Empire and an amusing medieval torture chamber could simply not be legitimate sources of interest for non-Germans. Later, standing on the quay by the bridge, rocking on my heels, contentedly staring at the great whirlpools, thinking of where the Danube had come from, and where it went on to, bratwurst in a crusty roll in hand, it suddenly seemed impossible not to set out to write a book that might convey something of this lost country.

A note on Germany and German

The modern states of Germany and Austria only cover part of the historic German land. The entire course of Germanic history has been an argument about poorly defined borders, sometimes with the most terrible consequences. I have, with a handful of self-indulgent exceptions, restricted this book to modern borders as it is within them that there are the towns and landscapes which remain a live issue for Germans themselves. Historically the areas now called Germany and Austria have been so entangled that I generally do not differentiate between them. A different book could have been written that encompassed everything from Zürich to the land of the remaining Volga Germans, and I would love to have written it, but it would have been at least twice as long and even more chaotic than what you are holding.

It is impossible to be consistent with German names, as at different times specific names have sunk into the English-speaking conscious one way or another. In the case of cities, to refer to München, Wien or Köln would be unhelpful and pretentious. In the case of individuals, where there is not a universal English usage I have always used German. Frederick the Great, Maria Theresa, Charlemagne and Charles V all stay familiar, but otherwise everyone gets to keep their German name. The Emperor means the Holy Roman Emperor and, after 1804, the Emperor of Austria; the Kaiser means the German emperor after 1871. These are all arbitrary decisions, but mostly they work and they have the overwhelming advantage of coming out just right in the end: Kaiser Wilhelm, a name with a century-long flavour of dastardly creepiness, is far preferable to the Emperor William, who sounds like someone from an unchallenging children's story.

Aside from names I have used almost no German words at all, in order to reflect my own language ability. The reader will therefore be spared the usual analysis of complex German concepts which cannot be translated into English, such as 'the sense of self-loathing and emotional collapse men feel as they walk down the

steps into a beerhall toilet', and so on. There are only two exceptions: Ratskeller and the unavoidable Schloss. A Ratskeller does not
sound terrific to non-Germans, but it is a restaurant in the cellar
(Keller) of the town hall (Rathaus) and tends to be decorated with
elk-antler chandeliers and serve artery-gumming food. A Schloss
can be a lightning-devastated tower on a crag or a pretty town-
palace festooned in allegorical figures; it can be a massive, ruinous
attempt to copy Versailles or just a simple country house. Words like
'palace' or 'castle' just cannot stretch to encompass Schloss.

CHAPTER ONE

From the land of gloomy forests »
Roman Germans » An alligator far from home »
I'll have some green sauce with that » The medieval car park

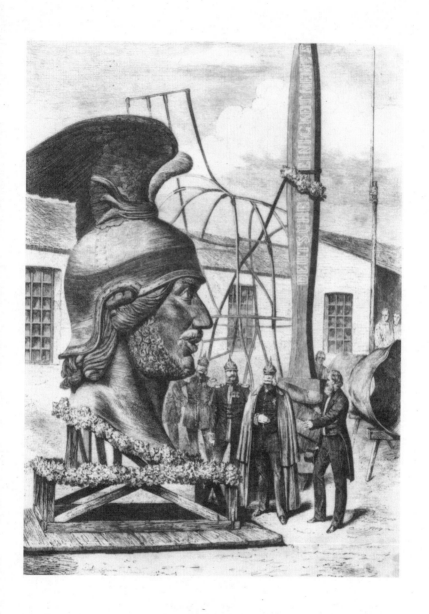

From the land of gloomy forests

There can be few better times to think about the myths of the ancient origins of Germany than when listening to the second act Prelude to *Siegfried*. This scarcely manageable piece of music creates in some five minutes a trackless, choked, gloomy forest, menace (specifically a sleeping dragon) and a sense of waiting – the many years during which dwarves and gods have been drumming their fingers waiting for the great (if borderline silly) events at last to unfold.

It is hard to avoid a sense of irritation mixed with relief that non-Germans have such a second-hand relationship with this music. There have been many great non-German enthusiasts for and interpreters of Wagner, but none have to take quite the same responsibility that Germans do for the drama's roots and meaning. There is something about all the elements in the forest Prelude very specific to German culture. English forests can be driven across so quickly that it's possible to miss them – and walking in them hardly counts as a form of exercise, with a playground, baked-potato salesman or nature table every ten feet or so. But in Germany it's still possible to stand on high hills and see nothing but trees, albeit very well-cared-for trees, rolling towards the horizon – a tiny fragment of the ancient forest. The dragon, dwarves and gods also seem convincing, part of a toy box of creatures lurking in the mountains and forests and repainted by generations of linguists, folklorists and composers, at the heart of any number of festivals and children's books.

The Germans have invested far more in their ancient past than the English, who have always had a more restricted curiosity about their origins. The two nations share much of the same primeval ice-sheet, giving its melting as a clear start date (southern Germany was clear of ice, making it annoyingly different even in the Pleistocene era), but then we go our separate ways. Undeniably much of the national story of England's origins is embarrassing. As a Roman colony Britannia was a hardship post and a bit of a joke. There has always been a last-ditch suggestion that the Romans may have left us at least the odd noble-browed, classically educated gene, but sheer lack of surviving information about the province shows the disregard in which its owners held it. As an obsessive fascination with the ancient past swept over Europe in the nineteenth century, British superiority complexes were simply not nourished much by such sorry stuff. And once the Romans left, Britain became a free-for-all, with wave upon wave of pleasure-seeking North Germans, Danes and Norwegians using it as a sort of chopping-board until the final ignominy of the Norman Conquest. In all this melee the figures of Arthur and Alfred bob up and down – the former invented by French poets, the latter a figure seen through so many layers of subsequent marauders that it is unclear whether modern England has any real link with him at all.

The very public and mortifying nature of England as a resort for axe-wielding immigrants has made its deep, early history almost unavailable to inspiring narrative except as a swirling and idiotic run-up to Magna Carta and then fast-forward to Macaulay's enjoyable onward and upward. For the Germans, however, the deep past has had a corrosive and disastrous effect. There can be few stronger arguments for the damage that can be done by paying too much attention to history than how Germany has understood and taught its ancient past, however aesthetically pleasurable it can be in operas.

All over Germany, partly entwined in the same obsessions as Wagner and partly in turn inspired by him, artists and writers tried to scrape away at the wholly unrecorded wastes of Central Europe to find some clues as to where they were from. The only real document, and perhaps one of the most unfortunate in European history, was Tacitus' *On the Origin and Situation of the Germans*, the *Germania*, a single copy being found in a Hessian abbey and sent to Rome in 1455, where its implications began to sink in. This book (far more full and interesting than Tacitus' *Agricola*, with its description of Britannia) has been tugged apart phrase by phrase. Lifetimes were devoted to extracting every last piece of ambiguous information, initially by Italian humanists, who did so much unhelpful work fabricating the myth of the Ur-Germans in the forest, before then passing on this disastrous gift north of the Alps. The book's existence *is* amazing – a seemingly well-informed, very precise account of what the Roman empire knew about the Germans, written in AD 100 or so and surviving, unlike many of Tacitus' other works, in spite of fire, weather and the whims of monastic librarians and copyists, over almost thirteen centuries.

The Roman empire had famously been unable to subdue the Germans, with its northern border stabilizing along the Rhine and Danube. Generations of German nationalists saw the *Germania* as the founding document of a German nation – one of 'pure blood' (in Tacitus' catastrophic phrase). Tacitus contrasted the Germans' specific virtues with their effete, immoral, toga-wearing neighbours' failings. The Germans are rugged, swift to anger, oddly honourable, simple and good fighters – albeit fighters who get rubbed out when they are stupid enough to engage with the Romans head on. The text delicately balances its impressions so that the Germans are formidable enough to explain why they lie outside the Roman empire and yet savage enough for it not really to be worthwhile subduing them. The tone is reminiscent of British anthropologists describing Africans – until very recently – giving them the same puzzlingly narrow range of designated activities (fighting, feasting, procreating) followed by great stretches of torpor.

The difficulty with the *Germania* is that it is in many ways a fantasy, although the book's absolute isolation means we will never know just how much so. 'Germania' implies a clear geographical and ethnic part of the world, but since the text's discovery centuries have been spent, sometimes with terrible results, trying to live up to an entity that in practice wobbles and veers about almost mockingly. Clearly many of the virtues, including the ruinous 'pure blood', are only there to provide a contrast with what Tacitus saw as the corrupt, polysexual shambles of Rome and are not meant as serious comments on the people who back in AD 100 lived in a vaguely understood and hostile bit of Europe. We will never be able to disentangle when Tacitus is passing on information based on a serious source (he never went near the region himself) or when he is simply making a smart point for home consumption: were German men *really* devoted and faithful to their wives, or is Tacitus just needling his friends?

The *Germania* gives a powerful sense of the inhabitants of that region being very different from those within the empire, and that must have been true. Within the empire there was a settled, road-using, tax-paying, centrally controlled population: across the Rhine were mobile, roadless, freebooting, semi-anarchic individuals in loose bands, living in clearings in an immense, thinly populated forest. The Romans loathed this forest and it was the site of one of the most famous military reverses in their history – the Battle of the Teutoburg Forest, in which twenty thousand legionaries and their commander were disposed of by Arminius ('Hermann the German'), a figure who pops up heavily moustached and frowning with recti-tude in various nineteenth-century sculptures and paintings.

This Roman hatred for Germania is gleefully reconstructed in Ridley Scott's film *Gladiator*, which opens with the post-Tacitus anti-German campaigns of the emperor Marcus Aurelius. When, in the opening battle sequence, the camera pans over a spectral, freez-ing, fog-bound forest, seemingly shot through a special depressive charcoal filter, and the caption *Germania* pops up, we know that we remain in the shadow of the Roman empire two millennia on. This is not the German forest of chirping birds, pleasurable footpaths and mobs of hiking old folk, but the light-deprived nightmare imagined by citrus-fruit and deep-blue-sea Romans, or indeed Californians. The success of this film has enjoyably reopened ancient and disrep-utable discussions about the nature of ancient Germans. Here they are shown as fabulously grungy, militarily brave but strategically idiotic, yelling mucus-flecked imprecations at the fastidious and dis-gusted Roman troops. Setting aside too obsessive a sense of realism,

Gladiator helpfully allows us to understand Russell Crowe's Roman general by having him speak English rather than Latin, while the poor Germans are doomed to gargle away crazily before their certain defeat, having been too stupid to post proper guards behind their lines.

But did these ancient Germans really exist? Is there anything to link the people on, say, the Frankfurt metro system today to these shaggy folk? The mischief injected by the *Germania* is to imply that there is – even down to the title of the book. To Tacitus 'Germania' simply meant an arena of un-Roman people, split into numerous tribes, often at odds with one another and addicted to fighting and feasting. It is odd in many ways that modern Germans didn't see Tacitus' vision as endorsing permanent backwardness, disunity, inanition and chaotic drunkenness as badges of racial pride. Instead it was used to imply a coherence and value to a block of land which to its inner depths was German. It also endorsed the idea of Germany as a land of forest and personal freedom, albeit a personal freedom confusingly entangled in contradictory idylls about unquestioning obedience to local chieftains.

But in practice so many people have wandered back and forth across the area now called Germany during the thousand years between the *Germania* and the emergence of a sort of real medieval Germany that the tribes talked about by Tacitus cannot be called German in any but the vaguest sense. A famous example would be the marauding but astute Vandals who seem to have migrated from, very roughly, Silesia (now south-west Poland) all the way to Spain and then on to Africa around the end of the Roman empire, imprinting, through their violent antics, their name on several languages. Or the Burgundians, whose eventual territory between what became France and Germany marks one of the great fault lines in Europe's geography, and who wandered through Central Europe, seemingly originating from an island off Sweden. We will never know how many of them there were, how much impact they had on the other tribes they carved up or intermarried with, indeed anything much at all. With the best research possible there are whole areas of Germany where the inhabitants and their tribal names remain more or less mysterious. Some of these people must have spoken a sort of proto-German, but only alongside numerous other tribes and any number of evil-smelling incomers carving their bearded ways through supposedly impenetrable forests: Huns from Central Asia, Goths from Sweden, swarms of Avars, Czechs and Sorbs coming into Central Europe from the East, each displacing further tribes, creating fresh societies, different religions, barely getting the hang of sedentary farming before being in turn pushed westward by yet further arrivals.

Conventionally these shifts of peoples over the thousand years or so from contact with the Romans to the final fixing of the Magyars in Hungary in about 900 is seen as a process with an end. But one of the oddities of German history is the degree to which no boundaries are ever really fixed, with each major national group and sub-group gaining power over its neighbour at different points and generating a variety of tragically overlapping myths as to who rightly rules over whom and in what area. The more these ancient tribes' barely visible trajectories were pored over, the more fraudulent, absurd, but also murderous patterns could be observed. For nineteenth-century nationalists, tensions between Saxons and Wends or Poles and Prussians which were entirely to do with modern power and privilege were instead rooted in some murky, elemental past. Everyone loved these mead-crazed ancestors in elaborate helmets banging their fists on banqueting tables and swearing eternal vengeance of some dark kind or another. There is a marvellous scene in Theodor Fontane's 1878 Prussian novel *After the Storm*, where in an obscurely traditional part of Brandenburg, two old friends, a pastor and a magistrate, spend a happy evening, clearly one of many, arguing over a tiny bronze model chariot from an excavation. Is this a richly characteristic piece of Germanic artwork, decorated with Odin's ravens – or is it the very quintessence of the great Wendish Slavic culture, the plaything of an Obotritan prince in an otter-fur cap, made at a time when the Germanic tribes 'lived under trees and dressed in animal skins', wielding crude flints? The two men argue back and forth drawing on an absurd range of linguistic and metallurgic evidence, with the pastor making the devastating point that even his friend's name, Vitzewitz, itself sounds awfully Slav. There is an obvious pleasure in seeing a great novelist at the height of German chauvinism making fun of this issue, but it also compresses into one short chapter all the problems of ancient Germandom. In practice Germany is a chaotic ethnic lost-property office, and the last place to be looking for 'pure blood'. As dozens of tribes arrived, left, intermarried and exterminated one another, it became impossible to know who spoke German as a sort of birth-right and who just decided it would be sensible to learn it – and whether the birth-right German had switched from Frankish or Danish or indeed Obotritan a generation before.

What should be local history or a fusty private interest could become horrible as state policy. At its most comic there was Goebbels' attempt to recreate the atmosphere of pagan Germany through the building of '*Thing*-theatres', enormous outdoor arenas incorporating heroic oak trees, craggy outcrops and the usual medley of nonsense, where people would congregate in the old northern manner and watch pageants of pure Germandom. It is a small satisfaction but a real one to imagine those who had voted for the Nazis having to sit in the cold and rain watching people in costume declaiming neo-Norse rubbish. The '*Thing*-theatres' were not a success and only a handful were built; they are now crumbled, disregarded or used for rock concerts. Infinitely worse was the neo-paganism of the SS, with its obsession with blood purity, runes, oaths, flames and temples. If the Third Reich had survived then we would not now be in a position to say just how contemptible this deep German engagement with the ancient past really was.

Roman Germans

These myths of 'ancient Germany' were confused in their own right, but they also had to share space with another equally baf-fling legacy: that such absolutely 'core' bits of the German world as Austria and the western Rhineland were fully integrated into the Roman empire, lying well behind the fighting lines so lovingly delineated in *Gladiator*. Towns such as Koblenz, Vienna, Worms and Augsburg (Augustus's town) all started out as forts built by Augustus or Tiberius in the first century AD while Regensburg, Baden-Baden, Heidelberg, Cologne, and many others were all either founded or taken over by the Romans somewhat later. This non-shaggy, non-foresty sort of Germany – all roads, bridges, jugs of olive oil and civic centres – offered an entirely different model and affected far too many essential German towns to be viewed as somehow fraudulent or non-German. It was an inheritance which gave Germans a direct access to Latin culture quite at odds with the programme outlined by Tacitus, even if it was an access no less silly than that channelling their forest ancestors.

The presence of occasional blocks of Roman architecture in places like Regensburg or Trier provided no actual link between their original, long-departed inhabitants and the people who happened to live there now. However bogus, these Roman associations remained deeply important to many Germans and this bogusness goes back so far that it almost becomes indistinguishable from the genuine. Most obviously this was through the existence of the Holy Roman Empire, traced to Charlemagne (742–814), who based his legitimacy on being the new 'Emperor of the West', reviving classical learning, copying Late Roman and Byzantine models, and being crowned in Rome itself by the Pope.

One of Charlemagne's most potent notional predecessors, Constantine the Great, had ruled as Emperor of the West in the early fourth century, from the ancient Roman town of Trier, where he entertained himself by feeding rebellious Frankish chiefs to the wild beasts in the arena. Out of sheer ignorance, I always used to think of Constantine as lolling in a court filled with incense, eunuchs covered with gold dust, elaborate gong and harp music, stifling heat and sunlight. This farrago of later Byzantine stereotypes is absolutely at odds with the young Constantine sitting in gloomy Trier, a tough, military city in a fragmented, warlord-inundated Europe, mulling over the possible meanings of Christianity. Trier was severely damaged in the last war but still has some curious Roman remains – the huge but coldly depressing Black Gateway and Constantine's palace hall giving some sense of the scale of Roman life even so far north. The palace hall has been so mutilated by architects, accidents and bombs that it is hard to respond to, beyond a basic, startled sense of awe that these walls have stood for some sixteen hundred years. Trier's place at the heart of German Christianity gave it a reflected glory over following centuries, with the Archbishop of Trier one of the seven Electors of the Holy Roman Empire.

This undoubted Roman aspect of German life has meant that many of the arguments carried on by Roman writers, avidly picked over by generations of German scholars, as to the relative virtues of the republic and the empire came as a sort of pre-made kit for propagandists. The Roman-inspired palaces and statues that litter the German landscape, built by far later rulers, may have come via the Italian Renaissance but they seemed too to have a local legitimacy – a feeling that for southern and western Germans here was a direct if complicated heritage. The Holy Roman Empire was a mass of contradictions, idiocies and inspired compromises, but it was *meant* to gain its validity from this ancient model. Latin remained the language of much of its business and its public pronouncements – not least as the only plausible way to bind together the Flemish and Polish, Danish and Czech speakers within its boundaries, but also as a mark of that fabled continuity. The Holy Roman Emperor (and his heir apparent, the King of the Romans) was understood to be operating in a line that certainly stretched back to Charlemagne, with Charlemagne's own extraordinary act of imaginative recreation providing what was willed to be a link back to a directly Roman world.

This obsession with Romanitas clutters museums with a seeming infinity of not terribly interesting Roman objects. One awful room in Mainz is filled with so many black pots that it implied a recklessly long-term joke by Roman merchants on the Rhine, amusing themselves by deliberately tipping load after load off their ships to puzzle later archaeologists. Of course, all this is a matter of taste and some find these rooms of coins, funerary inscriptions, battered statues and helmets totally absorbing. Occasional brilliant things have turned up – most strikingly a huge mosaic pavement found in 1941 in Cologne during building work on an air-raid shelter. But most of the 'German' Roman empire seems to have been pretty marginal (although, of course, absolutely hopping with artefacts compared to the fog-bound punishment posting of Britannia!). These were, with a handful of exceptions like Trier, just garrison towns founded to keep out trans-Rhenish and trans-Danubian tribes and protect the much richer heartlands of Italy and Gaul.

Once the Romans left, many towns were more or less deserted, with a squatter population drifting in and out. The great buildings slowly fell apart, were looted for their stones or had their foundations used for vegetable gardens. Sometimes a tribal prince would cohere with his band around a site and protect it, but there seems hardly any evidence of serious, long-term use and certainly no indication that anything new was built after AD 500 or so.

This Roman background has had a rich and contradictory effect on German history, with great German classicists, architects, poets and musicians responding in all sorts of ways. Much of it was also entangled in the cultural influence of Italy itself and not just with a specifically German Roman inheritance – although some Rhineland towns and the rulers of Bavaria and Austria have always loaded themselves down with fraudulent links to the Roman empire. The sense felt by many Germans from Frederick the Great onwards of being essentially a martial race was fuelled by comparisons with the Roman empire – but this could be balanced by any number of examples of very un-Roman German military incompetence. Hitler drew at least as much inspiration from the British empire as the Roman, wishing to treat the Slavs as the British had the inhabitants of India, although he ultimately treated them as the British had the Aborigines. But his legions were also meant to be Roman ones, and there were mad plans for 'veteran settler' colonies on the Roman model scattered along the Urals, much as Cologne itself had begun. Of course, Roman fantasies were not unique to Germany – rulers as diverse as Louis XIV and Mussolini have been similarly oppressed by them and a fake Roman style seeps into everything from the Jefferson Memorial to Alexander's Column in

St Petersburg. The legacy of Rome is ultimately so broad that it is something that pretty much anybody can use.

In the German case the rough, multinational structure of the Holy Roman Empire and its Emperor's claim, until its destruction in 1806, to be the descendant of ancient Rome, was often a source of some comedy as the Empire was so fractured and ramshackle. But it could also suggest that, as the Holy Roman Empire's upper reaches were run by German-speakers, Germany had some broader mission to rule the whole of Europe – that places as far apart as Belgium, Italy and the eastern Baltic were part of some birthright. Of course this was absolutely illogical as the heart of the Holy Roman Empire was the rude, foresty and completely hopeless zone which had gone to some lengths to refuse the Gift of Rome, but this was such an ancient fraud that everyone agreed to pay no attention to it.

In 1945 the Western Allies deliberately drove their top Nazi captives slowly through the ruins of Trier. The oldest German town, Augusta Treverorum, former residence of the Western Roman Emperor, it was now a virtual moonscape, with street after street of rubble and its great monuments seemingly beyond repair. Every now and then people can take actions of perfectly judged excellence and this drive through Trier is one of them. The Third Reich had been an attempt to twist together fantasies of pagan darkness and blood purity in the forest with the creation of a new Roman empire, its capital, Berlin, to be renamed Germania. The Christianity which was associated so early on in Western Europe with Trier was also ultimately to be expunged. There is a very thin satisfaction in thinking of what may have been going through the minds of the more mentally agile Nazis on their journey through Trier.

An alligator far from home

As the Romans were their own best critics, so many Germans could also point to the wholly non-military, private, aesthetic or democratic elements in surviving Roman literature. Rome's central role in

Christianity and the immense Latin literature stemming from it also meant the complexity of the inheritance was far too great to back any one meaning or lesson, however much individual German rulers or writers might have tried. Non-Roman Germany too has created a more benign legacy. Nobody in England has (aside from Kipling and one or two others) really cared hugely about woad-covered Britons resisting the Romans or about the post-Roman Mercian or Kentish kingdoms. Even the Norse invaders are restricted in popular memory to, at best, the opportunity to massacre monks in Lindisfarne and King Canute's not very interesting lesson in the limits of kingly power. But there can be no doubt that the ancient Germany glimpsed in Tacitus or in the fragments of clues about life in the chaotic melee of Dark Age tribes remained potent for Germans into the modern world. The forest as an authentic cradle and home of truth has been promoted by everyone from Goethe and the Brothers Grimm to Martin Heidegger.

This cult of ancient Germandom can still be felt in a very reduced way outside the faded Rhineland resort of Königswinter, with its somewhat haggard hotels and listless tour groups. Brünn-hilde is meant to have slept in the mountains to the east and there are appealing Wagner-related walks. The highlight is a hall on a mountainside, built in 1913 to commemorate the centenary of Wagner's birth. Its drum-like shape and ornate fittings are meant to feel unbelievably ancient: a chieftain's mead-hall with *Beowulf*-flavoured fixtures. Of course the building, in practice, screams out pre-war Jugendstil decorativeness and a dopey, pre-Nazi enthusiasm for which it should always be treasured. Inside cracked, ancient, early twentieth-century leather benches are available from which you can admire a bust of Wagner. Symbolist paintings of scenes from *The Ring* (some more inspirational than others) fill the walls, framed by rough-hewn wooden beams.

Clearly this mead-hall has had a challenge staying relevant to many tourists so the owners have added some further, not notably successful bits and bobs. Orchestral selections from *The Ring* are played continuously through speakers inside the hall. There is a stall outside selling honey from oddly ornamented hives, one having a carved and painted cartoon of George W. Bush's face covering its entrance so that the bees fly in and out of his mouth. There is also a massive sculpted dragon, presumably *Siegfried*'s Fafner, which visitors reach through a winding and notionally heart-in-mouth underground corridor. Sadly, the dragon is so lacklustre that you can almost sense the heavy hearts of those who initiated the project and came to realize that this feature could only anger or bore visitors. In a desperate, but happy, response to this the owners continued the dragon theme with a small reptile zoo. After wandering further and further from the site's original tribute to Hunding, Gunther and other Wagner franchise favourites, through the usual rigmarole of Gaboon vipers, Burmese pythons and anacondas – only appealing because the zoo had been there long enough to make each of these into simply huge specimens – I at last found happiness. In an outside pool floated, almost motionless, a Louisiana alligator of appalling size and blankness. It lay almost submerged, with the enjoyable result that the innumerable bumps and dents in its back armour created natural drinking pools for the bees from the nearby anti-Bush hives. Every now and then the alligator would sink a little further in the water and the bees would spring up into the air and hover, waiting for the pools to re-emerge. So an opera about Germany's farthest distant, mythical past, a past preserved in a short long-lost Roman text, had generated a fin-de-siècle attempt at a chieftain's warrior-hall, which had spun off beehives and an impoverished dragon sculpture, which had resulted in a creature with a far more ancient ancestry, but from the American bayou, being marooned for its lifetime in a concrete tank by the Rhine. We have certainly created a very strange world for ourselves.

I'll have some green sauce with that

If there is one subject on which pretty much anyone British or American will agree, it is horror at German food. As we ping some blend of sugar, salt and fats in the microwave or munch on curry-flavoured tortilla chips (a current British enormity), we will shake our heads about the unique awfulness of what Germans eat, topped off with a joke about what goes into the sausages.

It has to be said that much of Germany is made up of a landscape that does not imply much in the way of cuisine. There are bits of Pomerania or Brandenburg of a near-Dakotan awfulness – closed-down, wind-battered moonscapes dotted with little houses of a kind usually described as 'huddled', but which have in practice moved on to a stage where even huddling has been abandoned as a survival strategy. These houses imply worlds so circumscribed that the only activity consists of the husband waiting to hear the sound of the wife getting the circular saw going to carve up some more winter cabbage, giving him the chance to run over to the DVD player and put on his favourite disc of horses mating. These are the landscapes that so bedevilled nineteenth-century Prussian planners, who dreamed of settling further thousands of hardy beet-farmers, but who instead watched them head off by the million to have fun in America. These landscapes are matched by immensely productive ones such as the verdant stretches of Swabia or the famous Golden Meadow, set between two sets of Thuringian mountains, which gives a visitor a sense of being trapped in a child's picture-book farm of neat fields and orchards (with a certain amount of visual ducking and weaving to avoid the pharaonic heaps of mining slag and battered schnapps factories). But almost everywhere this is a landscape not unlike England's, reacting in the same way to relatively weak sunlight and frustrating northerliness.

Admitting that this is a land of pickle and schnapps and not a nursery for cooking greatness, the sheer oddness of broader German geography further conspires to make the achievements of lucky Mediterranean countries hard to compete with. The Germans must be the only major linguistic group *so* hemmed in (setting aside, as usual, the British and Irish), with long winters to the north, a reasonably temperate middle strip and then the climatic disaster of mountains to the south. Like some circling, trapped beast, German cuisine is goaded by its climate into turning out endless sausages, turnips and potatoes. Within these stifling brackets, there are big regional variations, with a patent gravitational pull from neighbouring countries. So in the north there is a cult for eating long-dead fish in the Scandinavian manner, whereas in the south there is a sort of unviable form of pasta. To the west you really do reach a point around the Mosel where the salads are genuinely attractive and fresh, whereas the further east you go the more likely you are to come across denatured, spiceless versions of goulash and the omnipresent *solyanka*, a nearly flavourless version of an in itself uninvolving Ukrainian soup. This aversion to spices is generally shared across Northern Europe. Every year Germany imports immense amounts of cinnamon and paprika – the sweet and savoury supplements to a thousand dishes – but it is striking just how little impact these clouds of old powder actually have – the taste is generally only just noticeable. The ubiquitous presence of paprika-flavoured crisps (the German equivalent of ready-salted) 'in the Hungarian manner' is a bane to all travellers as sometimes they will be the only option at small railway stations. These crisps taste horrible but also oddly unpungent and are a sort of insult to everything Magyar.

These orbital cultural pressures are what you would expect – this is a relatively low-self-esteem, ingredient-thin bit of Europe, hemmed in by other cultures with access to serious sunlight: it is melonless, basilless, oliveless. This means that for the heart of German cooking it would be rational to look in the central belt – and with remorseless logic this does indeed turn out to be true, with a region roughly from Frankfurt over to Regensburg turning out the classic German cuisine of genuinely lovely, densely flavoured sausages and stews. This is also where the cult of fine river fish comes from. I feel a bit shut off from this last since having my second-worst meal ever in Nuremberg (the cult town for good traditional German food). This consisted of a big blue carp, cooked so that its head and tail met, served with desultory boiled potatoes and parsley. It was awful. I remember once reading about streams in New Jersey so polluted by metals and chemicals that if you were to wash your hands in them, all the skin would come off in one go, like gloves. This fish seemed to have died in a similar way, the blue colour not helping. The effect wasn't improved by my, mistakenly, cutting into

the flesh, which gave off a smell like a vault tomb after flood water
has just subsided. I managed a couple of mouthfuls and swore off
any further engagement with mystical German freshwater fish, no
doubt to my loss.

In a tiresome, leading sort of way I said 'second-worst meal',
implying something to cap it. I once went with some friends to a
traditional Frankfurt restaurant which turned out to be a sort of
temple to German hard-core, with undrinkable apple-wine and
guests greedily tucking into blocks of lard on black bread. On the
disturbingly narrow menu, the only choices seemed to be between
cuts of hot fatty ham served with the notorious Frankfurt 'green
sauce' (an old enemy – vinegared chopped herbs), yet another
bratwurst of a kind that even I was getting bored with, or something described as a 'slaughterhouse platter'. In a spirit of fatalism
I went for the platter. This turned out to be a central ridge of sauerkraut flanked by two skin canisters, sealed with metal surgical clips
– the one filled with blended liver, fat and water, the other with
blood and a kind of mealy material. Sticking a fork in one caused
the canister to detumesce, jetting its content over the sauerkraut. I
recognized I was cowardly, but I couldn't eat even one mouthful.
The meal was rescued by my mucking about photographing the
slaughterhouse platter on a mobile, enhancing its ghoulish appearance by tipping a companion's untouched 'green sauce' all over it.
There seemed to be no pudding on the menu and the waiter denied
having any. When we pointed out that the people at the next table
were gorging themselves on vanilla ice-cream and raspberries, he
claimed that these were in fact bowls of heavy fat with raspberries
– but he may have been having us on.

I realize at this point that I am not making a brilliant case for
German food. But within narrow limits – narrow limits shared it
has to be said with the stunted cuisine of a certain high-quality off-
shore European group of islands – Germany does do some great
food. There is always a pig and a potato just around the next corner,
but there is a lot to be done with these two life-forms. Diced,
mashed, braised, fried, generally hacked about, hundreds of years
of semi-industrial ingenuity have gone into presenting potatoes and

their friends (root vegetables and cabbage) in a cheerful light, in innumerable soups, stews and roasts, with their unvarying but oddly satisfying sprinkle of chives or parsley.

And what Germans do with ducks and geese has to be tasted to be believed. Remarque's *All Quiet On the Western Front* (a book at least as much about food as about fighting) has a central scene where two soldiers steal a goose and cook it in a shed with almost no equipment at all: the pedantic detail engaged in by Remarque and the resultant orgy of eating make it clear that this was a goose that did not die in vain.

At this point I've probably been in more Ratskellers than most people in the world, and sometimes I can almost feel myself metamorphosing into a fat-necked, glassy-eyed and complacent townsman in traditional costume, wiping the back of my head with a napkin as I launch, breathing heavily, into a further, monstrous plate of thick bacon, sauerkraut and pan-cooked potatoes, drained down and emulsified by vast bocks of lager or a candlelight-filled glass of Riesling.

Sadly my own almost tearful, nostalgic enthusiasm for German food is not in practice shared by most Germans. Indeed, I am sheltered from the true impact of this stuff. Intermittent visits to Germany make huge bowls of 'farmhouse-style' potato soup or 'hunter-style' stew highly entertaining – but if I were doomed actually to live somewhere like Bamberg and settle in, it is clear that on such a diet I'd be both rapidly bored and (running not very far behind) quite quickly dead. Even in the most lovely surroundings – and nothing can perhaps be more lovely than Lübeck's Ratskeller, with its little wooden booths and crazy heaps of paraphernalia hanging from every surface – it is hard not to notice that many fellow guests do seem in shocking condition. Massive figures with girths and complexions like Gert Fröbe's Goldfinger and beards covered in bits of lager foam and pig are not perhaps ideal role models.

Sometimes I will be in some adorably traditional Hof – I remember a particularly stark dinner in Ingolstadt – and I will be more or less alone except for some boss-eyed, rheumy old nationalist in a feathered hat. Walking back down that ice-encrusted Ingolstadt street, I was stunned by screams of laughter, overturning furniture, group singing and blasts of jocularity from entrance-ways as the entire population of the frozen town lived it up inside the scores of Thai, Indian, Greek, Chinese and Italian restaurants crammed within the city walls. For at least a generation most active, smart, thin, forward-looking Germans have seen their traditional foods as a marginal if not dangerous aspect of their heritage, just as the core German vacation fantasy has been to abandon the pleasures of a brisk hike in the Harz Mountains in favour of being pleasured in a sweat-streaming Thai massage parlour. But that's another topic. Increasingly 'German food' is an abstraction completely at odds with the green curries, vindaloos and gnocchi actually consumed by most Germans, leaving only me and the elderly man in the feathered hat (who, on reflection, may have had a minor stroke) to tuck into their 'farmer-style' goodies.

One food area that remains alive and well, albeit only for Germans over about fifty, is the afternoon cake. Desserts with meals tend to be a bit perfunctory, even if the default adjective to match 'farmer-style' is the almost unvarying 'dreamlike' (as in 'dreamlike chocolate praline marzipan ice-cream nougat dessert'). Given the medical issues that crowd around the main course, it implies an almost cavalry-officer recklessness to further challenge Death by ordering such material. But this is because hefty amounts of sugar can always be taken on board on other occasions. Cake shops thickly scatter both Germany and Austria, surprisingly often run by refugees from the territories lost in 1945. Perhaps this is a very readily transferable skill – a cake-and-coffee establishment in Breslau can quite easily move to Goslar, providing at the same time a ready-made set of nostalgically decorative pre-Nazi-era pho-tographs. I used to plunge into these places with gusto but after a bad experience in Wörlitz I could stand it no longer. The hit rate for genuinely excellent cake was just too low: for every perfectly presented Sachertorte there would be five or six stale disasters with cream of a consistency reminiscent of the insulation foam injected into wall cavities. But this may be an unfair response, a cry for help from someone who after decades of heavy sugar use is finally hitting some serious hidden medical constraint.

The medieval car park

Speyer is a blameless little town on the Middle Rhine, in many respects teetering on the edge of dullness. But as its residents visit the chemist or nip into the pub, as they circulate gently through their normal rota of chores, all seem oblivious to the presence, crashed in the main square, of something which appears to be a monstrous fragment of a space cruiser from some *Battlestar Galactica*-style interplanetary war. This is Speyer's extraordinary cathedral – a much damaged, much repaired but still overwhelmingly potent thousand-year-old pile of stone, as much a great survivor of a lost civilization as Machu Picchu or the Acropolis.

Germany is dotted with such survivors, gnarled and bashed up, but pressing down in the modern era as goads and irritants, strange reminders of a prior German greatness. I think it is not unfair to say that the Middle Ages for modern England are fairly unproblematic – a set of dramatic monuments (Durham Cathedral, the Tower of London and so on) held in affection as remarkable repositories of national and local consciousness. Nobody seems to care hugely that they were built by colonial occupying forces – the genial, rolling tide of the English narrative ignores such complexities. The events of the English Middle Ages have little remaining impact except at the level of cosy stories, generally focusing around Robin Hood and Maid Marian – itself, oddly, a tale of colonial subjection in which Hood is battling for the right to have England ruled by a hearty and amiable foreigner (Richard the Lionheart) rather than a creepy, lying one (John). There is a compelling daffiness to all this, where even the most ludicrous setbacks (e.g. the Hundred Years War) become part of a brightly coloured tapestry of noble-browed achievement (the Black Prince, Agincourt, the Order of the Garter), moving the reader on to the next scene of Greatness.

This really isn't the Germans' story at all. The roots of their nineteenth-century fascination with the Middle Ages are very similar to England's, not least a shared enthusiasm for Sir Walter Scott's *Ivanhoe*, *Quentin Durward* and other bulky works, but also a broader literacy and growing curiosity about national history as a whole. A specifically German inspiration was Goethe's widely read essay on Strasbourg Cathedral, which he had visited in 1772, and which celebrated Gothic art as quintessentially German, oddly. For Germans the Middle Ages represented an acute degree of annoyance – a time that appeared to be one of immense achievement, of cultural confidence and national unity, in stark contrast to the chaos of small, weak states that followed and the growth in French and Habsburg military power and Italian cultural power that made the intervening centuries so shameful. In any quarter-way rational sense, the period was as completely irrelevant to modern German life as it was to English, but for specific German reasons discussions of the Middle Ages became profoundly politicized and damaging. As so much of modern historical practice – really the very idea of history as something to study and analyse – comes from Germany, the Middle Ages can be treated as a sort of laboratory for the uses of the past.

When Heinrich Heine wandered cheerfully through the beautiful little Harz town of Goslar in 1824, he was surprised to find that the great imperial cathedral there, built by the Emperor Heinrich III and his successors, had been knocked down just four years before because of lack of funds. At the same time the Imperial throne had been sold off at its scrap-iron value (through weird bits of good luck this in fact survived and is now back in Goslar). The area of the cathedral is now just a chunk of porch and a huge, dusty car park and it is very odd to be able to wander around in such a massive visual absence. If only the cathedral, which managed to hang on for over seven centuries, had kept going for perhaps another twenty years, it would have been saved, cherished and embellished with all the confused German Romantic love for the Middle Ages which smothered its surviving contemporaries.

For Germans the chaos of the Napoleonic era and the German

states' generally humiliating, vulnerable, shoved-about role in the fighting, created a strange paradox. For many writers, politicians, journalists and artists there was a strong sense that for Germans to take on France, Britain or even Russia they needed to be a single country. Modernity required the ending of the chaos of little states that split up the land in a way which, despite considerable rationalization under Napoleon, ensured national weakness. But Germany had always looked on the map like an explosion in a jigsaw factory – so the only model for this modernity was to go back to the early Middle Ages, where the dynasties of Carolingian, then Ottonian and finally Salian emperors from the ninth to the twelfth centuries, the 'First Reich', appeared confident, German and militarily successful. These emperors had created what seemed to be specifically German monuments – cathedrals, castles, palaces – and these dotted the landscape still, in reproach to their effete successors. So where English enthusiasts for the Middle Ages were at worst romantic Tories, yearning for greater social deference ('The rich man in his castle / the poor man at the gate'), and at best fancy-dress enthusiasts, some Germans thought they were looking at a serious political template.

This confusing nineteenth-century enthusiasm was to have profound effects. It was possible to love the Middle Ages from a deeply conservative, local, antiquarian, dormouse-like perspective, and also to love them from a nationalist, progressive, but still not very liberal perspective. This generated a tremendously powerful movement, the remains of which scatter Germany in happy and unhappy forms to the present – as much in the reverent and imaginative care with which so many medieval buildings were rebuilt after 1945 as in the repulsive dreams of the SS.

Early nineteenth-century Germany was scattered in ancient, unfinished great churches, stopped for reasons either technical (the architect's plans proved too mad and ambitious), financial (the town had been broken by the sheer cost of the building or by a poorly timed invasion) or religious (the Reformation had made the unfortunate building undesirable). The dominant feature of Cologne was for centuries not the cathedral as such, but the vast, slowly rotting crane that filled the stump of one of its unfinished towers. This shambolic building, with its half-made nave filled in with little huts and offices, came to stand as a reproach and challenge to German nationalists. Eventually over a billion dollars (including a massive subvention from the Prussian state) was spent in finishing it off – indeed the railway which runs alongside the cathedral had been long built while masons still fussed around in the scaffolding trying to carve gargoyles. What should have been a perfect symbol of Babel-style over-reaching, a celebration of German uselessness, became by the time of its 1880 completion a pompous and worrying sign that German megalomania was on the rise.

Major towns such as Ulm and Regensburg also had remarkable if spireless churches. On both a grand scale and a much smaller scale, a movement swept across Germany wanting to fix all these now suddenly unacceptable anomalies. In part this came from the general nineteenth-century obsession with tidiness, a wish to make everything just right. But it also came from a powerful desire to validate and engage with the Middle Ages – so the rebuilding became a wish for unity and a wish for serious autocracy.

Climbing to the top of the spire of Ulm Minster, the tallest in the world, as I once stupidly did, toiling up seven hundred and sixty-eight steps with an increasingly resented, not very good book about Goethe under my arm, is to come face to face with this nineteenth-century enthusiasm. As you are wrapped into a tighter and tighter set of staircases, winding up almost suffocated in blackened stone-work, so you are equally trussed up in the madness of a world that wanted to engage in such monstrous work. The only break in this strenuous vertical yomp is a fusty room lined with old photos of other sacred buildings from around the world. Some are simply famous and holy but most are chosen just for the heights of their spires – the only point made being the infantile one that Ulm's tower is *taller*. That the plans were closely based on the medieval architect's original demented drawings – the minster was always way too big for any plausible congregation Ulm could round up – hardly makes it better. However notionally echt the inside of the tower, it has the same atmosphere of industrial heartiness, of Victorians' waistcoated confidence in their own engineering prowess, as that experienced in a water-pumping station or viaduct. The spire also labours under the crippling weight of cheap historical hubris – Ulm itself was annihilated in the Second World War, shortly after Rommel's body was laid in state inside the Town Hall, the site visible from the gaggingly claustrophobic stone cage of the bird-shit-caked spire's pinnacle. This bombing left the new spire as one of the handful of objects still standing in a devastated landscape. The sense that the new, united Germany of the nineteenth century could best mark itself by completing medieval projects sensibly aborted at the Reformation shows the power of history to make people behave oddly. The temptation to treat the less than fifty years that separate Ulm Minster's apogee as a symbol of the new, imperial, united Germany from the catastrophe of Nazism and the destruction of the town it symbolized is a very great one – but, as the later parts of this book try to suggest, it is a temptation that must somehow be fought against.

CHAPTER TWO

Ancient palaces

What survives from the real Middle Ages is a range of, in practice, quite arbitrary objects based on luck and the durability of their materials. Ivories of great age, generally showing scenes from the Bible, have endured because they have always been valued but also because they could not decay and could not be reused. Very little decorative gold survives because centuries of embarrassing royal emergencies or changes in taste have taken advantage of its plasticity to remodel it or put it back into ingots or coins. Clothing, even precious clothing, has rotted, tapestries have faded, paint has worn away. Much of the texture and visual meaning of the Middle Ages is therefore lost – quite aside from the irreparable problem of our mental and spiritual equipment being so drastically altered by the intervening centuries that we can hardly engage with what we are looking at.

The massive exception to this decay and disappearance is stone, the stone which gives each cathedral or Schloss such seeming solidity, despite the remodellings, explosions and decorative efflorescences of later tastes. Palaces, always the heart of political and cultural life, even for the most itinerant of rulers, are one area where there can be no pretence about our real links with the Middle Ages. Hardly any survive in Germany, for the same reason that they generally don't exist elsewhere: because their sites have tended to take on a specific moral or even sacred aura which has led to later, improving generations keeping the site but razing the buildings and building fresh ones, leaving simply a medley of foundations, cellars and bits and pieces for historians to puzzle over. Any fortunate and wealthy dynast is going to express his generally delusive hopes for

the future by rebuilding his palace over the ruins of his dead
predecessors'. The exceptions are themselves so massively fiddled
with and adapted as to be almost unassociated with their origins.
The Wartburg, for example, was the fortress of the landgraves of
Thuringia, where *Tannhäuser* is set and Luther was to hide, translating the Bible into German and creating a revolution. Somehow,
chunks of the old twelfth-century Romanesque palace survived, but
these were so smothered in affection in the nineteenth century that
the genuinely ancient interiors were encrusted in medievalene-
flavoured gold frescoes celebrating a saint's life. These themselves
now have a sort of kitsch that makes their violent removal unthinkable. Almost all that is left untouched is a beautiful, undecorated,
cube-shaped space with a central pillar, the room used by the landgrave's bodyguards, pure, quiet and smelling of cold stone. Of
course none of this loveliness and clarity would have existed when
it was routinely filled with reeking, vermin-packed mercenaries. The
Wartburg became one of the quintessential medieval-modern sites
when in 1817 it filled with students commemorating the death of
comrades killed in the Napoleonic Wars but also using the occasion
to call for a united Germany. Unfolding the black-red-gold flag –
based on the colours used by the volunteer groups ('Freikorps')
fighting Napoleon – still used today, the students showed all the
confusion of their movement. The Wartburg somehow made the
leap from a mere provincial stronghold to the essence of Germany,
both a symbol of lost medieval greatness and of Lutheran pride. The
students wanted unification, but they saw it in anti-modern, anti-
Semitic and anti-democratic terms – a military sword-brotherhood
leading Germany to new glory. The event culminated in a book-
burning. The students were anti-conservative in as much as they
blamed German royalty for being backward and obscurantist – but
it was dangerously unclear whether this made the students forward-
looking or merely impatient with disunity.

In Goslar, in a perfect example of medieval crudity, the Emperor
Heinrich III (1017–1056) dumped his palace down right next to
the mountain where he got his silver supplies, so the metal could

be dug up, refined, turned into coins and handed over to him in bags with a minimum of fuss. The surviving palace building, next to the car-park cathedral site, sums up everything about German views of the Middle Ages. The building is, in all honesty, quite boring, if enlivened by massive nineteenth-century bronze statues of Friedrich I 'Barbarossa', the great twelfth-century emperor and delusive role model, and a grizzled Kaiser Wilhelm I. It survived for centuries after the medieval emperors abandoned it, as a city council room, a prison and a set of storerooms. Damaged by fire, neglect and general indifference, it then became (unlike the sad cathedral) a great beneficiary of medievalism. Following unification in 1871, the kaisers saw themselves as the true heirs to their Salian predecessors. This was gratifying to them and a way of getting away from their obvious Prussianness, unifying the new Germany under a neo-Salian cloak. The intervening centuries of sad disunity then simply became something over which a beautifully engineered bridge could be laid linking a glum, unimaginative military man in the present day (Kaiser Wilhelm I) with his glittering, armoured, charismatic predecessor Friedrich I over six centuries before.

This mad self-identification, closely supervised by Wilhelm I and his heir Crown Prince Friedrich, resulted in the Great Hall in the palace being completely covered in frescoes telling the story of Germany, from its mythical origins to the present day, but skipping over all the awkward disunity issues. There is no escaping the ugly stupidity of this room, the misguided twenty-year labour of an almost pulselessly untalented Dresden painter, but for those interested in the uses of history it is almost too rich a dish. It culminates in a monstrous fresco of Wilhelm I, with Crown Prince Friedrich and the infant future Wilhelm II, his withered arm carefully hidden, in a deranged apotheosis, backed by a glowing light with the ghosts of figures such as Frederick the Great hovering approvingly in the sky and flanked by delighted-looking European statesmen, Bismarck, Prussian generals and other members of the royal family. There is also the usual detritus of allegorical ladies, representing the usual implausible characteristics. The by-rote use of these women in paintings and sculpture to indicate Justice, Unity, various rivers and so on is one of the more wearying aspects of even the most superficial wander through any German town.

When unveiled this fresco must have been a bare minimum test of character for its initial, Friends-of-the-Kaiser audience. This is a picture that presupposes a viewer on his or her knees. Even one drop of irony would have been fatal and led to uncontrollable giggling. Now it seems so poignant – all that time, trouble and paint to extol a family and a set of values that would not last another twenty years. By the time the pictures were finished both Wilhelm and Friedrich had died and that gnome-like tot in a cadet's costume would be closing in rapidly on the incompetent sequence of decisions that would destroy his dynasty. This sense of futility is of course played out by dynasty after dynasty – so many incomplete projects, unexpected deaths, reversals of fate rack Germany that the Goslar paintings are painful merely because they are recent. The picture's effect is not entirely poignant though because of the ease with which Wilhelm I could be substituted for by Hitler – a figure also often painted in a messianic glow and who, when it suited him, was more than happy to call down the shades of Bismarck and Friedrich the Great to smile on him, and indeed name the operation in which he invaded the Soviet Union after Friedrich Barbarossa.

Charles the Great

The ground zero for the German Middle Ages lies in Aachen – a small town on the Belgian border devastated in 1944 but which remains the home of one of Europe's most extraordinary, alluring and mythifying buildings – Charlemagne's basilica. This great, battered octagon, with its gold frescoes, spooky shadows and immense candelabra is one of those places which comes at the hapless visitor from so many angles that it becomes immediately clear whole lifetimes would be required to wrestle with the twelve hundred years of cross-currents held within it. The overall feeling is very un-northern and cries out for a bit more wholehearted incense and sunshine to complete the effect. When Charlemagne (742–814) had it built as the chapel to his long-vanished palace, he was ruler of a vast empire, comprising much of modern France, Germany and Italy. He seemed to have established himself once more as the Roman emperor, a delusive, strange concept that inter-mittently haunted Germany's most ambitious rulers perhaps until as late as 1945. Given that the real Roman empire had caved in centuries before and was very little understood beyond its remain-ing ruins and a few statues and texts, the only model Charlemagne could copy was the continuing Eastern Roman empire based in Constantinople. So his palace chapel was based around and indeed probably built by craftsmen brought in from an Italy still soaked in Byzantine artistic ideas. So the building that kicks off German identity is in practice Italian and Greek.

This building's mental golden haze was further buffed up for me by listening to a performance of Monteverdi's *Vespers* there, which put me on the verge of derangement. During some of the less inter-esting passages in that beautiful but exhaustive work it was possible to mull over – aside from the core building's distinctive shape and the strange, solemn presence of Charlemagne's simple throne – just how much was really far later accretion. The chapel became the place where German kings were crowned, with Charlemagne's tomb acting as the crucial, mystical endorsement. In 1000 Otto III opened the tomb and found Charlemagne's nose had fallen off, his fingernails had kept growing through the tips of his gloves, but that otherwise he was not doing badly. The site's cultic power attracted serious relics such as Jesus' loincloth, and the cathedral (of which the chapel is now part) remains a major centre of Catholic pilgrim-age, with busloads of slightly tiresome and threatening people flocking in for key festivals. The old Carolingian core was soon swamped by chapels and assorted statues given by happy pilgrims who had come from as far afield as Hungary, generally with a greater sense of effort than their modern equivalents.

Charlemagne himself rather vanishes under this heap of later spiritual exertion. A major contributor to this is the gigantic

'Jerusalem' candelabrum that hangs in the octagonal chapel's central space, a gift from Friedrich Barbarossa to the memory of his great predecessor. These monsters are an acquired taste: only three remain and having accidentally collected the set by encountering the other two in Hildesheim and in Gross Comburg I am pretty sure that they are the twelfth-century equivalent of having a swimming pool in the shape of a guitar – less to do with culture and more to do with a kind of rampant sense of display. They couldn't be bigger, they couldn't be more opulent. Indeed, Barbarossa's candelabrum at Aachen was so heavy that it caused Charlemagne's original frescoes to slough off the inside of the dome, which makes it a funny sort of present. So the object that gives the place a big part of its atmosphere (and which, carping aside, is in its general effect magnificent) actually wrecked Charlemagne's design. The frescoes are now neither-here-nor-there nineteenth-century fakes (again, part of the manic German completist impulse) and the feeling of awe created in the interior is in fact given by a megalomaniac bit of twelfth-century metalwork, neither actually having anything much to do with an eighth-century ruler.

This accretion of later atmospheres which allow us to understand and enshrine leaders is of course at the heart of all history. Charlemagne as the founding figure in German history, however, is cotton-woolled more heavily than most by this process. As far as we can understand he would not have seen himself in any sense as German – he and his descendants were born in what is now Belgium, and would have viewed what is now France as more of their centre of gravity than what is now Germany. Indeed, while Charlemagne owned important German lands, he could more plausibly be seen as a sort of Hammer of the Germans, leading massively destructive and violent raids in campaigning season after campaigning season into what is now central Germany. As usual with such leaders, historians – who are generally rather introverted and mild individuals – tend to wish Charlemagne to be at heart keen on jewels, saints' relics and spreading literacy, whereas an argument might be made for his core competence being the efficient piling-up of immense numbers of dead Saxons. Perhaps his interest in saints' relics and Latin learning was comparable in importance to some modern, blood-boltered drug lord's collection of little crystal animals. A baffling example is his original tomb. Charlemagne chose to be buried in an ancient Roman stone box decorated with scenes from the Rape of Proserpina – an entirely bizarre, pagan and titillating choice presumably made just because the carvings were nothing if not pure class and the whole thing felt 'top of the range'. An embarrassed descendant replanted him in something more conventional and Christian-feeling.

One of the most pleasurably nauseating of the Goslar palace paintings is a version of the famous scene when, having defeated the Saxons' army, Charlemagne reaches their pagan shrine and destroys their sacred carved tree. In the painting the emperor is all frowning forbearance, the shattered idol has an oddly Hawaiian look (as though there has just been a brawl in a tiki bar) and the Saxons are marked out by their elaborate if impractical winged helmets and general shagginess. This sword-point conversion to Christianity for the Saxons was, theatrics aside, a genuinely critical moment in what turned out to be German history, and marked a step forward for Christianity that was to be a leitmotif for shaping the German experience at least for a further seven centuries. Late-nineteenth-century viewers might have seen the picture as an allegory of the struggle going on in Bismarck's Germany against Catholics and minority groups such as Sorbs and Poles to conform to the dominant Protestant Prussian ethos – these groups being viewed in much the same picturesque yet doomed light as the tiki-bar Saxons. What it wasn't, of course, back in the late eighth century, was anything even faintly to do with a united Germany – or indeed Germany in any sense. Nobody involved, of course, would have spoken anything understandable as modern German, the handful of people writing things down using Latin or Greek.

In the West there were some scarcely visible strands connecting Europe to the Roman empire, most obviously the Church structure, but from the Saxon lands north-eastward (in other words most of modern Germany) there was nothing but the same chaos of forests, tribes and general freakishness which the Romans themselves had

despaired of. Charlemagne and the rulers who followed him gradually carved out bigger chunks of land, but theirs were 'empires'
where the only real source of economic growth came from booty.
A successful emperor in the following centuries was one who could
kill off other tribes and bring their vulgar gold display pieces back
to his own palace to distribute among his leading henchmen. The
unsuccessful emperors, who tended not to last long, were too old
or too young or too incompetent to carry out this key mission.

Returning to the Goslar paintings, it becomes uncomfortably
clear how little has changed in some ways. Was Kaiser Wilhelm I –
absurdly if briefly known, at the urging of his grandson Wilhelm
II, as Wilhelm the Great, in plodding imitation of Charlemagne and
Frederick – really more than a war-band leader? He enriched his
followers and destroyed a range of independent states to his and
his entourage's advantage (with Bismarck, for example, simply stealing the King of Hannover's entire treasury to use as a bribe fund).
He did this with more sophisticated means than Charlemagne
but it is odd to see German rulers *still* carving out lands, still directly
copying their medieval predecessors. And, it is hardly worth
saying, the Third Reich (named in sequence from Otto the Great's
notional 'First Reich' and Bismarck's evanescent 'Second Reich')
was entirely devoted to plunder and land in a way that made
absolute sense of its medieval obsessions. The soldiers of the
'Charlemagne' Division of the Waffen-SS (themselves Frenchmen),
who died defending Hitler's bunker in the last moments of the
Third Reich, brought Germany's early medieval obsessions full-
circle in a very peculiar way.

Pious, Bald or Fat

Charlemagne's empire was therefore in no serious sense German,
but the repercussions from the splitting-up of that empire really
were significant. Over the course of a series of Carolingian rulers
almost unknowable beyond their occasionally having nicknames
(Pious, Bald, Fat and so on), gradually entities which approximate

to modern France and modern Germany took shape, with a border area between them, variously known as Lotharingia or Lorraine or Burgundy, and with wildly fluctuating boundaries, which was to cause trouble off and on for well over a millennium.

As reign after reign goes by, we really only have a very vague idea of what was going on. The records left are tiny, contradictory, chaotic, biased. In the Hall of the Electors in Frankfurt there is a hastily slapped-together, nineteenth-century sequence of paintings of all Germany's Emperors from Charlemagne to the end of the Holy Roman Empire in 1806. These paintings, until they reach rulers from the fifteenth century onwards are simply fantasy. But what a pleasure that they exist. How much better to feel that one emperor had a distinctive forked yellow beard, that another had an amusingly unlikely floppy hat, and so on. I hardly feel a purist about this – I just feel happy not to be a professional historian who really has to stare hard at the reign of Heinrich the Fowler, say, and must ignore his notionally flowing locks and chartreuse cloak, must banish fantasies of mead-halls, damsels and winged helmets, must dispose of all this picturesque accretion in favour of a handful of often woefully under-informed monastic chroniclers and the odd legal document.

The more one studies Charlemagne and his descendants the more awkwardly un-German they appear. Even the point at which Charlemagne's grandson Ludwig, known significantly as Ludwig the German, formalizes an eastern chunk of the old empire so that it covers an area approximating somewhere somehow vaguely like today's western Germany, does not help much. Not the least of the problems is the eruption of yet more raiders in the ninth century who do immense damage – both to the feeble towns of the period but also to any sense of Europe having some manifest destiny for itself. These raiders fit awkwardly into European history for this reason – they make a monkey of the onward-and-upward school and indeed carve out entire new countries and dynasties. In the British Isles the Vikings have always stood out as the worst nightmare, destroying monasteries, ravaging more or less at will, taking advantage of their ships to attack and retreat before any lumbering land army could engage them. And yet the Vikings remain a crucial part of several national histories, founding Dublin, re-founding York, making most of the north-west part of a Scandinavian sphere which comes to include Iceland, Greenland and even (very marginally) Nordic America. England or parts of England are, off and on, part of Scandinavia until 1066 – and even then William the Conqueror is himself a descendant of other Vikings who had carved out Normandy as a separate fiefdom. The Vikings are therefore an integral, important part of English and other histories – and yet they are equated in the end with ideas of helplessness and vulnerability, an affront to nationalist self-confidence.

All along the North Sea coasts the Vikings hacked and burned away, raising the same awkward questions wherever they went: were these people just archaic pirates or were they simply more successful than the societies that they first devastated and then intermarried with? The same problem arises with the unquestionably European Spanish Muslim 'Saracens' who raid and settle around the north-western Mediterranean. The 'Saracens' appear anomalous and strange and create histories which leave us drumming our fingers, awaiting their departure so we can contemplate a more neatly Christian land mass: and yet clearly they offer in Andalusia and Sicily and elsewhere a model of sophisticated civilization, contrasting rather strongly with the beer-and-skittles environment they laid waste to.

Some of the worst Viking pressure landed in northern France, which really became a wasteland – a miserable, wrecked place with each bright initiative thwarted by the scale, guile and ferocity of the Viking raids. It is hard not to feel sorry for rulers like Charles the Fat, Charlemagne's great-grandson, who were obliged to keep smiling through tears as they scraped together ever less potent resources only to have to suffer yet another round of slaughterhouse ignominy. Indeed, this could be one of the great unspoken themes of history – the shifty, embarrassing reigns that have littered the world, where the day-to-day business of marriage, ceremonial deference and rewards is played out, sometimes for decades, all headed up by someone widely viewed as an idiot. If

German history particularly could be entirely recast as a sequence of absurd, fruitless marriage alliances, farcically ill-timed switches in religious faith, chaotically managed, shameful battles, faithlessness and cowardice, how attractive it all would be. Of course, the work involved would be immense as all the historians who have been mesmerized by Charlemagne or Otto the Great or Friedrich Barbarossa would need to find entirely fresh skills – but what an entertaining narrative would follow of helplessness, bad luck, human folly.

The German lands were less overwhelmed by Vikings than elsewhere, but for the unflattering reason that the most obvious North Sea and Baltic coasts were impoverished and undeveloped places, dotted with pagan fishing villages of the sort the Vikings had gone to so much time and trouble to leave behind. Wherever there *was* some modest settlement, such as Hamburg, it found itself on the Viking list (almost completely destroyed, 845). Far worse for Germany were the Magyars, who sent immense cavalry forces out from the Hungarian Plain, wrecking a Bavarian army in 907 and for a further generation dominating Bavaria, Swabia and Thuringia, raiding at will as far as Lower Saxony and Cologne, while also engaging in fun detours to the Seine and the Rhône, invading northern Italy and reaching Rome in 936.

These raiders were themselves European or becoming European, but existed outside the big English, French and German historical narratives we have all been lulled by since modern history was invented. They appear to be brakes on progress – and yet Islamic Spain proves to be a beacon of classical learning; the Norsemen discover America; Normandy and its spin-offs (England, Sicily) are central to the Middle Ages, as is the stable and indeed crucial Christian Hungarian kingdom. So the horror provoked by the raiders is a confusing one – reasonable for those who were on the receiving end at the time, but more problematic in retrospect. The German Empire which emerges under the Ottos and Heinrichs in the following century is a response to these raids – all those dukes and other panicked figures clinging together for a while to generate a state which could defend itself. But, of course, the consequence was simply to put the boot on the other foot and create an aggressive, colonial Germany.

A very small town

The idea of a separate German area of Europe seems to have developed under the dynasties of the tenth and eleventh and twelfth centuries later known as the Ottonians, Salians and Hohenstaufens. The Saxon ruler Heinrich the Fowler, first of the Ottonians, restarted what became a fairly regular policy of raiding east and north against non-Christians and absorbing them into his territory. That this resulted in Germany was not the plan, of course, and the emperors continued to be distracted by involvement in Italy. Almost all the Emperors spent the bulk of their time in Germany, but Italy, particularly the north Italian towns, was a crucial source of cash and an association with Italy was important to their continuing (if patently absurd) sense of themselves as heirs of Rome. The medieval Emperors were peripatetic – in an era when London and Paris were taking on something of the flavour of capital cities there was no German equivalent. Aachen could be seen as Charlemagne's present to himself in later life, a reward for years of violent action, but none of his successors could afford to spend more than a short time in one place. Attempts to stabilize the court in a single city, such as Eisenach or Goslar, never came to anything as the Emperors needed to be constantly on the move, checking on their most important and therefore often most flaky and scheming supporters, denuding fresh areas of food and drink for their retinues of bodyguards, scroungers and clerics and, of course, leading expeditions into untapped areas of pagan backwardness.

This German failure to establish a London shows the extremely deep-rooted nature of German fissiparousness. There was something about this region – an issue not resolved in our own lifetime – that tended to splinter power and authority. It is also what makes it so enjoyable to wander around today – these fossil records of earlier political decisions, expressed in buildings and artworks, are scattered in a thousand different places, leaving all kinds of surprising traces.

One strange example is the miniature Harz town of Quedlinburg. This lovely place has been a backwater for about a thousand years, with even the 'New Town' area being established in about 1200, and maintaining ever since a sort of failure-to-thrive atmosphere. The town's claim to greatness is that it is the burial place of Heinrich the Fowler himself, who died in 936, and who endowed the town to look after his body. Ruled by a group of aristocratic nuns as an independent state, Quedlinburg was the traditional place where the Emperors would spend Easter in honour of their great predecessor. Heinrich hurtled around chopping up Bohemians, Magyars, Danes and disgruntled fellow Germans and creating the Holy Roman Empire, albeit in a less clear-cut form than later propagandists would have liked. As usual with these figures it is hard to know whether they are visionaries following a coherent plan, or gore-soaked maniacs splitting up loot with their mates. Quedlinburg came into political existence at the very beginning of the Empire and, through many ups and downs, survived until its final dissolution under Napoleon and digestion (a very minor snack) by Prussia. It is the acme of German obscurantism, but all the while, like so many such places, remaining oddly important.

I once spent a happy few days there and remember with some embarrassment standing in a bus queue waiting to go on the long trip over the hills to the former micro-state of Stolberg-Stolberg and realizing that I was trapped in a sick downward spiral of dependency on 'tiny Germany': the cult of marginal political entities that set itself, not always ineffectively, against the cosmic dreams of Hohenzollerns and Habsburgs. I turned my back on that bus to Stolberg-Stolberg, walking away, resolved that I really had to focus more on Prussia and Saxony and other big bits of Germany if I was ever to get anywhere.

In any event, the abbey church of Quedlinburg is in a perfect little residential Schloss on a hill with a tiny museum filled with all the things which give micro-Germany such a siren-song: a ballista, a narwhal horn, incompetent portraits of abbesses, a portable wooden prison, miscellaneous torture instruments – the usual. The entire state was there to generate just sufficient economic activity to pay for the nuns, to allow them to pray for Heinrich's soul. Wandering around the abbey itself, which I did first, I was struck by its austere beauty, its lack of the usual accretions. Until very recently it had been even more austere as many of the treasury items had been stolen by an American lieutenant in 1945, whose shame-faced family had only just returned them. But even so, the neatness seemed odd – with a simple, clearly modern stone marking Heinrich the Fowler's grave. What I had not reckoned on was that even in a dopey backwater like Quedlinburg the world of modern German medievalism never slept. Weirdly omitted from my guidebook (perhaps deliberately to add to the shock) was the crucial piece of information that in the 1930s the abbey at Quedlinburg had been deconsecrated, its congregation thrown out, and it had been turned into an SS shrine.

Heinrich the Fowler, German expansionist, Slav-killer, was to become one of Nazi Germany's non-Christianized patron saints. The abbey was so neat because it had been rebuilt – a medieval Gothic choir had been ripped out as too French (Romanesque being somehow authentically German), an eagle with a swastika in its claws had filled the main window and cult runic flags had hung from the interior walls. In an elaborate, characteristically absurd SS ceremony, with Nazi flags draped from every window on the route, leading grandees with Himmler at their head had processed through town to dedicate the temple, reburying Heinrich, his skele-ton wrapped in a swastika with a metal laurel wreath on the skull. The abbey served as a temple, with a permanent SS military honour guard on the tomb, until events in the wider world mercifully wound it all up. After initial American liberation, Quedlinburg fell into East Germany, where it returned to a level of peace and quiet to which its inhabitants must have been almost genetically inured. In the museum, aside from broken fragments of the stone Nazi eagle, there is a superb photo of local dignitaries, seemingly a priest, a doctor and a lawyer (the stand-bys of dozens of horror movies), at the reopening of the tomb to establish whether the Nazis had actually reburied Heinrich the Fowler. Of course the skeleton turned out to be a fake.

The idea that an early medieval ruler could really be an object of veneration is infinitely far from England's experience, where obsessions of this sort are more or less restricted to a vague sense of gratitude towards Alfred and his cakes. But then the entire circumstances of the two histories are so different. Very few English towns have any real record of their foundation – by the time anybody literate and interested came along (generally Norman) they had been populated and repopulated by waves of Britons, Saxons and Vikings over so long a period that they appeared immemorial. German towns can, however, often be given founding dates – and these can be mapped from Swabia north, north-east and south-east as each Emperor defeated his pagan opponents and turned over their settlements to their followers and created bishoprics. There were areas of genuinely new settlement too. There was a real population growth and ambitious schemes to clear parts of the Black Forest and convert marshes and heath into farmland.

Heinrich the Fowler was a talismanic figure for the Nazis both because he appeared to be on the right track and because of his role in Wagner's *Lohengrin*, Hitler's favourite opera: a pageant that could trigger off in his entourage unappealing spasms of excitement, as Heinrich beats his sword against a tree to mark the opening of a trial by combat or sings about how all Germans should gather together to defeat their enemies ('Never again shall anyone abuse the German Empire!'). This amazing opera is of course entirely rescued by its music, but it is doomed always to be a hair-raising experience in a way Wagner himself never imagined, as we remain unable (except through some unimaginable level of determined antihistorical effort quite at odds with being interested in the opera in the first place) to shake off the knowledge that Hitler was never happier than hearing the first bars of the Prelude.

Spreading the Word

Heinrich the Fowler carved out substantial new lands for his Empire
and restarted a process that became the basis for the German state
for the rest of the Middle Ages. Incompetence or inattention (not
least distraction in Italy) would sometimes retard this process, but
the essential task of the Emperors was to chew through Germanic
and Slavic tribes in the name of Christianity – a process with a
boundless frontier, making eleventh- and twelfth-century Germany
not unlike the United States in its development. This was the beginning of the great age of that long-lasting German phenomenon the
'fighting bishop', a scarlet-faced predator who, dabbing the meat
juices from his chin, was as happy grabbing his chain-mace and
stoving in some pagan chief as putting on a mitre and attending
vespers. These prince-bishops carved out huge lands for themselves
and formed an important part of the patchwork of ownership across
Germany. Their stern, hieratic images glower from hundreds of
expensive tombs scattered throughout the elaborate churches they
built. They always had a strange status because by definition they
were, once the medieval hierarchy became serious, unable to have
legitimate heirs, making their territories permanently prone to interference by the Pope, the Emperor and powerful neighbouring
dukes. They therefore tended to come from very wealthy aristocratic
families, with the occasional ascetic chucked in to please Rome. In
their lifetimes they could carry immense prestige, have fascinating
roles in artistic patronage and then not infrequently die in battle. By
the time Napoleon at last kicked them all out they had become a
powdered and rather unwelcome joke, but for centuries, wherever
there was yet another bout of anti-Slav bloodletting or a fresh pagan
temple to demolish, these lip-smacking, armoured figures would be
on the scene with their expensive horses and luxurious, intermittently pious retinues.

The early patronage of these bishops can still be seen, dotting
the landscape, despite war, greed, time and bad luck disposing of
so much. In the north Saxon town of Hildesheim the cathedral is

decorated with the remarkable initiative of Bishop Bernward – two doors decorated with scenes from the lives of Adam and Eve on one side and Jesus on the other, created in about 1010. The figures themselves have something of the air of a talented primary school project, for some bizarre reason permanently memorialized in about two tons of bronze, but I don't mean this badly – there is something so tentative yet direct about the little figures, married to a sense that for over a thousand years people have been staring at Adam and Eve's unchanging bliss and degradation, that makes these doors genuinely holy objects. Exuding a similar, eerie atmosphere, in the cathedral of Erfurt is a strange bronze man, made in the same period, holding a candle in each outstretched arm – he is not a brilliantly finished object, but to stand in front of him and think how long he has been carrying these symbolic sources of light gives an uncanny sense of being directly linked, through his sheer persistence, to an incredibly older age.

These Emperors were still presiding over, in world terms, a pretty small place. Western Christendom could have fitted into a side-pocket of the Chinese Empire of the period. It was a provincial joke compared to the Muslim sphere, with a city like Baghdad on a different scale to anywhere like Aachen or Cologne. By 1050 or so the settled German world consisted of just the western part of modern Germany, with a sea of heathen opponents from Holland to most points east. Bremen was one of the great centres for missionary work, sending out recklessly brave figures to try to save the souls of pagans who remained at this point both numerous and feisty. Major expeditions to Schleswig and Mecklenburg in the tenth century and Iceland, the Orkneys and Jutland in the eleventh all produced results, although there was occasional spectacular backsliding. Areas that had become Christian would fall out of the habit, needing fresh missionaries and fresh punitive raids. For a long time there must have been a fascinating admixture of pagan practice lurking in the interstices of Christian Germany. This era was very far from laying down an immaculate tarmac of Christian faith, as the Empire spread along the top of the Alps and into what is now Austria or moved up towards the Viking countries. Monasteries tended to be in the vanguard of settlement, with the landscape pinned down by castles and churches in an ever denser network. As the fighting frontier moved on, what was left behind was a rich religious blend of festivals, decorations, evangelism and threats that must have seduced and frightened surviving, leaderless pagans into the Christian fold. Surviving land grants, legal documents and other papers give some sense of this rolling process, whereby a burned-over and traumatized 'front' would become first a new defensive zone and then a fully settled duchy. The problem the Emperors faced with these dukes was never really resolved until the end of the First World War and their final abolition. Because the Emperor himself was always so closely associated with the frontier, either its expansion or its defence, he never had a chance to settle down or gain a power base of his own sufficiently impressive to quell either the prince-bishops or the major dukes, who could become very powerful and mutinous indeed. By the seventeenth century, when the role of Emperor stabilized in Vienna, it was way too late, even setting aside the impossible religious issues which had come up by then. It was also never very clear how desirable such boundless sway would have been in any case.

These dukes, margraves and so on administered the territories being carved out in the great annual summer campaigns. Under the Ottos and Heinrichs the irreducible building blocks of Germany – the ducal territories and the Church lands that supported the great bishoprics – gradually took shape. These lands were named on the whole after one of the tribes who had surrendered – hence through a series of linguistic mangles that take us a long way from what might have been something faintly akin to their original pronunciations, the Bavarians, Saxons, Frisians, Swabians and so on are memorialized forever in states, regions and islands which otherwise offer no trace of the real nature of their previous inhabitants.

This is also the era when, although it remained true that Western Europe remained a bit of a joke by international standards, the Emperors began huge building projects on such a pharaonic scale that clearly Europeans were beginning to feel on the verge of some kind of greatness. Many of these buildings, such as the palaces already mentioned, or Otto the Great's huge cathedral at Magdeburg, have disappeared or been built over. The most powerful remainders are the three magical cathedrals on the Rhine – Mainz, Worms and Speyer. It is impossible to wander around Mainz Cathedral without wanting to know more: the sheer drama of the place – the colossal ambition that lay behind the Rhine cathedrals, the arrogance of the electors' tombs and their sense of theatre, in Mainz's case most memorably in its geometrically complex, gloomy, Piranesi-like east end, guarded by a lion statue of imperishable charisma. These buildings were consciously created to display the unbridled power and prestige of the Holy Roman Emperor – through the manipulation of thousands of tons of stone, through the forcing of entire communities into their construction. Speyer was designated as the Salian Emperors' personal church, where the dynasty would always be buried. Needless to say, this did not work out, but it is still unbeatable to go down into the crypt (itself an architectural marvel, a forest of pillars in its own strange world, untouched by sunlight for nine hundred years) and see the plain slabs of Conrad II, Heinrich II and Heinrich III. The actual sites of the tombs had in fact been lost but in 1900 they were found and reburied in their current, theatrically minimalist site. This project was one of those antiquarian bits of spookiness at which Germany has always excelled. In Dr Frankenstein-style scenes, photographs show wide-eyed workmen under the direction of black-clad figures, animated by a queasy blend of scientific concern and just wanting to have a peep, pull up the lids from the ancient tombs. Heinrich II and the others were duly shown to be mere oblong piles of trash, dotted with odd bits of gold or ivory. Pocketing these goodies for museum display, the antiquarians then reburied the Emperors, adding a further chapter to Germany's airless enthusiasm for the Middle Ages.

I have always found it impossible, if by even the broadest definition I am close to the cathedrals, not to jump on a train and have a further look. On one babyish occasion I even zoomed between all three in one day just to see definitively and finally which one I liked best (I couldn't make up my mind in the end). Despite much later rebuilding, not least thanks to Louis XIV's army blowing the front off Speyer, all three churches continue to give a sense of a remarkable and *new* civilization. Like all such buildings, one could argue that they are disturbing objects, with every stone made from the lives of those destroyed by the expanding Empire that wished to enshrine itself through their creation. Much of the cost would have been directly paid for by the profits from raiding and forced tributes from crushed tribes. Their cold presence, after so many vicissitudes, still glowering in the twenty-first century, gives a unique sense of what the most ferocious, dynamic element in eleventh-century Europe really must have been like. There is also the curdling sense that it was this sort of arrogant, violent, missionary impulse that was intrinsic to Europe and has never really gone away. These are important subjects and, the interior of Speyer Cathedral on a dark winter evening, the nave dimly ticking over with weird echoes, susurrations and occasional candle flames, is the perfect place to contemplate them.

It would be a mistake to think of the Church as just an expression of imperial power. In parallel were the whole worlds of monasteries and parish churches, of a society operating to religious as much as seasonal rhythms. Freising, in central Bavaria, remains today as an attractive reminder of this complex, inward, sophisticated world. The headquarters for the Bavarian church, it will always be associated with Otto of Freising (1114–58), a Cistercian monk who led an absurdly interesting and varied life, studying philosophy in Paris, extending and stabilizing German Christian rule (and wine-making) around what is now Vienna, going on the catastrophic Second Crusade with the Emperor Conrad III, and writing an invaluable history of the German Empire from the time of Heinrich IV to the coronation of Otto's patron Friedrich I Barbarossa. Standing towards the end of this long (if patchy) period of imperial greatness (the era which would so hypnotize the nineteenth century), Otto brings a certain seriousness to the imperial enterprise, however much it might have in practice been just an annihilatory land-grab.

The crypt of Freising Abbey shares with Speyer a sense of an ancient and very brilliant Salian culture, with its mysterious pillar wreathed in carvings of armed men being eaten by monsters. The main part of the abbey's interior unfortunately looks as though something has gone horribly wrong involving a collision with several trucks filled with icing sugar, having had an extreme rococo makeover to mark its seven-hundred-and-fiftieth anniversary. However deplorable this vandalism might appear, at least it is a happy indication of just how little the eighteenth century cared about the Middle Ages, viewing them simply as old, weird and grubby.

I wandered around Freising after a heavy blizzard one January and found myself in the hills above the town en route to the oldest brewery in the world (founded in 1040) – a patently feeble-minded task as the age of the brewery has no impact of any kind on the taste of the beer (I once stayed in a hotel in Erfurt that boasted the smallest brewery in the world, a similarly nugatory claim). Walking through the silent hills, with spires just visible, skeletal trees dotting the snowy landscape and the occasional wisp of smoke, I found myself irritably wondering why genial but essentially pointless little birds like bullfinches could bomb around in the fir trees surviving the winter whereas I would be dead of exposure within twenty-four hours. Suddenly, I realized where I was: I seemed to be walking through Breughel's *Hunters in the Snow*, but with the dark, purposive figures of the hunters replaced by an out-of-condition publisher. Then I arrived at the brewery's lorry delivery ramps, and my little late-medieval moment evaporated.

In search of a bit of sunshine

German engagement in the crusades was both intensive and peculiarly ill starred. At the end of the eleventh century there seems to have been a sort of brimming-over of confidence and religious zeal, a sense of spare capacity in Western European culture that allowed for a series of ambitious strikes against the Near East, an attempt to bring the Holy Places under Western Christian control. There was no doubt that this was a religious rather than colonial enterprise –

there were much closer lands available for settlement which were entirely ignored and for most crusaders the region of Jesus' late activities would have appeared hot, dusty and tiresome. The crusades were always at heart a French/Norman undertaking with important English, Fleming and German help. The positions of the Germans in Europe made it difficult to get to the Holy Land, the relatively easy ship journeys of the other combatants being replaced by arduous marches of months upon months through Hungary and the Balkans, men and supplies being shed left and right through ambush, accident and exhaustion.

The First Crusade is most notorious in Germany for the massacres of the Jews in the Rhineland towns through which many soldiers passed, given a new sharpness of focus by the nightmarish events of the twentieth century. Jews formed a special category in medieval Germany – they were not extirpated like heathens because they had such a specific and important historical role within the biblical narrative – and yet their presence behind the lines of a militant and missionary Christianity moving steadily east across Europe was always an unstable one, with the Jews offering a critique and question mark over its violent, absolutist claims. The complex, important and ultimately disastrous relationship between Christian Germans and Jewish Germans passed through a horrible phase in the Rhineland cities, as in Cologne, Mainz, Worms and Speyer enraged mobs slaughtered Jewish residents, whipped up by the same logic that was pushing crusaders overseas on their strange mission to attack the Muslim states. In a German context, where religious difference remained a defining aspect of the Empire, there is throughout the Middle Ages something nasty and bristling about attitudes towards Jews – a nastiness best characterized by the 'Jewish sow' sculpture on the wall of the City Church in Wittenberg, with Jews suckling from a pig and a rabbi gazing into its arsehole. This foul object just happens to survive at Wittenberg but was common elsewhere – there is still one in Regensburg for example, and there was a strikingly prominent 'Jewish sow' maintained for many years by Frankfurt's city government on the main bridge (Goethe remembered it with disgust).

What is perhaps strange in so violent a missionary-militant society was that there was not more violence against Jews. Perhaps the ancient nature of the Jewish communities, which could often be dated to the Roman empire and followed the line of old Roman forts along the Rhine, was a factor. Or the decentralized structure of Germany made concerted attacks more difficult. Or the special protection (in return for money) they received from some of the authorities. In any event Jewish German communities were always very small, tangled up in a welter of demeaning restrictions, but somehow endured in the face of sometimes serious viciousness.

A semi-comic element of bad luck plagued German engagement with the crusades. The First Crusade had been successful, through sheer religious fervour, military shock tactics and great good luck (all histories of the crusade are a heated exchange about how to portion out these three elements), taking Antioch and Jerusalem from the Muslims in a series of astounding bloodbaths. There is an argument that this was in fact a disaster for Europe (as well as for Islam) and that if only the First Crusade had been roundly crushed then an awful lot of time and trouble over many subsequent generations would have been saved. The later history of the crusades is a farce of misdirected effort, semi-heroic forlorn hopes, loopy visions and total failure. The Islamic world, as soon as it had adjusted to the shock of the arrival of hordes of sweating Northern Europeans, had the resources to push them back to a coastal strip and stymie all attempts to carve out something worthwhile. Louis IX of France wandering about in a swamp in the Nile Delta, carried in a litter by four strong men with a special hole cut in the seat to allow his dysentery to freely and immediately express itself, sadly rather sums up the crusades. The Emperor Conrad III was crucial to the hopeless Second Crusade, which settled down to take Damascus, found that even this one city was far too strong for it, and petered out.

Friedrich I Barbarossa himself was meant to be one of the super-crusade bringing together Friedrich, Richard the Lionheart and Philip Augustus: the Emperor of Germany, the King of England/ Duke of Normandy and the King of France in a single, overwhelming commitment to the Holy Land in response to earlier fiascos. In 1188, in an emotional ceremony in Mainz Cathedral, the elderly Friedrich pledged himself and his followers to recover the Holy Land. Unfortunately, Friedrich's formidable army, having cut its way through the Danube countries, met disaster when Friedrich either had a heart attack or drowned falling from his horse while crossing a Turkish river, leaving his army to be hacked to bits. The legend grew that Friedrich, asleep in a mountain cave, would awake at Germany's greatest hour of need – a legend unfortunately based on a sixteenth-century misprint, typesetting incompetence being as old as printing itself. The legend had in fact been first attached not to Friedrich I but to his grandson Friedrich II, the last of the truly extraordinary medieval Emperors, the exuberant, polyglot 'Wonder of the World'. By the time historians discovered this mistake it was all far too late and countless statues, paintings and frescoes – including a particularly hilarious one in the Goslar palace with Friedrich awakened with joy at German unification – feature the wrong man.

Expeditions continued to go to the Holy Land and – in the delusive belief that this might somehow be easier – to Egypt, despite its only glancing involvement with the life work of Jesus. The crusaders lost their last mainland toehold in 1291, long after any real hope or vision remained. One tiny chink of light had been provided when the Mongols crashed into modern-day Iraq in 1258 and an excited group of emissaries went to see the Great Khan in the hope of a Christian–Mongol alliance against Islam. As we will see, this was a sadly delusive initiative.

Before moving on, I would need to have a heart of stone not to mention the Count of Gleichen. This blameless Thuringian crusader chose to portray himself on his magnificent funerary slab in Erfurt Cathedral flanked by both his wife and his mother. At some hard-to-pin-down point this turned into the idea that the count, Ernst III, had in fact been bigamous. This in turn became a story of how in the Holy Land he had been enslaved by the Saracens but then rescued by a beautiful Turkish maiden, whom he married and brought back to his Thuringian Schloss. After working through a few issues with the countess, who had been faithfully waiting for years, the count was rescued by the Pope, who gave him a special dispensation to be married to them both.

The story has several glaring weak points but of course the subtext (or just text) of three-in-a-bed, wimples, chainmail and harem-style inventiveness lends it permanent value. A musical based on the story which is currently touring Thuringia seems unlikely to take full advantage of the more lurid possibilities available to it. Erfurt is a very beautiful town but not a place where anything much has ever happened. In front of its spectacular main churches there is a magnificent open square (created by accident when loads of houses burnt down) where the Emperor Napoleon and Tsar Alexander I met. Otherwise it has always been absolutely somnolent. This provided a challenge for the usual late-nineteenth-century artist called in to paint the usual frescoes for the staircases of the Bismarck-era neo-Gothic city hall. He resolved it by only featuring made-up events: so he painted a couple of scenes from *Tannhäuser*, which was supposed to happen fairly nearby, and an excellent, if fictional, moment from the Faust legend where some Erfurter students are astonished by the doctor conjuring up the giant Polyphemus. The centrepiece, however, is the lucky Count of Gleichen, shown ecstatically kneeling at an altar in rapt and rather weedy contemplation of God on his safe homecoming. Clearly the whole situation was too much for the artist, Eduard Kämpffer, who recklessly threw in an extra twist by painting the two wives, kneeling on either side of praying Ernst, eyeing each other with a certain heat. It must be enjoyable to live in Erfurt and constantly find excuses to run into the city hall to pay parking fines, enquire about loft-insulation grants and so on just to get another reminder of the pious count's fun home life.

Thrust to the east

Despite having a strongly farcical element, the crusades and the idea of the crusades became quickly grafted onto existing German ideas about the shifting German–pagan frontier, much as it proved a fruitful idea in Spain for the next four centuries. German crusaders still went to the Holy Land and they supported an important military order there, the Teutonic Knights, but the latter's great effort and lasting, highly contentious contribution to Germany was not in the Near East, but in Central Europe itself.

The very name 'Teutonic Knights' immediately taps into a rich pageant of pre-moulded images – of some Grand Master with a huge red beard, in full armour, enjoying some hapless novice, taking great slurps of wine from a bejewelled goblet between profane curses, pausing only to be confessed by a pliant priest. This sense of the Teutonic Knights as in some unique way completely out of control, of course, comes in part from the experience of the twentieth century – the use of their cross on German military equipment, the idea of 'Prussianism' as something at the heart of the German fighting ethos and a general feeling that the Knights prefigured Wilhelmine and Nazi soldiers in some rather foggy way. The Knights' black legend is at the heart of Eisenstein's anti-German medieval movie epic *Alexander Nevsky*, where to Prokofiev's unbeatable music the Knights, in deathlessly spooky costumes (a bishop smiling approval all the while), toss Russian babies on the fire.

I have no particular brief to restore the Knights' reputation; my only thought is that their cult of violence does not seem to have split off much from the general standards of the entire period. Their traces are creepy – the vast brick fortresses of the Baltic and the indefinably sinister atmosphere of their heraldic shields, dotting churches from Marburg to Riga. Part of their horror is attached to the name itself, which sounds fiendish but is really just a romantic translation of the perfectly boring Deutscher Orden, 'German Order'. Over centuries they promoted German rule, albeit at a time when the Empire as a coherent entity had collapsed and when the Knights ruled their territories in practice as independent princes. They completed the conquest of much of the north-east – the territories that became East Prussia and the Baltic states. They smashed up the surviving, unaligned tribes which separated the Empire from the formidable and extensive Christian Poland and

pagan Lithuania, thereby creating one of the defining relationships
that dogged Europe for centuries.

All the difficult preoccupations with the Teutonic Knights come
together in the Hessian town of Marburg – a place of almost ridiculous beauty, with the upper town like a Hollywood set for *The
Student Prince*. After the death of the austere, self-damaging young
widow Elisabeth of Hungary in 1231, the Knights were given the
task by the Emperor Friedrich II of setting up a shrine to honour
her name in Marburg. Elisabeth's example of selfless work with the
poor and sick left a profound impression on her contemporaries,
particularly given that she was only twenty-four when she died of
penitential exhaustion. The launching of the cult by Friedrich II
himself in a ceremony of solemn hysteria, personally laying a
golden crown on her corpse's head, was one of the highlights of
his reign. Pilgrimage to her tomb flourished and the town grew up
around the beautiful early Gothic church the Knights built for her.
Remarkably, at the Reformation, Marburg's rulers decided *not* to dis-
mantle the fittings of the pilgrimage church, although the pilgrims
themselves were sent packing. So, through this striking piece of
semi-humanism, we still have an intact church with many of the
lovely gifts of statues and altars as well as Elisabeth's gold relic
casket. The Knights' headquarters are still scattered around this
church and are now mostly university buildings, with the odd
appealingly stereotypical creepy turret. One of the many striking
aspects of Marburg is the row upon row of grand masters' funeral
shields, complex and eldritch in the German manner, as well as the
tombs of the Dukes of Hesse. These cold rows of stone men are in
themselves a great assembly of medieval art, although so regularly
spaced as to have the air of a hospital, albeit one not following 'best
practice' as everyone is both in insanitary full armour and dead.
More surprising is the presence of the tomb of Paul von Hindenburg – the warlord of 1914–18, the quintessential Prussian, the
disastrous, cynical, dim President of the German Republic who
reluctantly handed power over to Hitler and then died.

Hindenburg became a German national hero when he defeated
an invading Russian army in 1914 at the Battle of Tannenberg, so

called because it mirrored the devastating defeat suffered by the Teutonic Knights when fighting the Polish-Lithuanians in 1410 and which ended further eastward German expansion. An immense monument to the 1914 battle was set up and Hindenburg and his wife were buried there in a Wagner-inspired, pseudo-medieval Nazi set-piece, explicitly linking both battles of Tannenberg, the Teutonic Knights and the Third Reich, in that queasy love-death way which any other regime would have considered comic. With the Soviet advance in 1944 the Tannenberg monument was blown up by the SS to avoid its being defiled and the Hindenburgs were hustled westward for the same reason. Indeed in these months a motley collection of corpses were on the move, including many of the principal Hohenzollerns, whose successors had so rapidly mishandled their legacy. Friedrich Wilhelm I, Frederick the Great and Hindenburg all wound up in Marburg, after reluctant agreement from its American administrator. The Prussian kings went home once the coast was clear after 1989, but Hindenburg, in an unlit alcove tucked behind the main doors, seems set to stay for ever – the East Elbian Germany he came to personify is now forever part of Poland, no Germans remain there and the Battle of Tannenberg will never be celebrated by anyone again. So it is appropriate in an icy, strange way that the perfect product of the Teutonic Knights' carving out of German lands in the east should end up under a big plain slab surrounded by the crests of the grand masters of the order, hundreds of miles from home and with all of his and the Knights' visions finally erased.

CHAPTER THREE

Walled towns

The modern German landscape holds innumerable traces of the Middle Ages, however frequently patched up or picturesquely re-imagined. The best vantage point from which to see this landscape, in places such as the Stauferland or Mosel Valley, is from the unmedieval comfort of a train, where these rich, complex worlds of agricultural patchwork, fortified houses, parish churches and small castles drift by the window in a sort of pageant of semi-fraudulent medievalness. In Germany this process is much helped by chaotic political and economic history – because whole regions have in turn come to greatness and then waned completely, often being left behind in a pickled, vegetative state with their town walls intact or with just too little economic vim to be bothered even to knock down their last watch-towers or fill in a defensive ditch. These military and religious fragments are so evocative, even if it is not always clear of what.

A fine example lies on the picturesque mayfly-dotted River Kocher south-east of Schwäbisch Hall. Wandering through this characteristic, clottedly rich Swabian landscape, there suddenly comes into view an impressive hill topped by a magical fantasy of what a medieval stronghold should look like: the monstrous bulk of Gross Comburg, stuck like an inverted vacuum cup to its hilltop, a perfect set of walls sheltering an ideal towered church and ancient administrative buildings. Founded as a monastery for aristocrats in the eleventh century by the crippled contemplative Duke Burkhard II, Comburg shows how the critical factor in survival and success lay in securing a suitable hill-top – a factor as crucial for Bamberg as for Prague or Salzburg (or indeed Durham or Assisi or a thousand other examples). It is as though medieval towns can be sorted into two kinds – those on hills and those on rivers (with hybrids of the two such as Meissen or Prague being just right). I found myself so obsessed with Gross Comburg when staying in the area that I would find quite spurious reasons for going back down the river for one more look, or crane my neck from the train in a frantic attempt to get another fix. It is an odd comment on how little we really know about the Middle Ages that the loveliest building in the complex, a squat octagonal Romanesque wonderwork, has left no trace of its purpose – a special chapel, a reliquary, a library? It is fair to say that this perfect building over which tremendous care and thought must have been lavished will always remain completely mysterious.

Town walls were often massively expanded and strengthened, right down to the mid-nineteenth century. Walls defined German towns, giving protection, but also sifting who belonged and who did not. These walls were always problematic as they required so many troops to defend them. In a world in which there were simply not that many people and most were busy shoeing horses, pickling cabbage or making clothes, the headache of armed men, either as mercenaries or as town units put together only by reducing the numbers of blacksmiths and so on, was never resolved. The Middle Ages (and indeed much of the entire period up to the seventeenth century) was a time in which individual urban settlements were responsible for their own fates. Generations might go by with no danger of any kind, but then a war would break out and those towns which had failed to maintain and elaborate their walls or who had failed to keep cutting-edge equipment in the arsenal were doomed to disaster.

Most town walls were taken down – most spectacularly in Vienna with the huge urban development of the Ring or more usually as in towns such as Trier or Münster where, with a much weaker economic heartbeat, they could only manage to turn them into leafy walks. But where a town was pretty much failing completely, such as Mühlhausen, the walls remain and it is still possible to wander the battlements from turret to turret. In times of anxiety, these walls would have been reinforced by ditches, spikes, water barriers and outlying redoubts. In the face of a serious threat of siege all the houses and trees in the zone outside the walls would have been destroyed and the rubble and timber brought inside. But all this activity became snared in the same problem – how to man all these features, even with a population swollen by the terrified inhabitants of the surrounding countryside flocking in to eat up all the reserve food supplies. And how long could you hold out until a relieving army chased off the marauder? There must have been numerous occasions, at least until the Thirty Years War, where city fathers must have had some pretty fingernail-gnawing conclaves. With rival Emperors, for example, or a truculent local duke, issues of allegiance were insuperably hard. If the job of the city fathers, huddled in their rather elaborate town hall, was to protect their own property and that of their fellow citizens, would this be best achieved by simply surrendering and getting good terms? Or would this result a year later in the Emperor, say, arriving in the town and having all the city fathers pulled to bits with red-hot tongs for treason in front of that self-same rather elaborate town hall? Would closing the gates and initiating a siege result in everyone being half starved and then massacred anyway or would it be seen as the heroic act which turned the tide against an, as it turned out, evanescent threat? When religious issues lumbered into view in the sixteenth century the problems became even worse, if possible. Was it better to go down fighting for the faith in an era where occasional exemplary slaughter was the order of the day, or could an allied army packed with bishops and incense be just over the horizon? Standing on one of the towers of Mühlhausen or up in the battlements of Gross Comburg, albeit buoyed by holding a bottle of Sprite, it is easy to feel the loneliness and gloom of the town watch.

The principal pooled efforts of towns were in building and maintaining their churches and their walls. The churches were a key defensive element – in the race with ill-intentioned horsemen the best response was the conquest of space brought about by watchmen high in the tower and the conquest of time created by church bells, which could sound alarms that might be heard fifteen miles away. Wittenberg and a handful of other towns still have their military platforms set dizzyingly high in their towers, their watchers presumably always teetering on the verge of either boredom or madness.

The walls were meant as much to keep the townspeople in as keep enemies out. A curfew would be called each evening and the gates all locked – only specific individuals had the right to reside within the walls at all, so guarding the walls did not merely have to do with external threats. But it must have been a grim life – particularly that of the solitary sentry whose job it was probably to be killed, but to make enough noise in the process to alert his friends. The dullness and threat is perfectly imagined in the guards at the beginning of *Hamlet*, who at least had the lucky shot of seeing something interesting, or in Dino Buzzati's 1930s novel *The Tartar Steppe* where the main character spends the whole story in the pointless exercise of sentry duties in an ever more thinly manned fortress, only to be lying in led, decrepit and sick as, at last, on the distant horizon a monstrous cloud of dust heralds the arrival of the long-promised invaders.

Other superiority complexes

This monstrous cloud of dust became the reality for Germany in 1241 with the advent of the Mongol hordes. It cannot be emphasized enough just how tiny Europe and indeed Christianity as a whole remained. Europe's cities stayed very small compared to those in Asia or indeed even parts of a still unguessed-at America. Shoved into a small corner of Eurasia, their outlying defences in the Near East reduced to almost nothing, Spain still substantially in Muslim hands and the Mediterranean dominated by Muslim corsairs, there was no preordained reason why specific areas of Christian culture should have survived at all.

And yet there was clearly a confidence and brilliance about

German culture, for example, in the first half of the thirteenth century, which is conveyed absolutely intact today. Magdeburg's tremendous, gnarled cathedral remains one of the great symbols of Christian eastern colonization and arrogance. Following the accidental burning down of the previous cathedral and palace in 1209, work began on an ambitious replacement. What exists now took many years to complete, somehow survived the annihilation of Magdeburg in the Thirty Years War, was used as a stable by Napoleon and devastated in 1945. But despite these vicissitudes or perhaps because of them it seems an authentic survivor of an extremely remote time, the heart of the extensive Archbishopric of Magdeburg, with an explicit military and missionary task. The cathedral was a vast expression in stone of Christianity's commitment to converting or destroying the pagan tribes to the east and was a sort of high-medieval religious version of the Pentagon. It is impossible to imagine its impact on the small, simple heathen settlements – its size must have appeared non-human.

The general medieval atmosphere of Magdeburg is pretty much restricted to the cathedral itself, though, and one or two ravaged monastery sites, the rest being acres of Stalinist concrete. When I first came to Germany just after reunification, I used to take a short cut down a notably dank, empty and dreary alleyway to get to the cathedral. It is one of the more confusing aspects of the New Germany that this same alley should now contain a shop guarded by a dummy dressed as one of Elizabeth II's bearskin-hat guards promoting a shop called *Teatime Treats: British Food and More*. So many generations of nationalists and communists would find this ghastly that its very existence is something to celebrate, however embarrassing and odd.

If Magdeburg is the harsh frontier face of the thirteenth century, then Bamberg, in what is now northern Bavaria, is the genial face of German civilization. Of course the town has grown up, mutated and developed over many centuries and does not look even faintly like its earlier self, but it does still keep its original structure, with a major religious building on each of its hills, a monastic hospital, a cathedral, a bishop's palace, with the red-tiled houses filling the crowded

spaces between. The cathedral is clearly a later homage to the Imperial cathedrals on the Rhine, with the same oddity of a choir at either
end and towers on each corner. Apart from its being so atmospheric
you want to nuzzle your face against the stonework with gratitude
(or perhaps not), the cathedral has lurking inside it the Bamberg
Rider, the first full-sized equestrian statue made in Europe since the
fall of the Roman empire. It was carved around 1230 and nobody
really has any idea who it is meant to be. I like it so much *because*
nobody knows who the rider is: given that whoever it was must have
been extremely important, historical accident has much improved it
by converting him into a contemplation of human vanity. Needless
to say the Rider was a nationalist and Nazi favourite, as indicating
a pure German fountain for Renaissance-style achievements. The
Rider has rather fallen on hard times because of this earlier abuse,
but its size and strangeness, alongside a range of other great sculptures (devils hauling the damned into Hell, elaborate tombs, figures
of the Church and the Synagogue – the latter erring and blind-
folded), lie at the core of a town which remains an acme of German
medievalism. It has a bridge over a cheerful little river, a town hall
painted with ancient heroes, gnarled pubs (with apparently a greater
consumption of beer per head than any other town in the world) and
lovely monastery gardens.

While in Bamberg, I remember delusively trying to work out
how my family and I could move there, despite our having no suitable skills and no ability to speak German. Perhaps I could have set
up as the new landlord of the Ram's Head, grown a luxuriant moustache and – steadily wiping the bar with a cloth and frowning with
inward concentration – ignored the taunts and execrations of the
furious clientele as they failed to make me understand their drink
orders. The air would be thick with the smell of burning sauerkraut,
possibly unhelpful sarcasms from my wife and the sobs of our
children picking over their plates of fried sow stomach. We could
have been a rainy and cold but no less deranged version of the
unfortunate American family in Paul Theroux's *The Mosquito Coast*.

But to return to the past, German settlement had carried on vigorously in the thirteenth century, with armies, monks and settlers

chewing through what is now Brandenburg, Saxony, Pomerania and Austria, solidifying earlier, more isolated bits of conquest. The major rulers of these territories proved almost impossible for any central authority to control and famous figures such as Albert the Bear in Brandenburg and Henry the Lion in Saxony were more or less independent. They were much helped when Emperors chose to live in Italy or went on crusade or became variously ineffective – the slightest loss of concentration would result in the resulting space being filled by gleeful dukes.

While the Teutonic Knights continued to extend their grip over the Baltic coast and create cities such as Danzig (Gdańsk), Riga and Reval (Tallinn) as well as what became East Prussia, the thirteenth century marked a clear consolidation of Germanness. Numerous tribes – Sorbs, Lusatians, Pomeranians and so on – had been ploughed under and Germanized, but this relentless processing now seized up in the face of better-organized opponents. Partly through their own natural evolution and partly in the face of the German threat, the groups that became the Poles, the Czechs and the Hungarians were ever more capable of resisting further German encroachment, not least through cunningly accepting Christianity themselves. Individual groups of Germans would continue to move forward into Central Europe, at the invitation of particular rulers, as freelance minor enterprises (or, later, under the wing of the Habsburg Empire), but broadly the shape of the German-speaking lands had now been set – and would stay roughly the same until the German-made disaster of the 1940s resulted in almost all the far descendants of these settler communities being killed or expelled.

The irruption of the Mongols in the 1240s threatened to change this whole eastward drift – indeed it threatened to devastate European Christianity completely. It is easy to laugh at the Mongols' bizarre superiority complex. The crusader emissaries sent to them in the hope of forming an anti-Muslim alliance were horrified to discover that the Mongols did not understand the idea of 'ally', only really using the term 'slave-subject'. On the face of it these strange, townless flocks of horsemen could not have been a threat to settled, organized, urban traders and soldiers. But by the time they turned their attention to Europe they had already devastated China, a civilization of far greater density and sophistication than Europe, if it is possible to gauge such a thing. They had smashed to pieces the powerful states of Central Asia and subjugated Russia (in scenes brilliantly imagined in Tarkovsky's film *Andrei Rublev*) – and Mongol-descendant groups would go on during the following two centuries to bust up India, Iran and the Ottomans, leaving emptied, burnt-flat towns, pyramids of human skulls, and noblemen crushed slowly to death beneath Mongol feasting-platforms all over Eurasia.

Could Europe itself have been wiped out? Given the extreme nature of this crisis it is odd, and an interesting example of Europe's own superiority complex, that Europe's closeness to disaster is not now more widely known. After all, Russia remained under Mongol rule for centuries, setting it on a drastically different path from the rest of Europe – although how different has been the source of end-less, debilitating and unresolvable arguments down to the present day, with everything unfortunate about Russia being blamed on its 'Asiatic' inheritance. Europe's entire political and cultural history could have gone the same way when worryingly big numbers of Mongols crashed into Poland and Hungary in 1241. A mixed force of Poles, Silesians and Teutonic Knights was annihilated at the Battle of Liegnitz by Subutai and the Blue Horde, with the survivors hauled off into captivity and never heard from again. The entire resources of the Hungarian kingdom were mobilized against the southern of the two Mongol armies and again the result was a mas-sacre. Given the chaotic rumours that had filtered through to Europe about what the Mongols did to those who crossed them, there was a Christianity-wide panic. Subutai had Europe defence-less before him, with a battle method that Europeans could not deal with as their heavy cavalry were simply shot to bits by mobile Mongol horse-archers before they could even bring their weapons to bear. Annexing Hungary, Mongol armies marched into Austria, reaching Wiener Neustadt, poised to drive on into Bavaria or north-ern Italy. But then a freakish turn of fate came to the rescue – the Great Khan, Ögedai, died in Karakorum and the principal Mongol generals around Eurasia had to pull back. Hungary remained under

Mongol supervision for a few years, but the invaders never returned and we will never really know why. One ingenious and plausible suggestion was that in Mongol terms Europe was fairly marginal and boring – even the Hungarian grasslands, on the face of it ideal for their simple needs, were rather paltry when you already owned North Asia. And, to add further insult, you could have more fun loot-wise in bigger, glossier spots such as Baghdad rather than in Wiener Neustadt. Just how much further the Mongols would have got is a crucial what-if in Europe's history. Perhaps the sheer density of walled cities as they moved further west would have stopped them, but it is cheery to know that this never had to be put to the test.

A brief note on political structures

The great size of the Empire and its wildly conflicting requirements always made a strong, unitary structure implausible. Even the most dynamic and talented of its rulers were worn down by the relentless travel required to keep its regional dukes in order. Even when a capital of sorts was created at Vienna, this was merely a reflection of its being a local powerbase for the Habsburg family itself. Imperial functions scattered across Germany, with Wetzlar, Frankfurt and Regensburg having key roles and other cities, such as Schwäbisch Hall, acting as mints. The Empire fits awkwardly onto modern maps as its most important cities included such un-German places as Brussels, Dijon and Milan. The vision behind it (and the idea of an Emperor rather than a king at its head) was always steeped, as already discussed, in a self-conscious and entirely delusive sense of Charlemagne and his successors as true inheritors of Constantine the Great's Empire of the West.

The Holy Roman Empire was always therefore a work in progress – it *should* have included places like France, England, southern Italy and Spain (and at some periods through personal inheritance its rulers did absorb or threaten these places) because that would have replicated the original Roman empire from which it drew its legitimacy. This all seems a bit mad now as there was such a long gap between the collapse of the Western Roman empire and Charlemagne picking up some of the pieces. But the Empire's rulers were entirely serious, particularly as this forged the crucial link with Rome itself and the Pope, who also based his supremacy over all other bishops, on his inheritance from the Roman empire, also rather dodgy, and sprinkled with low-comedy fakes such as the 'Donation of Constantine'. The ruinous clashes between Salian emperors and popes in the eleventh century which caused such violence and civil war within the Empire stemmed from this sense that both rulers were the inheritor of this spiritual power, whereas people like the kings of England or France were many rungs lower down, effectively jumped-up barbarian chieftains. That these kings were so wealthy and increasingly strong (and indeed developing their own maximalist ideologies in relation to each other or to the Empire) was seen as a tiresome and transitory nuisance rather than as facts which the Emperor needed to acknowledge in any serious way. Similarly the Emperor was always many rungs higher up the hierarchical ladder than even his most powerful subjects within the Empire. As the rulers of Prussia or Saxony became ever more formidable, the Emperor tried to ignore these political realities in favour of an often ridiculously unrealistic fantasy about his own Caesar-style omnipotence.

The Holy Roman Empire was so massively devolved therefore because its rulers had little choice. Within Germany large parts of the empire were in the hands of more or less independent marcher lords who had, with their own followers, built substantial states. At different times and under various circumstances they could be very respectful of the Emperor and share all kinds of military and, later, religious concerns but this respect was based on being given a level of freedom which in England had been beaten out of the regional aristocracy by the end of the fifteenth century. The colonial nature of Germany also meant huge swathes of important land were in the hands of the once missionary Church. Fighting bishops ruled sub-stantial towns and had their own revenue and troops, from Cologne and Mainz to Magdeburg and Freising. In addition various towns earned privileges which made them directly responsible to the Emperor. This was a huge source of strength for the Emperor and something ferociously resisted by the dukes whose land tended to surround these places. The status of Free Imperial City created miniature semi-republics across Germany, ranging from important towns such as Lübeck, Frankfurt, Nuremberg and Ulm to much smaller places such as Esslingen and Mühlhausen. The huge imperial eagle set in a stained-glass window in Ulm's minster is a perfect example of this local autonomy – a successful lucky charm against greedy neighbouring potentates wanting to encroach on a rich town. Behind their walls these semi-independent cities could thrive, safe in the knowledge that their ruler was a man based in Austria, often preoccupied with fighting the Turks and unlikely to bother them too much.

Ducal territories tended to get split in inheritance disputes, creating an anarchy of competing claims, all mediated through the structures of the Empire which, once individual castles owned by 'free imperial knights' were thrown in, was able to absorb hundreds of separate political fragments. There is a wonderful CD-ROM of the Holy Roman Empire as it was before Napoleon abolished it and to anyone who grew up with a London or Paris unitary-state mentality, cruising around its voluminous, brightly coloured maps on a computer screen will provoke something like carsickness. Areas such as Swabia (which was thick with the micro-territories of those sturdily independent Free Imperial Knights) are a wilderness of tiny bits, of fantastically sub-divided and almost meaningless fragments, each reflecting its own complex history. To walk across Germany was to walk past countless boundary markers; to try to get your boat up the Rhine was a sort of absurdity with tolls payable to a wide range of noble families and towns who happened to own a little bit of river bank. I once despairingly stared at the sheer irrationality of a map of the blameless little margraviate of Ansbach (in the Ansbach museum – one of the dullest in Germany), as even this statelet owned for arcane reasons bits of fields in neighbouring states, or specific customs rights here or there. The Dukes of Württemberg owned territory that looked like a cruel accident – bubbles of land all over the south-west, most almost valueless and many in the hands of local notables who took an innocent pleasure in thwarting all attempts by the dukes to make some fiscal or geographical sense of their inheritance. Ludicrous efforts were made by the dukes to protect a handful of enclaves they had inherited in eastern France – none of them more than a herd of pigs and a broken-down church, but of great strategic interest to the duke's fiscally desperate, constrained and humiliated court.

But it was the major units, not the brightly coloured detritus, that called the shots. The Empire was established in a recognizable form with the issuing of the Golden Bull in 1356 by the Emperor Karl IV. The Bull laid down definitively that from then on the post of Emperor was to be elective, albeit with a seriously constrained electorate of only seven individuals, each owning major territory. There were the three religious lords: the Archchancellor of Germany (based at Mainz), the Archchancellor of Gaul and Burgundy (Trier) and the Archchancellor of Italy (Cologne, oddly). There were also four secular lords: the King of Bohemia, the Count Palatine of the Rhine (ruler of a scatter of rich territories based around Heidelberg), the Duke of Saxony and the Margrave of Brandenburg. This line-up changes at various points, with some removals and some additions. The ceremony of choosing the new Emperor happened in the Free Imperial City of Frankfurt. The whole area where the ceremony happened was destroyed in 1944, but rebuilt in the sort of over-tidy approximation which inevitably marks these projects. If only it could be possible to allow some of these immaculate fronts and roofs to slump and decay a bit into a better flavour of what we expect buildings from that era to be like. The electors would come in from their territories, huddle in a special chapel and then vote. After a while, with one serio-farcical exception, this meant voting for a member of the Austria-based Habsburg family. The new Emperor would then be presented on a balcony in the central square, the Römerberg, to a huge crowd, eager for the ox-roasts and fireworks that followed. This was one of the great events in the lifetimes of Frankfurt's citizens and a source of immense pride. This prestige continued even after the

Holy Roman Empire had ended, with Frankfurt the logical choice for the parliament of the nineteenth-century German Confederation as it continued as one of a handful of 'free cities'.

German tribes

When we think of the Middle Ages at all, we are most of the time thinking about the earlier Middle Ages – the tenth to the thirteenth centuries. However obscure many of the events and however much is missing or misunderstood, there is a fascination in seeing our world gradually coming into focus – cities being founded, countries developing recognizable boundaries, a social organization that makes sense after a fashion. One impossibly difficult area is trying to work out at what point the groups cheerfully called tribes at the beginning of the period (Saxons and so on) evolve into something approaching nations. This is of course an exquisitely tricky issue of nomenclature today, with a foggy and chaotic argument over, say, 'tribes' in Africa. In the case of Germany the disappearance of these tribes seems in the end just to be an effort of pseudo-intellectual will by historians. The assumption seems to be that tribes are old-fashioned and embarrassing, that a 'tribe' is un-German and unchristian and that language and conversion ends that tribalism – so Sorbs, Wends, Old Prussians and so on stay tribal not least because they shun the blessings available from stopping being Slavs. This was an issue that never really went away, having a baleful impact on Nazi thinking – and there could be an argument that one of the reasons the Nazis were so obsessed with the Middle Ages was that it allowed the entire arena to come into view, with Germans representing civilization and Poles (who had in reality controlled a massive state for centuries) becoming once more 'tribal' and outside the pale of civilization.

We all yearn for rows of historical pigeonholes, but perhaps the answer is that the tribes however defined never really went away. Most people had a primary allegiance to their families, then to their parishes and guilds. These in turn had an allegiance to their duke

– payments of cash, goods and many hours of their time. At various points individuals would have been more or less aware of these obligations. A bad harvest would make payments in kind a potentially fatal issue and one that required complex negotiation. The sudden presence of hostile armies would require serious actions from individuals that had not been required – beyond regular and perhaps quite desultory weapons practice – for generations. A crusade would create quite other obligations – and there were many bursts of recruiting aside from the big, set-piece crusades, whose numerical descriptions (the Fifth Crusade and so on), like a highly successful movie and its less worthwhile sequels, were only given by nineteenth-century historians. As usual, we don't really know, but it is odd not to imagine that enthusiasm for crusades ran throughout entire societies, soaked in Church teachings, inured to pilgrimage as an aspect of life, fascinated by stories of exotic lands. Some of this can still be felt in crusader tombs or in surviving sculptures of the Holy Sepulchre, such as the lovely one in Gernrode, and which once dominated many more churches.

Crusades clearly required a complicated level of commitment, at once personal, tribal and universal, and there's no reason to imagine that these different identities could not be reconciled just as they are today. An individual crusader was seeking individual salvation, but he was also representing a community to which he hoped to return years later with the odd Umayyid helmet and a bag of dried fruit. He was leaving because he was obliged to as a subject of the Duke of, say, Bavaria, and he was doing so as part of the universal Christian quest to wrest Jesus' neck of the woods from the infidel. He would be thinking as an individual but also as a subject part of a tribe – and certainly not as part of a notional German nation.

Tribalism is so awkward in German national thinking because it always remained so extremely difficult to *be* German. A Bavarian or Styrian was conscious of a range of allegiances but not of a specifically German one. This was also true in England, but it was a confusion that seems to have been resolved – although, again, the evidence is worse than useless – some time in the fifteenth century at latest. In England the counties were always too small and had too little practical meaning to allow for much wholehearted commitment – it was rare after the Dark Ages, except perhaps as a result of the Victorian county-based regiment system, to give your life for Kent, say. Some counties, such as Yorkshire or Cornwall, have strong identities, and some regions, particularly those with borders with Wales and Scotland, had serious meaning because of the requirement to fight for them. But even at their most powerful, the individual English territorial lords, however crucial as military organizers and as heads of society, had an allegiance to London that cut across and undermined their regional power-bases. Increasingly being called duke of somewhere became an expression of where some of your revenue came from, rather than implying that you lived there all the time. Political significance in the end meant being at the king's court and that increasingly meant London.

Germany remained entirely different and only in the poorly managed and indeed disastrous form attempted in the nineteenth century did it even try to create a roughly English state, and even then with all kinds of mad incongruities. For example the Senior and Junior Princes of Reuss were rulers of a few valleys in Thuringia from at least the twelfth century, a once key area of fighting between German settlers and pagans. Every male member of the family was called Henry as a homage to the Emperor Henry VI's patronage, which was crazy enough, but, even worse, every male member was issued with a number rather than just the ruling prince, throwing up such challenges to sanity as Henry LXVII. Every century or so a decision was taken, in the manner of sweeping back an abacus, to start the numbers again. The princes managed to make themselves a constituent part of Bismarck's notionally unified and excitingly modern Germany in 1871, still running their micro-domains under Henry XXII and Henry XIV respectively till these were finally stamped out in the revolutions of 1918 after a zany run of some eight hundred years. At what point the inhabitants of the Reuss lands ever actually shook off their local selves and substituted a non-tribal and grown-up national Germanness must remain forever unclear.

At a more serious level, Saxon, say, or Bavarian identity must have always remained in effect tribal – more than just local, but a long way short of national. Oaths were to their individual dukes or margraves or knights. Justice and obligations were almost all local, and the Emperor was a generally distant figure. It is crucial to emphasize again how variable this atmosphere would have been, how external events would have sometimes made an allegiance uppermost in people's minds or how much it would simply be a given. Historians on the right have tended to see the medieval structures as a lovely, graded sequence of harmonies; those on the left – a view popularized by the East German state – as a repressive system punctuated by popular revolt. Both models seem suspect because they give the historians a sort of ownership – clearly these were societies fairly different from our own, but there seems little reason in practice not to think of them as just as sophisticated (or unsophisticated depending how jaundiced one feels), with a mass of chaotic impulses, good and bad leadership, good and bad luck, all held in check by sets of agreed norms which generally hold and which sometimes break down.

It is striking in the history of most towns how much time over the long term is spent in peaceful attempts to organize life sympathetically for their inhabitants, punctuated by really very occasional disasters (a terrible fire, a call-up for an army that is subsequently massacred). For me it would seem rather appealing to live in one of these well-ordered places, with their specialized trades, their rivers with little bridges, their astonishingly small ecological footprint, their elaborate clothing codes and their beautiful walls, mansions and churches. Or at least it would for perhaps two or three days before the general levels of illiteracy and provincialism became too wearying and for perhaps four or five before you were expelled or burnt as a witch.

Famine and plague

The optimism of the central Middle Ages (the 'high' Middle Ages as they are sometimes called, with the implication of a top point on a graph or on a rollercoaster) comes sadly undone in the fourteenth century. The crusades had more or less given up and the Emperor was no longer the powerful figure he had been, but life for the hundreds of self-supporting, fairly small-scale regions of Germany had continued to be tolerable, with a rising population, reasonable security and established systems of justice. All this changed for the unhappy generations arriving after 1280 or so. One striking fact that cannot be ignored when spending too much time wandering around local churches in Germany is, through the sheer density of memorials, the unfairness of your fate based on when you were born. Sculptures and, later, paintings stare back at you asserting or even boasting their subjects' secure, civic, prominent and enjoyable existence. But other birth dates intersect with the most ghastly events. Indeed, more often than not memorials tend to come from prosperous times and a lack of memorials means something has gone seriously wrong – that the community has temporarily lost its enthusiasm for marking its own providential happiness. We are ourselves of course acutely aware of this in the twentieth century, where specific age groups suffered millions of deaths while in some parts of Europe others could come through almost unscathed – and in others of course, such as Poland or the western Soviet Union in the early 1940s, there was no generation left undevastated.

The first half of the fourteenth century was a comparable nightmare, with similar or worse percentages of dead (albeit in a much smaller overall population) to those experienced in Central and Eastern Europe in the Second World War. In some places the Thirty Years War was to offer something similar. Within the period for which we have worthwhile records these three points (the 1340s, the 1630s and the 1940s) are the worst times to have been alive in Central Europe's history.

The crisis of the fourteenth century began with an immense famine. It seems to have rained and rained and rained. Crops completely failed over huge areas. It was so wet that salt could not be dried to preserve meat. Transport was always too poor to allow for much food to arrive from non-afflicted areas, but in any event there were hardly any of these. People were driven to eat the seed corn needed for the following year's crop. It has been suggested that the story of Hansel and Gretel stemmed from this awful time. Germany was at the heart of a general Northern European torture. There had always been famines, but this was the one that became known as the Great Famine, killing off an unknown but massive number of people. Having absorbed such a nightmarish blow, Germans then had to face the Black Death in 1349 – a still mysterious epidemic that swept across Eurasia, killing many millions. The statistics are conjectural but prosperous places such as Bremen and Hamburg seem to have lost up to two-thirds of their inhabitants, whole villages ceased to exist and were never re-founded, entire regions became depopulated. The combination of the Great Famine and the Black Death seems to have reduced the number of Germans by about forty per cent. It is perhaps the event in Europe's history least possible to visualize. Some historians have suggested that Europe's civilization, that of a vigorous intellectual life, of the great cathedrals, of an expansive and outward-looking world, should be viewed as coming to an end by 1350. Buildings such as Bamberg Cathedral should perhaps be seen much as we look at Machu Picchu, as fascinating remnants of a dead culture, even if in Europe's case they were reused by subsequent inhabitants. Though probably too extreme, it is a useful way of thinking about just how much we really have in common, as 'Europeans', with this earlier period – we yearn for continuity as it makes us feel happy, but perhaps that continuity is there in a more tentative way than we would like to think.

Records are very poor, the ashen comments of some of the surviving monastic chroniclers aside, and people were too busy dying to express what they felt in much art, so we are very ill-equipped to envision what happened. The most convincing and enjoyable imaginative account is Hermann Hesse's 1930 novel *Narcissus and Goldmund*, which is set in part around his old school, Maulbronn, in Swabia, the only surviving complete monastic complex from the period in Germany and still a famous centre of learning. So beguiling and textured is Hesse's novel that the era of the Black Death has a substance and plausibility which is, of course, a total hoax. Equally, Bergman's Black Death film *The Seventh Seal* seems so *likely* that much of the emotional upset of the movie's end is as much to do with being suddenly shut out from its world as with the fate of the characters. And yet its real concerns are with gloom in Sweden in the 1950s, just as Hesse's real interest is in the integrity of the individual in a Germany which integrity was under acute threat. But it is easy to be too purist – I have yet to read any proper account by a real historian which doesn't make the Black Death completely dull, unavoidably shackled as historians are by the lack of sources. Hesse makes it all likely, palpable and horrifying.

Where a million diamonds shine

Mining has a strange and central place in German life. British mining, with the exception of Cornish tin mines, is deeply bound up in the miracle of the nineteenth century: the monster, industrial miracle of many thousands of men bringing the basis for Britain's wealth up to the surface. This great tale, the founding story and a reality for entire counties until only thirty years ago, has absorbed and made invisible earlier mining. Germany too has its great seams of coal and iron and a heroic industrial story, but it also has a vigorous and peculiar sense of an older life lived underground, not least of course because there were more fun things to find there (silver, jewels, kobolds, feldspar, archaeopteryxes), and these built up a set of potent folk myths which have imaginatively invented mining not as a horrific, dangerous, back-breaking operation, but as a fantasy of untold wealth, of secret spells and curses, of Germany underground as a part of the national story.

The world of historical or even contemporary mining is unvisitable: the rhythms, the clothing, the skills, the companionship cannot be approximated by a quick zip down a lift wearing an orange overall and hard hat. Heine tried it in 1824 in the Harz mines at Clausthal and was clearly terrified by the sense of a dripping, alien, slippery world of specialized beings who understood the layers, the lack of light, the poisons lying around, the brittle props. In one of the great surreal moments in early nineteenth-century

German literature Heine is taken into the chamber where the Duke of Cumberland – Queen Victoria's unappealing uncle and the future King of Hannover – had attended a special banquet. His feasting chair was made from heaped ore and he had sat there surrounded by lights and flowers and serenaded by zither-playing miners. Now the chair lay abandoned in the dripping darkness. It would be wonderful to know if it is still there, calcified in the abandoned works.

Where a major seam was hit, and under the right conditions, a town could sit on its find and maintain its privileges and wealth, such as the blatantly named Freiberg (free mountain) in Saxony which keeps hauling out various ores today; unlike Goslar, whose Rammelsberg mine had generated the silver that had made the Salian Empire possible but which at last, after over a thousand years, packed up its mining operations in 1988, replacing them in the British manner with a visitors' centre and museum manned by a handful of the original workforce.

The most vivid sense of medieval mining comes from the old German monastic settlement of Kuttenberg, now Kutná Hora in the Czech Republic. Much enhanced by industrial haze, one of Central Europe's strangest pieces of architecture wobbles into view, as you walk towards the old town, like a very grey version of the Emerald City. The spires of St Barbara's Church are a set of vast witches' hats, seemingly floating free of any town or indeed any base. The church was built in the fourteenth century by the German silver miners as a symbol of their good fortune. The town itself is fairly standard post-Thirty Years War Habsburg, complete with superficial baroque features and a sinister old Jesuit educational complex. The medieval mines are best indicated by a church tower which has lurched to the side at an alarming angle having many years ago partly fallen through into the honeycombed diggings under the town.

The Kuttenberg Hymn Book, decorated by Matthew the Illuminator in the very late fifteenth century, has a sensational page showing the entire mining process – the bottom third filled with a suffocating rendering of cowled figures clambering about underground, the centre filled with horse-turned winches and miners washing themselves or hauling sacks of ore. The top of the picture – a riot of accidental proto-communist sarcasm – features beautifully dressed figures rubbing their hands together and listening to music as they watch the ore being sorted.

St Barbara's itself has a set of frescoes, badly damaged (and thereby, of course, much enhanced) of miners at work, not in any immediate way sacred or even self-aggrandizing. The pictures simply show miners as they were, underground, in their special clothing, the heroic point of their own story, but protected by their church and their saint. To come face to face with these frescoes naturally gets you nowhere near the experience of mining, but it does make apparent something quite difficult about the Middle Ages: that there was a level of day-to-day, sophisticated expertise entirely comparable to our own, that technology always operates in perfect synchronization with its users, and that these silver miners were just as capable, just as aware of their world and its dangers and limitations as we are. Medieval miners were a closed-off little planet, as specialized as their close cousins (also protected by St Barbara) who worked siege engines or made explosives, but in a world of little movement they could define entire communities, set a pace and a range of values and self-sufficiency which deeply marked their towns. These mines, many of whose origins remain quite mysterious (who first dug in the right place?), continue under German feet to maintain a sort of odd potency.

As a literary idea the stifling world of underground pops up everywhere, from Hoffmann's 'The Mines of Falun' to Hebel's 'The Unexpected Reunion' (one of Kafka's favourite stories) and Kafka's own 'The Burrow'. The Grimms have figures popping out from underground – little black manikins, but most famously of all the Seven Dwarves, whose mine (where a million diamonds shine) is – admittedly rather notionally – meant to be some miles east of Bonn. Most overpowering of all must be Wagner's Nibelheim – accompanied by some of the most implacable, frightening music ever created. Wotan and Loge descend through a 'sulphurous cleft' into Black Alberich's dictatorship where the Nibelung dwarves are cursed to work without end digging up gold. The screams of the tortured miners and clanging of tuned anvils create a sort of fever of dread.

By the late nineteenth century, German mines were raging away, spitting out millions of tons of coal and iron in the same manner as the British ones. And in the same manner the essential accident of sitting on vast seams of industrial stuff became confused in the minds of nationalist boosters with a sense of virtue. Symbolically and actually this German romance with the underground world came to a sick close with Mittelbau-Dora, the underground factories built into the Harz Mountains, a real Nibelheim, created by Albert Speer and Wernher von Braun, where armies of workers assembled the V2 rockets, a story harrowingly re-imagined by Thomas Pynchon in *Gravity's Rainbow*. Walking around the site of Dora is one of the very worst experiences available in Germany and perhaps the world. The freezing tunnels are still heaped with thousands of tons of scrap rocket parts and collapsed gantries, half flooded with eerie, crystalline water and mostly bricked up – an entire underground town with every pick- or drill-mark in the endless corridors made by the labour of slaves, of whom some twenty thousand died. Unlike many of the Nazi sites, Dora, because of the nature of its physical space, feels hideously close – only sixty or so years separate us from its full function. The V2s may have gone on and mutated into Apollo rockets and space shuttles, but lurking here in the southern Harz is the original evil lying behind it all. Its creators, Speer and Braun, respectively ended up writing bestselling exculpatory memoirs and being loaded with honours as the father of the moon landings.

CHAPTER FOUR

The tideless sea

Günter Grass's novel *Cat and Mouse* is set during the Second World War, substantially among a group of teenagers who meet to chat and swim one summer on the half-submerged wreck of a Polish ship sunk at the beginning of the war off the Baltic coast. There is one particularly nauseating scene where boys take turns to masturbate on the deck and, in a bravura passage, Grass creates a sort of phantasmagoria blending images of fresh semen, iron rust and hungry sea-gulls. I first read *Cat and Mouse* many years ago, but its effect has been rather fundamental. The German Baltic may be the magic land of amber, of Casper David Friedrich, of Vladimir and Vera Nabokov walking along the beach, of the Hanseatic League, of Thomas Mann's schoolboys with sealskin satchels racing along town dikes. And yet, whenever I thought of going to the Baltic I wound up thinking of *Cat and Mouse* and going somewhere else.

This is an odd aversion, not just for the associations above, but because as a child I had for many years – for reasons which are complex but really uninteresting – a copy of a terrific sixteenth-century Venetian map of the Baltic on my bedroom wall. This map represents the acme of its genre – accurate enough to appear pleasing and decorative, but not something you would want to navigate by, despite the fraudulent reassurance of compass points and what pretends to be a precise scale. The designers have not yet noticed the most startling thing about the Baltic Sea – that it looks like a crusader praying on his knees. The map pullulates with the stuff you would hope to see – sleds, monsters, pagan shrines, knights fighting bison, wolves fighting reindeer, pretty shields to mark kingdoms and bishoprics. There is even a little inset claiming to show part of Greenland – a country inhabited by two men with spears seemingly in Chinese clothing and, discouragingly, with the shattered remnants of a ship bobbing in the surrounding waters. To the map's left a generous chunk of the Norwegian Sea is included, mainly as a virtuoso class in drawing implausible sea monsters of a kind I've always loved and which was the real source of its longevity on my wall rather than any enthusiasm for things Baltic. A mass of armour, snouts, flippers, snaggly teeth, they fight each other, munch thoughtfully on ships, attack – oddly – giant lobsters; they have bull-, lion-, horse-faces and generally set such a high bar of excitement that the open ocean has always been, for me, in practice a bit of a letdown.

In the later Middle Ages the dominant city of the Baltic was Lübeck, the head of the great trade and mutual-protection society, the Hanseatic League. Ships from this city and its associates spread through the Baltic, Norwegian and North Seas. My love of trading cities battling in my breast with distaste for the Baltic, I at last wound up spending a few days in Lübeck. The sea itself fulfilled my worst ideas about it – a listless, grey mass without tides or proper waves, it implied a children's dystopia in which there was *no point* in building sandcastles, as there was no tide to threaten them. Indeed the entire rhythm of seaside activity seemed completely violated. The beau ideal of a beach for me was one of those Cornish coves which can only be used at low tide, each turn of the tide chasing refugees with deckchairs and towels back up the cliff paths as outcrops convert back into islands, reeking sea caves fill again with sea, and the most elaborate child-made systems of channels and fortifications are swept away. The Baltic, despite occasional dirty storms, seemed to offer an outrageously dull contrast, as though under a spell of peculiar illegitimacy and malice: Baltic children doomed never to walk on expanses of wet sand, never battle the invading sea, only engage with the most highly constrained flotsam and jetsam. Metaphorically of course it had a superficial appeal, but like all open-target metaphors (stagnancy, unchangingness, lack of ambition) it failed through its own obviousness. I briefly perked up thinking how Sibelius drew inspiration from water, but this, sensibly, proved to be Finnish lakes, a very different proposition.

Just through my own ignorance I was amazed by the monstrous size of the ships going into Lübeck's port – a shuttle-service of Swedish and Finnish boats transporting an infinity of containers filled with everything needed for Scandinavian consumer capitalism. This Hanseatic continuity made me very happy – through centuries of vicissitudes, fires, bombs, trade rivals, changing patterns of world commerce, Lübeck still controlled a big chunk of the Baltic trade.

The Hanseatic League is a relief, reading about the Middle Ages, as it is a recognizably modern organization. Here, at last, are people who are not kings and queens or peasants or soldiers. They are interested in weights and measures, rational bargaining, new products, workmanship, profit – all the things widely disregarded by spittle-flecked fighting monks, for instance. Cities like Lübeck, Hamburg, Bremen and Danzig, and Hansa colonies such as Reval (Tallinn) and Riga, set up one of the key tensions in German life – between the aesthetics of the merchant state and that of the royal/military state. Each city was a small republic run by a group of rich (sometimes very rich) families. Their republicanism was a bit provisional: as elements in the Holy Roman Empire they were after all guaranteed by the Emperor, without whom the city states would have been snapped up by surrounding predatory princes. But the jigsaw nature of the Empire meant that specific bits of territory tended to take on the colouring of their principal function, rather than being mixed up as they were in England or France, so royal or merchant or religious towns tended to have widely different flavours. Somewhere like Lübeck was therefore in its entire manner a sort of reproach to late-medieval royal towns such as Meissen or religious towns such as Mainz, although of course all engaged in trade and had major markets.

This sense of Hanseatic self-sufficiency was perhaps exaggerated further by the Reformation as the towns tended to all become Protestant, but in many ways Protestantism's outer trappings merely reflected an early Hanseatic manner. Pre-Lutheran portraits also tend to show people wearing sober, dark clothing. The heaping up of plain, flat brick fronts shows the clear Baltic origins of Lego: the quintessential post-Hansa toy. A world lacking stone for building but instead devoted to turning out millions of bricks simply had to come up with Lego at some point, and much of Lübeck is like being trapped in Legoland itself.

These merchants were callous and predatory, working cooperatively but enforcing the sort of extra-territorial rights in places like London which the British themselves would later enforce in places like Hong Kong. Hanseatic business lay in timber, pitch, amber, bulk goods of different kinds. While kings and princes were lying around in piles of hunting dogs and underage mistresses, the devout, pensive, intensely hypocritical Hanseatic merchants were creating the outline of a modern economy, the links that would prove so crucial in, for example, the later establishment of the British Royal Navy, made possible by Baltic supplies. In a world in which most people moved about very little, the Hanseatic merchants were peripatetic on a startling scale, with tentacles spreading from Novgorod to Hull and from the Arctic to the river systems of Northern Europe. All these Baltic cities are best seen through their habitual mist of rain – Riga's and Lübeck's and Bremen's roofscapes come beautifully to life in a steady drizzle, all that green copper and mercantile rectitude. With the sun out they seem a lot less interesting and a bit exposed – the coach parties and road signs coming through more strongly than the green spires and the stacks of brickwork.

The League eventually fell apart in the sixteenth century, having for years been outpaced by the ocean-going economies of the Atlantic countries and by the new banking skills of Italy, but it survives in odd ways. Bremen and Hamburg remain separate provinces within Germany, the last survivors of the old Free Imperial Cities. Lübeck had kept its independence too as late as 1937, although the rest were mostly gobbled up in wave after wave of acquisitive princely and religious wars. Danzig, disastrously, maintained itself as a separate, mainly German-speaking city state after 1918, another goad to rival nationalisms, and finally wound up with its Germans expelled from the shattered ruins and reborn as the Polish city of Gdańsk. Other Hanseatic – but with an admixture of Teutonic Knight – cities such as Tallinn and Riga lost some of their Germans after 1918 (some forming a particularly virulent, bitter element within the Nazi Party) and the rest in 1945. The German cities still refer to themselves as 'Hanseatic' with their city badges festooning every conceivable surface, suggesting that a specific set of virtues is understood by the term.

These continuities of geography and trade were oddly shown up in 1945 in Lübeck where the Swedish legation in the devastated town (there to protect the interests of Swedish sailors and merchants) became the venue for a panicked, sweating Heinrich Himmler's deluded attempts to broker a deal with the Western Allies to form a sort of UN–SS united front against the Russians. Needless to say this did not work out.

The curse of Burgundy

Perhaps more than any part of the world, Germany has attracted makers of elaborate maps. Germany's fame as a creator of atlases for the rest of the world is in fact just a self-evident side-effect of its own painful, historic thirst for means to patrol its own thousands of internal boundaries, sub-divisions and reallocations. The portrait of a figure holding a map has always been a cliché of command for kings, generals and surveyors, but in a German context, with every frontier a provisional one, it has held a specific resonance, culminating in the defining wartime photos of Wilhelm II poring over a map with Hindenburg and Ludendorff and then of Hitler and his entourage – indeed Hitler clung to his maps through thick and thin as a means of understanding the world, almost as a form of early computer game, a finger pointing or a gesture across a paper surface meaning the elimination of thousands of lives.

Maps can easily become a sort of sickness – a simplifying process defining nationalism, ambition, failure. This is not just true of Germany, but it has had a particularly sharp effect there both internally and in relation to its neighbours. Germany has always had disastrously unstable western and eastern boundaries, whereas seas and obstreperous Danes blocked up the north and mountains prevented it spreading south: not to mention the smaller eastern ranges that failed to keep German rulers out, but nonetheless protected a separate Czech culture and language.

The western border issues are so complicated that too detailed a contemplation of them would probably bring about a nervous breakdown, but they are so important – indeed one of the principal machines for generating Europe's history – that they need a certain amount of thought. I think it is easier to deal with the whole course of Lotharingia/Burgundy's history in one section rather than keep returning to it.

By the time of Charlemagne's death in 814 it is impossible to talk about anything that might be called either France or Germany, whatever generations of nationalist historians in either camp may have said. Charlemagne inherited what became northern France (Neustria) and south-eastern France (Burgundy and Provence) and north-western and central Germany (Austrasia). He added southern France (Aquitaine, Gascony and Septimania), southern Germany (Alemannia and Bavaria), northern Germany (Frisia and Saxony) plus the Kingdom of Lombardy (north and central Italy) and border territories further east. As Charlemagne and his descendants all came roughly from what is now Belgium both the French and Germans have proudly declared them ancestral to their own countries, whereas in practice the Carolingian kings would have been puzzled by both. At the Treaty of Verdun in 843 Charlemagne's grandsons carved the Empire into three, creating what would become broadly a French-speaking realm and a German-speaking one. Sandwiched in between however was the inheritance of Lothair I (hence Lotharingia or Lorraine – land belonging to Lothair).

Lotharingia if put through a computer projection through the following twelve hundred or so years would wobble, lurch, intermittently vanish, re-emerge and bulge in all kinds of fantastic ways.

It could be seen as thriving or withering depending on the relative healths of the regimes to the west or east. If the King of France was feeling expansive it dissolved but if the King of France was in decline (and for great stretches of the Middle Ages he was) then it grew. Just as the French had a tendency to want to colonize eastward into Lotharingia, so the Germans wanted to colonize eastward into Polish and Czech lands and the Poles wanted to colonize eastward into Ruthenian and Lithuanian land – a motor that explained much of Europe's history. The Holy Roman Emperor would sometimes be deeply engaged in Lotharingia, but would often be tangled up in fighting further east, would sometimes be a minor, would sometimes live in Italy and through inattention would let Lotharingia crumble.

This zone tended to fill up with all kinds of unstable semi-independent organisms with doubtful allegiances. Even extremely vigorous rulers such as Otto I (who perhaps more than anyone made a clear border between France and Germany plausible) had to battle shifty Dukes of Lorraine (and indeed a murderous Archbishop of Mainz, up to his neck in at least two plots to have Otto assassinated). As France and Germany both went through extended periods of central royal helplessness with their principal subjects carving out often very convincing states (such as Normandy or Flanders or Bavaria), the central Lorraine (or Burgundy) zone became simply one of many headaches or givens, depending on what else was going on. If it was to become ultimately a crucial European fault line then it is fair to say that until the fourteenth century it was one among many. That the region would turn out to contain independent states in the Netherlands, Belgium and Switzerland would have been a surprise – there were plenty of other entities that could have made it through just as plausibly. At any point in modern history the accident of Luxembourg's survival would have caused astonishment. But, of course, the real problem is that nobody was looking forward to a time when Germany (which did not exist as a single piece) and France (which was also fractured) would grind against each other to such horrible effect.

Perhaps the key turning point was the slightly odd decision by the French King Jean II in 1363 to leave Burgundy, which he owned as duke, to his younger son. This created within a generation a powerful state between France and the Holy Roman Empire and with many geographical points in common with the original Lotharingia. It straddled the formal boundary of the Empire – essentially northern France, the Low Countries, a sprawling version of modern Luxembourg and roughly the modern area of Burgundy split between the Duchy of Burgundy to the west and the County of Burgundy to the east, with the stuff in between Luxembourg and Burgundy filled by the lands of the Duke of Lorraine. These lands remained sometimes somnolent but at other times crucial to the rhythm of Europe's history until Alsace-Lorraine and some little chunks of eastern Belgium were definitively settled into French and Belgian hands respectively in 1945.

The ins and outs are beyond my scope – they would swamp this whole book. Burgundy as an independent state is rather an appealing idea, and in portraits from the fifteenth century and in some of the atmosphere of cities such as Beaune and Dijon, Bruges and Brussels there are clear traces of its existence. A key English ally in the latter part of the Hundred Years War (and helper in burning Joan of Arc), Burgundy reached its height of power and prestige under Philip the Good, creating a specifically Burgundian fur/ velvet/armour aesthetic visible in images made by Burgundian painters such as Jan van Eyck and Rogier van der Weyden. Of course Burgundy was a grasping and violent place on a par with everywhere else, but if it had remained stable and independent then subsequent history would have been different in ways we cannot really imagine. This stability collapsed with Philip's death and the ten-year fiasco of his son Charles the Bold's reign. Incidentally, with all these rulers, suffixes such as 'the Good' or 'the Bold' are merely tags which have congealed in the historical records, the initiatives of often anonymous sycophants or detractors, usually many years later, and clung on to by nineteenth-century historians to make life more interesting. In his own, extraordinarily intemperate and violent life Charles probably got called many more things than 'the Bold' but in any event, burning and massacring and lashing

out at everyone in his neighbourhood, he was finally cornered in
Nanzig (Nancy) by vengeful Lorrainer and Swiss troops. With
Charles's death in the battle his heir suddenly became his teenage
daughter – whoever married her would scoop the lot. The French
king wasted time taking over the bits of Burgundy which historically belonged to France (the duchy) while Frederick III, the
Habsburg Emperor, wheeled out his son Maximilian for a quick
marriage and the Habsburgs overnight became Europe's greatest
family, with Maximilian owning land (with some friendly gaps)
from the North Sea to the fringes of the Hungarian Plain.

Later history played out this situation. The Habsburg lands
(as they now were) created a highly desirable, hard-to-defend belt
of land. It was intermittently very wealthy – particularly what
became slowly the Southern Netherlands/Belgium; it gave many
rulers complexes about the Habsburgs having a plan to rule the
whole of Europe, whereas each ruler in practice spent his life
battling with a fragmentary and unruly shambles. The Habsburgs
always ruled the land independent of their function as Holy Roman
Emperor and indeed the sheer weight of rule meant splitting their
inheritance, particularly once it included the entire Spanish Empire.
This split meant that in the later sixteenth century, for some fifty
years a very attenuated version of Burgundy – the 'Spanish Road'
– lay in Spanish hands. This was a wobbly little selection of valleys
and bridges allowing troops to be fed from the western Alps up to
the Netherlands where they could be massacred by rebellious Dutch
Protestants. It seems unlikely many of these Castilian musketeers
particularly enjoyed the undoubtedly bracing and varied scenery.

The problem of 'Burgundy' lay in its unresolvable nature.
The French kings always saw the border as a joke imposed at a time
of French weakness – a zone up to and even beyond the Rhine
legitimately French but which cunning nobles and interlopers had
prised away. As the French king with greater or lesser success
rubbed out independent-minded lords inside France, it always
became a temptation to apply similar discipline to legally dodgy
but in some cases slightly plausible Burgundian territories too. The
joint Franco-German names for many of the towns lying between

Paris and France's 'natural' borders on the Rhine (Mainz/Mayence, Aachen/Aix-la-Chapelle, Trier/Trèves, Koblenz/Coblence and so on) reflect a competing set of nationalist fantasies fuelled by maps. This seemed to peak first with Louis XIV grabbing or smashing up as much as he could, but reached its apogee under Napoleon where it all became an official part of France. With the clearing up of the rubble of tiny German states in the same period, the way was clear for a matching German nationalism to which, approached from the other direction, French 'Burgundian' pretentions were intolerable.

With Napoleon's departure further doomed efforts were made to fix in place this awkward band of territory. Belgium came into a stable existence in 1830 under British protection. Luxembourg, a piece of land linked to the Dutch king, stabilized in 1867, nearly provoking a war and to everyone's surprise somehow becoming independent. The remaining 'Burgundian' issues fuelled Franco-German hatred down to 1956. The Moselle–Saarland territories were always fatally wobbly and changed hands repeatedly, with much of the Saarland tantalizingly in French hands in 1814 but taken away again as punishment for Napoleon's brief reappearance, then handed to Austria, who gave it to Prussia, who used it to invade France in 1870. A gloomy chunk of woods and coalmines, the Saarland was batted back and forth, with the French always hoping to hang onto it, before a final (we must all hope) referendum in 1956 returned it to Germany. The rest of the Burgundian territory, before reaching the mercifully neutral Swiss border, consisted of Elsaß-Lothringen/Alsace-Lorraine, the dramas around which formed a classic piece of pseudo-medievalist, map-fuelled idiocy, killing and displacing countless individuals in pursuit of terrifying levels of abstraction. The French may have picked through this territory in a piecemeal, cynical and opportunistic fashion, but the key cities of Metz and Strasbourg had for practical purposes been French for centuries. Bismarck, wanting to make some tangible and crushing gain from the Franco-Prussian War, decided to annex a chunk of the Moselle valley and Alsace, creating the Reich Territory of Elsaß-Lothringen, forcing out some hundred thousand French refugees. Most of those who remained spoke German dialects and it was probably no worse being ruled from Berlin than from Paris. But the effect *in* Paris was transformative. So great was the sense of anger and humiliation at Alsace-Lorraine's disappearance that no government could ever view Germany as anything other than its permanent and bitter enemy. The first French act of the First World War was the suicidal charge of thousands of troops into Alsace-Lorraine in a bid to get it back. So, over five hundred years after Charles the Bold's death Lotharingian–Burgundian issues continued to dominate Europe. The French got the territory back in 1918 and then had it taken from them again in 1940. The Free French used the Cross of Lorraine as their symbol, and in the spring of 1941, in the Libyan desert when the very idea of destroying Nazi Germany must have seemed hideously distant, General Leclerc of the Free French swore that he would never put down his weapons until Metz and Strasbourg were liberated. Leclerc achieved just this in the winter of 1944 – an extraordinary piece of single-mindedness but also the end of over seventy years of mutual trauma and weirdness based on spending far too long staring at maps and thinking about history.

I once went to an architecture exhibition in Frankfurt of some of the Nazi plans for how they would rebuild Europe once victory had been finally secured. Inevitably at the heart of it was Strasbourg – with a great, mad map packed with triumphal gateways and axial military routes smashing through the old town, celebrating Straßburg, the Reich's true western frontier. This sort of rubbish has gone on now for so many centuries that it can only be hoped that 1945 represented a fundamental defanging of Europe, which might at last allow these issues finally to fall asleep.

Happy families

The history of much of Central Europe can be explained through the fates of just four families: the north-east-German Hohenzollerns, the east-German Wettins, the south-east-German Habsburgs and the south-German Wittelsbachs. These families mattered so much because their grandeurs and miseries dictated from the High Middle Ages to the end of the First World War who would be responsible for count-less fates across a swathe of territory that extended across the whole of mainland Europe. Generation after generation found themselves through these families' marriages, victories, defeats, reforms and tax needs, either better off or worse off. Of course there were many Germans who dodged these people, living in the rubble of political bits and bobs (and often very appealing bobs, of course), but gen-erally even these territories had rulers either themselves related to these core families (such as many of the prince-archbishops) or doomed to cringe before them in a more or less unappealing way just to keep in business.

Only in a computer game (perhaps not, in all honesty, a very profitable one), called something like *Liege Lord*, could the im-mensely complex patterns created by generation after generation of these families' goings-on be adequately expressed. Whole chunks of the families would sometimes break away, fortunate marriages would conjure up huge new territories, a political or religious decision could in a snakes-and-ladders manner dazzle or ruin in a few weeks. But always the motor for the families was the fecund mum. Only through a male heir plus ancillary sons and daughters for dynastic marriage could the show stay on the road. Accidents, gayness or lunacy could blow devastating holes in the family trees (which were kept up obsessively and, even by the seventeenth century, had reached demented levels of multifurcation), but if children kept coming the dynasty was safe. And so over centuries the Habsburgs, for example, would sometimes bloom into myriad archdukes and eligible girls, the former stuffing up the army and Church, the latter putting a layer of drone Catholic piety into many an unfortunate husband's previously amusing court, and at other times would flatline, teetering on the verge of extinction, with predators on all sides waving their own family trees to explain their sudden interest in ascending this or that throne.

Dynastic history is very unfashionable. Attempts to explain

history through national rulers, their marriages and children has an air of simple-minded idiocy now, merely gossip of a particularly pedantic kind. But this is a shame. Perhaps it could be said that it is defeated not by its chattiness, but the degree to which its chattiness comes from the sheer impossibility of conveying court life in its real, kaleidoscopic complexity. This was a world in which the ruler had huge power, but in which that power was hedged by advice from family – the way that brothers and sisters would convert for the next generation down into father, mother, aunts and uncles, the way that wildly different longevities, experiences, mental aptitudes would shape court life, decisions for war, decisions for marriage, building decisions, religious decisions. All this weighs down dynastic history so heavily that it can hardly move. As readers we can understand someone like the Emperor Charles V, we can concentrate on understanding his personality, his aims, his piety, his interests – but can we really fully encompass his often shadowy kin, his leading nobles, his changing and mercurial relations with a huge gallery of family and other figures, shifting through the years in their levels of influence? It is just too much; there are too many things going on. Any quarter-way coherent account of the reign of Charles V would need to be many thousands of pages long, just to give a sniff of the atmosphere of his complex, fascinating reign. It would need chapter after chapter just to give a sense of what was felt by those who compared him to his grandfather, the unbelievably canny and beguiling Maximilian I. In any event nobody could write such books and nobody could print or read them, and so instead we cling to the single figure of the ruler, flanked by his barren or child-generating consort, and with the odd shadowy brother or uncle or mother who may or may not have carried huge influence in casual, invariably unrecorded conversations, not to mention great, barely sorted piles of noblemen, confessors, tutors, visiting royals who at different times may (or may not) have done so much to shape real European history, almost unnoticed by the blankly staring or hunting-obsessed oddball who happened to be on the throne.

Of course, even allowing for the huge oversimplification created by clinging to crowned heads, German history is just endlessly more interesting and funny simply because the Wettins, Hohenzollerns, Wittelsbachs and Habsburgs between them generate a madly complex gimcrack of genealogies, competing, interrelating, rising, falling, dying on the battlefield, going mad, doing nothing much at all. This provides a pleasure denied to those whose interests are narrowed to the no doubt instructive, but also tiresomely unitary histories of France and England. English royal history is mad too, but it is after a bit just not nutritious enough: only four murdered kings (with a possible fifth) in almost a thousand years, a clearly defined core inheritance, and no really serious internal conflict for three and a half centuries. How can this possibly compare to, say, the mind-blowing switchback-ride of the Saxon Wettins?

German royal history is of a very different kind from Britain's. Probably since the death of William III in 1702 it has been possible in Britain to ignore the monarch – the real story lies with parliament and a network of soldiers and businessmen. In Germany this was not the case. Some of the hundreds of rulers dealt with very small territories in which they could do as they liked, sometimes creating brilliant courts without which European culture makes little sense. Others were very substantial, commanded great armies and settled the fates of millions. This extreme diversity is impossible to encompass, even while admitting a general failure to understand their flanking families and advisers. A slice through any given month in Germany's history could turn up a staggering array of rulers: a discredited soldier humiliated in an incompetently handled battle in his youth, still carrying on his gloomy, undermined reign forty years later; a genuinely pious archbishop obsessed with designing his own monumental tomb; a clearly sickly boy whose regent hopes will die soon in the – as it proves mistaken – belief that he will grab the throne; a half-demented miser, obsessed with alchemy, leaving whole rooms of correspondence unopened for years; and so on.

This characteristic of Germany provides the core of its strange historical flavour – a flavour progressively altered by Napoleon and then Bismarck. It comes up at every key point in its history – what *will* the individual reactions of a host of rulers be in the face of the next challenge? Will they be resolute? Does being resolute turn out to be a bad plan? And resolute against whom? Is a ruler just too old/too young to seize an opportunity? Or too mad? Or ill-advisedly in the Holy Land, or fighting the Turks and unable to get back in time? Does loyalty lie with the neighbour whose palace is further up the river or in the next valley or does it lie with the Emperor in Vienna? Or with the brother who is Archbishop of Würzburg? These anxieties meant that each of the great convulsions in Germany's history, from its meaningful founding in the early Middle Ages perhaps even until the fall of the Berlin Wall (and therefore, presumably beyond), was peculiarly, unstably reactive. The lack of a defining focal point (a London, a Paris) led both to chaos and to space for great creativity and potential entertainment.

It is possible to get too hung up about this point. In, for example, the genealogical multiple pile-up of Swabia with almost every hill under its own prince, it is possible to imagine a feudal version of Jorge Luis Borges' infinite library, a world of so many hundreds of rulers that every variation of behaviour is possible, or indeed certain, in any given moment. So somewhere a ruler with a huge grey beard is dying surrounded by his weeping family and retainers; somewhere else a bored figure is irritably shooting bits off the plaster decorations in the ballroom; another is making an improper suggestion to a stable boy; another is telling an anecdote about fighting the Turks, staring into space, girding for battle, converting to Calvinism, wishing he had a just slightly bigger palace, and so on. This dizzying multiplicity makes each of hundreds of castles a frightening challenge – with the possibility of the guide making my head explode with the dizzying details of how the young duchess had been walled up in a tower for being caught in a non-spiritual context with her confessor and how as a result the Strelitz-Nortibitz inheritance had passed, unexpectedly, to a cousin resident in Livonia who, on his way home to claim the dukedom, died of plague in a tavern near Rothenberg thus activating the claim of the very odd dowager's niece, long resident in a convent outside Bamberg. But it is probably time to move on.

Rampant folk costume

The Germany of the later Middle Ages has much more body and texture than earlier periods. Of course physically this is substantially an illusion – everything has been much rebuilt and every town has been through so many paroxysms since, but something that *might* approach a flavour of the fifteenth century still hangs around some places. It is impossible not to be aware that earlier survivals – cathedrals, monasteries, fragments of palaces – are not unlike dinosaur bones or objects crashed from outer space. They have been so abused, denatured, worn, encrusted and their whole social and political context so heavily scoured away, that they appear as strange, isolated and unfathomable, often in very winning fashions. But while there are many wars, plagues and fires between us and the fifteenth century, it was clearly a time when there was a level of urban pride and a confidence about how buildings should appear – what was appropriate to a market square – that a sort of ideal of town living was created which many later generations were happy to reconstruct after later disasters.

Schwäbisch Hall – a town really just called Hall, but with the *folklorique* Schwäbisch (Swabian) added in the 1930s – is a perfect example of this illusion. A famously successful and prosperous medieval town, it was a mint for the Emperor and a maker of salt. It kept its independence as a Free Imperial City until being folded into Württemberg by Napoleon. Hall sits on a steeply pitched site over a little river, a landscape of high, wooden-framed houses. It is impossible not to be taken in by the sheer agreeableness of every-thing, with the little covered bridges, the herons fishing in the middle of town, the battlements, the bright colours, the lovely churches. Hall even had the surprising distinction of having been home to Germany's only portrait painter who, lacking arms, painted his commissions with his feet. And yet, behind the charm, here is a town which has been devastated by fires, bankrupted by Swedish troops in the Thirty Years War, suffered long periods of total fail-ure. The town as it now appears has been through a lot. And as so

often with cute, well-maintained little German towns, it had a concentration camp nearby and a Messerschmitt factory. Today its
cuteness is paid for with a slurry of cash from a mortgage-company
headquarters, carefully tucked out of sight down the river.

For me these towns have an infinite appeal – they are scattered
around and come from the general complexity and prosperousness
of late-medieval German life. Despite political mayhem, the arteries
of trading routes stretching from Britain to Turkey, from Africa to
Russia, all wound their way through these German towns, with
their inns, markets and specializations, like mule-pace conveyor
belts rolling through mountain passes, down river valleys, around
great forests, with each walled town representing both safety and
sales for hordes of carters, porters and merchants. Periods of
extreme bad luck have tended to preserve some of these towns in
aspic, but others have simply decided that their appearance in a particular era represented a sort of ideal of 'townness' and kept the
layout of walls, gates, market place, town-hall square and big church
through thick and thin, sometimes with a minor convulsion of new,
posh, classical buildings popping up in the eighteenth century, but
generally left alone. Marburg, Freiberg, Hall, Hildesheim, Gmünd,
Weikersheim, Goslar, the list is more or less endless.

What is so attractive about these towns is that we can mentally
populate them. There are realistic and engaging pictures from the
fifteenth century, carved, drawn or painted, of their inhabitants –
Northern Europe comes suddenly to life through the work of artists
who, through changes in taste and technology, have – almost incidentally to their true purposes – memorialized forever the sort of
people who walked through these markets and worshipped at these
churches. This was achieved initially through carving – the great
proliferation (a striking feature of Germany) of large images of the
Passion. We can be grateful that medieval woodcarvers and sculptors had no serious interest in what Jesus and his friends might
actually have been wearing in the hot and dusty conditions of the
Holy Land in the early first century. This frenzy of German carving
then shifted into an absolute explosion of religious painting of the
same themes after about 1500, and it is impossible not to notice,

wandering from regional museum to regional museum, that almost every little parish church seems to have bought a fresh altar-piece around 1505, implying a monstrous sweat-shop of skin-tone specialists, good/bad thief aficionados, Golgotha experts. As these images of the Passion were created for the societies their audiences and creators lived in – much like the contemporary tableaux, festivals, plays on religious themes – they are accidentally full of things for us now to love. Thank goodness that at crucial moments in the Passion soldiers were required to guard Jesus, taunt him, divvy up his clothes, snooze in front of his tomb. Thanks to this grace note in the Passion story we have whole armies of late-medieval soldiers preserved in their chaotic medley of equipment, with their science-fiction-inflected sallet helmets, their chain mail, padded jerkins and studded chest-pieces, still holding swords and crossbows and arquebuses. This unstandardized hodge-podge of metal, leather bits and pieces and pinched, harsh faces once populated a thousand town walls, with their reinforced gates, curfews, alarm bells, crenellations. Similarly, thank goodness, Jesus deals with a wide range of haut-bourgeois scoffers: merchants, judges, lookers-on, all similarly preserved like insects in amber by the artwork that includes them, with their showy hats, lovely capes, decorative belts and clasps and rather odd coloured tights.

These townscapes can be seen so clearly in the background to painters from the Van Eycks to Dürer – a world of charismatic turrets and spires, stone and wood bridges, substantial merchant homes. In *Laughter in the Dark*, one of Nabokov's Berlin novels, there is a millionaire who wishes to create a monstrous movie cartoon which would animate Pieter Breughel the Younger's *Proverbs*, allowing the entire townscape and its myriad inhabitants to drop their frozen poses – to let go of the eel's tail or continue firing a crossbow at pancakes on a roof (a Flemish proverb I really am not going to research). Of course, this idea is both mad and pointless, but it becomes almost oppressive wandering around Schwäbisch Hall or Marburg's crooked, spooky Upper Town: this is a world that has left such a full, vivid, textured record of itself that it seems almost touchable.

As an imaginative game this era is fun, but as real life it is naturally a disaster. Many modern Germans are happy at the drop of a wimple to put on period clothing – Schwäbisch Hall is particularly guilty of this. The whole country indeed is a mass of festivals in which people in strange outfits struggle at various olden-times pursuits, play extinct musical instruments, engage in tasks such as making salt in needlessly laborious ways, or try to persuade people of the virtues of foods mercifully no longer current. This behaviour would almost be enjoyable if it were self-contained, if Schwäbisch Hall were to insist *all* its inhabitants act as though they lived in 1500 and for the duration was sealed from the outside world, with roadblocks and police helicopters, treating it as an introvert sort of game. But, naturally, the point of doing this is to attract tourists – so, perversely, Hall disappears under a welter of people dressed in Tommy Hilfiger leisurewear and waving digital video cameras, with the occasional smocked figure selling horrible pies or wearing gauntlets and a falcon completely lost in a chaotic ruck of idiocy very precisely dateable to 2010.

At worst though, this low self-esteem pageantry is harmless and perhaps even poignant. Long shorn of its Nazi-tinged folkishness, the dressing-up is so compulsive because it represents a time without the horrors of the modern age. In the Schwäbisch Hall town museum there is a very strange painting of the immaculate sixteenth-century square at night in 1871, filled with the town's entire population cheering the creation of the German empire and their absorption into it. The painting is almost black, but has an electric light behind it which illuminates the flags and lamps and fireworks. The message of the picture is very clear – in this intensely locally patriotic little town, here is the town square, site of so many earlier great happenings, now witnessing a fresh page in its history. Of course the museum also has photos of the same square in the 1930s filled with immense, billowing swastikas, hanging from the same windows and poles, festooning the inns and the church. People in Schwäbisch Hall did terrible things across Europe in the 1940s and these people and their descendants still live there – clinging to a more brightly coloured and hopeful past seems a very good idea.

Imperial circles

These quite small, very vigorous but also vulnerable towns were a crucial part of a sort of cultural human chain that reached from northern Italy up to the Dutch coast, shifting ideas and objects back and forth on a mixture of carts, panniers, barges and backs. This was a thriving world, well policed, heavily armed and watchful but, aside from occasional disastrous outbursts, one in which it was plausible to travel with reasonable safety. Most people only moved very short distances with goods being passed along by many hands, their value increasing with each exchange. But of course the most serious money could be made by holding onto your goods and pushing them along greater distances at your own risk, without dozens of impeding middlemen. This mix of the local and the long-distance traffic created different kinds of fortunes, from the great merchants of Antwerp or Nuremberg to countless more petty figures in the interstices. This is the world that can almost be stepped into in some of Dürer's drawings – of water meadows, craggy walls, church towers doubling as watch towers, irregular streets and tiled roofs. It can still be glimpsed in all kinds of places – parts of Bamberg or Quedlinburg or in some of the rebuilt set-piece areas of Münster or Frankfurt.

In the fifteenth century the Empire was reduced to near chaos by the failure of its Emperors (crucially Sigismund and then the long-reigning Frederick III) to pay it sufficient attention, as they retreated into their core, directly owned lands. This led to the crucial invention of 'imperial circles' late in the century – groups of duchies and smaller units who would cooperate both in protecting each other and in representing their members' interests with the Emperor. Started by Maximilian I with a great meeting at Worms, the details took years to settle but ended with a semi-plausible structure of imperial courts (based in Wetzlar and in Vienna and with unfortunately clashing jurisdictions), a system of somewhat consultative meetings and a serious tax base for what was from now on recognizably the Holy Roman Empire.

Some of the resultant atmosphere can still be felt in Regensburg, in the Imperial Assembly building there. For many years the assemblies were peripatetic, meeting in Worms or Nuremberg or wherever was convenient. The shift to Regensburg did not take place until the late seventeenth century, but effectively the institutions remained until Napoleon disposed of them so it is a pleasure to wander around a place so completely soaked in a semi-archaic but not unworkable spirit of compromise and deference. This small but beautiful wooden-ceilinged room with its Imperial symbols is much enlivened by a torture chamber in the basement with rack, stocks and spooky lighting – gleefully set up by some unknown anti-Catholic benefactor with a small crucifix on a stand in the corner to give it an air of monkish hypocrisy. Even allowing for this splendid bonus (and a surprising one – Regensburg is itself a very Catholic place), the surviving Imperial Assembly Hall keeps its dignity and interest. It is impossible, sitting there and thinking about it, not to feel that there has been a conspiracy of odium heaped on the Holy Roman Empire. It did after all last in its mature form some three hundred years, and before that, in all sorts of mutations, many centuries more. It suited German nationalists to hate it naturally enough, as it was nothing if not multi-ethnic and decentred, but we should not take their ideas on this at face value any more than on anything else. It certainly fused into place a sort of fusty bureaucratic obsessiveness (perhaps best explored in Kafka's *The Trial* and *The Castle*, both of which have far deeper than mere twentieth-century roots). It is true that some legal cases literally took centuries to be resolved in Wetzlar with waiting lists for new hearings that could outlast lifetimes. But equally it held together under the most extreme stress: not just the Reformation and the Thirty Years War, but an astonishing array of fighting, shifting alliances and so on, none of which ever really – until Napoleon's arrival – questioned its overall existence.

The 'imperial circles' limited the sovereignty of individual members with even substantial states such as Saxony or ecclesiastical Cologne hamstrung, but it also protected hundreds of chips and fragments, the semi-independent abbeys and castles that proved in many ways to be some of the great facts in Germany's existence – the reasons for the admittedly unwilling tolerance for different religious opinion after the Reformation that allowed, after immense amounts of fighting, for a diversity enshrined in national jigsawism. One crucial imperial circle, for example, was the Netherlands (both north and south) and that circle held the roots of the nationalism which ultimately created the Netherlands and Belgium. It may be that this structure delayed nationalism in Germany, an unhappy contrast with dynamic England or France – but until the late eighteenth century nobody seems to have even thought of such an idea. One of the pleasures of being German must have been watching the failed attempts of wave upon wave of Habsburg Emperors to try to impose a sort of hegemony over their Empire, attempts which always backfired hopelessly, leaving the happy inhabitants of the Mergentheim lands of the Teutonic Knights or the county of Öttingen-Öttingen to get on with their relatively blameless lives. This may have been an arrangement to outrage London or Paris centralists, but in the light of later developments it certainly has now regained its charm.

Habsburgs

I have a clear memory of my sixteenth birthday, which fell on the same weekend as that of a German school friend. Swapping notes about our birthdays I had rashly gone first and said that I had celebrated it at home with my parents and sisters, we had a Chinese takeaway and I'd been given Simon and Garfunkel's *Greatest Hits*, all of which of course had thrilled me ('Feelin' groovy!'). The German friend then countered by saying that he had been given a motorbike and had slept with a friend of his mum's. I certainly remember feeling out of my depth on hearing this, but it seems unlikely that it caused such psychological damage that it set me onto a path of dependence on German history as such.

I also remember the previously mentioned trip to Alsace and the effect it had on me, but again this seems inadequate. In the end perhaps Germany was a displacement activity. I moved to New York in my twenties and, much as I enjoyed being there, reacted to this environment not by a wholehearted embrace of American culture but by heading off in a different direction – by learning German, or trying to learn German, and by getting soaked in German writing and writing on Germany. My bible was always Claudio Magris' extraordinary *Danube*, his set of essays following the river from a squashy field in the Alps to the Bulgarian delta. This set me off on years of loosely Austro-Hungarian reading: particularly the great spasm of regret that followed the disasters after and during the world wars and which ruined the multi-ethnic worlds: Stefan Zweig, Gregor von Rezzori, Joseph Roth, Arthur Schnitzler, Robert Musil, Franz Kafka in a way. I was particularly struck by Rezzori's *The Snows of Yesteryear*, which despite having an appalling title (itself fleeing in dismay from the German title of *Flowers in the Snow*) is a great book. He writes in a series of vignettes about life in the northern Bukovina and its capital Czernowitz (now the far western part of Ukraine). This area was almost a parody of Habsburg diversity, with an astonishing blend of Germans, Jews, Galician Poles, Roma, Ukrainians and Romanians, beautifully described by von Rezzori in an era (the 1920s) when already, as a newly acquired part of Romania (with the city renamed Cernăuţi), this diversity was coming under strain. The Second World War killed or expelled almost everybody, leaving, after a totally fearful series of events, only Ukrainians. The book ends with von Rezzori wandering around the modern town (now Chernivtsi), scarcely able to recognize it.

This is a perhaps roundabout way of saying that in the end I can best trace my interest in German things much less to Germany than to Austria, or more precisely the Habsburg lands. The Habsburgs were always far more than German because they ruled such an absurd array of territories, but it was through my interest in them and a sense of loathing for what happened after their disappearance – with the rival nationalisms they had once managed with fair success tearing each other to pieces well into the 1990s – that Germany came into view for me. As so often throughout most of its history, the real action was in Vienna with the bulk of Germany following behind – a fact that remained true in, alas, ever worse ways into the twentieth century.

So for me the Habsburgs are everything – despite their on the whole rather disappointing personalities, particularly in the final centuries of their astonishingly long period of rule, where even fighting Emperors such as Leopold I have left an oddly colourless legacy, swamped by their role and practising a sort of glum yet fervent religiosity of an unenjoyable kind.

Some of the earlier Habsburgs took full advantage of the opportunities open to them though and their great shrine is the Tyrolean city of Innsbruck. Innsbruck is in many ways a large, dull, functional place, with the battered air all mountain cities have, where the annual corrosion of ice, wind and salt causes subtle but depressing damage everywhere. It is really not enjoyable as a whole, but it has two sensational things in it worth any amount of gloom.

The Emperor Maximilian I died in 1519 having spent a long and enjoyable life, fighting, having children, feasting and fixing up marriages for his own children. His reign has the air of a vastly prolonged international card game where through debonair luck and skill Maximilian winds up with virtually everything. He even had the pleasure of living long enough to sort out his grandchildren's futures and see a fresh round of Europe-wide dramas result, a soap opera of staggering complexity. Sadly Maximilian died before the episodes where it fully unfolded, that the marriage of his son Philip the Handsome to the Castilian Joanna the Mad was going to have the sensational result of their six children turning into two emperors and four queens. The Habsburgs through Maximilian were to pick up Spain, the New World, the Low Countries, Franche-Comté, Hungary, Bohemia, most of what is now Austria, parts of Italy and chunks scattered around Germany. His only loss was Switzerland, which went its own wacky way after the Battle of Dornach in 1499 and need concern this narrative no further.

There is a pleasure in life about Maximilian which is extremely winning, although perhaps misleading. He knew so much, did so much, travelled everywhere, enjoyed the Renaissance as it filtered across the Alps, he spent time being fawned on by toadying humanists while he mulled over whether decorative schemes should show him as a descendant of Aeneas or of Noah, he had Dürer paint his portrait. The last years of his life were spent in part indulging in the unbeatable hobby of designing his own tomb in Innsbruck. Well aware of his great achievements, he wished to make a memorial of such size and grandeur that it would last forever. Consulting various humanists and artists he came up with an immense structure placed at the centre of the Court Church (the church itself built by his successor) with a kneeling figure of himself on top. This is impressive enough, but the real pleasure comes from the array of twenty-eight huge bronze standing figures around the tomb, a blend of real predecessors, contemporaries and mythical ancestors. Some of the sitters were alive still – and indeed Maximilian himself lived to supervise and approve some of their statues. They are about seven foot high and cannot really be reproduced in photographs as it is their texture (bronze doubling as cloth or flesh or indeed as armour) and sheer volume that make them so startling. Much of the emperor's scheme was unrealized – not least the major setback that he himself ended up buried elsewhere. Some of the statues can claim to be the greatest German art ever created: King Arthur and King Theodoric were made in Nuremberg by Peter Vischer the Elder to designs probably by Dürer and sum up a sort of hyper-stylish brilliance that can hardly be improved on. It is perhaps these figures most of all that make such a sad mockery of their thousands of nineteenth-century sculpted successors as Germans tried and completely failed to regain this Gothic-Renaissance spirit. Some of the other statues are simply beautiful records of clothing and hairstyles. There is an old King of Portugal who, happily, left no record of his appearance and had to be shown in full armour to conceal his face – a terrifying sort of Renaissance robot. There are some cheerful absurdities too – the dark patina giving way to shining bronze at Rudolph I's glowing groin, as numerous fingers over the centuries have found it impossible not to touch his prominent codpiece. And there is the amazingly dressed Polish princess Zimburgis of Masovia (Maximilian's grandmother) who was so strong she could straighten a horseshoe with her hands and pull nails from a wall.

The other all-action spectacular in Innsbruck is Schloss Ambras, the home of Maximilian's great-grandson Archduke Ferdinand II, ruler of the Tyrol and Further Austria (which from a British point of view is actually Nearer Austria, a medley of territories based around the Black Forest). Ferdinand had a most enjoyable life: fighting the Turks, ruling Bohemia, illegally and secretly marrying a banker's daughter of acteonizing beauty, and collecting great piles of armour, weapons, pictures and curiosities, many of which are still in the rooms he built to display them. His great collecting rival was his nephew, the Emperor Rudolph II, and after Ferdinand's death in 1595 some of the collections were moved to Rudolph's gloomy Schloss at Prague (where they in turn were looted by Swedish soldiers during the Thirty Years War). Enough remain though to get a strong sense of Ferdinand as a sort of civilized, restless Action Man. The weapons and armour are heaped up every-where, with sensational helmets and famous pieces, such as armour owned by Louis II, King of Hungary, who was killed by the Ottomans together with three-quarters of the Hungarian nobility at the Battle of Mohács in 1526. Most armour is, of course, not that interesting – but the idea that the armour of the famous Louis, Ferdinand's revered uncle, was part of his collection suggests the reality of family, violence, luck and inheritance in sixteenth-century Austrian life.

Ferdinand's own great moment with the Turks was the success-ful defence some thirty years after Mohács of the last Christian parts of western Hungary and his whole life was spent in the shadow of further possible advances by the Turks (there are trophies on the walls of Ottoman quivers, bows and shields). Each cam-paigning season could see devastating setbacks, heroic last stands and hideous accidents and these would have been chewed over ad nauseam by Ferdinand and his guests. Just as he was building the enormous 'Spanish Hall' at Ambras news came through of the Battle of Lepanto, where finally Christian forces managed to deliver a serious blow to the Ottoman navy. This is commemorated at Ambras with huge, rather tabloid paintings of the key commanders and enough of the atmosphere remains to feel how these were topics of personal and immediate interest rather than historical events.

Aside from portraits of members of the Habsburg family (some marvellous, some less so), Ambras is also famous for Ferdinand's obsession with oddity: paintings of the Canary Island family entirely covered in thick hair (a little girl painted à la Velasquez but with a face like a monkey's), a court giant's suit of armour, a picture of a Hungarian nobleman who survived a lance through his head (it enters through the back of the skull and comes out his eye – this dreadful picture is impossible to look at, like a three-hundred-and-fifty-year anticipation of Otto Dix). There is also a painting of a dwarf thought to have jumped out of a pie at the wedding celebrations of William V of Bavaria to Renata of Lorraine, a fine example of the period's rather plodding sense of humour – imitated presumably in many dozens of other ever more minor Renaissance courts, where dwarves must often have been ruefully brushing bits of pastry off their shoulders. It goes on and on: a crucifixion made from coral and seashells, another made from an old tree root, con-cave mirrors, Indian daggers, a North African kaftan from about 1580 which looks as though it was made in about 1970, a lime-wood skeleton in a mincing, gleeful pose. There is very little in the whole collection that could be described as beautiful, but its strangeness more than makes up for it. Ferdinand and Rudolph between them, with their great wealth and unlimited curiosity, created one of the crucial bases for the scientific revolution. Their interests may have had a fairground-sideshow element to them, but entangled in astronomy, alchemy, weird forms of medicine, the Ambras collections still give off a strong sense of a dangerous, alert, restless era and of individuals fizzing with the possibilities open to them. Later Habsburgs may in many cases lull everyone to sleep, but in Innsbruck at least there is a reminder of the sort of brilliance that made them so formidable and so hated.

CHAPTER FIVE

Sieben köpffe Martini Luthers

Vom Hochwürdigen Sacrament des Altars / Durch
Doctor Jo. Cocleus.

Martinus Luther
Siebenkopff.

Doctor · Martinus · Luther · Ecclesiast · Schwirmer · Vsisirer · Barrabas

Spires, turrets and towers

Free Imperial Cities are the real heroes of Germany. At different points in the Middle Ages they managed to pull themselves clear of local princes or were created directly by the Emperor and from that point on maintained themselves, often through considerable luck and ingenuity, as semi-independent states. Responsible only to the generally distant and distracted Emperor, they dotted the chaotic landscape of the Holy Roman Empire, a gleeful, mercantile contrast to their palace-bound ecclesiastical or secular neighbours.

These cities' distinctive landscapes in part appeal so much because they have a sort of toy-town geniality – the city square, the town hall, the posh shops, a tinkling fountain – but also because they seem relatively sane and reasonable. They must have in practice often been bigoted, stifling places, obsessively hierarchical and tiresome, but so much of what is valuable and worthwhile about Germany stems from them that clearly something went right within their walls.

It is hard to generalize about these cities. Some were hardly cities at all and simply sat there rather residually, just about fending off their neighbours. Others were very compact – a small dot on the map like Regensburg seemed hardly worthwhile, but around 1140 when the Regensburgers built the only bridge for many miles across the Danube they had a happy goldmine which made them rich, with strange multi-storey merchants' houses accumulating like a chemical side-effect of the bridge. Ulm and Straßburg were also quite compact places with riverside locations, able to dominate their bits of the Danube and the Rhine respectively – Ulm's Danube fortifications and protected fishing village, however rebuilt, still showing its autonomous, rather threatening position.

Others had sprawling patchworks of territory – Nuremberg and Hamburg, for example, having a core of land with other fragments (some themselves quite important) scattered around. There were severe limits in many cases on their independence. However much they might bristle with weapons and towers they only thrived as entrepôts for their regions and as such needed to get on with those around them. Even within the towns there were all kinds of exclusions and oddities – monasteries or cathedral chapters could own large chunks of land within the walls, the Emperor himself and imperial officials would have a variety of rights (most famously the imperial elections in Frankfurt and the imperial parliament in Regensburg). Sometimes the towns had what could be seen as horrible fungal spores. Nuremberg was cursed in the late Middle Ages by the Hohenzollern family having got hold of an old fortress in the centre of town. The townspeople and the Hohenzollerns competitively built fortifications against each other, adding ever more elaborate platforms, walls and crenellations in case one side or the other tried to make some decisive move. Ultimately the Hohenzollerns were defeated and much of their Schloss demolished in the fifteenth century, but it has left Nuremberg with a peculiar (if, of course, marvellous) mass of stonework hanging over the town.

Cologne had been the main city in the territories of the Archbishop of Cologne, one of the most important princes in the Holy Roman Empire, an Elector and owner of one of the most ancient of Northern European Christian titles. But in 1288 the Archbishop backed the wrong side in a mind-blowingly complex territorial dispute (squaring off against, among others, someone called the Count of Loon) and wound up captured in battle and kicked out of the city forever. From that point on Cologne was a Free Imperial City with the archbishop himself, over several centuries, obliged to sulk, gnash and flounce out in Bonn.

The Free Imperial Cities were so remarkable because while not truly independent they nonetheless had a sort of civic arrogance that expressed itself in lavish display, spectacular town halls, considerable patronage and a wish to compete with each other in ways that made the Empire into one of the great cultural flywheels. Of course the contribution to this atmosphere made by princes, kings and archbishops and the imperial court itself was not slight either, but the sheer density of buildings, gold work, beautiful fountains and generally alluring forests of steeples, turrets and towers made these places startling at a time when Berlin was scarcely a twinkle.

Nuremberg is in many ways the most tragic example. Of course it will always be the city of rallies, laws and trials and will never shake these off. Arriving there for the first time I remember being amazed that I had no sense in advance of what this great townscape looked like – a city as vivid and important to European culture as Siena, say, but which is now a perfect example of how cauterized from the mainstream Germany became in the twentieth century. For Germans themselves it is a townscape which stands for the quintessence of tradition, the perfect echt German town (one of the reasons it so appealed to the Nazis). Featured on a million German tea-towels, cheap prints, beer mugs and table mats, Nuremberg could probably not be identified in a photo by almost anybody in Britain or the United States. And yet here is the home of Dürer, one of the great mapmaking, sculpting, goldsmithing, armour-creating cities – in the Renaissance probably one of the most interesting and absorbing places in the world and still preserving, however much restored, a mass of city walls, bastions, spires, sinister little streets, giant public fountains and so on. Visiting Dürer's house is a predictably dismaying experience (this may have been where his kitchen was, but perhaps not), but there are still scattered around the town (which was severely bombed) some interiors of merchant homes, filled with lovely carvings, decorations, great oak tables and objects of value and interest. My favourite Nuremberg object is the world's first true extant globe, the 'Earth Apple', made by the cosmopolitan Nuremberg freebooter Martin Behaim in 1492. Haggard with age and incompetent restoration, the 'Earth Apple' still magically preserves a just pre-Columbus age, the Atlantic still littered with fake medieval fantasy islands like Saint Brandan and Antilia, which irritated mariners would continue to clean off their charts for years to come; a world in which Zanzibar and Madagascar are the same size and (most importantly) Cipangu (Japan) is an easy sail westward from the

Azores. Behaim was involved in schemes with the Emperor Maximilian to sponsor a trip to reach Japan and China and there is even
a letter from the summer of 1493 on Maximilian's behalf recom-
mending Behaim and others to the King of Portugal for such an
expedition. But four months beforehand Columbus, acting on the
same false hunch about Asia's accessibility, had already returned to
Spain, changing the entire course of human history and beaching
the 'Earth Apple' and its world view forever. It is curious that one
object should preserve Nuremberg's expertise (metalwork, cartogra-
phy, painting, information), ambition (the city's symbols thickly
decorate the South Pole and the globe was clearly an element in the
city's relations with Maximilian) and eventual failure (made at the
exact endpoint of the Middle Ages and the opening of the new Atlantic
trade world which would convert Nuremberg into a backwater).

Almost as magical is the extraordinarily complex bronze
reliquary for St Sebaldus (in a church which in itself is one of the
most complicated, beautiful and moving in Central Europe), a phantasmagoria the size of a small car, crawling with statues of saints
and flowers, dragons and boys and all held up on the backs of huge
bronze snails (symbols of man's slow progress to meet God). Its
creator, Peter Vischer, includes a genial image of himself in his working clothes. The extremely cautious Reformation in Nuremberg
protected the shrine from being smashed to pieces or melted down,
as so many were.

And none of this faintly impinges on Nuremberg's German
Museum, a monstrous set of halls originally built in the nineteenth
century cataloguing all aspects of German cultural life (rank upon
rank of oboes, saints, goblets, Tyrolean masks). This museum has a
wearying completeness which rather swamps the beautiful things
in it – what I chiefly remember now is the sheer pleasure of finding a mock medieval stained-glass window donated by Bismarck
and featuring himself in full plate armour in one corner, both an
honour to one of Nuremberg's old specialities and a fine example
of the patently demented nineteenth-century German sickness of
identifying over-heavily with the Middle Ages.

The Free Imperial Cities each tended to specialize and become famous for some attribute – the mighty bankers of Frankfurt and Augsburg (the amusingly named Fuggers), the saltworks and mint at Hall, shipping and fish at Hamburg and so on. There were roughly seventy-five Cities altogether; some thrived, some blew in completely. Some were so pointless it is unclear how they survived beyond perhaps a sense that they were not worth the trouble (Bopfingen is a town whose name is on relatively few lips). Nuremberg had been sitting pretty as a crossroads of the Holy Roman Empire but as the patterns of trade became more sea-based and more enamoured of the Americas and Asia many of these inland entrepôts lost their vitality even before the horrors of the Thirty Years War. Indeed one of the reasons Nuremberg is so attractive is that it became frozen into inanition and a byword for antique charm and also for economic failure, a dilapidated shadow taken over as a minor gain by Bavaria during the Napoleonic Wars.

The struggle to survive meant that one by one the Free Imperial Cities became absorbed by their neighbours. One group, Basel, Bern and Zürich, became the core of Switzerland and went off on a different tangent. More were grabbed by the French in the 1550s, most notably Wirten (renamed Verdun), Metz and Tull (suddenly Toul). A particular massacre occurred in the Rhineland in the 1670s and 1680s when Louis XIV came up with totally absurd rationales for absorbing, often in the wake of immense violence, places like Cambrai, Kolmar (Colmar) and Straßburg (Strasbourg).

One odd latecomer was Bremen, established as a Free Imperial City from the rubble of Swedish-ruled north-west Germany in 1646 and somehow managing through all kinds of setbacks to maintain its semi-independence to the present, still keeping in a cathedral outbuilding as one of its odder attractions the mummified bodies of a couple of Swedish troopers: a collection added to later by other lucky cadavers, including that of an English adventuress with orange fingernails and a bewitching chocolate complexion generally referred to as 'Lady Stanhope'. The major massacre came in the dying throes of the Holy Roman Empire in 1803 when Napoleon sat and dealt out the cities to his favoured, slavering German allies, who could now at last rule proper contiguous territories. At its lowest point Bremen was absorbed by France and, alarmingly, found itself turned into Brème, capital of the French department of Bouches-du-Weser. This was reversed with France's defeat, but many of Napoleon's new German countries stayed, albeit in highly adapted form, and with them went the Free Imperial Cities that had been snaffled, with Augsburg going to Bavaria, Ulm to Württemberg, Dortmund to Prussia and so on. Coming out the other side of Napoleon's period only Bremen, Hamburg, Frankfurt and Lübeck managed to get back their independence within the German Federation. Frankfurt fell in 1866 through supporting the Federation in favour of the Austrians and against the Prussians. After Prussian troops occupied the city the last bürgermeister, Karl Fellner, killed himself. This endlessly inventive and complex place (its appeal now heavily disguised by annihilatory bombing and post-war redevelopment) just became swept up as an extra piece of Prussian booty – its specific urban traditions irrelevant to the behemoth that now absorbed it. Lübeck clung on until its council took the admirable decision to ban Hitler from speaking there. When the Nazis came to power this proved a bad mistake and in 1937 Lübeck was tossed to the Prussian province of Schleswig-Holstein to make up for Prussian land lost to Hamburg when the latter's territory was reorganized. Lübeck's subsequent rather enthusiastic Nazism and its position on the front line between east and west in 1945 meant that it was doomed to stay as an aberrant part of Schleswig-Holstein. This left, at the end of the war, American-occupied Bremen and British-occupied Hamburg and these have kept their tangled and often semi-broken autonomy going, with Bremen even still owning a territorially separate port (Bremerhaven) as a last, genial reminder of the geographic craziness which once made Germany such a confusing but nourishing place.

A birthplace and a death-house

Martin Luther was born in the Thuringian mining town of Eisleben in 1483. His birthplace is one of those richly enjoyable fake heritage disasters that strew the German landscape. Luther's family only lived in the house of his birth for a few months before leaving town, and the house burned down in the seventeenth century. There was a sufficient shock locally that a new house was built carefully inscribed as his birthplace, but which looked completely different. As nobody had cared about these things when the rather transient Luther family had been in the original house nobody knew which room the prodigy had been born in. To paper over the house's tenuous – indeed non-existent – links with Luther its owners appealed for keepsakes from the great man's life, ultimately scraping together some short letters, a lovely fifteenth-century Bible and some uninvolving medallions. They then put in a pretty hall decorated with the usual paintings of various Electors and princes. This shambles somehow lurched on into the nineteenth century, when the Prussian king took an interest, and in the late nineteenth century a Prussian official, appalled by the house being jumbled together with others and being insufficiently 'picturesque', ordered its surrounding buildings demolished.

The Pope himself would volunteer a thin smile of sympathy at the sheer difficulty in keeping going such a woefully marginal and inauthentic sacred site. Driven to distraction, the current birth-house regime decided last year to go for broke. Now visitors wander into a room featuring a crib and some rather new-looking furniture. Hidden speakers provide quintessentially late-fifteenth-century noises – clopping hooves, groaning cart wheels, barking dogs. And then: a baby cries (little Martin!) and his mother sings a lullaby.

By sheer bad luck I was in Eisleben for the annual festival celebrating Luther's birth. Around the chunky statue of the man himself in the market square the usual cast of figures dressed in sacking drank mead and listened to minstrels singing rude songs very roughly of the right period. The feedback from the stage speakers would certainly have woken up the infant reformer in his cot. Sometimes it seems as though the entire generation of German students who had vaguely sympathized with the Baader-Meinhof Gang back in the '70s are doomed to act out the rest of their lives as blacksmiths, tumblers and flagoneers at these sorts of witless festivals, travelling from town to town in a constant, anxious quest for marginal anniversaries at which to sell candles, honey and fruit brandies. Curiously, another entire generation seems to now also be following in the footsteps of their elders – perhaps as part of an ever-burgeoning government protection programme where reformed terrorists and now former GDR narks keep their freedom but are forever cursed to work as minstrels or town criers. A grim, completely fed-up-looking man dressed as Luther sat off duty, drinking in the hotel bar.

Luther's links with Eisleben were fairly tenuous, then. Despite this, Luther always acclaimed it as his birthplace and at the end of his life came back to adjudicate a land dispute, give a final set of sermons in the beautifully gnarled and imposing church, and die. This means that as a 'combi-ticket' you can buy discounted entry both to Luther's 'birth-house' *and* his 'death-house' while not walking more than a hundred yards. Given how Luther-related sites, some fascinating, some not, sprawl across Germany, this has a real soup-to-nuts attractiveness to it. Of course, by the time of his death Luther was very famous, so the 'death-house' is, while wholly fraudulent too in its furnishings and lay-out, at least the real thing, and as such less fun.

At the time Eisleben was part of the County of Mansfeld, one of Europe's industrial hubs, churning out copper and silver dug from mines of amazing, suffocating nastiness. Luther's father had a senior role in these mines and there has been endless and in the end useless speculation as to how important Martin's unusually capitalist background was in shaping him. There is also the curious and again irresolvable backdrop of printing as a mature business. Is Luther feasible without printing? Jan Hus, a great but ultimately unsuccessful and executed reformer, had in the early fifteenth century been without access to printing. But there are simply too many variables to say what the key differences were, or what it was about Luther's lifetime that made such a huge change in Europe's religious existence feasible.

The problem is that the entire nature of Luther's work – and of those around him or influenced by him such as Zwingli, Melanchthon and Calvin – cannot be viewed with neutrality. The assumption for many generations of Protestants that somehow Luther represented the future and that Protestantism was inherently progressive and dynamic continued to create a gravitational field of great persuasiveness until very recently. The Germany unified after 1871 was then almost torn apart by Bismarck's feeling that the southern, Catholic parts of the country were in some sense backward and unpatriotic, despite Baden, for example, being as dynamic and clever as anywhere. Weber's famously idiotic *The Protestant Ethic and the Spirit of Capitalism* assigned specific virtues to Protestantism even as places such as Catholic Belgium appeared suspiciously able to handle heavy industry, research, financial planning and colonialism. The great majority of the world's Christians – who of course always remained Catholic or Orthodox – looked on with mixed amusement and irritation at the mad conceit of Protestants.

So powerful remain the original roots of Luther's appeal, however, that it *is* almost impossible to shake off this providential story: of a Germany mired in backwardness and corruption snapping suddenly into black-clothed, unshowy modernity. Catholicism itself of course furnishes so much of the critique itself. The principal church of Halle, for example, was built by Albrecht von Hohenzollern, one of the most powerful men in the Empire: Elector of Mainz, Archbishop of Magdeburg, brother of the Elector of Brandenburg. This church was built to mark the triumph of Catholicism over Protestantism (it went Protestant shortly thereafter). The church now features two marvellous Cranach workshop paintings on the altar, both prominently showing Albrecht himself interacting genially with a selection of saints, each helpfully holding their usual symbols: St Christopher with baby Jesus, St Catherine with the wheel she was broken on and so on. Given how many of the figures are young women who were either friends of Jesus or who died terribly martyred in his cause, it is fun to see how the painter follows the Cranach inability to paint women as anything other than erotically depraved. In any event, Albrecht looks the very model of jewelled-glove Catholicism, barely able to stand beneath the weight of vainglorious doodads – sufficient in himself to provoke the Reformation. That Albrecht was in fact a clever and ambiguous figure stands no chance in the face of this sort of association with silks and loose women.

The devil's bagpipes

Protestantism and the Papacy spent centuries in a sort of mutual death grip across Central Europe and to a strange degree they supported each other. For example, it suited both sides to view the Pope as a figure of eternal and superhuman authority who had enjoyed unquestioning authority until undermined by a renegade Wittenberg monk. The Catholic fight-back then became the struggle to re-establish this ancient and God-given role in the face of devil-inspired heretics – the idea behind one of the most famous of all pro-Catholic cartoons with Satan playing a bagpipe shaped like Luther's face. For Protestants in turn it added a sense of bravery and style that they should be taking on such an implacable Monster of Corruption, lounging in hypocritical luxury in Rome guarded by zombie trooper monks. In practice the Pope had always had to deal with challenges to his authority with heretics, anti-Popes, fresh and disturbing innovations. Indeed the hundred and fifty years running up to the Reformation were plagued by great clouds of bizarre ideas, unstable sects, feverish visions, witchcraft, demented processions. Bohemia was torn apart by battles against a series of picturesque heretics, part of a long tradition of defiance of papal authority. After a while the Pope must have dreaded the arrival of the next postal delivery – or rather the Popes must have, as quite often there were two rival ones. So, oddly, the threat of Protestantism opened the way for a much more shrill and genuine Papal harshness than had been possible before. As Protestantism became more entrenched, Catholicism reacted with ever greater violence.

The Reformation itself famously began in 1517 in Wittenberg – today a small, quiet town but then the site of a new, freethinking (or relatively freethinking) university of just the kind that was sure to cause trouble. In a good example of how later periods improve on the past the most striking feature of Wittenberg (aside from its poisonous 'Jewish sow' statue on the side of a church) is a nineteenth-century addition to the rather plain original palace chapel to the doors of which Luther nailed his 'Theses'. This huge, completely mad tower, with massive Gothic letters running round it screaming out 'A mighty fortress is our God', makes Wittenberg startling and impressive in a way that none of the real buildings do. A stream of Lutheran tourists pours through the town, providing its only visible source of income. The famous doors are overwrought replacements (the originals finally coming to grief during the Seven Years War) but despite all these embellishments there is something exciting about the sense of this small town really breaking Europe apart. The wood-panelled rooms in which, whenever Luther was in town, he and his wife held court to their many visitors have been preserved and been tramped through by the curious and pious ever since (most wonderfully Peter the Great's signature is still visible on a piece of woodwork).

In the end it is impossible to disentangle the drama of the Reformation from the events it seemed to provoke: no doubt political events, particularly the usual rows between princes and the Emperor, would have occurred anyway, but from now on all these had a fresh, religious tinge. Once Luther had established a convincing critique of the Pope and one which various German princes would support, for reasons both religious and cunning, anything could happen. Protected by these princes – most crucially by the Elector of Saxony, Frederick the Wise, in his palace fortress outside Eisenach – Luther became a force of nature, pouring out pamphlets and translating the Bible into German (and thereby establishing the idea of German as a written language rather than just a mass of peasant dialects).

Protestantism mutated rapidly into many forms, some uncontrollable by Luther himself but digging into a rich mass of previously existing anarchism, peculiar private religious practices and so on. All subsequent events became seen as something to do with Luther. The most important of these events centred on the Thuringian town of Mühlhausen, one of the key bases of the Peasant War but much later also birthplace of Johann Röbling, the architect of the Brooklyn Bridge – although he left when he could.

Answering Luther's call for reform, peasants, farmers and clergy across a broad band of central Germany, convulsed by intense religious feelings, rose up and started massacring the authorities. Similar disturbances had occurred before but the divisive religious issue gave these riots a new sort of momentum and it is not an exaggeration to say that this was the single greatest revolt in Europe before the French Revolution. Scenes of scarcely credible savagery engulfed region after region. Mühlhausen became the headquarters of one of the leaders of the war, Thomas Müntzer. A mystic and thoroughly impractical figure prone to visions, he was never really in charge – but Karl Marx and Friedrich Engels noticed him centuries later and decided he was a good communist stand-in despite his top-to-toe religiosity. This meant that the German Democratic Republic loved him – here was a German who could give Germany an impeccably communist pedigree. The lucky chance of his having fought on communist-controlled territory and the anniversary of his birth falling in 1988 provided a last gasp of excitement for the GDR, with Mühlhausen being turned into a sort of secular shrine to him. Some of this has now been cleaned up, but Müntzer remains an oddly omnipresent figure – and a fascinating example of how rapidly (only eight years after Luther's theses) the Reformation began to run completely out of control. Müntzer was only squatting in Mühlhausen as he had already been kicked out of more mainstream cities such as Prague. The Peasants' War really lasted so long because Imperial troops were away in Italy with Charles V thwarting a French invasion. As soon as the devastating Battle of Pavia had crushed the French, troops began to be moved back over the Alps and were available to dispose of Müntzer and his ragged, desperate supporters at the massacre of Frankenhausen. The GDR commissioned the totally ridiculous, if compelling, largest oil painting in the world at the site of the massacre, created in the 1980s in a vaguely sixteenth-century style but having more of the atmosphere of a Terry Pratchett novel. Under the sort of numbing title that now makes the GDR sound so quaint the painting was called *The Early Bourgeois Revolution in Germany.* The fighting ended with the proto-communist yet oddly religious revolutionaries chopped to bits. Müntzer was captured, tortured and executed in Mühlhausen, his decapitated body left on display as a reminder to the town's surviving citizens to behave.

If the Pope dreaded hearing of more setbacks, Luther himself wound up fairly inured to bad news. What he had seen in conservative and measured terms soon turned out to have unleashed a crazy mass of individuals, many working on the basis that the Second Coming was imminent. Luther hated the Peasants' War and ended up a violent supporter of the status quo and thereby, perhaps inevitably, made Lutheranism into only a single if important strand in an ever-wackier patchwork of belief.

The ruler of the world

A complicating fact in the Reformation was the new Emperor, Charles V. This extraordinary man is now a rather dim figure but he holds a place in the sixteenth century comparable to Napoleon or even Hitler – in the sense that his decisions and actions held a sway across Europe of a quite exceptional range: until the arrival of Napoleon there were no figures of such grandeur and reach, with even Frederick the Great being a sort of provincial amusement in comparison.

A Burgundian from Ghent, Charles had a rise to power that was madly vertiginous. In a sequence of dynastic accidents, Charles first inherited the Burgundian lands in 1506; then became King of Spain with places like southern Italy and America thrown in; then on the death of his grandfather Maximilian he also inherited all the Habsburg lands in Austria, followed by picking up the role of Holy Roman Emperor in 1519 through outrageous bribery. In a series of moves therefore he became over some nineteen years quite incalculably powerful, with Mexican loot pouring in and a messianic sense of being the God-given ruler of the whole Christian world.

Charles was thoughtful, well educated and brave and even spent his spare time wisely – for example sleeping with a Regensburg innkeeper's daughter, who subsequently gave birth to what turned out to be Don John of Austria who destroyed the Ottoman fleet at Lepanto, a sex act somewhat uneasily commemorated with a statue and plaque in Regensburg today. Charles marks, through changes in styles of portraiture (which are of course completely deceptive) but also through the nature of his education and his own aspirations, something new and a bit more modern. His predecessor as Emperor, Maximilian I, has the same air of Burgundian, fifteenth-century chic as the English kings Edward IV and Henry VII – rather remote and hard to fathom. In his great portrait by Dürer, made shortly before his death, all gloom and furs, Maximilian seems like a medieval wizard. Charles gave the impression of being very different – an impression greatly enhanced by his firmly new-fangled portraits by Titian. He spent his entire reign on the move – there is it seems hardly an inn on an attractive town square anywhere in Germany where he did not take up residence at some point or other. Motivated, well financed and tireless, he patrolled his varied inheritance, which in Europe stretched with some minor gaps from Gibraltar to Transylvania. He fought everyone and everything – he carved out a new substate in north-west Europe from a mixture of inheritance and conquest, thereby unwittingly inventing the Netherlands just in time for it to rebel against his successors; he battled the Turks, he battled the French.

Above all, at the Diet of Worms in 1521 he listened to Luther's arguments about reform: and rejected them. This may have been a delusion, but it had been felt at least possible that Charles, with his immense power and prestige, could have brokered a deal which would have reformed the Papacy (something which many faithful to the Pope would have been happy with) and involved Luther in the process. But instead he opted for repression. Luther had been present at Worms under Imperial protection and he now fled to the safety of the Elector of Saxony's Schloss.

Charles's decision to root out Protestantism split Europe (although this may have already been inevitable – we can never know) and ensured his own failure. It is one of the very odd facts of life in far western Eurasia that nobody has managed to unite Europe in the way that the Chinese emperors or Ottoman sultans did their lands. It is perhaps one of the strongest argument for being sceptical even about the very idea of a 'European' culture, that anyone who has attempted to create a single political culture seems to have provoked an almost unconscious, automated counter-reaction that foils him. Charles certainly felt that he was on a mission to unite Europe and then destroy Islam – the marriage of his son (the future Philip II of Spain) to Mary I of England should have resulted in England being added to the Habsburg domains (a plan only foiled by Mary's failure to have a child and then her death). But it does seem that, whatever the stated motives of those involved, there is a supra-dynastic element in European life that steps in to dispose of anyone wishing to rule a single, unified, giant land. For Charles the nightmare was the French, whom he repeatedly thrashed (most gleefully at the Battle of Pavia in 1525, when he even managed to capture the French king) and from whom he picked up Milan as a further piece of property, but who just kept on coming and ultimately exhausted and humiliated him.

It is here that the Reformation becomes most murky and interesting. Clearly religion was a magnificent weapon in any fight with Charles V. The Holy Roman Empire crawled with princes and knights who were horrified by the possibilities open to Charles – the most powerful ruler since Charlemagne. We simply cannot attribute clear motives for anybody involved (although one can point to certain rulers who manoeuvred in a more shockingly cynical way than others), but a break with Rome was a clear way to keep Charles at bay. Equally, in a society soaked to the top of its head in religion, the immediate appeal of Luther was to many individuals genuine and overwhelming. The speed of events is amazing, from Luther hammering up his theses in 1517 to the Edict of Worms in 1521 which outlawed Luther and his views and started the process of killing people.

★

Important switches to Protestantism were everywhere in the same years, including one odd convert, the gnarled old reprobate Ulrich, Duke of Württemberg, a chaotic, brutal and nasty murderer, kicked out by his disgusted subjects, who converted to Reform and, despite an almost incredible further series of demeaning and half-baked adventures, died in charge of his old duchy and safely succeeded by his son. Württemberg is a fun state as it seems so often to represent everything grotesque about Germany: its dukes and then kings were a picturesque lot and the core of Stuttgart and their other castles and palaces are fine backdrops to the world of a medium-to-small state that was both buffeted by fate and yet also had its fate made far worse by its rulers' ineptitude. But whatever its future travails, here was a genuinely Reformed state – home in the Old Schloss in Stuttgart to perhaps the earliest purpose-built Lutheran royal chapel, a simple, grave, magical little place created by Ulrich's son, where I worshipped once with three or four elderly parishioners, the scarcely breathing residue of a religious movement that tore Europe apart for centuries. The boggling Ulrich's motives can never be plumbed, but the end result of his decisions – and those of more serious figures such as Frederick the Wise – was a split within Europe that became permanent.

Charles V simply had to fight too many people and deal with too many complex political issues – not least stemming from being King of Spain, a country whose language he could never speak properly, but whose multifarious interests in America and the Mediterranean had as much call on his time as events in the Holy Roman Empire. The booty pouring in from America is one of the most astonishing features of the age. On the last of his major journeys from Nuremberg, Dürer travelled in 1520 to the Netherlands to attend Charles V's imperial coronation at Aachen. While there Dürer saw in Brussels the just arrived gold treasures taken from the defeat of the Aztecs (Dürer also saw a walrus, hauled in by fishermen back from the Arctic, whose head he magnificently drew). It is useless, but interesting, to ponder whether during the Diet of Worms the following year, Charles V was thinking more about Luther's heresies or more about the sacks of precious metal he now owned, so valuable that they changed the shape of the entire European economy.

In any event, Charles's absences proved fatal. Reform spread, as Luther, aided by a band of equally compelling preachers, by his own widely spread writings and by the startling propaganda images of Lucas Cranach the Elder, inspired a great swathe of Europe to throw off papal authority. Entire states switched allegiances, formed defensive leagues and awaited the Catholic onslaught. These were years of horrible persecutions, with the Low Countries under a reign of terror and all mention of Luther's name, let alone writings, under absolute ban. But Charles did not rule directly over all his territories. The Heath Robinson workings of the Holy Roman Empire and the patchwork, chaotic nature of his inheritance made his every action almost absurdly complex and uncertain. Shortly after Luther's death in 1546 the principal Protestant defensive organization, the memorably named Schmalkaldic League, overplayed its hand. The Protestants had taken advantage of Charles's numerous distractions to intimidate and mop up some remaining Catholic territories, but goaded beyond endurance, Charles temporarily threw off his other tormentors and at the Battle of Mühlberg crushed the Schmalkaldic Army, led by John Frederick I of Electoral Saxony, the nephew of Frederick the Wise.

With Wittenberg under siege (the ultimate Lutheran shrine and still home to an embattled Cranach), the war ended disastrously for the Protestants, who were broken as a political force. Terms were dictated at the 'armed' Diet of Augsburg, ringed by Charles's Spanish troops. Still, however, Charles could not shake off the indirect nature of his rule over the Holy Roman Empire. He could be as horrible as he liked to places like the Netherlands and Spain, which he personally owned. But he had to acknowledge that the Electors and their associates whether hostile or friendly (like the Catholic archbishops) just would not wave goodbye to their own semi-independent status. Short of invading each state and slaughtering each one's ducal families Charles could not impose his will, even in the triumphant era enshrined by Titian in his somewhat unrealistic 'Battle of Mühlberg' portrait of Charles as the armoured, horse-borne champion of true Catholicism (feeling poorly, he had in fact been carried to the battle on a litter). The Lutheran rulers maintained their separate status – subsequently enshrined in the Peace of Augsburg in 1555 with Charles's brother Ferdinand.

Charles came close after Mühlberg to making a coherent Holy Roman state in Germany, but even so it was a hopeless project and the mass of separate major and minor states clung on. Then, in one of the most startling and dramatic scenes in sixteenth-century history, Charles V stood before his key lieutenants in Brussels in October 1555 and announced his retirement from all his remaining titles and disappearance to a Spanish monastery – worn out and despairing, mocked by continuing French and Protestant feistiness, he threw in the towel and through his actions made himself a rather more attractive figure than his most significant pan-European successors. But this late capitulation did not alter the overall disaster of his reign – the violent tangle of his shambolic inheritance would be worked out over the following two and half centuries.

Within the Holy Roman Empire, the Peace of Augsburg admitted a sort of fretful exhaustion after a generation of violence. It conceded the idea that the ruler of each state, small or large, could chose between Lutheranism and Catholicism – but all this at the expense of anything else more radical, which remained absolutely forbidden. Of course, this simply meant that Calvinists and others went underground or clung to friendly territories such as Switzerland or the Netherlands (which from now on really became a separate place – a broad strip of aggressive Protestantism hemmed in by forcibly re-Catholicized and burnt-out Münster to the east).

Charles V's decision to split the Habsburg empire into two branches, one based in Madrid and one in Vienna, meant that the Madrid branch became obsessed with the Mediterranean and America, crushing dissent in the Netherlands and handling the miserably antagonistic French. Vienna focused on fighting the Turks but also, under the long, listless but artistically fecund reign of Rudolf II, more or less drifted to sleep, with its alchemists, astrology and gloom – perhaps best summed up by the sensational pages of painted calligraphy by Joris Hoefnagel and Georg Bocskay, designed for the

Emperor to leaf through, with its mirror-writing, minutely observed caterpillars, toadstools and – most weirdly of all – a black page with words in white and a sloth chewing a twig.

The serious excitements in the world were therefore elsewhere and Rudolf II's slumbers (his rooms filled with unanswered letters) allowed a multitude of German states not to maturely settle down as Protestant and Catholic, but instead to fester.

The New Jerusalem

If the Peasants' War had made the more extreme aspects of the Reformation unappealing to many possible converts and shaken Luther into a more moderate pose, then the astonishing events of 1534 had a similar effect on north-eastern Germany.

The Westphalian town of Münster is a hard place to criticize. Its air of provincial gloom can at least in part be blamed on its devastation in the war, but it has probably never been a very fun spot. It has a permanently honourable role as the base of Bishop Galen, one of the few leading churchmen to speak out categorically against the Nazis. In stark contrast to the modern town – a steady drift of German consumerism under headachy skies – Münster in 1534 became the focus of apocalyptic hopes and fears. Anabaptists, extreme Protestants who believed in the total separation of their Church from any state authority at all, began to gather in Münster from all over Europe and, having taken over the town, made it into an independent kingdom of virtue, awaiting the brief period before the world ended and the present Godly dispensation came to an end. Their leader, John of Leyden, was in fact King of the World and the people of Münster the Chosen of Israel. Opponents were executed, all goods held in common and men could have as many wives as they wished – partly so as to allow lots of children to arrive and boost the number of Israelites as fast as possible to 144,000 (a mystical number) but partly, it is impossible not to think, because the Israelite rulers could not believe what they could get away with. This blood-soaked, highly unstable entity persevered into the following year in an environment that must have been unpleasantly like West German experimental-theatre productions of the 1970s. The Anabaptists were always fighting for their lives in the town against ever-larger besieging forces, but even if left alone it is hard to imagine that Münster could have ever stabilized into more than anything completely horrible. Having declared themselves a final, elect group with no further members, the Münsterites awaited Heaven's sword. What they got instead was Franz von Waldeck, a classic fighting prince-bishop (in his portrait a startling amalgam of out-of-control warrior and Church grandee), with his own Protestant sympathies but with no time at all for polygamous communists. With a substantial princes' army he stormed the town's defences and destroyed the New Jerusalem.

For generations the story of Münster became the nightmare of what could happen when social order broke down. It destroyed the Anabaptists as a serious movement, generating freakish gangs of Bible-neurotic killers like the Batenburgers (not to be confused with the pink and yellow sponge cake, which is spelt Battenberg), who roamed the Low Country borderlands murdering non-believers, using secret signs and enjoying polygamy in between times. These and their ever-crazier and more disgusting splinter groups, such as the sinister-sounding Children of Emlichheim, had all been rounded up and executed by the 1580s, but their continuing existence was very helpful in imposing an almost sheep-like docility among Lutherans, obediently clustered around their rulers for fear of something worse.

But another response to Münster came from the Mennonites, who combined some Anabaptist ideas with an extreme sort of quietism – a total rejection of the state in all its forms and a private community existence in communion with God. This set of beliefs – in its way just as startling and novel as anything put forward by the colourful Münsterites – had a profoundly valuable future. In the face of aggressive persecution by understandably unsympathetic princes, Mennonites spread around the world – to the Ukraine, to Manitoba, to Pennsylvania (in part as the splinter group known as the Amish), to Paraguay and to Iowa, creating an extraordinary and enduring critique of all national government. Their survival, sometimes under horrific threats and sometimes under far luckier conditions, is one of the great stories from this German religious explosion, albeit in its sheer quietness not one much appreciated or thought about.

There was also the Family of Love – a network of outwardly conforming individuals who followed an intensely private religion and scattered across north-western Europe – keenly aware that, as persecution grew ever more violent, they could best achieve religious reform in secret and thereby avoid being carved up or burnt. Members ranged from Breughel the Younger to the keeper of the lions in the Tower of London.

The fate of the captured leaders of the Münster commune was an unpleasant one, as can be imagined. Repeatedly abused and tortured, John of Leyden (separated from his surviving fifteen wives – he had earlier beheaded one) was with two key associates stood on a platform in the centre of town and, in the compulsory presence of the entire population, had pieces of himself pulled off with giant, specially made red-hot iron pincers. He was then beheaded and cut into quarters. The remains were then shut inside huge iron cages and hauled up the side of St Lambert's Church from which, over the years, bits would sometimes tumble – a constant reminder to the people of the town not to even think about rebellion or heresy.

The modern reason for coming to Münster is that these cages, extraordinarily, are still there. As you wander around the town, thoughtfully munching a pretzel, suddenly: there are the cages. The idea that these things through so many years have endured (presumably restored at intervals) as a sort of permanent memorial to ghoulish cruelty, both official and rebel, had appalled me for years and it was odd, having thought about the objects so much, actually to see them. The only disappointment was going into the church and finding that there were no postcards. In one of those many moments where my lack of German has proved so valuable I spent ages working out from my dictionary how to ask the forbidding lady at the little cash desk: 'Do you in fact have a postcard of the flesh-cages, perhaps hidden in a drawer? I will pay you well.'

By the time I had worked out a plausible form for 'flesh-cages' I realized that this request probably would not be viewed as a funny one. I was reminded of the time wasted in Dessau once, staring at the uninformative website for the Junkers Aviation Museum. This place was a long tram ride out of Dessau and appeared only to feature the Junkers civil airliner from the 1930s (the famous, slightly dull one, with corrugated metalwork and three engines). Rather than fritter a valuable afternoon at what felt like it could be a corporate bromide almost as numbing as the Audi museum in Ingolstadt, I pored over my dictionary working out how to say over the phone, 'Excuse me, but do you in fact have a Ju87 "Stuka" dive bomber tucked away somewhere?' before I realized that I probably wouldn't be able to understand the coldly formal reply.

An unhappy wine merchant

One very odd aspect to many European countries, not often noticed, is that if you start in their top north-wests they are generally unattractive, gloomy, harsh places – but if you travel south-east life gets better. This is drastically true in Scandinavia, but more curiously it works for Spain, Italy, France and Greece – all start out blustery, a bit cheerless and marginal or indeed too mountainous to have more than a scattering of wiry farmers (Galicia, the Savoy Alps, the Pas de Calais, Epirus). But then they get sunnier and more pleasurable, packed with wine, melons, olives and a plausible, regular outdoor existence. This curious longitudinal range is critical for these civilizations – it gives them a spread of experience but also (if it is possible to see a country as an organism, which of course it isn't except in wilder nationalist tracts) a sort of hopefulness: a feeling of ownership over types of food and life. It is not as though the entire population of Calais, say, actually moves in a catastrophic rush (as though on some destabilized raft) to the Mediterranean edge, any more than huddled Savoyard shepherds hanker to move from the Alps to Italy's heel. Indeed the focuses of these countries (Madrid, Paris, Rome, Athens) all suggest some deep geographical compromise – access to a warm or even warmer south and its good-ies allied to a studied decision to ensure that south's political marginalization.

As this is a book about Germany it will not take much time to realize that this is a country with a different framework. As its inhabitants flee southward, away from the grimness and pickled fish of the north-west they do not find themselves in some golden land of sunshine but, instead, crash into the implacable, sterile and unhelpful Alps. It is, of course, impossible really to say what role this plays in German life. I will talk later about the generalized sick longing for Italy that has so animated German culture, but it has certainly meant that for most of Germany's history its principal competitors have been blessed with a much more attractive world (setting aside Britain as simply a basket-case on these issues), most strikingly in relation to wine.

For much of Europe, civilization has been intimately and hap-pily tangled up with wine – the essential element in wave upon wave of cities, cultures, ways of life. With different histories Spain, France, Italy and Greece have been united in being great conveyor belts for wine, drinking immense amounts and exporting it to less happy environments. Germany has always been proud of its wine production but it is on a tiny scale (perhaps a tenth of Spain's, for example) and it battles constantly against a cold, rough climate and a short summer. Germany does have some fabulous wine areas. The train trip from Koblenz to Trier down the Mosel Valley is a hymn to grapes with every tiny jut or near-vertical slope stuffed with vines. For non-drinkers it might seem a rather depressing mono-culture – the Mosel must have looked very pretty before wine wrecked it – not unlike driving through an oil-palm or rubber plan-tation. But for those, like me, in favour, it is a grapey Angkor Wat.

I once had a friend who in a moment of genial self-hatred decided to become a wine merchant in London specializing in German wines. I never dared ask what the deep roots of this deci-sion were – perhaps just a profound idleness, or a pathological wish to fail. I once visited him in his shop in north-east London. This was some time after the grotesque Austrian anti-freeze-in-the-wine scandal and when the British market was starting to be flooded with cheap Australian and Chilean wine. Ranks of pretty bottles lined the walls, their Gothic lettering, riot of umlauts and baffling labels alienating all but the toughest wine completist. Attractive maps of the different, rather small German wine regions were pinned on the walls. Some plastic bunches of white grapes and little wooden barrels decorated the windows. There was an eerie lack of clientele.

One of the many perks of having no customers was of course that he could easily lock up the shop (or indeed just leave it open) and have a long lunch somewhere. Once he took me to a nearby cafe used by taxi drivers which did spectacular all-day breakfasts. We worked through throbbing piles of black pudding, bacon and beans with a couple of dinky half-bottles of very expensive sweet German wine. He gloomily explained how until the First World War for most people in England drinking wine meant drinking 'hock' (German Rhine/Mosel white) or 'claret' (French Bordeaux red). Twentieth-century events made it patently weird to keep on drinking hock and it vanished almost overnight, never to re-emerge. As a historian once put it, German white wine just 'tasted too much of steel helmet'. All that remained was the utterly and totally cheap end of the market, exemplified by Blue Nun and her friends who, despite a bad press, have spread a lot of happiness over the years.

My friend's vision had been that German wine had hit such a low that, with ever more British people drinking wine, racked as ever by our childish national craving for constant novelty, they would turn to his expertise: only a small increase in enthusiasm for Rheingau Riesling would float his entire business. This turned out to be not true. In fact the situation just got worse and worse. I lost touch with the friend in the 1990s but can't help thinking he has retrained by now.

The need to find those rare slopes of at least intermittently sun-friendly land means that vines pop up all over the place. Towns like Würzburg have vines coming down to the railway station and curled around its fortress. The little former Free Imperial City of Esslingen, just outside Stuttgart, has vines stretching from its hill-top crenellations to the road and there cannot be anything much more pleasant than walking past them. The marginality of much of German wine-making makes it a bit more heroic and perverse than that of the substantial, sun-kissed producers – as though the whole thing is just an effort of cultural will to fit in with the expectations of classically trained post-Roman states. But it has its own magic. I like drinking wine but I'm hardly an obsessive. A glass of wine in Würzburg one evening had me in tears – admittedly against a back-drop of exhausted hysteria from clambering all over this sensational town – but also driven by its delicious, benign clarity. This was as nothing though compared to a tiny underground restaurant in some old monastic vaults in Speyer which served a white wine that had been decanted into glass flasks and kept buried in ice for hours and which tasted like some magic, if possibly untrustworthy, potion from Grimms' fairy tales.

The final wine outpost lies around Meissen in Saxony, so far north-east that you feel every grape needs to be individually coaxed and pleaded with to plump up at all. I was staying at a guest house with two straggly and stunted vines immediately outside the window and there was clearly a sort of chic within the town about the absurdity of growing wine in such an un-Mediterranean envi-ronment. The blissful pub which showcases this wine, the Vincenz Richter, has something of the air of a moonbase or Saharan fort – the last place before things get worse, a final glass of wine before moving into the leaden, grain-alcohol skies of Prussia and Poland. I think I'd be entirely happy eating my dumplings and gravy, surrounded by President Hindenburg ashtrays, rusty swords and agricultural tools, slurping a thin and steely bottle of Vincenz Richter. I even tried to buy some to take back home but so small is the crop that all they could – in polite bafflement – offer me was a monstrous display bottle of rosé which had clearly decorated the bar for some time and lost much of its colour even in the weak sunlight. I still have it as a sort of talisman as I write now – I'm sure undrinkable.

CHAPTER SIX

The Golden City of the Faithful »
The land where the lemon blossom grows »
Black armour » The King of Sweden's horse »
A surprise visit from an asteroid

The Golden City of the Faithful

In the later sixteenth century something really does seem to go wrong with Germany. After the Peace of Augsburg in 1555 there was the most extended quiet patch recorded in Central Europe's history, lasting until 1618. That this should be so shows just how much the region's default setting has always been either war or preparation for war, both at the instigation of its own rulers and through the unlucky role of being a natural arena for others. Some countries could last centuries hidden behind mountains or the sea without fighting on their soil, but it seems that everybody took turns to ravage Germany. This long peace oddly does not call up any sort of golden age – it was a poisonous and unproductive peace, filled with bitter religious disputes (many between different Protestant groupings), an ebbing of cultural and intellectual initiative, an economic silting-up and a growing assumption that a major war might clear the air.

Much of this atmosphere is caught and preserved in the town of Lüneburg, in Lower Saxony. This had been a crucial part of the Hanseatic League despite being so far inland. One of the largest medieval industrial sites in Europe, Lüneburg churned out immense amounts of salt, the mining of which riddled the ground beneath it and only fully stopped in 2000. Salt was the crucial element in northern commerce, needed in infinite amounts to preserve food for the winter but controlled by a handful of major producers. Lüneburg's close links with Lübeck can still be seen in its Lübeck-style architecture – the strange, stepped brick house-fronts – and the intensely mercantile atmosphere, with its storehouses, canals, ancient crane and austere churches. In the later sixteenth century

Lüneburg began to seize up as salt became easier to ship from else-where, merchants focused on more interesting things (such as trading with America and Asia) and the centre of the world shifted. This ghastly feeling was available to the burghers of towns across inland Germany – places with easy coastal access were getting richer and richer while much of the interior began to decay. It didn't seem to matter how violently the Spanish attacked the renegade Netherlands, both sides (maritime, outward-looking) just seemed to become ever wealthier. The Netherlands even took over most of the Baltic trade, as the Hanseatic League fell to pieces. As so often, an old and pretty town centre in Germany is a strong indication of an ever more decrepit economy. Lüneburg dwindled into an ever less important place: by the time of the Second World War it was happily not even significant enough, despite its convenient location, to be worth bombing. It re-entered history briefly as the place where Heinrich Himmler – recognized by his British captors in his pathetic disguise – killed himself.

A startling effect of this neglect can be seen in Lüneburg's one great building – the town hall. Through a combination of economic gloom and inertia, much of the inside of the town hall has been kept in its late-sixteenth-century condition, when a final great decorative effort showed off the town's grandeur just as it ended. I'd be hard pressed to find quite so much allegory stuffed into any other comparable space, whether painted or carved, and the famous rooms offer a glimpse into a lugubrious world in which everything is an emblem, every virtue is clunkingly spelt out, every monarch a fountain of justice. One hall has its ceiling covered in hundreds of standardized pictures of great kings from the past, dark walls are covered in a seeming infinity of family shields, an obsessive geneal-ogy of local rule. The most stifling and glum of all must be the fusty tangle of the old archive room, with its ancient desks and walls stuffed with year after year of dated record boxes (1601, 1602, 1603). That they should exist is, naturally, astonishing, but I felt a part of me suddenly quite keen on the sort of commercial, royal, social confidence that might simply set fire to the whole lot and start again. Surely at some point all this must have looked rather embarrassing? Why did Lüneburg so completely lose that desire for change of the kind that, for example, drove Catholic architects in the following two centuries merrily to tear out centuries of Bavarian church fittings and fill up the lot with zooming white marble angels, barley-sugar pillars and ceiling vaults filled with implausibly sunshine-style blue skies?

The Great Council Room, a mass of carved wood panelling and lovely old benches, is a scarcely credible survival, clinging on through four hundred and fifty years of changing fashions, warfare and drunken nightwatchmen dropping their oil lanterns. The room gives off a rich sense of only just being vacated by serious, dark-clothed, heavily bearded and ruffed patricians, fresh from mulling over profound splits within the Protestant camp and the annoying growth in enthusiasm for, say, Moluccan spices or Peruvian silver over their own honest and practical local product.

Much of the character of all these rooms comes from the tireless work of Daniel Freese, a jobbing painter who trundled around north Germany turning out maps, devotional works, coats of arms and allegories as the need arose. Freese in many ways exemplifies the crisis in German culture in that he picked up so many commissions while not being terribly good. One can only hope that at least some Lüneburgers laughed at his earnest allegory of justice, with Prudence helping the ruler judge when faced by Anger (with a flaming sword), Lies (with a devil behind her head), Suspicion (blind and handless), Calumny (arrow instead of tongue) and Invidiousness (snakes for hair) plus the usual duller figures of Wisdom and Victory.

But it is Freese's tabloid or infant-school sensibility that makes his paintings for the Great Council Room so striking. Here, accidentally preserved in all their clumsiness, are core-samples of the brain of the late-sixteenth-century Protestant. Created in the 1570s and ranged around the walls they show a world of Last Things, of a religious struggle in which winning could not be more important, and where enemies would literally be doomed to eternal torment. In one mad vision the Second Coming sweeps away, like an enthusiastic housemaid, a tangle of losers: figures representing Death,

Turks, the Pope, Eastern Orthodoxy and the Devil. These evil characters give way in another painting in the face of the glory of a vast, orange and turreted Golden City of the Faithful, presided over by God, picked out by Freese in an infantile orgy of glaring colour which, for most sane observers, can only make lying in a pile with skeletons and fat popes seem a better housing option.

At the centre of the room is Freese's most poignant work: a painting of the Emperor Maximilian II flanked by the solemn, ermine-robed Electors (in reality, a pretty variable bunch). Maximilian died in 1576 after a fairly short reign and this painting must have been made shortly beforehand. The tragedy lying at its heart is that Maximilian probably represented the best opportunity for some form of religious peace. Sympathetic to Lutherans, sceptical of papal authority, he seems miles away from the incense-laden Jesuit fodder who made many other Habsburgs such bywords for dull-minded bigotry. Like many important rulers across the Empire, he toyed with changing faith and, given how riddled with Protestantism the areas he directly owned and ruled – Austria, Hungary and Bohemia – had become this would have been as sensible as remaining Catholic. Incredibly – at least in the light of later recalcitrance on this issue – he urged the Pope to agree to married priests. But he was much distracted by fighting the Ottoman empire, pressured by a host of more devout Austrian and Spanish relatives and in the end did little more than continue a tolerance which could always be suspended. His reign held the chance that Central Europe as a whole might have become Protestant, but in the end he disappointed his fans. His children were educated in Spain in the worse strains of Castilian black-clothed gloom and he himself died suddenly in Regensburg en route to a pointless invasion of Poland. For both Protestants and Catholics the fervent hope had been the end of the schism, with one side backing down and being converted. Maximilian's reign made it clear that this would never happen. Protestantism reached its greatest extent, but huge blocks of Germany remained Catholic, allowing both sides to imagine that with missionary persuasion stumped, warfare might do the trick. The doom-laden atmosphere preserved in Freese's pictures, visions of plague and starvation and the end of the world, lashed on by economic failure and paranoid religious certainties, made an unappealing world in which to live.

The land where lemon blossom grows

Standing contentedly in front of the cooker making a risotto, drugged by clouds of scent from newly torn-up basil and listening to Vivaldi's *Gloria*, it is hard not to think that my interest in Germany may have been a wrong turn. Inputting ROME on the airline booking site instead of BERLIN and clicking YES would have created an entirely different book. I'd be in better health, pleasantly tanned and filled with Mediterranean laughter, instead of what I've got. A friend who could speak both German and Italian fluently claimed to feel his personality change quite drastically when using these languages – the former making him punctilious, waspish, acrid, remote, extremely polite, the latter making him expressive, promiscuous and a pleasure to be with. Regardless of the truth of this, it is certainly hard not to feel wistful about the South when wandering around Germany – olives and lemons trump root vegetables, and sunshine makes a monkey of all those low, lugubrious clouds. This is a common problem for many Germans, who have always had a fraught but important link with the country from which the Alps almost mockingly bar them.

Both German and Italian historians had immense difficulties dealing with this relationship. For example, two of the most powerful German rulers of the Middle Ages, Otto the Great and Friedrich II, spent much of their time not in Germany but in Italy, the latter indeed living most of his life in Sicily and giving off little indication that he had much interest at all in Germany. Many of the Emperors spent large parts of their reign in Italy – partly because from Charlemagne onwards the Pope was crucial to their mystique and partly because they really did see themselves as reviving the Roman empire, which had, of course, been more famous for its substantial Italian component than for its German. This Italian inheritance has latterly pleased nobody – no nationalists could have much time for it. If Friedrich Barbarossa, for example, was so intensely German and such an Arthur-like hero, then why did he spend so much time pursuing his Italian inheritance (and indeed get beaten by the Italians in the process)? There is an absorbing computer game where you can pretend to be Friedrich taking on the Lombard League, complete with castles, navies, trebuchets and the fruity German accent of Henry the Lion who pops up on the soundtrack – already replete with sword-clangs and dying cries – to say, 'Zo zorry, Barbarossa, but I mussst now betray you.' The game is gleefully set up so that your German armies are snuffed out every time by the Veronese. I gave up in disgust in the end, lacking the martial stamina and men-leading skills that would make me an inspirational figure of a kind likely to wake from my mountain tomb in Germany's greatest hour of need.

This link between Germany and Italy was expressed in all kinds of dynastic tangles over the centuries, but the Reformation really fixes in place a cultural and political loop of great importance. In the later sixteenth century the split between a northern, Protestant Germany and a southern, Catholic Germany meant that two artistic spheres tended to give the north close links to the Netherlands and Scandinavia, the south a gravitational pull towards Italy. These separate worlds were reinforced quickly by the near monopoly on serious cultural activity enjoyed by the Church and princes, with forms of worship, palaces, marriages and so on having to conform to confessional needs. The tragedy for Protestant Germany was that this created too thin a texture for much of anything, with Calvinist areas such as Switzerland and the Palatinate banning and destroying all religious images. The high point of image-making in the northern and central towns based around the Cranachs churning out stuff collapsed with their deaths: the money and the inspiration just no longer seemed to be there. So embarrassing is this artistic failure to later nationalists that attempts were made in writing about the barren seventeenth century to rope in Rembrandt as a German painter – a desperate idea but also indicative of the Low Countries' continuing, peculiar role within the Empire as being somehow *nearly* German despite all evidence to the contrary. Catholic Germans did the same, with Ludwig I of Bavaria's hall of German heroes, the Walhalla, including a bust of a rather uneasy Rubens.

Southern German and Austrian culture seems to have similarly weakened during the long peace but with the major difference of having open religious access to all of Italy. Of course, German culture had never really been something quite separate, with even the hard core of Germanness – Dürer, the Holbeins, Altdorfer, the Cranachs – being in all kinds of ways thoroughly Italian-influenced. But there was a clear process in the later sixteenth century whereby the sort of turreted, spooky gloom I like so much gives way to something smoother and more brightly coloured and, indeed, give way to actual Italians, who clustered thickly as musicians and decorators throughout the Catholic German lands, perhaps most famously Giuseppe Arcimboldo whose strange faces made from fruit and vegetables have become a sort of shorthand for Rudolf II's dysfunctional reign in Prague.

This fascination is most enjoyably seen in the Antiquarium, built for Duke Albert V of Bavaria in his Munich palace. This Renaissance hall, the shape of a giant, lightly compressed Swiss roll, has been much tampered with (and substantially rebuilt after a disastrous air raid), but it sums up the delights available for Catholics through their direct links with Rome, the greatest source of patronage and artistic ideas in Europe. It is impossible not to feel, walking purposefully about on the marble floors, admiring the exhausting ranks of Roman portrait busts, a sense of certainty buoyed by faith, plus the usual confusion provided by the display in a vigorous, Christian context of objects from a pagan culture. Albert drifted along in a fog of intense religious feeling while amassing great piles of ancient coins, Egyptian items and treasures, and leaving almost farcical debts on his death in 1579.

There was really no serious artistic alternative to Italy at this time, with much of Protestant Europe either directly antagonistic towards art in most forms, or on a permanent war footing or (in England's case) continuing with its strange inability to impose its eccentric art forms on its more sophisticated neighbours (with even

Shakespeare disregarded in Germany until Schlegel began his trans-
lations of the early nineteénth century). The last great specifically
German painter, Adam Elsheimer, grew up in the Lutheran city of
Frankfurt in the 1580s but moved (almost inevitably) to Venice and
then Rome in his early twenties, dying a Catholic ten years later.
Much of his genius emerged from working with Italian painters and
his magical pictures are *somewhat* German in tone (he certainly saw
Altdorfers in Munich and perhaps in Regensburg), but such is the
gravitational pull of Italy that it is hard to square actual human
experience with the demands of nationalism. The very notionally
somewhat possibly German Rubens was also in Rome and a friend
of Elsheimer's, but then the whole issue of national allegiance
becomes chaotic in the seventeenth century, with the two greatest
'French' painters, Claude and Poussin, managing somehow to live
respectively some fifty and forty years in Rome (Claude is a particularly unlikely Frenchman, born in the then independent Duchy of
Lorraine, raised in the Habsburg Black Forest town of Freiburg and
then living in Italy from his late teens).

Elsheimer left very few paintings and they are scattered around,
in Berlin, Vienna, Munich, Braunschweig and elsewhere, but I am
always alert to the hope of seeing one (one indeed has just been
added to the Braunschweig collection paid for by a football lottery!).
My favourite is *Jupiter and Mercury in the House of Philemon and Baucis*
in Dresden, a never previously painted subject from Ovid, where the
gods come to earth in disguise to try to find good people to save
from the flood which will destroy all sinners, and find only one old
couple, Philemon and Baucis, with the decency to welcome them.
In this tiny, but incomparably vivid and warm picture, Jupiter and
Mercury manage somehow to be both plausible humans yet ineffa-
bly god-like as their elderly hosts make them their meal. At various
times I've looked at this picture (including, as a happy surprise, at a
London exhibition of paintings chased out of Dresden following the
disastrous floods of 2002). I always wind up feeling pathetically
upset that such a painter should have died in penury in Rome aged
only thirty-two. As the sixteenth century curdled and ended, with
different religious ideas digging in and preparing to fight, it was

clear that a south-eastern, Italy-linked Catholic Germany was in the ascendant, together with the important Rhine Catholic electorates of Trier, Mainz and Cologne – the last ruled invariably by members of the Bavarian ducal family from 1583 onwards. This resurgence was an unattractive surprise for a Protestantism that continued to see itself as the self-evident future.

The appeal of Italy has, of course, been a virtual constant in German life and at different times caused more or less confusion. Was German culture to be found in its own resources (the cult of Dürer, of Nuremberg, of northern gloom) or in being, in effect, subjugated by a greater southern culture? Waves of fashion (confused immensely by the irruption in all kinds of ways into German life of the France of Louis XIV) played mayhem with later nationalists. These deplored the Italians who played music for the Habsburgs, built palaces and churches, designed clothes and painted portraits and ceilings, giving a particular style to cities such as Munich, Salzburg and Vienna. This in practice happy cross-fertilization throws up hundreds of examples, but two from the eighteenth century sum it up.

In 1706 the twenty-one-year-old Georg Friedrich Händel, raised in Halle and Hamburg, headed off to Italy and reacted to what he found there with some of the most beautiful music of the entire century: cantatas set in myth-riddled, brightly lit Italian landscapes, sung in Italian, perhaps most perfectly *Apollo e Daphne*, and a sort of summation in music of the world created in Elsheimer's landscapes a century before. Händel could not be more German, but he was able to make a sort of brilliant concentrate of Italian sensibility, with a cantata such as *Aminta e Fillide* being composed to be played in a private garden outside Rome for the members of the appealing-sounding Arcadian Academy. Arguments about how German or Italian he really is are just too confusing to have any value. Particularly as he was in fact British.

Heading in the other direction half a century later, Giambattista Tiepolo, the greatest living Venetian painter and in many ways the last of his line, was invited to Würzburg by the prince-bishop to design ceiling paintings celebrating Würzburg's standing both in the Holy Roman Empire (a previous bishop had married Friedrich Barbarossa to Beatrix of Burgundy) and in the wider world. Even without Tiepolo's ceiling paintings the Würzburg Residence would be an astounding building – a genial response to Versailles and frivolously self-indulgent, as the prince-bishop was by almost any international yardstick a very unimportant person. Tiepolo painted Barbarossa's marriage with everyone looking Venetian in amazing silks and with no concession of any kind to the chillier and more northern medieval context, and with his usual dwarf and dog in attendance. The mind-disordering follow-up to this though was the ceiling over the grand staircase, painted to glorify the prince-bishop and showing images from the entire planet, a continent along each side in a mad but beautiful hymn of praise to a man who, in practice, had no links of any kind to American alligator-hunters, Nubian princesses or Asian wizards. It remains the biggest fresco in the world as well as the funnest. Würzburg was badly bombed in the war and the town now only has isolated reminders of its time as a tiny capital city but, through the enterprise of an American soldier getting sheets of canvas hauled over the palace's devastated roof, the fresco itself was rescued, enshrining a mixed-up German and Italian world that seems impossibly remote from the strident and exclusive nationalisms that were to follow – and indeed that would swallow whole such screwy little spots as Würzburg.

Black armour

Tucked away in disregarded corners of provincial German museums are works by an early seventeenth-century Flemish painter called Sebastian Vrancx. In my ever more heedless and chaotic travels I would find myself remembering them quite clearly when far better or more beautiful pictures had already been mentally filed and lost. Vrancx's pictures are highly disturbing images of powerlessness. They show groups of armed men who have achieved absolute superiority over other groups of armed men – through ambush or sometimes through wearing a particularly satanic sort of black bullet-proof armour. The pictures show the immediate aftermath of the point where one side bests the other: some of the defeated side are already dead, sometimes already being stripped of their clothes and weapons; but many others are on the point of losing their lives and express their terror through hopeless flight or turn and face singly an implacable group of attackers. This scene is watched by an assortment of winners who, confident that the survivors will be mopped up and killed by their confederates, are chatting or taking off their armour. It is the matter-of-fact nature of these pictures that is so disturbing – this is just a day's work to those involved. The viewer is doomed to hunt through each painting looking for some survivor of the defeated side who might reasonably hope to escape: except that Vrancx has thought of this and filled every corner with despairing encounters which will result, if the spell hovering over the unmoving figures were to be removed for only five minutes, in the execution of all the losers. It further adds to the sense of unease that Vrancx is not a very good painter: he is a sort of stolid, gloomy version of his contemporary Pieter Brueghel the Younger. Also surprising is that there is no sense that the winners have any moral advantage – the viewer is not invited to celebrate any specific triumph such as Spain's victory in Velázquez' *The Surrender of Breda* where, having neither enthusiasm for imperial Castile nor hatred for Dutch freedom, you still get a happy lift from the general air of congratulation. Instead, with Vrancx, there is a grim fantasy of an almost meaningless but lethal encounter, painted by a diseased individual. The very worst is his little picture of a group of cavaliers (all floppy hats and lovely buff jackets) encountering a group of men in black armour, also on horseback, who, impervious to the cavaliers' pistols, are clearly just about to kill them all.

It is odd thinking of specific dukes or princes being shown some pictures by Vrancx by one of their procuring agents and giving them the thumbs-up. But they must have matched a sort of reality. I was once wandering through the freezing rooms of the Schloss at Ingolstadt and suddenly there were those identical black suits of armour, in terrible silent rows, like so many lightly decorative, deactivated robots. Dating from the Thirty Years War, these suits were serious body-armour's last outing before the twenty-first century: unwieldy, expensive, unbeatably macabre. Wandering around these rooms, filled with the horrible armour, with pikes, halberds, wheel-lock and matchlock guns, Vrancx's pitiless early seventeenth-century world seemed quite plausible and real – as indeed it was for much of Central Europe.

The Thirty Years War has almost no place in the British imagination because of the wise decision of James I to stay out of it. By doing so he betrayed his only living daughter, wife of one of the crucial if idiotic early protagonists of the war. This seems quite acceptable given the fate of everyone else who delusively felt at different times and – such was the war's duration – even in different generations that their engagement in the fighting would tip the scales. The horror of the war lay, among other things, in the way it perverted and destroyed the efforts of all who entered it, regardless of their motives – whether deeply religious, completely cynical or helplessly vacillating, everyone was ruined by the conflict. It left between a quarter and a third of all Germans dead and even in relation to the twentieth century must, as a percentage of population, be the worst man-made disaster ever experienced in Europe.

All the labyrinthine details of the fighting hold their distressing interest because of this futility: nobody gets what they want and everybody dies. The Dutch (in as much as their eighty-year conflict was entangled in the mere thirty-year one) gained their independence from Spain, but only after generations of the most hideous fighting and at the cost of giving up the southern Netherlands (Belgium). The French ended up turning themselves into a threat to the rest of Europe of a new kind, making other rulers nervously finger their ruffs at the monster that had been unleashed. After half a century of being a disunited and helpless shambles, France emerged from the Thirty Years War on its own 'special path' of militant, chauvinistic arrogance. But even in France's case, the architect of the new military policy, Cardinal Richelieu, was dead before any treaties had been signed.

There is no limit to the fascinations of the Thirty Years War, but to plunge into its details would unbalance this book entirely.

The central point is that this was a war with origins which were genuinely about religion. There have been attempts to make it an economic war or come up with other class or Realpolitik reasons, but it is clear that most of those involved in its initial stages felt that what they were doing was steeped in prayer and missionary zeal. It was to mutate into something else, but by then there was no going back. In a peculiar way the conflict cried out for some top-level hegemon to weigh in. The unacceptable idea that had afflicted Europe in the mid-sixteenth century was of the Habsburgs ruling everywhere in the manner of the contemporaneous Ming Dynasty. But this threat was now replaced by a strange Europe in which nobody in whatever coalition was able to end the fighting, or indeed even faintly impose order. Each year the war chewed further through this world, wrecking city after city and making whole regions of countryside empty of inhabitants for many decades.

I was raised as a Catholic but wound up (as there are not that many English Catholics) going to quite aggressive Protestant schools. In the end, being bombarded with Protestantism won through and I have always seen the Thirty Years War as an exciting tale of how Protestantism comes so close to disaster but is saved by the wonderful Gustavus Adolphus. I imagined the Catholic enemy as a sea of credulous Austrian peasants egged on by serpentine, leering Jesuits. This unsophisticated picture was somewhat challenged by actual visits to Catholic Germany, where an Imperial commander such as the Count of Tilly, a blood-caked Protestant-slaughtering freak, I had reliably understood, appeared to enjoy open public recognition, with attractive statues, buildings named after him, and so on. In Munich's Odeonsplatz, for example, seeing if I could find the spot where Hitler stood in the famous photograph of the crowd cheering the outbreak of the First World War, I became far more interested in the presence there of a massive, sombre statue of Tilly, the saviour of Catholic Bavaria from blood-caked, etc. Protestants.

It is this mutual sureness in 1618 that is the origin of the disaster of the war. During the long interval of peace, both Protestants and Catholics had come to share a mirror image of disappointment: that their true faith had failed to topple the other and that compromise meant the compounding of that failure – a failure answerable in Heaven. Maps conveniently colour in Protestant and Catholic states, but of course these are a polite fiction. Both faiths' lands were peppered, often heavily peppered, with heretics – even the heartlands of Habsburg real-estate in Austria and Bohemia were stuffed with Protestants, sometimes rural and obscure and sometimes rich and powerful. Even very Lutheran cities such as Frankfurt never lost the knowledge that they owed their independence to their direct relationship with the Emperor (even if he was the odd Rudolf II) and that a reasonable degree of latitude towards Catholic worship was needed. Even worse, the Protestant camp was split over the severe, iconoclastic form of Calvinism, which had scooped out and destroyed almost every religious image ever made in countries such as the Palatinate, Scotland, the northern Netherlands and much of Switzerland. For many Lutherans, the Calvinists were so threatening and unacceptable that they would rather support the Catholic Imperialists in any conflict.

One of my happiest possessions is a very fetching photo of my wife grinning in front of the window in Prague castle where the Thirty Years War began, with Imperial emissaries being thrown through that window by enraged Protestant Bohemians in 1618. The Bohemians used the concessions made to them by the weak Emperors Rudolph II and Matthias to elect their own king, Friedrich, the Calvinist ruler of the Palatinate (married to James I's daughter Elizabeth). This unfortunately for them broke against a profound wave of Catholic revanchism. This had already begun in areas such as Tyrol where the Archduke Ferdinand had split his time in the late sixteenth century between collecting ambitious, sensational paintings and expelling Protestants, looking on in some dismay while first his fairly reasonable brother Maximilian II enjoyed being Emperor and then second his nephew Rudolf II, who retreated into his own private and gloomy world. Ferdinand's brother, Archduke Karl, tried something similar in Styria (south-east Austria), splitting his time between founding the Lipizzaner stud, whose oddly dancing white horses continue to provide doubtful entertainment for tourists in Vienna to this very day, and expelling

Protestants, first blowing up their churches, then making great bon-
fires of their books and scattering corpses from their graveyards all
over the roads. But even Charles had in the end done a deal with the
Protestants. A more squarely Catholic, Jesuit-inflected world came to
full fruition when Karl's son Ferdinand II became Emperor in 1619.

The terrible sense of single purpose in Ferdinand II contributed
hugely to the events that now unfolded, but the sort of *va banque*
provocation of the Bohemians was also something new – a deliberate attempt to break up the Empire and lock into place a
diminished inheritance for the Catholic Habsburgs after their long
period of inanition. As soon as he could raise an army, Ferdinand
invaded Bohemia, with an old campaigner, the Count of Tilly, who
had fought the Dutch or the Turks for much of his life, as commander of the Catholic League army. The result was a disaster for
the Bohemians and their small scattering of Protestant allies (many
Protestants stood on the sidelines, either through being fearful and
broke like James I, or through dislike of the Calvinist Prince of the
Palatinate, or through a genuine, prudent anxiety about war).

Wandering around Prague today, which is in so many ways a
supersaturated solution of the great achievements of nineteenth-
and twentieth-century Czech nationalism, it is strange that so much
of what is built there – so many of the churches and institutions
and what make Prague so pretty – are in reality symbols of Czech
abasement and failure. The ruinous Battle of the White Mountain
destroyed Bohemian identity – the execution of many leading
Bohemian nobles, the confiscation of their property, the digging-up
of anything smelling even faintly Protestant or anti-Habsburg. A
country well on the way to becoming an at least semi-independent,
Protestant Central European state disappeared for three centuries,
instead becoming a mere Austrian colony, with Prague a German
city. This central catastrophe raised the stakes in the fighting incredibly high – a rich, serious, dynamic part of Central Europe had
been reduced to an experimental laboratory for the most extreme
forms of the Counter-Reformation, its landscape dotted with Jesuit
colleges and Marian shrines. The Czechs even had to cope with a
church dedicated to Our Lady of Loreto, named for the absurd hut,

notionally Mary's, which in the face of infidel invasion of the Holy
Land flew up into the air in 1291, landing first in Croatia before
heaving itself up once more and crash-landing in Italy. There is
a surely intentionally hilarious painting by Tiepolo – for obvious
reasons Loreto features little in sacred art – which looks like story-
boarding for Dorothy's house caught in the twister in *The Wizard
of Oz*. In any event, in the wake of the Battle of the White Mountain, the sort of people who had plans for building a Loreto
shrine moved in and we look elsewhere for inspiration until the
arrival of Smetana and Dvořák. The threat of a religion imposed on
them by people who worshipped flying huts must have provoked a
desperate resistance in the surviving Protestant states.

The King of Sweden's horse

As there is hardly a town in Germany without an intense feeling of
local pride there is hardly a town without its own museum. These
can sometimes be just incredibly boring, with a handful of glazed
visitors dragging themselves through exhibits on local geological
issues, the invariable reconstructed apothecary's shop, something
about spinning and cloth, some old hats and an engraving of things
going wrong in 1848. Wandering from room to room, trying not
to catch the eye of other equally somnambulant figures (and, in
all honesty, there are sometimes few enough) and trying not to
panic as a room filled with weights and scales approaches, it is
hard not to see the whole thing as a cruel trick – a religiously
inspired attempt to mock the futile nature of human existence.
These museums tend, because of the political nature of so much
German history, to emphasize the non-political – so there is a huge
enthusiasm, for example, for all aspects of Early Man, with reconstructions of huts, lots of business with things made from reeds or
flint and dummies of hirsute families squatting around a fire preparing their simple fare. Sometimes there are engaging reconstructions
of mammoths or other fun creatures, but on the whole you are
left simply with a puzzled sense of the surety all curators have of

hair-lengths for early humans for whom all evidence derives from skeletons: and why do they *all* look like West German university lecturers of the early 1970s?

While these museums can be stupefying they have to be persevered with as in all the tedium there is always some treasure. Treatment of the twentieth century can only be interesting and varies greatly, often thoughtful and intelligent and only very occasionally cursory in a disturbing way. Once I was wandering around a nadir of the city museum experience when, suddenly, it became all worthwhile: in the midst of the usual, space-filling slap-in-the-face exhibit of 'toys of yesteryear' (dolls, wooden bricks – there is no need even to *mount* the display, let alone keep its temperature steady and its shunned glass cases clean), there was a board game from the early 1940s called Bomb England. The lid was only partly off but showed a nicely rendered British Isles, with Ireland properly neutral and little squares with all the towns marked – it looked like a dice game with better points for getting to more far-away targets, such as Glasgow or Belfast. It was eerie and unsettling, but also exciting – I have always loved board games and I even rummaged around briefly inside my own little moral box, examining the issues involved in stealing Bomb England: it would give much more pleasure in use than trapped in a desiccated museum, objects are designed for use not exhibition, conceivably I had some rights as a representative of a victor power, and so on. I was held back by cowardice and a nagging anxiety that the game might be missing some crucial pieces.

In any event, this is a preamble to a serious return to the Thirty Years War. Ingolstadt is a town in northern Bavaria and in many ways the sort of acme of medium-sized, self-conscious German urban pride. Stuffed with money from the upper management of the Audi works (and with large teams of highly trained shopkeepers adept at getting that money circulating in the town through the sale of fur coats, elaborate underwear and long-haul package tours), Ingolstadt has great churches, serious city walls, characterful pubs and a magical Schloss which houses, among other things, the Bavarian Army Museum. For me this last was meat and drink – what could possibly be more fun than following the military twists and turns of one of Europe's most persistently turncoat and confused fighting organizations? It had been snowing heavily and as, a little before lunchtime, I waded through the drifts filling the grand main court-yard, it was impossible not to notice that, some three hours into the museum's opening time, mine were in fact the *only* footsteps in the snow, meaning that on this February day I was the *only* person in Europe who found the travails of the Bavarian army funny.

By contrast, at the other end of town is the much more charac-teristically sleep-inducing city museum – a mass of things so dull that I can now recall none of them. But the place may have been put together by a curator of genius, who understood that if you have one really great thing to show, then you don't want to confuse vis-itors with anything else. Fill up the space with engravings of market day, cannonballs and apothecary equipment, because all this is just a frame for something unique.

The 1620s were a nightmare for Protestants. After the initial catastrophe at the White Mountain, Catholic forces had moved for-ward, devastating all attempts to stop them. The Protestants were painfully disunited – Saxony, fatally, a powerful Lutheran state, first joined the Imperialists and then stayed neutral, through the venal idiocy of its drunken ruler Johann Georg I (I cannot afford yet another digression, but I will develop later the uplifting theme of Saxon political and military incompetence – a theme so consistent that it provides a perfect refutation of any sense at all that Germans have some inherent thirst for or brilliance at warfare). England con-tinued to be neutral and there was chaos and dissention in the Protestant command that ushered in disaster after disaster. It was in the 1620s that the remorseless, savage nature of the war became apparent as it disposed of the reputations and lives of all involved. Most of the initial Protestant champions or those willing to support their cause were neutralized, destroyed or chased away, from the Savoyards to the Transylvanians. The Elector Palatine's territory was eradicated, taken over by the Spanish and Bavarians. Admit-tedly a highly unstable psychopath, the dashing, implausibly titled Bishop of Halberstadt, a key Protestant champion and a prince of

Brunswick-Lüneburg, after careering around Northern Europe and having alarming paintings made of himself, died 'his vitals gnawed by a gigantic worm', according to Catholic sources. The Count of Mansfeld, leader of the main Protestant army, after endless humiliating defeats, packed up and left for Dalmatia, where he died. The Danish king tried to rescue the Protestants (egged on by England and France) and was quickly beaten by the Emperor's startling new champion, Wallenstein, a military contractor of genius and a Protestant who had brushed himself down and become a Bohemian Catholic so as to grab many of the immense chunks of formerly Protestant Czech land being handed out by Ferdinand II.

The sheer misery of this period set the pace for what was to follow, with rival armies living entirely through plunder, ruining both friendly and unfriendly territory through their insatiable depredations. Armies marched and countermarched across Germany in a warp and woof of ever-greater density, in the end debauching most towns and villages aside from occasional, bristlingly defended neutrals such as Hamburg. Wallenstein was particularly wedded to the wrecking of territory, both to pay for and feed his troops and to spread terror, but it was a model pursued by all sides. Ultimately armies became the almost zombie-like murder collectives of Grimmelshausen's great novel *Simplicissimus*, published in 1668, long after the war had ended but written by someone who had himself been entangled in the fighting since the age of ten. While sometimes the story gets lost in feeble fantasy, much of it has a ghastly, documentary air as gangs of marauding troops slaughter villagers, torture them to extract hiding places for money (and then kill them anyway), ambush one another, but all with no sense of purpose, of a beginning or an end – warfare as an unvarying and unstoppable way of life.

Once the Danes were finally ejected from the fighting in 1629 it appeared as though Protestantism had no further resources. The Imperialists as a first move announced that all territories which had become Protestant over the previous seventy years (mostly former religious lands) would be returned to Catholicism, and it appeared that any surviving Protestant territories (most importantly

Brandenburg and Saxony) would only co-exist under sufferance. This was a period of huge satisfaction in Vienna and provoked a lot of extra-long masses – much of the Empire was in ruins, but at least they were now Catholic ruins. The nadir was the destruction of Magdeburg – a powerful Protestant fortress town that Tilly totally erased, with some twenty thousand of its inhabitants and defenders killed, leaving it a shattered ruin with a remaining population of about four hundred. This outrage was used to galvanize Protestants in thousands of cheap, less cheap and highly elaborate engravings (all battling with the same problem of how, with rather crude means and in black and white, to represent graphically buildings and people blown into the air).

It was at this point that, for Protestants at any rate, one of the most exciting events in all European history happened. The previous year the King of Sweden, Gustavus Adolphus, had arrived on the north coast of Germany with a small but highly trained army, driven to intervene by a desire for self-aggrandisement but also by a wish to help his fellow Protestants. The effect was astounding and I can never look at my Gustavus Adolphus beer mat without emotion. Initially he was ignored by the Imperialists as just another doomed Scandinavian interloper. But unfortunately for the Imperialists, even without Gustavus the tide was turning – not least because the Dutch had overcome the worst of the Spanish attacks on them, and were becoming a dynamic, wealthy and vengeful Protestant element, and the French had resolved their own internal problems and had a limitless well of anti-Habsburg feeling to draw on.

But it was the Swedes who caused astonishment. Using new mobile tactics Gustavus destroyed the Imperialists' main army under Tilly in the autumn of 1631 at the Battle of Breitenfeld, and in the following year, at the Battles of the River Lech (where Tilly was wounded) and Lützen (where Wallenstein was defeated), the Swedes ruined the Catholic cause so completely that even over a further sixteen years of fighting it never recovered. Gustavus himself died at Lützen so his active impact on Europe was only some fourteen months, but it was enough. The Protestants would never be strong

enough to defeat the Emperor absolutely but the idea that Central
Europe could be in its entirety re-Catholicized became ever
more unlikely and indeed religion as a basis for fighting between
Christians was discredited and dropped.

This is where the Ingolstadt museum comes in. In the chaotic
aftermath of the Battle of the River Lech, Imperial forces fled inside
the walls of Ingolstadt, where Tilly died. The Swedes then besieged
the town but without success, Gustavus eventually lifting the siege
and marching on to his eventual death at Lützen in Saxony. But
before he did so he was nearly killed when his horse was shot from
under him. This sort of lucky escape is such a common cliché of
history books that it is tempting to think of a parallel version which
would privilege the horse: so that later, at the Battle of Lützen,
'the horse's rider was shot from over him' would be a happy and
much-whinnied at outcome. In any event, after their heroic defence
against Gustavus and after the Swedes had gone, the Ingolstadters
opened their gates, grabbed the king's dead horse and mounted its
skin – and here, nearly four centuries later, the horse remains, standing on its battered legs. Of course, it is not in great shape – it had
after all been shot from under the king so the Ingolstadters were
not working from perfect material; there is also a wealth of patches,
stitch marks and dark spots, as though over the intervening years
several drinks have been spilt on him. He has been through a lot,
but here is the horse, preserved as an object of mockery and local
Catholic pride, the focus of banquets, a classic seventeenth-century
memento mori, as curious a preserved historical animal as Stonewall
Jackson's horse Little Sorrel in the Virginia Military Institute or the
elephant skeleton sketched by Goethe in Kassel, but far older than
either and in its sheer haggardness speaking volumes.

A surprise visit from an asteroid

The latter parts of the Thirty Years War are remorselessly grim. The
fighting became so complex, the alliances so fraught with mutually
excluding special deals about ownership of this or that town, that

it is nearly as unenjoyable to read about as it must have been to endure. From being the heroes of the middle part of the war, the Swedes now became horrible parasites, drifting around Central Europe destroying everything they encountered, spreading plague and famine. If it is any consolation to fair-minded and neutral modern Swedes, it has to be said that most 'Swedes' were in fact Scottish mercenaries or prisoners captured from other armies. Nobody had any real way to pay for these troops so they tended simply to gravitate towards whoever was on the march, just in the hope of getting some food in a countryside that could no longer support large groups and where many towns were now almost empty.

A key point in the war was reached in the small Swabian town of Nördlingen, one of a handful of places that have until today kept their entire city walls. Aside from being a battlefield site, Nördlingen has a second, very peculiar claim to fame. Some fifteen million years ago, when Germany was a balmy, sub-tropical place filled with the grunts and whistles of proto-elephants and giant turtles, a nearly mile-wide asteroid smashed into Nördlingen (or at least its future site), making a crater some fifteen miles wide and having an impact comparable to an inconceivable 1.8 million Hiroshimas. Not so much as a proto-elephant's trunk tip survived. Really oddly, the shape of the crater is still entirely clear, with pretty fields stretching in every direction, rimmed by a scrumpled partial circle covered in trees. The impact created millions of tiny diamonds that suffuse the region's geology and make a kind of shocked quartz stone called suevite, which Nördlingen's sensational church is made from. Babyishly I thought for a few moments that the church was made from rocks from outer space, but even the reality is peculiar enough. The town itself is a perfect circle, with the huge church tower in its exact centre, lying in the far, far bigger circle of the crater impact. As I walked clockwise in the steady arc of the town walls and the tower bells struck the hour I had the sick strange sensation of having become an element in some unmanageably large, inconceivably ancient and utterly unknowable mechanism.

The people of Nördlingen all have something of this air as it is a place so trapped by its past, by its stifling walls and towers and olden-times buildings, that it exists (like nearby Rothenburg) only to be pumped full of tourists, fed in a steady circulation through a mass of pubs and minor sights. The townsfolk are therefore obliged to operate in a coded framework of geniality which must be almost insufferable – like being the little people who pop in and out of the doors of one of those Bavarian barometric cottages to show whether it is rain or shine. But the battle was real enough. In 1634 Nördlingen was threatening to become the new Magdeburg – an isolated Protestant stronghold under siege from an Imperial–Spanish army. Since the destruction of Magdeburg the war had turned so violent that when the Catholic soldiers in, for example, the lovely fortress of Würzburg had surrendered honourably the Protestants slaughtered them all anyway. Nördlingen was holding out in desperation and an army of Swedes and their German allies were more or less obliged to try to rescue them. The battle could not have been more badly handled and the Protestant armies were ruined and the town taken and ravaged.

While this was a painful moment for the Protestant cause, the nightmare now is in seeing that despite Nördlingen the war went on for a further *fourteen* years. Imperial forces thought that they had their enemies on the run, but in fact this was just a fresh but final high point in their fortunes. If only Ferdinand II had managed a comprehensive peace now (which would have been very hard, but not impossible) then the war might have ended – but he and his son Ferdinand III (who fought at Nördlingen) carried on and forces (not least France) turned against them. As in so many wars, the psychological high point had come and gone with none of the protagonists noticing.

As the war progressed, armies on the whole got smaller. Neither side was able to create a knock-out blow, with the Protestants (now fully supported by an increasingly out-of-control France) holding off Imperial forces but never seriously threatening the Habsburg core. Negotiations for ending the conflict dragged on for years, and the war ended with the painful coda of the mainly Swedish Protestant army at last breaking into Bohemia and attempting to liberate

Prague, where the trouble had all begun. The Swedes tried and failed to fight their way across the very same Karl Bridge whose approaches are now so plagued with amusing 'human statues' covered in metal paint and with less than competent jugglers. Unable to break through the defences of the Old Town, the Swedes turned back (looting the castle on the way, which explains why such quantities of Rudolf II's collections, including some prime Arcimboldos, are mysteriously to be found in Stockholm). The Swedes could not get through because the Bohemians now saw them as the enemy: the inhabitants of Prague were no longer Protestant – staked out by the Jesuits and taken on innumerable school trips to visit the Church of Our Lady of Loreto, they had in the twenty-eight years since the Battle of the White Mountain, like something from *The Invasion of the Body Snatchers*, been turned into fervent Catholics.

The Thirty Years War had long lost its primarily religious character by the time it ended and indeed it marked the point where Protestant and Catholic remained fundamental units of political and religious life across Europe, but not in a way that would again provoke open warfare. Wars would now be fought for dynastic and economic reasons and the fervour that had made the great issues of 1618 seem so profoundly important had burned itself out. The successors to the initial princes and commanders, all of whom had now died, were far more cautious or cynical.

The room in Münster where parts of the Treaty of Westphalia was signed is still there – a grand, solemn space lined with portraits of dignitaries, appropriate in every way to the weight of what was witnessed here, aside from a confusing, dried-out human hand lying on a desk, presumed to have been severed from a malefactor at some point in Münster's history. The envoys came from all over Europe, and the result was a triumph for the northern Netherlands and for Switzerland, who were now both fully recognized as independent states. Sweden received large blocks of fairly useless Baltic and North Sea German coast – the only valuable bit being Bremen, which managed in the end to fend the Swedes off. But Swedish ownership further boxed in and excluded most of Germany from a direct role in the new global economy. The existing multiplicity of

German states acknowledged the Emperor's role as head of the Holy Roman Empire while reserving the right to carry out their own foreign policies, an arrangement that was to last under all sorts of stress and strain until the arrival of Napoleon some hundred and fifty years later. The Emperor abandoned any attempt – perhaps never serious anyway – to convert Germany into a unitary state comparable to Spain or France or England.

For most German states the war had been nothing but a disaster and many areas never really recovered until the nineteenth-century population boom and industrialization set them off again. Many great cities sank into a deep sleep. There is a painting in the Nuremberg city museum, made to commemorate the banquet marking the final departure of the Swedish occupation troops in 1649 (after the payment of an immense fine), a sea of men in the black-and-white clothing of the period, trying to put a brave face on a hopeless situation. As elsewhere in Germany, most of the inhabitants of Nuremberg had no experience of anything *except* war by this point and the Swedes left behind an utterly ruined place – one of Germany's great Renaissance cities reduced to a rotting museum piece, something for which we can be grateful now, but which doomed the Nurembergers themselves to irrelevance until their miraculously pickled Germanness caught the eye of nineteenth-century nationalists.

The trauma of the Thirty Years War has been overlaid by later traumas. It remains a key part of the German historical memory but its terrible theatre of helplessness was to be re-enacted again in the Napoleonic Wars – and this was to be a further model and warning that did such ruinous damage to Germany's idea of itself in the modern age. For generations of German historians, arguments about the nature of the Thirty Years War were central to the making of Bismarck's Second Reich, with Gustavus Adolphus a sort of honorary German trying – apparently – to create a unified Germany, but thwarted by Catholic Habsburg bloodsuckers. This shrill and Protestant reading of the war was a parallel, intellectual version of the struggle between Prussia and Austria for ownership of Germany and fed the poisonous idea that only Protestants could be real Germans.

For pre-Bismarck German rulers who valued and clung to the Peace of Westphalia there were profound lessons about how to run their states and how to avoid the sort of uncontrolled rampages that had done such damage. There is a famous propaganda print of the 1630s of alarming modernity, showing an armed man in fashionable clothing gesturing in despair at an allegory of War: a hideous monster – a sort of dragon covered in metal armour, breathing fire and squatting on a pile of corpses. By 1648 this creature had eaten most of Germany and there was simply not enough left to keep him fed – the war had ended in a bitter exhaustion and stasis within Germany from which it would take generations to rebuild. In the war's later stages, too, it had become clear that whereas its religious aspects had been so discredited that its initial causes had been after a fashion resolved, there was something else far worse unleashed by the fighting. For the mass of tiny territories around the Rhine, the nightmare for the next two centuries was to be a predacious, immensely powerful France.

CHAPTER SEVEN

Hourglasses and bird-eating spiders »
'Music to Escort the Dead from this Life' »
In the time of powdered wigs » Damascened yataghans »
'Burn the Palatinate!' » Catholicism goes for broke

Magne Parens rerum, cui se Natura volentem
  Subijcit, et dominos collocat ante pedes,
Respice, Natura quá nil præstanti[us] omni,
  E BARBERINAE stemate Gentis APEM:
Hãc vti Lyncèidum, ppiori lumine lustrans,
  Disposuit Tabulis, explicuitq́ labor.
Cæsiadẽ Genio sacrum stimulante laborem,
  Palladis et promptos arte iuuante viros,

Maxima dum tereti surgunt miracula vita,
  Maioremq́ oculus discit habere fidem,
Quis norat quinas in Hybleo corpore lingie
  Atque leoninæ proxima colla iubæ,
Hirsutosq́ oculos, binásq́ ad labris vagina
  Ni facerent artis dia reperta noua
Sic decet, vt dum te mirãdu suspicit Orbĩ,
  Et mage mirandã se Tua præstet APIS

Panchas   IVST[VS]·RIQVIVS. LYNCEVS·BELGA DEDIC C.E

Hourglasses and bird-eating spiders

The political events of the seventeenth century are preserved as a state of mind in the tremendous sense of gloom that pervades surviving artwork and writing. As usual it is impossible to disentangle waves of fashion from actual events. German art has always loved corpses, guttering candles, emblems of human folly, dances of death, and there is no reason to pin them to specific disasters. But there is an intensity in the seventeenth century that pervades much of Europe in different ways. In England, for example, for all their differences, the morbid yet highly pleasurable mysticism of writers such as Burton, Vaughan and Hobbes is rich with an atmosphere of poorly lit alchemically tinged lives of a kind which must have been in practice rather grim but is an endless pleasure to read about now in a comfy chair, with a drink and some suitably gloomy viol music playing through a good speaker system.

Tangled up in this sense of melancholy is the immense diversity of 'cabinets of curiosities' or 'wonder cabinets' which still dot the German castlescape, either as collections that have permanently survived since the Renaissance or as painstaking reconstructions, the work of modern enthusiasts in love with the idea of such things. I could really spend all day and every day with these collections. They were once common across much of Europe, but events or fashion dispersed them or folded them into later museum collections. They were particularly sheltered in Germany by the sheer diversity of ossified old courts, still filled with stuff which would have been binned or burned centuries ago in London or Paris.

Rulers have always had an interest in paying for useless yet exotic objects and the origins of these cabinets are obscure. They were an attempt to systematize and display things which were otherwise scattered around odd corners of palaces. Their point was hardly in any sense scientific – the items were purely there to give visitors a vague shiver and to convey the owner's prestige and humanism. Of course, for objects to come from far off they had to be bony or dried, not smelly or soft. This gave a strange, dusty impression of an outer world – consisting of ostrich eggs, nautilus shells, narwhal tusks, bits of coral, the skeletons or skins of snakes and so on. Coming into Europe through Venice or Antwerp (later Amsterdam), these things were often a very minor aspect of a merchant's wares and had passed through many hands to reach the European interior. It would be interesting to know, for example, at what point it became decisively clear to everyone concerned that unicorn horns were in fact narwhal's tusks – a knowledge long available only to a handful of Norwegians and Shetlanders, who may well not have been asked. Was there an awkward silence when these prized objects (very rarely washed up on far northern Atlantic coasts) ceased to be magical, or just a polite agreement to pay no attention to such ideas? They would have been part of the general, encroaching battle to continue enjoying traditional medicine, magic and astrology in the face of ever more plausible scientific scorn.

A spectacular wonder cabinet remains in the schloss at Gotha, assembled in heavy wooden display boxes and packed with skulls, mummified frogs, weird charms, bottled goodies, crocodile eggs. Particularly in the smaller courts there must have been intense competition to get hold of slightly bigger bits of fire coral or an even odder-shaped fruit and at big social occasions a tension as to whether your proud collection would provoke laughter from some ducal heavier-hitter passing through. The acme of these collections was definitely in Prague where Rudolf II in the late sixteenth century almost disappeared under fantastical bits and pieces.

Of course in their 'raw' form these objects could only get you so far. Once everyone had a piece of coral it became merely a prestige baseline rather than something that could be boasted about. So the next step was to try to decorate it, and the Renaissance became a great era for absurd treatment of these blameless tropical objects, once merrily floating in the vivid sunshine of the Red Sea, but now just desiccated blobs vulnerable to improvement by itinerant, very odd craftsmen in some draughty Thuringian Schloss. Ungainly cups, weird banquet centrepieces, spooky objects to bring out after dinner or contemplate in a religious-mystical way, these mutant combinations of gold and coconut husk or silver and conch-shell left the mere sad world of dried-out frog corpses far behind. The artists who turned out these objects of course fought against the very same problem that the older, simpler assemblies had wrestled with – that once everyone had an ostrich egg with a silver model ship balanced on top of it, they would become merely boring. This fuelled a sort of arms race, with Venetian suppliers pouring in sacks of tropical detritus which could then have bits of precious metal and jewels stuck to it to make ever more demented table settings. In parallel came ridiculous acts of miniature prowess, such as carving a three-dimensional crucifixion scene, jammed with mourners and soldiers, on the inside of a walnut (a Flemish speciality) or the crazy misuse of ivory to make spheres inside other spheres, carved from a single piece in a crescendo of meaningless virtuosity.

I am going on about these things too long – I pretend to despise them, but really I could only be happy with a nautilus-shell drinking cup. As with so many of these objects, the tragedy lies in their museum status. How can an East Prussian backgammon set made from ebonized wood decorated with mythological scenes and with each counter made from amber carved with the faces of Greek heroes *sit unplayed with in a museum cabinet?* I can only hope corrupt officials or curators every now and then take these things out and actually use them, drink from them or just chuck them around for fun – with the occasional privilege of hearing the spectral crunch of a nautilid shattering on the parquet – for it seems a shame they should just pine away forever behind glass. The decorative arms race finally caved in under the sheer absurdity of Augustus the Strong (1670–1733), the Elector of Saxony who, with money pouring in from his hideous porcelain factory and from defrauding the Poles (whose king through chicanery he had become), decided to go for broke. When many of his contemporaries were sharpening up and reforming their armies, he spent much of his revenue on mistresses, lovely palaces and daft trinkets. He was aided in this last aim by the services of the great Badenese goldsmith Johann Melchior Dinglinger, who blew astounding sums making such monstrosities as a giant cup made from a block of polished chalcedony, dripping with coloured enamels and metals and balanced on stag horns, or creating repulsive little statues of dwarves by decorating mutant pearls, or a mad but magnificent object called *The Birthday of the Grand Mogul Aurangzeb* in which dozens of tiny figures made from precious stones and metals fill the tiny court of the Mogul, itself made from all kinds of spectacular and rare stuff. This delirious thing (not paid for by Augustus for many years as the money sort of ran out when a Swedish invasion swept through a virtually undefended Saxony) simply ended the tradition. Looking at it today in the head-spinning Green Vault in Dresden, Dinglinger's fantasy seems a long way from the relative, bluff innocence of a yellowy whale tooth in a little display box – but it was the same tradition endlessly elaborated.

Aside from sheer, sickly excess, what also did for wonder cabinets was Europe's ever-greater knowledge and global reach. Germany was necessarily a bit player in this, albeit an interesting one, and the process can be traced through the seventeenth century as a remote and uncertain knowledge of much of the world was transformed by voyaging and then publishing. A world in which a group of nobles could stand gawping around a titchy bit of fire coral was replaced by immense amounts of often poorly understood information which slowly solidified into the great scientific universe. Humble wonder cabinets became, as it turned out, the rather dodgy building blocks for systematizing the natural world. Symbolically this could be made to start with one of Adam Elsheimer's works: a little, charming but highly inaccurate picture of a lynx made for the Rome-based Academy of the Lynxes in 1603. This amazing organization was the first in the world to have a recognizably scientific basis – a wish to voraciously scoop up and assemble all natural objects (not least through hundreds of paintings and drawings, a 'paper museum') as a sort of preliminary to understanding the world. The Lynxes were mostly Italian (most famously Galileo) but there were interesting German elements: Mattheus Greuter from Strasburg, who engraved both Galileo's newly discovered sunspots and the first image ever taken from the newly invented microscope, a compelling and peculiar one of honey bees; Johannes Schreck from Constanz, who ended up in China having become a Jesuit, taken a Chinese name and advised the last Ming emperor on calendar reform; or Johannes Faber from Bamberg who spent years supervising a huge and wonky compendium of pictures of Mexican animals.

The Lynxes fired a sort of starting gun for a sustained and increasingly scientific assault on the world, sifting and mulling over everything from humble mushrooms to the astonishing supplies of dried, pickled or sometimes living things brought back in increasing profusion by Spanish and Dutch navigators from the New World. It is in this sense unsurprising that Greuter among many other things worked on designs for globes, following in the footsteps of his distinguished German predecessors Behaim (the world's first globe), Etzlaub (creator of the great Rome Pilgrimage map), Waldseemüller (inventor of the word America) and Mercator (creator of a plausible flat map). It is surely odd that the world should have been so deeply shaped by the inhabitants of a country with such limited access to the sea.

This ferment of investigation and the profound sense of chaotic decompression – both from having access to a far wider world and from being in turn assaulted by a mass of new data from that world – had a profound effect across the whole of Europe. In Germany it was all somewhat second-hand except through the Dutch networks of northern Germany and the Habsburg networks which entered Germany in both the north and the south-east. As in the example of the Academy of Lynxes, German scientists were not restricted to their home towns. Mercator, for example, was Flemish but, suspected of heresy, had to flee Spanish rule and did most of his remarkable work safely ensconced in the Duchy of Cleves; Johannes Kepler was kicked out of Graz by the future Emperor Ferdinand II for refusing to convert to Catholicism.

Despite the nightmare of the Thirty Years War, there is a sense as the seventeenth century progressed of a Germany which, through travels but mostly through increasingly reliable books and maps and engravings, had a strong sense of the outer world, a world in itself so exotic and diverse, so filled with religions and practices and ideas that challenged European ones, that this must have been (if you were leisured, safe and smart) a highly stimulating period to be alive, both scientifically and practically. Peppers, pineapples and potatoes began to nudge their way into European diets (the last of these more or less redefining Germany). The seashells which had so prominently featured in older wonder cabinets merely as name-less, geography-free oddities were being systematically engraved and named by the Bohemian Wenceslas Hollar in the 1640s and in every area description and labelling were marching relentlessly onward. In a limited way it is regrettable that Europeans found themselves lying in such uncontrollably large piles of data, objects and stories as the century went by. Of course this inpouring of stuff was the basis of the scientific revolution, but it was also an early indication, like a clammy change in atmosphere before a storm, of Europe's coming role as despoiler and chewer-up of the whole planet. What started with funny bits of coral passed through dozens of hands and taken over the Alps as a minor aspect of a mule's load ended with wholesale global misappropriation. But even setting that aside, part of me would love to share that very narrow, igno-rant but questing and excited seventeenth-century world, with its dense allegories of skulls, mirrors and soap bubbles, its strange blend of obsession with the classical world and a wish to heave its way out of the merely antiquary: where a small group of savants in a dark, barely candle-lit room could handle a mutant lemon and mull over its properties (perhaps accompanied by some sensation-ally introvert piece of music). Of course the problem with all such reveries remains that the reverer assumes he would be one of those savants, when in practice the chances are that he would be in quite some other part of town dying of glanders or some other grotesque horse-handling-related illness.

As usual, an individual must stand in for a more complex, slow

and ambiguous process, but a fine finale to the intellectual enrich-
ment of *things* in these times is shown in the career of Maria Sibylla
Merian. This great naturalist and painter, having spent many years
in Frankfurt and Nuremberg studying caterpillars and butterflies,
moved first to a pietist community in the northern Netherlands,
then to Amsterdam and then in 1699, in her early fifties, in a boggling change of scene, to the new Dutch colony of Surinam on
the northern coast of South America. This conjunction between
a remarkable, highly experienced researcher and artist and New
World jungle resulted in one of the greatest, most blindingly
coloured of all works of natural history: *The Transformation of the
Insects of Surinam*. To be honest, this marriage of exotica and the
somewhat decadent, lurid pallet of traditional flower painting of
the same period is a bit hard to deal with. But, looking at these
pictures, even through streaming eyes, we have clearly entered the
modern world, even down to Merian's enthusiasm for making
creatures fight it out for our enjoyment, as in her immortal image
of a giant waterbug eating a frog or a spectacled caiman battling
with a false coral snake – the latter a riotous decorative pattern of
coloured/armoured scale varieties. There is one, very odd picture
of a pink-toed tarantula eating a hummingbird which, as far as can
be known, seems to be the origin of the term 'bird-eating spiders'
to describe the more completely ghastly, teddybears-on-mescaline
giant South American spiders as, aside from Merian's painting, there
is no evidence of their *ever* eating birds. It is a short walk from these
images to modern television documentaries. Her meticulous paintings of fruit, flowers and – above all – insects seen as living creatures
rather than pinned specimens are themselves a sort of new world.
In two centuries the 'cabinet of curiosities' had been swamped by
a revolution in how Europeans were allowed to see and use the
world. How could the poor old Duke of Saxe-Gotha-Altenburg
impress his smart guests as he pottered down the darkened corridors to open the creaking door to his mouldering selection of
half-mummified rubbish, when one of his more scientific-minded
friends could unveil a full-colour copy of Maria Sibylla Merian's
Roots of the Cassava with Rustic Sphinx Moth, Caterpillar and Chrysalis

of Tetrio Sphinx and Garden Tree Boa, a picture so alien, bracing and garish as to induce a sort of excitable nausea in all those who come face to face with it?

'Music to Escort the Dead from this Life'

Some small courtly towns are simply unimprovable and Wolfen-büttel in Lower Saxony is one of them. As you get off the train you immediately see, laid out for your pleasure, a lot of rooks mucking about in the trees, fish plopping in a pretty stream and an ivy-covered restaurant called the Crown Prince. Wolfenbüttel by this point can already do no wrong and its sensational Schloss, pink-painted arsenal, library – the Herzog August Bibliothek – and city church are almost extras – certainly less significant than the ideally named DVD rental store, the Herzog August Videothek. The town's perfection comes from its having been abandoned by the Dukes of Brunswick in 1742 and since then left substantially just to pickle. Leibniz and Lessing both lived here (with Lessing running the great library), as did Michael Praetorius, composer and compiler of the *Dances from Terpsichore*, a huge sequence of beautiful, graceful and pawky tunes assembled in 1612. Praetorius is probably unique among major composers in having made his fortune not from his music but from having helped thwart an assassination attempt against his boss, Heinrich Julius, Duke of Brunswick-Lüneburg, a brilliant, profligate, witch-burning drunk who died – much hated – of alcoholism shortly after *Terpsichore* came out.

I mention Heinrich Julius because he and his successors show perfectly the dazzling variety of options available to Germany's rulers. There were simply so many of these rulers and with such wide interests that anything could happen. Even within each major Schloss there is often this same air of fevered diversity, of stylistic chaos, inadequate funds, cheap and shoddy artists, fire damage and quixotic bequests that mirror the infinitely varied soap opera of princely rule. The sheer size of many a Schloss is one area of puzzlement: even if you have filled an entire tower with mad relatives and their keepers, and filled another with an unstable coalition of illegitimate babies, housemaids in trouble and sullen, blackmail-minded stable lads, there were still acres of rooms to give purpose to. Mutinous younger brothers would move out, entire decorative schemes would fall out of fashion, one regime wants harpsichords and wig-powder, the next wants the whole place looking like a barracks. The staff must have been nothing if not flexible. Sometimes the place would fill up with children, sometimes all the men would clear off to fight (this was a particular issue for the Dukes of Brunswick, who had an amazing propensity for being murdered or dying in battle). Entire reigns could be spent in the shadow of the long-lived widow of two dukes ago, her powerful personality and old-fashioned mourning clothes dominating the court for decades. Families would pour in and pour out, the latter sometimes assisted by plague – with one reign spent in a banqueting hall filled with entire cooked deer, elaborate jellies and a court orchestra, the next shrinking down to just a sallow, wigless old man with his cutlets and a single candle.

These vagaries are perfectly expressed in Wolfenbüttel, where the unlamented Heinrich Julius was succeeded by his son, the even worse Friedrich Ulrich, who was so drunk and so profligate that he was even deposed for a while by his strong-minded mother. He then handled the delicate issue of the Thirty Years War in such an abject way that while he dithered friendlessly the entire duchy was ravaged by any passing forces, both Catholic and Protestant, scratching around for diminishing loot and food. But help was at hand: with Friedrich Ulrich's death in an accident in 1634 and no successor, complex negotiations led the Emperor to choose a distant cousin as the new duke, August the Younger. This adorable man was named 'the Younger' to mark him off from a deceased elder brother – an increasingly odd and confusing designation as his eyes became more rheumy and his beard more Father Christmas-like, remaining the Younger until his death in his late eighties. He entirely changed the atmosphere of dissolute chaos and spent some thirty years adding to his collection of rare manuscripts and mulling over a lifelong obsession with chess and secret codes. His books have been re-housed in a rather pedantic Victorian building and are almost too beautifully looked after: there is none of that wormy, bibliomaniac atmosphere that makes Duke Humfrey's Library in Oxford or the old library of the Frankesche Stiftung in Halle (with its early eighteenth-century German–Persian grammar books!) such sources of perverse enjoyment. Augustus' collection, however, with his handwriting on the books' spines and his astrological globes is not without its chiaroscuro glamour. And the idea of the scholar duke, taking full advantage of his money (and of the total prostration of the era in which he reigned – possibly a time when more money could have been spent on basic assistance to his subjects rather than on books, but never mind), is one repeated across Germany, and is no more and no less characteristic than the red-faced hunting-crazed ducal boor.

Almost exactly the same age as August the Younger was the prince of the Reuss dynasty Heinrich II Postumus (a related burden to being called 'the Younger': his father died before he was born), who ruled the tiny territory of Gera in eastern Thuringia. This enjoyable man looks almost exactly like Augustus, with the same air of gloom and darkness and the white beard. He ruled prudently, built a large Schloss for himself looking over the town, above the raging White Elster River, and spent much of the last period of his life choosing suitably gloomy little epigraphs for himself which he had inscribed all over his copper coffin ('Naked came I out of my mother's womb, naked shall I return thither'). To have had the privilege – as the Thirty Years War raged – to come to such a theatrical sense of self-belief is something which should be admired for all time. After his death the greatest German composer before Bach, Heinrich Schütz, who had long been associated with Heinrich, and had indeed been born in another Reuss-ruled town was commissioned to set the epigraphs to music, producing in the process the *Musikalische Exequien* (which could be translated for its sense as 'Music to Escort the Dead from this Life'), one of the most beautiful and moving of all German choral works. Sadly, the story that Heinrich listened to the music before his death is almost certainly not true – it would all be perfect if it were, as he stage-manages his own departure (piles of black velvet, a memento mori or two to hand) with a morose severity teetering on the edge of camp. Indeed it is hard not to feel angry with the musicologists who established that Schütz wrote the music after his patron's death.

Heinrich's Schloss is now a sad place: it was blown to pieces in Nazi–Soviet fighting in 1945 and not reconstructed. The German communists built a rather grim restaurant on the site – one of those places which proves the rule that the more panoramic the view the worse the food. One pre-Postumus little tower remains – plus as a happy extra a children's climbing frame in the form of a castle, a witty, titchy echo of the elaborate monster that features in engravings. It was frequently pointed out that the rulers of the small German states enjoyed a great advantage over places such as Prussia or Saxony because they were too insignificant to do anyone much harm. This was absolutely true with Reuss-Gera, tucked away in its sleepy hills.

In the time of powdered wigs

After August the Younger's death in 1666, Wolfenbüttel returned to its old chaos with two brothers ruling jointly (the elder was duke but could not be bothered to do the work) and some amazingly bad political plotting that, after many twists and turns, resulted in foreign invasion and complete humiliation. The figure at the heart of this was Anton Ulrich who, on his elder brother's death, eventually became duke in his own right in old age. Despite being on the verge of disaster for chunks of his career, Anton Ulrich in a more vigorous way seems a highly appropriate son for August. He extended the library and appointed Gottfried Leibniz to run it, employed the Ghanaian polymath Anton Wilhelm Amo and built up a superb gallery of paintings.

The absolute archetype of the silk-clad, massive-wigged late-seventeenth-century grandee, Anton Ulrich sneers haughtily from portraits and busts and waves goodbye, with an imperious gesture, to all that darkened room/contemplating a skull mentality. Indeed, there seems an unbridgeable gap between the two generations – a chasm opened up not least by the disastrous stylistic impact of Louis XIV's new palace at Versailles. At a stroke the palace made all existing structures obsolete, hick and pitiful, unleashing an immense, ludicrous campaign by various rulers of really quite small territories, such as the Prince-Elector of Cologne or the Landgrave of Hesse-Darmstadt, to conjure up something similar. This littered the landscape with useless and often unfinished structures and caused local building contractors to scratch their heads in wonder as they had to mix up yet another immense vat of stucco and order a further gross of stone nymphs. A state such as Braunschweig-Wolfenbüttel could not even imagine competing directly, so the duke confined his court to copying the sartorial aspects of Versailles, with astonishing wigs, lovely shoe buckles and acres of patterned silk.

Quite a bit of Anton Ulrich's powder must have sprung from his face in a spasm of shock when he learnt of one of the period's great bolts from the blue. With the sudden death of the childless William III and accession of his sister-in-law Anne (also childless after horrific numbers of miscarriages and young deaths), the English throne was going to fall vacant. Through a quirk of genealogy of a type common in Germany, this top job would fall, on Anne's death, to the nearest suitable Protestant. This was deemed to be Sophia of Hanover, the clever and wonderful daughter of Elizabeth Stuart, herself the daughter of James I, who had, after the humiliation of the Thirty Years War, spent a long exile having tons of children. So some fifty years after Elizabeth Stuart's death everything at last went right for her.

But not for Anton Ulrich, as the lucky winner was, following Sophia's own death shortly before Anne's, Sophia's son George, the head of the other branch of the Welf family, Duke of Braunschweig-Lüneburg and, through the payment of terrific bribes, Prince-Elector of the Holy Roman Empire. So in one those dynastic swirls which I have generally tried to shelter the reader from, two rather daft and marginal bits of Lower Saxony suddenly went their different ways, with one branch, from its new bases in

Hanover and London, ruling a large part of the world, and the other remaining daft and marginal. Anton Ulrich at least had the good fortune to die a few months before the whole ghastly sequence came to its final fruition with George's coronation.

I mention August the Younger and Anton Ulrich, both because they are rather sympathetic, but also because they, far more than the wonder-cabinet collectors, move Germany towards the whole brilliant, intimidating world of paintings and sculpture which still fill so many small towns, almost unobserved by non-German or non-specialist eyes. The sheer quantity (but also quality) of intellectual and cultural power lurking even in a backwater such as Wolfen-büttel remains astonishing. Anton Ulrich's pictures were moved to Braunschweig, where they can still be seen, and form the basis for one of the oldest museums in Europe. What is so fascinating about the collection is that it remains hung so that the core of pictures are Anon Ulrich's own, with his fervent, late-convert Catholicism very much to the fore, but uneasily allied to his enthusiasm for nude orgasmic female death, Dido, Cleopatra and Procris all juddering away. A surprisingly topless Circe, several Venuses, Diana, Potiphar's wife and Eve herself festoon the walls, and Jesus' no doubt admirable qualities are completely upstaged by the repentant yet oddly clothing-free prostitute he is converting. This is all presided over by a particularly louche and beaky-nosed sculpted bust of the duke.

Like so many collections of this period it seems to have no protection whatsoever against floods of boring minor Dutch works (which could presumably be transported over to Wolfenbüttel quite cheaply on carts), which raise questions about the static nature of these collections. They could so readily be thinned out with the vigorous use of lighter-fluid in a way that would make them immediately more appealing. Although, to be fair, the duke's collection is a minor job compared to what needs to be done with the collections of the Dukes of Hesse-Kassel. There, teams of grim, asbestos-suited men with flamethrowers could be employed for weeks with tough-but-fair instructions to look out for skating and tavern genre scenes and witless bits of flat landscape.

Damascened yataghans

Up on a hillside high above the town of Passau is the little pilgrimage church of Mary of Mercy. It is reached by walking up some three hundred and twenty steps, itself an important part of the pilgrimage. I've probably spent too much time staggering up penitential stairways in southern Germany, but this really is the worst. People are parked all the way up; some are clearly praying but others could as well be having some form of seizure or been marooned there for days. I have never been able to work out the etiquette issues around gasping and puffing past someone in a prayerful state – there could not be a better example of where an English culture of panicked privacy gets completely unstuck in a more gestural zone of Europe. The view from the top makes everything worthwhile, banishing all anxieties about shortly needing help from Medivac helicopters manoeuvring through steep hills. To see the swollen, bulky, green River Inn, all the way from the Swiss Alps, slotting into the side of the rather smaller, blue – or, to be honest, blue-grey – River Danube, itself all the way from a squashy field in Swabia, is one of the greatest map-obsessive's sights in Europe, beaten only by being able to stand in Passau itself on the concrete of the thin V of land where the two rivers actually first touch.

The Mary of Mercy chapel was interesting enough in itself for its little ex voto paintings thanking Mary for rescue from drowning, lightning, fire, robbers and runaway coaches. But what seemed truly startling was a small plaque left by the Emperor Leopold I, giving thanks for the deliverance of Europe from the menace of the Turk. During the 1683 siege of Vienna, Passau became a temporary main base for the Holy Roman Empire and, following the Allied victory over the Ottoman army, Leopold wanted to leave a sign of his gratitude there ('Mary of Mercy' – or 'Mary Help' had been the Habsburg battle cry). Leopold spent his long reign fighting virtually everybody – every frontier of the Empire was under threat – but in the end his life was about defending the rest of Europe against the Ottomans.

This core Imperial competence hardly featured in English ideas about Germany but Habsburg Catholic militancy was in practice far more important an ideology for taking on the Ottomans than for taking on Protestants. With the Habsburg court in Vienna working its way through its unvarying annual calendar of masses, processions, movements between palaces, an entire elaborate astrological wheel of almost Qing complexity, in the short breaks most of the discussions were about the state of the alarmingly near frontier with the Ottoman state.

For centuries the serious defence of Christian Europe was undertaken by the Poles and by the Austrians. Of course, the Ottoman role in Europe was always a complicated one. If such a huge chunk of Europe was under stable, long-term rule from Constantinople (including Greece, Europe's notional cradle) then how could the bits of Europe that happened to include French or Italian people be *more* authentically European than the Ottoman bit? The constant affront and military threat presented by the Ottomans stemmed from their having since at least the fourteenth century simply been more powerful than other Europeans. At a time when England was engaged in endless, futile fighting just to try to absorb some parts of western France, the Ottomans ruled the Mediterranean from the Adriatic all the way, clockwise, to Morocco. At the critical Battle of Mohács in 1526, the Ottoman army was, including smelly but effective irregulars, almost twice the size of its Christian opponent and with three times as many cannon. In the near-contemporary Battle of Pavia, which pitted the main French army against the main Imperial force (perhaps unfortunately, given the imminent arrival of the Ottomans), both armies were less than half the size of the Ottomans' Mohács force. Despite some occasional, exciting Christian successes such as the naval Battle of Lepanto in 1571, there was never any hope until the end of the seventeenth century that the Ottomans could be seriously dealt with. The Emperor's job was to hold the line and not lose even more territory. Every year Ottoman raiders would sweep through the tiny Habsburg remnant of Hungary and the zone east of Vienna, snatching many thousands of slaves. The old frontier is still dotted with church towers with their

'Turkish bells' to warn of imminent attack. And there was always the knowledge that if Vienna fell, the Ottomans could sweep up the Danube to Salzburg, then Passau and then debouch in a welter of kettledrums and scimitars into Bavaria. This remained a serious threat and is reflected in an Austrian landscape that still bristles with castles and armouries. It was also reflected in the massive Military Frontier – a zone running eastwards from Slovenia, attracting settlers through freedom of faith and no serfdom. This was filled with Serb, Croat and German troops, ruled from Graz and designed to hold the line against the Ottoman armies in Bosnia and Hungary. The Frontier was financed by Habsburg crown lands, hence mainly Austria – but for many German soldiers across the whole Holy Roman Empire service on the Turkish frontier was an important source of excitement and reward, and the Emperor stood at the head of a highly complex, often tense framework, an unstable set of alliances and blandishments that, it was hoped, would be sufficient to keep the Ottomans at bay.

There are few stranger survivals of the Turkish wars than the great armoury at Graz, capital of the frontier dukedom of Styria. There has been a certain amount of fixing up and rebuilding but this gloomy, suffocating building gives an alarming sense of the planning needed to counter the Ottoman threat. Over several floors there is nothing but row upon row of standardized weapons – hundreds of breastplates, powder horns, muskets, boar-spears, helmets, pistols, all absolutely utilitarian. There can be few other places in the world where there are so many old-fashioned ways of being killed. This was a real frontier and a place where the Austrians only just hung on – in one disastrous year crop-eating locusts, plague and Turkish raiders disposed of thousands of Styrians. Huge markets were set up by the Turks to sell the glut of Christian slaves. As Graz itself gradually relaxed and became a military headquarters rather than a front-line fortress, the arsenal's importance drifted downwards but somehow the weapons have stayed intact as a peculiar and awful reminder of Austria's origins and its specific form of militancy.

The great change came as the Emperor Leopold I's reign stabilized in the 1650s. There was a new confidence that the Turks, despite still being able to field armies that were massive by European standards, were at last beginning to wobble. They found themselves under pressure from several fronts, most importantly from Russia, which spent the next two centuries steadily doing the serious work of wrecking the Ottoman empire. The great siege of Vienna in 1683 was a slightly despairing final attempt by the Ottomans to move the frontier further west or at least cripple the Habsburgs. After two months the Ottoman force, together with its Crimean, Wallachian, Moldavian and Hungarian subject allies, was decisively beaten by a mixed Polish–Lithuanian, Austrian, Swabian, Saxon, Franconian and Bavarian force. The siege is one of those frustrating historical events that have left no trace – Vienna was then encased in huge and now demolished fortifications and the battlefield is now hidden under streets and houses. Much of the fighting was carried out underground, in ghastly sets of tunnels, dug and counter-dug as Ottoman sappers attempted to get under Vienna's walls and blow them up and Imperial sappers armed with bombs, pistols and knives tried in turn to countermine their opponents.

It was during this astonishing emergency that Louis XIV took advantage of the Emperor's distraction to attack western Germany – on the one hand a peculiarly contemptible act, but on the other a curious indication of the degree to which, of course, the Ottoman empire was in practice a European great power much like any other. Clearly there were important chunks of a notionally solid Christian bloc not totally fussed at the idea of Vienna's fall.

The siege and battle at Vienna were the sensation of the period and there is hardly a Schloss or museum throughout Germany which does not have engravings of the battle or plans showing the layout of the Imperial 'Holy League' forces. The hill above Vienna, the Kahlenberg, which marks the meeting of the Polish and Imperial forces before they swept down into the Danube valley to destroy the Turks, remains a spectacular place, with a special restaurant, a Polish pilgrimage church and a very moving nineteenth-century inscription listing the king, Emperor and major princes who doffed their helmets to each other on that day.

To a striking degree that victory had depended on Poland – a country which gained very little from having helped the Austrians and which was to be carved into oblivion, not least by the Austrians, in the coming century. Again, this offered a curious limit on any sense of a concrete European or Christian 'culture', with Poland, a powerful and impressive Catholic entity for centuries, treated as being as much of a predatory target by Austrians, Hungarians and Russians as their new, formerly Ottoman lands in the south-east.

The best location to get a sense of these wars with Turkey (that in this period ended with the Habsburg takeover of the bulk of Hungary and Transylvania) is, oddly, in the far-off Rhine city of Karlsruhe. This is in many ways an unappealing place. Its layout is in the shape of a lady's fan, with the streets forming spokes out from the focal point of a tower in the palace of the Margraves of Baden-Durlach – an absolutist idea which *only* makes sense from the palace and makes walking around the town a mind-bending challenge, like being trapped in a drunken, lurched version of a grid system. Karlsruhe has the odd fame of being the town where Fritz Haber at the end of the nineteenth century worked out how to fix nitrogen, thereby inventing artificial fertilizers, thereby summoning into existence roughly a third of all humans alive today – a discovery that makes all others seem merely provisional and paltry.

But, trying to restabilize a bit with more normal history, the pride of Karlsruhe is the 'Turkish Booty'. This amazing display of Ottoman weaponry is part of the haul taken by Margrave Ludwig Wilhelm of Baden-Baden, also known as 'Turkish Louis' (as featured tirelessly on local wine, chocolate and schnapps packaging), after the crucial post-Vienna Battle of Slankamen, fought in 1691 in what is now the Serbian Vojvodina. Louis's mixed German and Serbian force destroyed a far larger Ottoman army, inflicting some twenty thousand casualties and permanently ending Ottoman offensive power (although their defensive ability was to keep them going, albeit mutated and contracted, right down to the present as the Republic of Turkey).

The 'booty' is perfectly displayed and leaves in the shade the sort of objects in the rest of the museum I would generally spend happy hours with (a sawfish saw, a crocodile skull, an amber jewel box, a wax and glass rendering of the Fall of Troy, the usual). It is also wittily juxtaposed with a modern sculpture of a Turkish-German taxi-driver carrying his taxi under his arm like a farmer carrying a small goat. There are double-edged axes, war banners, composite bows, kettledrums, whole chests of weapons, chainmail, leather quivers, campaign tents, sipahi armour, Persian flintlocks and – two words that do not come up much but must therefore be all the more savoured – damascened yataghans, the fathomlessly elegant Ottoman long knife, sometimes carried as a set of two crossed across the chest. If there is a hopelessly Orientalist child lurking inside so many of us, then these cabinets of eastern cruelty bring him thrashing to the surface.

There is also a painting from 1879 – pedantic and lurid in the academic German empire manner – of 'Turkish Louis' on a ramping charger looking down in disdain on the corpse of his chief opponent, Mustafa Köprülü, the picture contrasting Western strength (all armour, warrior comradeship and frowning rectitude) with Ottoman softness: parrots, turbans, a panicked Negro, a cowering houri, and some terrific damascened yataghans. While, naturally, shaking my head at the picture's witless nastiness I did spend rather too long contemplating its follies. It seems fair to admit that the picture had the appeal of the 'Turkish Booty' perfectly nailed.

I once went to a lecture on empires which made a point that is obvious but that has since bugged me: that at the frontiers of empires the soldiers, farmers and traders are all very familiar with each other but are generally very remote from the rulers and capital cities and that the line on a map hides a porous, vigorous reality. The Habsburgs and Ottomans were eye to eye for centuries – the Serb and Croat troops of the Military Frontier were familiar with Ottoman Bosnia, Royal Hungarians in Bratislava/Pressburg were well aware of the plight of other Ottoman-ruled Hungarians. There was a sufficient, if small, interchange of envoys, and traffic through Greek middlemen, for both sides to know each other's societies. One of the rather tense pressures in being a Habsburg envoy at the

Ottoman court was that while in normal times you were heaped with jewels, if war was declared you would be made into a galley slave or something similarly dead-end for the rest of your life.

We still today live in the shadow of Habsburg propaganda – a feeling that Ottoman south-east Europe was not real Europe, that it is more murderous, more mysterious and somehow worse, when of course it was a highly sophisticated and brilliant society, with its great fortresses such as Belgrade and Buda, its trading cities such as Salonika or Smyrna and, of course, Istanbul, a city which today still exudes a residual greatness entirely comparable to Vienna's. In terms of civilization it is quite hard in some moods to know who to have sided with during the Siege of Vienna: a fairly tolerant world of silks, sherbets, harems, zithers, tinkling fountains and tulip festivals lit by wandering tortoises with candles on their backs, or a world of gloom-ridden 'brocade Catholicism' in which, for example, Viennese Jews were not allowed out of their homes on Sunday mornings because they were Christ's murderers. There is a part of me that would be much happier in curly slippers, sipping coffee and watching camel-drawn artillery trundle past. It is curious if unsurprising that it is Austria that leads the block of European Union countries violently opposed to Turkey's entry – a sort of pip-squeak epilogue to 'Turkish Louis' and his exploits.

'Burn the Palatinate!'

These political flows are in the end impossibly deep, complex and inexplicable but, for whatever reason, just as Europe was in the final phase of the Thirty Years War it had the horrific bad luck to give birth to Louis XIV. As the war's dazed survivors tried to rebuild their towns and kick trade routes back into gear with some non-homicidal commerce, this ghastly man was growing up and rubbing his hands together at the financial and military machinery built for him by Richelieu and Mazarin. With this he was to make life entirely miserable for western Germany, along with many other places.

It is one of the chief pleasures of culture that it remains so specific to nation, class, region or time and that it cannot be faked. Louis XIV has never had many English admirers, so it is easy to fall into a long tradition of not admiring him. England had a fun role in ruining the later part of his reign but the real issue is a cultural one: what made Louis the arbiter of taste, architecture, music and design no longer seems interesting or even plausible. As with so many things, too much time has gone by even to see him vividly as a monster, to fully appreciate the enormity of what he did. When I think how much time I have wasted wandering around Versailles over the years – a sort of cold and inhuman nightmare of a place – it is hard not to feel that, despite it all, he does keep us all in his freakish orbit even three hundred years after his death. But the sheer absurdity of his court, with everyone watching the king shitting or admiring his ballet moves (dressed as Sunshine), or sitting around watching pageants at which representations of the rivers of Europe (the Rhine, the Danube and so on) bow down before the Seine – did really *nobody* laugh?

Louis ruled from the age of five to just before his seventy-seventh birthday, and once he got into his stride, it was misery all the way. This was expressed in military ways and in cultural ways. From the German point of view the military misery came from Louis being someone who, like many unattractive people, spends too much time staring at maps. On almost invariably quite spurious grounds he wished to expand France's frontiers to its 'natural' boundaries – the Pyrenees, the Alps and the Rhine. The human cost of this completely arbitrary, and indeed mad, vision was incalculable – there is probably no good way to work out how many thousands died just in order to grind the borders of France forward into what are now on the whole marginal, sleepy, resort-oriented places, with the exception of a bit of the north that later turned out to have some significant (but still inadequate) coal supplies on the Belgian border. Whether providing Zola with a suitable setting for *Germinal* is an adequate return on Louis's investment we cannot judge. Indeed what is odd about Louis's endless efforts is the smallness of the results (aside from the barely settled and abortive Louisiana) at a time when England was creating the basis for the future United States and Austria taking over the whole of Hungary and Transylvania. The futility stemmed from these geographical borders *not* being natural in any sense and Louis being so widely loathed that vigorous coalitions could always be thrown up against him.

The German nadir came in the 1680s when Louis chewed through the edges of the Holy Roman Empire, armed with absurd legal documents drawn up by shameless lawyers giving him the right to take over various towns, including the previously independent and genial Straßburg. Straßburg had managed to stay neutral throughout the Thirty Years War but it now fell to Louis's deranged greed – thereby inaugurating a key aspect of Franco-German hatred only resolved in 1945. Louis himself was quite happy to ascribe his motive as purely 'glory', a glory expressed in babyish pageants, ceiling paintings with wearying allegorical elements and so on. In the later 1680s, in order both to force the Empire to accept his thefts along the frontier and to impose his own candidate as the new Elector-Archbishop of Cologne, Louis moved his forces moved across the Rhine and devastated all the helpless major towns. Mainz, Koblenz, Worms and Speyer were wrecked (under the banner 'Brûlez le Palatinat!') with a deliberate emphasis on destroying them as centres of civilization, so that even if they did not end up owned by France they would form part of a ravaged zone protecting the frontier. Their inhabitants were herded out and every building of value or importance burned down. The damage to Speyer Cathedral, for example, was so bad that it was not until 1850 that it was entirely restored (having in the meantime been further smashed up by the French during the Revolutionary Wars). Of course, later layers of devastation hit all these towns in the 1940s so it is hard to get a sense of how bad it was. The most famous ruin left by the French remains the picturesque shell of the Heidelberg Palace, so loved by generations of tourists and painters, but itself a side effect of extreme, sour violence.

It would be unreasonable simply to place all blame on the French for these catastrophes – Louis had plenty of clients among the local rulers who were happy to egg him on in a faithless way – but these wars were fought for such baffling abstractions that they raise curious questions about our attitude to warfare as a whole. For many people there is a *point* to much European fighting from Napoleon onwards – there are clear, if contestable, motives and meaningful, if often tragic, sequences of events. I have always found it impossible to discern such ideas in the wars fought between the opening, religious phase of the Thirty Years War and the outbreak of the French Revolution – everything seems to be just the result of the ghastliness of scoundrels dusted in wig-powder. Louis's actions really start off this harsh period, with its obsession with a 'balance of power', a balance which varied according to which country you were talking to and which still treated territory as a question of personal ownership. Indeed, one of the ways of salvaging the era's politics is to look out for the strange, often small signs that as the eighteenth century progressed, this assumption of royal ownership became undermined by genuine nationalism – a feeling of belonging to a state rather than belonging to its owner. Historians tend to heave a sigh of relief when spotting something along these lines – for example in the late eighteenth century the more than dynastic unease that greeted the Emperor Joseph II's failed attempts simply to swap Austrian-owned but tiresome and far-away Belgium for Bavaria, shunting off the Elector of Bavaria to Brussels and tacking Bavaria onto his own land. This idea was greeted with outrage by both Belgians and Bavarians and we are clearly now, even before the French Revolution, on track for nationalism to break out all over the place. Instead, all that the Emperor got as compensation was a small chunk of near-empty agricultural land along the River Inn, thereby later on giving Austria the opprobrium of being Hitler's birthplace, with consequences too complex and sickening to muse on.

Back to Louis: the other disaster, as already mentioned, was cultural. Looking at the chilly shell of Versailles today, it is hard to imagine what an impact the court there had had and the general cultural focus provided by wigs, elaborate coats, huge amounts of meaningless ritual and hunting on a grotesque scale. Wigs have done a lot of damage to the image of the period. The rulers during the Thirty Years War and the English Civil War are all portrayed with their real hair, whether shorn or lank; then it disappears under wigs for a hundred and fifty years, giving a strange, permanent sense of modernity to those earlier rulers denied to their bizarre-looking successors. Of course fake hair is not a valid indicator of character, particularly through the heavy filter of fawning court portraiture, often of indifferent quality. Louis XIV has a central role in disseminating this absurd headgear, so that even sensible and cunning operators such as William III have heads almost swamped in brown bubbles. As it becomes so hard to get a sense of the personalities of these rulers, it becomes easy to assume that they are all merely lizardy cynics. They present themselves in a style which is no longer comprehensible. The audience who can pick its way unself-consciously through the ideologies in these pictures has died long ago and we now look on at such displays with hostility and boredom, oblivious to the white-silk-clad shins and unsubtle comparisons to Mars or Apollo.

What remain are the huge monuments built to ape Versailles. Whether such monsters were the result of rulers having more money or whether more money was gouged out of the peasants *in order to pay for them* can never be resolved. In any event, as areas of Germany recovered economically as the seventeenth century ended and the eighteenth century began (even if bits were always being blown up by somebody or other), a lot of this money went into pointless copies of Versailles. As the Versailles model ruled Western Europe until the French Revolution, this was clearly an important change. All over Germany genial, turreted, rambly castles were cast aside in favour of immense rectangles with carvings of weapons on top. Palaces at Kassel, Ludwigsburg and Brühl stay today as symbols of French cultural dominance, a shorthand (or rather longhand) for a particular kind of remote autocracy, intimidating and depressing.

Catholicism goes for broke

As I mentioned earlier, I was raised a Catholic, went to Protestant schools and came out the far end as a sort of Protestant. It may well just flatter my self-image to be sitting in the cool rationality of a whitewashed Lutheran hall church humming something by Bach but – like a former alcoholic diving face-first into a tray of liqueur chocolates – there is something that makes me get on planes to south Germany, hastily book into a hotel and jog down the street to the nearest baroque pilgrimage gross-out. I would like to say that my favourite painting in the Kunsthistorisches Museum in Vienna is Rembrandt's austere self-portrait, but really I know I have come home when I see Rubens' delirious whopper *St Francis Xavier Preaching*, with the saint as a sort of wizard, fixing up the ill, curing blind folk and blowing up a Chinese temple – its josses shattering to fragments to the dismay of the cringing, top-knotted idolaters – all backed up by a troupe of sensational angels. In a spirit of self-scrutiny I would have to say that I have always liked childish special effects and refreshed Catholicism on the march has them all.

This Counter-Reformation faith was astonishingly self-confident. Many ancient and important churches – the Comburg monastic church; Freising cathedral – were in the seventeenth and early eighteenth centuries made completely unrecognizable by shocking makeovers in white stucco, glowing marbles and gold-leaf. The geniuses at doing this were the Asam brothers, among the greatest theatrical decorators in Europe, who turned the inside of churches into a wilderness of special effects: beams of light, flying babies, immense heroic bishops, clouds, martyrs, candy-cane pillars. When it works well – as in the tiny church they made for themselves in Munich, the Asamkirche – it is wonderful, but it *does* require a steady nerve and constant restoration. I once made the mistake of wandering into the church of St Emmeram in Regensburg and suddenly felt as though I was at the scene of an accident and was required to do something urgent to help. ('It's too late to save the early martyr, but this putto's still breathing; in God's name, does anyone have any gold paint?') For me it may have been the kebab talking but, far from zooming heavenward, everything the Asams had done at St Emmeram implied an explosion in a chemical-weapons factory.

The general tone of this church is added to by the survival of rows of skeletons of minor saints, lolling in provocative, Rita Hayworth-like poses in glass cases along the walls, held together by rotting brown body stockings and with rhinestones for eyes. Most of these *Scooby-Doo*-like horrors were chucked in the skip years ago, sometimes through revolutionary violence but also through Catholic renewal movements which have often taken a cold view of this sort of performance, but here and there a few survive. Worse still, if you are looking to be frightened stiff by outdated aspects of Counter-Reformation faith (not high on some people's to-do list), is the cathedral museum at Freising. Oddly, I was the only visitor – and indeed even the elderly ticket-seller soon vanished – so that didn't help the generally eldritch atmosphere. Going down some harmless-seeming stairs, I was entirely surrounded by very old and complex crib scenes and a seeming infinity of wax Baby Jesus dolls. In the low, murky lighting it was hard not to imagine that the missing ticket-seller had run off to flip the mains switch. I would be found dead in the morning, as in one of those wonderful scenes in science-fiction films where the pathologist turns to the policeman and says, 'This man didn't die of a heart attack, Inspector. He died of fright.' Only then would they notice the thousands of tiny hand marks all over my skin.

The struggle though with deriding this stuff is that it is illegit-imate to say that the world of singing babies on plaster clouds and saints' corpses put in poses similar to those of the women painted on the sides of Flying Fortresses is uniquely ridiculous and apart. This was a highly self-critical, confident and dynamic faith, centred as much on the Habsburg and Wittelsbach families as on the Pope, with huge resources and at its ideological heart the mission to fight the Turks and root out heresy. It was as much an expres-sion of this to camp up church interiors as to commission, sing and play some of the greatest music ever composed. There is nowhere more baroque than the Archbishopric of Salzburg, a state dedicated in its very being to breathing in and out Catholic triumphalism. There in the 1670s the Bohemian violinist and composer Heinrich Ignaz von Biber produced his great cycle of 'Rosary sonatas', one for each of the mysteries and designed to be played at services of contemplation for the archbishop and his circle. The impact of this eerie, serene, strange music must have been extraordinary (although it seems even more extraordinary now, as the final *Passacaglia* rather oddly shares the same ground bass as John Barry's theme tune for the James Bond film *On Her Majesty's Secret Service*). Biber was clearly a sort of ecstatic genius in this music, but he was equally able to write completely terrible 'funny music' made to sound like drunken musketeers or battles being fought, presumably aimed at some of the rougher military types in his audiences. With equal fervour Haydn's great masses, such as the *Missa Sancti Nicolai*, written a century after Biber, inescapably have, however much we might pretend otherwise, tiny wax fingerprints all over them.

In the end it was Catholics themselves who tried to tidy up so much of this world for themselves. The Emperor Joseph II, the zealous, cheerless reformer who caved in through overwork in 1790, was at the core of his job description meant to protect the Catholicism of convents, hermitages and superstition. Despite being very devout himself, he was driven mad by the endless particularisms that would make even a small town a mass of tax exemptions and special privileges, with Imperial officials struggling along next to vast, well-provisioned monasteries filled with aristocratic idlers. Something of this world can still be felt in Oxbridge colleges, where individual privileges mean that on the same street one college can be on the verge of bankruptcy while at another college it is stuffed giraffe neck, Château d'Yquem and a lap-dancer for every table. Joseph swept away much of this closeted exceptionalism from his territories, closing over five hundred monasteries, pinching the Bishop of Passau's lands when the man's corpse was barely cold and banning the sale of Christmas cribs. He died hated and reviled and left behind merely another threadbare set of patched semi-reforms. The southern (and Rhineland) German landscape remains awash with the debris of layer upon layer of Catholic religious reform. Hulking monastic buildings may often now be government offices or wine bars, but they crop up everywhere, and remarkable numbers are still filled with monks, who bounced back after Joseph's and Napoleon's utmost attempts to dispose of them. These often bizarre churches too have sometimes been neglected, overhauled, bombed or burnt down or refashioned. Each change left its scars, but each in effect celebrated *another* failed attempt to rationalize and firm things up: still a wilderness of private superstitions, virtual polytheism and cheap lighting effects and with a sort of resilience that has managed to survive the most terrible circumstances.

CHAPTER EIGHT

The descendants of Cyrus the Great

Sitting in southern Bavaria, quietly reading an excellent short biography of the Emperor Joseph II, I was struck by an incidental sentence mentioning what it was about pre-Napoleonic Germany that most infuriated the ghastly anti-Semitic Bismarck nationalist historian Heinrich von Treitschke. What he really hated were the tiny states that puffed themselves up into a towering froth of glory on the basis of nothing at all – singling out specifically the grotesquely overblown monuments of the Princes of Hohenlohe at Weikersheim. Of course, within moments of reading this, I was on a series of aggressively local and slow trains, panting with excitement, impatiently staring through the window for a first sight of something which had received such a worthwhile endorsement.

The territory of the Princes of Hohenlohe was so small that it appeared on the map to be monstrously hemmed in by its hardly king-size neighbours, such as a little outcrop of Mainz and the headquarters of the Teutonic Knights. Hohenlohe-Weikersheim is essentially just a single pretty Franconian valley with the idyllic River Tauber running through it. The tragedy of Carl Ludwig, the prince in the first half of the eighteenth century, was that his only son died in a riding accident. The helpful result for modern purposes was that his line became extinct (absorbed by another Hohenlohe territory in a geographical convulsion unnoticed by a wider world). Carl Ludwig's activities at Weikersheim were therefore accidentally preserved as the town became itself a marginal element in an already marginal territory, with its own micro-capital elsewhere. His family really were *very unimportant*. One inspired ancestor had created a wonderful 'hunter's hall' at Schloss Weikersheim in around

1600, a miracle of animal-killing celebration, with dozens of ceiling paintings showing the slaughter of everything from boar to lynx to ostrich and with the walls decorated in life-size plaster bears, moose, deer and – incredibly – an elephant of unique, baggy oddness and with real tusks. This man's son had played an undistinguished role as a Protestant leader in the Thirty Years War and the Schloss had been badly smashed up – but then in 1709 Carl Ludwig arrived.

The result was a deeply strange, almost neurotic response to Versailles which, for a change, is just completely charming. It is immediately possible to see what made Treitschke so cross, but equally for that very reason important to embrace it as everything most fun about Germany. The life-sized gold statue on horseback of Carl Ludwig is alas no longer there, but otherwise everything is as it should be – the gold statue stood at the end of a vista of formal gardens, flanked and applauded by statues of his notional precursors: there is a turbaned Cyrus the Great, Nimrod with a sceptre, Julius Caesar in armour and Alexander the Great with nice hair. If this is not mad enough, then the major classical gods all sit around on the beautiful orangery looking down in approval on Karl Ludwig – Zeus with his thunderbolts, Mars with a drawn sword and so on. There is also a wan, plump and patently insincere figure of Peace – and a lady I couldn't place (Dido?) sitting on an elephant nearly as charismatic as his friend, the genial Trunky, back in the hunter's hall. Beyond this heroic ensemble lie fields of barley, orchards, vineyards. There is also a set of grotesque statues modelled on the commedia dell'arte work of Jacques Callot, of comic dwarfs in various household roles, the precursors to an unhappy nineteenth-century Thuringian invention that was to swamp the world: the garden gnome. Weikersheim shines with a sort of happy daftness which should be everyone's ideal. Sitting in the town's little main square (the only square in fact) with a fountain tinkling and a peacock scratching about on the steps of the tiny town bank, it is hard not to feel in some sort of fairy-tale fantasy.

Naturally the reason that Treitschke picked on poor Weikersheim was to offer a pathetic contrast to his manly, visionary and adored Prussia. Prussia has ended up with its values being blamed for the disasters of the twentieth century, its heartlands absorbed into Poland and Russia, its people dispersed or killed and its very name banished after 1947. But in Treitschke's vision (and that of so many late-nineteenth-century nationalists), while Karl Ludwig was busy fussing over which heroic military ancestors to put where, the real business was being done by that mustelid predator Frederick the Great in his epochal 1740 invasion of Silesia, the event that threw down the gauntlet to the effete, Catholic Austrians over who should rule the Germans. This challenge was finally answered in Prussia's favour in the decisive Battle of Königgrätz in 1866 that expelled the Austrians from any further role in German affairs and laid the path for German unity under Prussian rule. This providential path had a sickening plausibility, and indeed mesmerized Hitler, who saw himself for unclear reasons as following in Frederick the Great's footsteps, his bunker decorated with a portrait of a man who would have found almost every one of Hitler's actions disgusting, evil or absurd. This vision was quite at odds with the reality of Prussia as an often progressive, quite vulnerable and sometimes marginal place.

Of course it is possible to go too far. I was in Potsdam some years ago, visiting the new Prussian Museum which had just shyly opened there. This was a parody of quietude – Prussia as a land of rustic carts, folk-craft and embroidered dresses. There was even a special exhibition on Prussian pressed-flower collections and monastic herbal medicine, with little knobs to jiggle which then squirted the scent of rosemary, say, or sweet lavender into the air. The effect was outlandish – even those most friendly towards Prussia's complex reality had to concede that militarism featured *somewhere* in the state's make-up.

But the issues around Prussia have always been closer to Weikersheim than any German nationalists are ever likely to admit. There was a substantial aspect of Prussia which was genuinely introvert and admirable, not least the Pietists in Halle with their religious, educational mission, still beautifully preserved in the Franckesche Stiftung teaching collections, which include – by way of digression – an attic room filled with wigs, pictures of basilisks, a giant model of the solar system, pickled geckoes, a little dog made out of seashells, wax heads, a dried cow-fish, a speculative engraving of the Ark of the Covenant, an opium pipe, shoes from around the world and, hanging from the rafters, the best and biggest stuffed crocodile ever, an ancient, gnarled Behemoth which, if it fell to the ground, would detonate in a great cloud of evil-smelling dust.

But even Prussian militarism was as much the result of weakness as anything more aggressive. Repeatedly in its history, Prussia was threatened with extinction – its Elector was the weakest of the seven, Berlin a very small place, and clearly the real axis of Germany ran Cologne–Frankfurt–Munich–Vienna with spurs to Hamburg and Dresden. Much of Germany's life for most of its history was not reliant on a grim, dark, flat area of the north-east. Brandenburg (the heart of Prussia) was always being overrun and the Thirty Years War had been a disaster of helplessness as Swedes and Imperialists ignored its boundaries, contemptuously burning and killing more or less at will.

For one generation, however, Prussia was different, because of Frederick II 'the Great' (1712–86). Building on the work of his cunning predecessors (their portraits featured in sequence on a special series of small matchboxes before me now, a valuable aid as the monarchs are almost all called Frederick or William or both), Frederick took advantage of an accident – that the Emperor Karl VI had no male children. Karl had defined much of his reign by weary negotiations to get everyone in the Empire to sign the Pragmatic Sanction which would allow the Empire to fall to his daughter (impossible under unchallenged early medieval laws). Of course, in the usual parental tragedy, the parent's wish only has force while the parent is alive and the young, devout Maria Theresa's attempt to inherit on her father's death was always going to be difficult. Frederick, just on the throne himself, stuffed with cash and brilliantly drilled troops inherited from his borderline-insane father, Friedrich Wilhelm I, decided to alter Prussia's status for good – by invading Silesia. This is now a moderately significant industrial region of Poland, but in 1740 it was a key Habsburg territory, with a large, well-off and taxable population. Taking Silesia both enhanced Prussia greatly and did permanent damage to the Habsburgs by wrenching away a block which had before always been closely linked to neighbouring Habsburg-owned Bohemia and Moravia.

The subsequent wars, latterly in conjunction with Britain and Braunschweig, were a series of dazzling encounters whereby Frederick held off sometimes unbelievable coalitions trying to destroy him (most memorably in the Third Silesian War, where he had ranged against him the Russian empire, France, the Habsburg empire, Sweden and Saxony). Through brilliant generalship and luck, Frederick held on to Silesia and Prussia notionally became a great power. But after Frederick's death what is striking is just how rapidly Prussia became a minor and helpless country again (with a long run of pathetic kings, also featured on my little matchbox collection – indeed the rest of the set until the matchboxes run out in 1918 consists only of painfully weak or narrow figures). Napoleon swatted Prussia aside, destroyed its army, occupied much of it and considered abolishing it entirely (a fate only avoided through the personal intervention of the Tsar). The Prussians recovered their élan after Napoleon's disasters in Russia and played a significant role in his final defeat (most famously at Leipzig and Waterloo), but it would be impossible to claim that they were more than the beneficiaries of events way beyond their control – Napoleon was defeated by Russia, Britain and Austria with Prussia only given room even to breathe by the actions of these other countries.

Not to run ahead too far into the nineteenth century but Prussia after Waterloo had no further serious combat victory until the storming of Fort Dybbøl in the 1864 war with Denmark (itself an engagement engineered by Prussia's Austrian allies to make the Prussians feel better about their under-performing army). So if you bracket the heady little two-decade eruption of Frederick II's fevered violence, Prussia stays a generally vulnerable and, if not minor then certainly rather marginal state, a curious wild card in the manner of Sweden, and not faintly comparable to France or Britain or its opponents within the rest of the Holy Roman Empire.

At a time when the Qianlong emperor was taking over the whole of Xinjiang, the British marching all over Bengal and Canada, the Russians exploring eastern Siberia and Alaska and whole Silesia-size bits of land were being settled almost daily in the future United States, the activities of this rather odd flautist, galloping about on the north German plain with smoking bits of Prussian trooper whizzing about his ears, seems perhaps less than impressive. Frederick was, after all, only saved in the Third Silesian War by the lucky death of the violently anti-Frederick Tsarina Elizabeth and her replacement with a short-lived Prussophile loony. If she had survived then Prussia would have been crushed and perhaps dismantled completely. As it was, this amazing fluke was forgotten about and only the dazzling defensive victories remembered, providing an entirely misleading picture of Prussian strength for later generations.

The Tsarina Elizabeth's death only came back into its own in 1945, when the Nazis drew inspiration from it. Hitler, rather weirdly comparing Roosevelt and Elizabeth, imagined on hearing of the former's death that this would in the same manner undo the coalition ranged against him. It is curious that so many of the creepier type of German nationalist drew such succour from Frederick – the apparent lessons of his greatness creating a ruinous will-o'-the-wisp that led on generations of rulers and their sycophants. Frederick's true lesson was perhaps that in the end Germany was defenceless against its serious neighbours, and that he could heap brilliant tactical victories up to the ceiling and still be just much less important than the more heavily resourced and readily defended countries around him.

Frederick's Sanssouci Palace and gardens at Potsdam are now his main legacy – with most other aspects of his reign politically or physically erased by the twentieth century. The palace's general prettiness and sense of happy enjoyment bring Frederick very close in spirit to the orangery of the Prince of Hohenlohe, with lots of curves, glass and mythological trinkets, but with the rococo extras of a later generation. I could happily spend weeks wandering around the park at Potsdam (with its Chinese tea-house – the direct descendant of the lovely Chinese 'mirror room' still extant at Weikersheim). I was last there shortly after Frederick's body, after many indignities, had finally been buried according to his wishes – next to Sanssouci and by the graves of his favourite hunting dogs. A large group of Germans on a tour were being shown the new funerary stone, and several of the older tourists were in tears. It can hardly be possible to imagine the range of confused and difficult emotions that could have provoked such a response.

Frederick's actions *did not lead* to Bismarck's empire. Far too many events intervene and almost every aspect of what happened in the 1860s would have been entirely alien and baffling to Frederick. He may have been hailed as the descendant of Mars, Alexander the Great and so on with a bit more plausibility than Carl Ludwig of Weikersheim, but in the end Frederick II shares more of Carl Ludwig's engaging marginality than later and unattractively excitable figures have tried to suggest.

Drinking chocolate with ostriches

The later Habsburg rulers are a strikingly feeble bunch. It is as though the great effort of their dynasty – the defence against the Turks – was finally wound up with the siege of Vienna, and Leopold I's successors could afford to be a lot less vigorous. In the dismal sequence of dull or incapable figures who get us through to the end of the First World War, there were two potentially brilliant rulers – Leopold's son, the Emperor Joseph I, and his great-grandson, the Emperor Leopold II: both in their different ways dynamic, far-sighted and interesting. Oddly both died young after such very short reigns that it almost suggests a Vatican plot (perhaps with poison powders hidden inside finger rings) to keep smart decision-makers out of the way.

The nature of the Habsburg ruler was peculiarly important because of the personal nature of the entire Imperial arrangement. Britain or France could, within measure, afford some pathetic monarchs because they were both nations with identities that could transcend the king, however powerful. Indeed, there is an interesting question in the course of the eighteenth century about the general low quality of monarchs, who across so much of Europe form a sort of parade of malfunction. The revolutions of the end of the century tend to be given economic and social roots, but they might at least in part stem from the strangely helpless notional keystones (from France to Tuscany to Saxony-Poland) who created such a general atmosphere of decay.

Within the Empire there was a particularly unforgiving environment as there were so many potentially fissiparous elements all held in orbit by the Emperor, both within Germany and within the non-German Empire, with the Emperor separately being King of Bohemia and King of Hungary, the latter with a medley of territories spreading from the Carpathians to Slavonia. The one later Habsburg who really commands respect, oddly, is Maria Theresa, plus her fun husband Franz I. Maria Theresa tends to come across badly in relation to the other two great women rulers in eighteenth-century Europe (the Tsarinas Elizabeth and Catherine) because she looks such a pious frump. Her taste for particularly inert court portraitists (a taste shared by many later Habsburgs, whose features are almost lost in clothing and routinized symbolism) has not helped. But although she lacked the swagger of the Russian rulers, there is something both heroic and likeable about her. The appalling circumstances of her coming to power make an exciting start, a teenager battling for her inheritance, surrounded by the faithless wolves who had promised her father they would protect her. The sheer novelty of a woman in such a position, refusing to give in, rallying her generals and the aristocracy, dealing with defeat after defeat and somehow still fighting her enemies to a standstill is one of the great, completely unexpected epics. The humiliation of the creepy Bavarians is a particular pleasure, with Duke Karl Albrecht, aided by his French friends, spending his entire treasury and the lives of thousands of his subjects to force his way into the Empire and get himself crowned Holy Roman Emperor as Karl VII, only to find it all turning to ashes with Maria Theresa's troops occupying Munich and his unmourned death following after only three years in the job.

These sorts of reversals of fortune, startling dashes and amazing battles make the eighteenth century semi-fun to read about, but in the end the lack of ideology and the sheer childishness of the motivation make it all a bit hard to take seriously. Having constantly to remind yourself that ownership lay at the heart of what made Europe tick and that the glory of the ruler was the *point* of history becomes through endless repetition a rather unconvincing mantra. With Maria Theresa, though, it really is still possible to glimpse what was at stake: her legitimacy as a ruler in a world of predators in wigs and elaborate cloaks. That she holds on to her inheritance and indeed (despite in the end having to concede the loss of Silesia to Frederick the Great) makes Vienna into a great city and the Empire into the heart of Western civilization is a happy and surprising result.

After that rococo bankrupt, the so-called Karl VII, died in the shame and obloquy of his ambition, it was clear that the new Emperor was going to have to be a man despite Maria Theresa's claims. And this is where Maria Theresa's adorable husband came in. Franz Stephan had been Duke of Lorraine, but in a complex international swap of a kind that raises severe doubts about how interesting history really is he found himself as Grand Duke of Tuscany instead, after the death of the almost unbelievably disgusting and incompetent Last of the Medicis. This swap, incidentally, ended the important history of Lorraine as an independent state, as its new, Polish ruler only got the job on the basis of Lorraine then becoming part of France on his death.

With so many figures from this period it is almost impossible to judge their personalities – their martial or ecclesiastical attributes in their portraits and their immense cloaks and hats simply swamp them. But wandering around Vienna, Franz Stephan's picture is always turning up on palace walls and, however festooned in wigs and medals, it still shines through that he was an amusing chump. There is something about his eyes and the general, self-indulgent set of his mouth that makes him look enjoyable to meet.

After the Austrians had given the Bavarians a final crushing at the Battle of Pfaffenhofen (with Hungarian irregulars looting Munich), it was agreed that Franz Stephan should become the new Holy Roman Emperor (because he was a man) whereas Maria Theresa would be queen regnant in Bohemia and Hungary and Empress through her being married to Franz Stephan. This arrangement fooled nobody as she was patently in charge, exercising immense (if sometimes chaotic and rather narrow-minded) sway.

What makes Maria Theresa and Franz Stefan so appealing is their genuine love for each other. To be interested in dynastic history at all is to be forced to deal with a great welter of human misery, of frosty, vicious or even murderous marriage arrangements, of hundreds of women having to pay a very high price for having access to enchanting lapdogs and pretty tea-sets. There is hardly a palace which doesn't in the end reek of cruelty and inadequacy. By contrast, Maria Theresa and Franz enthusiastically turned out piles of children (mostly called Maria) and – when she was not inspecting her troops on parade before they were beaten by the Prussians and when he was not engaged in standard-issue philandering and collecting minerals – spent as much time together as possible.

This most charmingly survives in the unexpected environment of the zoo in Vienna. Just next to the Habsburg summer palace at Schönbrunn, the zoo has its origins in Franz's enthusiasm for all branches of science and still features the rococo pavilion built for him and Maria Theresa to enjoy breakfast together, drinking cups of chocolate surrounded by parrots, zebras and (those quintessential rococo animals) ostriches. Even the layout of animal houses, radiating from the pavilion, has been kept and there can be few luckier creatures than the hippos and giraffes still entangled in this ancient decorative arrangement.

Franz's death has had as much impact on Vienna as his life, as Maria Theresa commissioned portraits to remind her of him and worked to preserve his huge if miscellaneous collections of minerals, curiosities and animals. He remains in all his glory at the heart of the Natural History Museum in Vienna, with his great portrait surrounded by savants, fossils and collection cabinets, looking just as teddy-bear-like and self-indulgent as though he were alive today.

But, in the long tradition of Habsburgs enjoying the chance to design their own tombs, Maria Theresa (who wore black for the remaining fifteen years of her reign) had a brilliant time working on one of the most excessive of them all. There can be few greater pleasures in life than wandering around the Capuchins' Crypt, where so many of the Habsburgs are buried. Maria Theresa's tomb was up against some considerable competition from her own father and mother. The former – the ineffective Karl VI (for whom we must be grateful anyway for building the Karl Church and the State Rooms, two of Vienna's most fun pieces of architecture) – and the latter, Elisabeth Christine of Braunschweig-Wolfenbüttel, had gone nuts with their tombs, miracles of proto-Goth with skulls wearing crowns and metal women's faces suffocated in metal-gauze mourning veils. To solve this problem she simply had designed a tomb of infinitely larger size than those of her parents, in the form of a bed with figures of herself and Franz waking up at the End of Time and greeting each other, as though just about to hop up and head to the pavilion for a nice breakfast. It is silly, but still very moving – and a likeable end to an attractive reign.

More competitive tomb-building

I am always happy in Mainz. For many long years, visits to the Frankfurt Book Fair could be cheered up by a quick train trip up the River Main. Mainz has been repeatedly ravaged by invaders since its origin as a bunch of Roman military tents and it is possible to imagine a gene in many of the inhabitants that would allow them simply to roll their eyes fatalistically as the next Vandal, Hun, Swede, Frenchman, Hessian or Imperialist marched in. On the banks of the Rhine at the river junction with the Main, awkwardly close to France (which was always threatening to turn it into Mayence), the city used to bristle with fruitless crenellations, ditches and towers. Its readily pinpointable river location meant it was ravaged by bombers in the Second World War and rebuilt in an often glum, utilitarian way. As with similar medium-sized towns such as Hannover it is, under the circumstances, impossible to complain about this rebuilding. It at least creates an arena for the enthusiasm of the post-war German state in supporting traditional shopkeepers, protecting them with restrictive opening hours and discriminating against out-of-town megastores, which means that places like Mainz and Hannover still pullulate with the core German competence of mindlessly buying tons of stuff. Far more than old buildings this buzz of shopping, to me at any rate, gives a direct feeling of continuity with the older Mainz – although of course its citizens were then buying things like wooden shoes or pig's trotters for dinner rather than fur underwear or dodgy all-in holidays to Thailand.

Mainz is famous as the birthplace of printing – commemorated with an excellent statue of Gutenberg and a notably boring museum, although not as boring as the gauntlet thrown down by the endless, totally without interest Roman objects that cram another of the museums. But Mainz's other claim is as the capital of the old ecclesiastic Electorate of Mainz. Like many territories, it was made up of a chaotic mass of geographical oddities, owning chunks of surrounding land and valuable rents in others, and even the far-off Thuringian town of Erfurt (which still features a rather forlorn little monument to one of the last Electors, in a stiffly bewigged cameo, now a hangout for understandably disaffected Erfurter skateboarders).

The Electorate of Mainz was not very big but it was always very significant as its ruler, the Archbishop of Mainz, was the most important cleric in Catholic Germany – indeed, apart from Rome, Mainz was the only town that could be referred to as 'the Holy See'. He was Archchancellor of the Holy Roman Empire, which put him in charge of several key institutions, not least the ceremonies in Frankfurt around choosing each Emperor. He was also the director of the Electoral-Rhenish Imperial Circle and generally too of the Upper Rhenish Circle. These defensive groups were crucial to the vain attempts to keep out invaders and roped together the military potential of everything from chunky (or at least meaningful) territories such as Hesse-Kassel, Cologne, Koblenz and Frankfurt down to scraps like the Abbey of Prüm, whose sole asset in the event of foreign invasion was a pair of sandals apparently once worn by Jesus.

Like the other significant ecclesiastical territories before they were swept away after the French Revolution – Cologne and Trier being the most politically important, also being Electorates – Mainz was a very odd place. Strikingly, it was not motivated by sex. Each ruler was by definition celibate (and indeed was in practice too, with the odd spectacular lapse) and on each ruler's death there needed to be a fresh election. These were not dynastic states, in other words (although other dynasties often meddled in them), and therefore, in a peculiar way, a bit progressive, albeit with eye-wateringly large bribes changing hands before each appointment. This lack of sex around the court tended to create a unique atmosphere blending intense piety, greedy, rather blatantly compensatory building projects and heavy drinking. Long before they were disposed of after French invasion, the ecclesiastical territories were viewed as a medieval disgrace by many, not least the secular rulers who dreamed of carving them up (Hesse-Darmstadt eventually lucked out and swallowed Mainz). Predators were kept at bay because the ecclesiastical territories both biggish and tiny were crucial to the Habsburg family and at the heart of the running of the Empire. One oddity of the Reformation was that many of the key princes had become Protestant – the big exceptions being the Habsburgs themselves and the Wittelsbachs in Bavaria, plus at the end of the seventeenth century the outrageous reconversion of the Albertine Wettin family in Dresden, just so they could become Kings of Poland. This meant that the many ecclesiastical territories were out of the orbit of Protestants and part of a separate Catholic hierarchy linked to the Habsburgs.

This gave free rein to the immense numbers of Imperial Knights – rulers of tiny territories with totally mysterious origins in the dying days of the Carolingian Empire and whose comically minor but legitimate nobility allowed them to dominate appointments in the Catholic Church. These knights (who have no British – let alone American – equivalent) often lived in towns, only visiting their native castles in the summer months, and many lived in Mainz, which was once famous for its many borderline tumble-down knightly mansions. These knights had many children who

filled innumerable jobs in the Church, sometimes brilliantly, sometimes indolently or corruptly, in such proliferation that you could
probably create a chart using them to express the entire range of
possible human behaviours.

The importance of these people in the Empire meant that,
despite much of the chunkier territory being in fact Protestant,
the Empire as a whole had a strongly Catholic air, dominating the
institutions which ran it, just as the Emperor himself was always
Catholic. Bismarck's and Hitler's antipathy towards Catholics as
un-German, disloyal and unacceptable was – for two men so crippled by historical concerns – oddly unhistorical, therefore. The rule
of the prince-archbishops meant that Rhineland Catholicism was
deeply entrenched in a way that Protestants could never expunge.

The inside of the cathedral at Mainz has much of the atmosphere yearned for by makers of science-fiction films where the hero
enters the hold of some long-abandoned spaceship – a cold, grand
and bracing mournfulness. And preserved along its walls are statues
to some forty of the prince-archbishops, from the thirteenth
century to the eighteenth, again with an air of alien beings in
stone or marble pods, and presenting an extraordinary catalogue
of the sculptural style of each era. The tombs start with suitably
monolithic, harsh warrior bishops, then they get more genial
with Renaissance emblems, followed by the ruffed austerity of the
seventeenth century, and then everything goes mad, with life-size
white marble skeletons, figures of Father Time, winged skulls, blub-
bing putti, extravagant folds of clothing, all positioned to be hit to
advantage by shafts of real sunlight. One friend I once went round
with bailed out, queasy with horror, at about 1680, but I remained
bouncy and immune throughout – by the early eighteenth century
the Electors' tombs are entirely out of control and indeed strongly
anticipatory of the fine moment in Fellini's *Roma* where the Vatican
holds an excitingly modern ecclesiastical fashion show featuring
neon-clad, roller-skating priests and entire reliquary skeletons of
saints hanging like the Andrews Sisters from the sides of a jeep.

Just as the tombs they wound up being tipped into were the
most enjoyable, so the eighteenth century as a whole was the apogee

of fun for these rulers, who had a tremendous range of costumes to wear and intricate ceremonial occasions, both religious and political, for which to kit themselves out. It was an era of substantial armies and serious fighting, and ever more decisions were being taken in distant Berlin or Vienna, so their power was far less than it appeared, but that probably made the ecclesiastical electors' jobs even more pleasant. A classic minor noble family who made good were the von Schönborns who, from their original base in a scarcely visible piece of territory in Franconia, managed to scatter their seed all over the place, winding up with an extraordinary range of bishoprics and archbishoprics. Blending a vigorous, conspicuous piety and extreme acquisitiveness, the Schönborns were the men in the control room of the immense gift-that-goes-on-giving of the traditional Catholic Church. As late as 1918 the government of the new state of Czechoslovakia was confiscating half a million acres of Schönborn land and even today a Schönborn, who fled with his family from Czechoslovakia as a baby, is the Cardinal Archbishop of Vienna, offering a rather odd continuity.

The world owes a lot to at least three Schönborns – Lothar Franz and his nephews Philipp Franz and Friedrich Karl (one strange trait of these families is their necessarily indirect connections). All the time that more normal eighteenth-century rulers spent marrying off their children, selling their subjects as soldiers or trying to blow each other up, the ecclesiastical ones could spend in agreeable building projects, collecting art and paying for music (perhaps most famously the wonderfully named Hieronymus von Colloredo, Archbishop of Salzburg, one of Mozart's early sponsors). Lothar Franz managed to be both Elector of Mainz and Bishop of Bamberg. Lothar Franz loved building palaces and gardens, for example the 'Favorite', a crazy mass of fountains, pyramids and pavilions looking over the Main and Rhine which was humourlessly burned to the ground by the French during the siege of 1793 (admittedly, in the same year Prussian artillery managed to smash to pieces one of the cathedral towers and in 1857, as a key German Confederation fortress, Mainz was the unlucky location of a powder magazine which exploded taking another chunk of the town with it – this is a place used to rebuilding). Lothar Franz's most magical survival is the New Residence in Bamberg, a perfect Baroque wonderland next to the great cathedral. His nephews aimed – successfully – at topping it with the New Residence in Würzburg, where they took turns to be bishop, but there is something slightly dopey about Bamberg's palace which makes it more fun room-by-room than Würzburg, even though the latter is obviously one of the wonders of the world.

Chief joy of Bamberg's New Residence is the Imperial Hall. These odd rooms litter the German landscape and were built to express the unique role of the Emperor in the rulers' lives – the grandest possible space reserved specifically for visits by the greatest ruler of them all. Of course, Bamberg, however much I myself would like to live there, is objectively not an important place and in fact in the remaining century of the Empire's existence after the Imperial Hall was completed no Emperor ever got round to visiting it. And it is probably just as well. This huge, fabulous room was subjected to many years of labour by the Tyrolean painter Melchior Steidl to create the ultimate illusionist ceiling painting of the empires of the world, flanked by giant portraits of the usual scattering of German Emperors. There is one point in the floor where you are meant to stand and experience the full illusion of hundreds of figures, clouds, clumsy allegorical elements and so on whirling up into the air. The beauty lies in the way that the illusion doesn't work at all – the colouring and figures are all rather babyish, and very far from creating the sort of vertiginous lift that was Cortona's or Tiepolo's *specialité de la maison*. The result is a sort of queasy disaster with the opposite illusion – that by standing on this specific spot you are in danger of being crushed by a heaving mass of glowing tat. It is – in an environment where you are being barraged by generally brilliant and exciting works of art – a thrilling relief to encounter a grade-A disaster and speculate over the years of awkward silences and insincere praise which must have followed its unveiling.

There is a very striking photograph of the Imperial Hall in the First World War when it was used as a military hospital (one of the odder contributions to the war effort by the Bavarian royal family, who had taken over Bamberg in the general early-nineteenth-century territorial free-for-all). Aside from the normal suffering of a front-line soldier at this time, it seems an astonishing extra psychological grinding of the mill-wheel, to have to lie on your back, staring up at such a lurid oddity, the duff brainchild of a long-dead cleric.

Chromatic fantasia and fugue

Every town is doomed to be imagined under the conditions in which it is visited. For me the eerie expanses of the Hindenburg Park in Ingolstadt will always be dark and snowbound, while in the suburbs of Magdeburg, where I once spent a happy few summer days in the spare room of a couple of elderly flower-obsessives, everything was brightly coloured. Even the notoriously drab, Stalinist town centre seemed to me cheerfully tinged with my hosts' pansies and sweet peas. This rather arbitrary tagging of individual towns (this one blustery and louring, that one light and sparkling) was a problem with my method of criss-crossing Germany and only regularly returning to the really big cities, but it did give a specific extra dimension of vividness to each place which would have been erased by careful, seasonally paced encounters.

Köthen, a small town in Saxony-Anhalt, formerly the leading town of the micro-principality of Anhalt-Köthen, suffered from this through an alarming combination of dreary weather and a winter Sunday morning visit. Like so many such places it had known moments of greatness and notoriety – in Köthen's case as the home of the nineteenth-century ornithologist Johann Friedrich Naumann and the Naumann Museum, one of the principal temples for European bird-lovers, filled with beautiful watercolours and sinisterly old stuffed birds in crowded glass cases. Even for someone with no interest in birds at all, it has one sensational case heaped with hundreds of taxidermists' glass bird eyes on wires, for every size from a warbler to an eagle owl, which seemed to me one of the great (if accidental) artworks of the twentieth century. Köthen was also the home for some years of Samuel Hahnemann, who seems to have quite randomly made up many of the precepts of homeopathy while practising his surprising branch of medicine there. Now a deeply depressed place, Köthen has lost more than a quarter of its population within a generation and this, coupled with the continuing low levels of religious observance in former East Germany, meant that Sunday mornings offered nobody any reason to leave bed. Wandering Köthen's streets, I felt that it had been emptied in some disturbing and total accident which would, with the almost tedious inevitability of the genre, result in my being attacked by red-eyed flesh-eating zombie children around the next corner.

The only sign of life was a distant sort of hurdy-gurdy, fairground noise of an enjoyably creepy kind. After wandering through empty, battered and confusing streets, I at last came out in the main square. Here there was a truly brilliant church – a spindly, blackened oddity with thin towers capped with little hatlike roofs and every appearance of being an alchemically minded giant's stove. The fairground music was coming from a very battered stage erected by the church on which, really oddly, a troupe of teenage girls wearing spangled electric-blue majorette costumes were kicking up their legs to a selection of Prussian and Austrian marching tunes while a colossal, ill-shaven MC leered and giggled at the microphone, very much like the puppet-master in *Pinocchio*. Watching this spectacle were a scattering of semi-derelict morning-after men and some clearly rather uneasy yet supportive mothers come to cheer the girls on. It was like being trapped in a particularly irritating art-house movie from the sixties or seventies with a snearingly anti-capitalist message.

Moving on from this strange scene I reached the real reason for being there – the bleak, battered, unkempt ducal Schloss, its moat stuffed with dead leaves and even its handful of ducks managing to give their quacks a depressive timbre. Here Prince Leopold, the territory's ruler and a Calvinist, had in 1717 the brilliant idea of asking Johann Sebastian Bach to live in Köthen as Master of the Chapel, having already pinched a set of top musicians from the disbanded Prussian court orchestra. Bach had spent an unhappy time turning out religious works (and being put in gaol) in Weimar and was happy to work instead for a man whose very religion made him abhor church music of any kind. So for six years, for whom Prince Leopold should be thanked as long as music is played, Bach sat around turning out some of the greatest and most enjoyable material ever invented: everything from *Air on a G String* to the Brandenburg Concertos to the solo works for violin and cello to the *Well-Tempered Clavier* to the crazily cheerful and tiny *Badinerie*, kicking off what became the German secular music world in which whole lifetimes can be spent. Here Bach wrote my favourite piece of keyboard music, the *Chromatic Fantasia and Fugue*. On the piano it can sound merely emollient and virtuoso, but on the harpsichord it is like having some witch's basket dropped in your lap – a demented series of sounds from some other world. Usually it seems a good idea to be interested just in pure music and to ignore a composer's often pointless biography, but it was genuinely exciting to feel that the *Fantasia* must have been heard in these rooms, the man himself crossing and re-crossing this courtyard, climbing these spiral staircases, entering this dank and austere chapel.

Wandering or rather shuffling around the fabulous little Bach museum – wearing the outsize grey felt slippers still issued to visitors walking on historic parquet floors in the former Eastern Bloc, one of the Soviet Union's smaller legacies – I was as happy as a clam. Even if Bach actually wrote the *Fantasia* in a pub down the road I didn't care. Here, in one place, was the triumphant vindication of Germany's odd political structure – a little Calvinist statelet (Anhalt-Köthen) near enough to other small and medium states to filch for a bit a renowned composer and a top-quality orchestra for him to work with, and to change his life and the lives of everyone since who has even faintly liked classical music. When the prince died, still only in his thirties, Bach returned to Köthen to play the music for his funeral, unveiling several parts of what would become the *St Matthew Passion*. It is clearly not practical and probably undesirable, but there is definitely part of me that would feel it alegitimate use of the rest of my life to shuffle, in the style of some religions, in my shaggy slippers round and round the rooms of Köthen Schloss as an act of seriousness and focus and gratitude. But my attention began to wander. It was nearly lunchtime, and a peculiar version of the Radetsky March rescored for synthesizer was drifting across from the main square.

The Strong and the Fat

It is conventional in histories of Germany at this point to start talking about Prussia so that everyone can start gibbering and rolling their eyes with fear. Instead I thought I would write about Saxony. This part of Germany has always been one of my favourite places. It was one of the first I stayed in, shortly after the Wall came down, taking a room in a student flat in the south-east of Dresden, an area which, with its soot-caked late-nineteenth-century shop fronts and apartment blocks, its newspaper kiosks and battered trams, all arranged along a particularly beautiful stretch of the Elbe, seemed to me, even under the harsh conditions of the time, to maintain a vigorous argument for the wonders of urban life. A pub, placed slightly madly close to the river's edge, was defiantly marked on its outside wall with the heights over the centuries where Elbe flooding had wiped it out. I remember drifting in a happy daze around Dresden, Leipzig and Meissen.

This happiness came in part from the sense that this was Germany *profonde*, an area crucial to the great cultural and political moments that define Central Europe, but also tucked away to such a degree that I felt genuinely almost alone. I'm not sure why that feeling should be desirable, but in the context of the recent collapse of East Germany (with the trains all still marked as being run by the Reichsbahn, unchanged since the Third Reich) the ground seemed historically still warm and it was exciting to be engaged – to my own satisfaction at least, if to nobody else's – with a historical sense of what had really happened here.

The fundamental pleasure of Saxony lies in its hopelessness. It is as characteristically German as Prussia and yet as a political entity it failed in all it did. Saxony's history appears somewhat marginal, and yet this is the place that gave us Schumann, Wagner and Nietzsche. Despite woeful frivolity, insanity and mismanagement it clung on to its independence, never quite going under, until the last wholly unmourned king abdicated at the end of the First World War. At least while within the confines of Saxony it is possible to think of an alternative Germany – wayward, self-indulgent and inept in a way that gives hope to us all.

As with all the more serious German states, the more one finds out about Saxony's history the more absorbing it becomes, acting as a parallel and just as completely realized world, with many bizarre actors and events entirely comparable to the histories of England, say, or Spain, and impossible to go into too much detail over without accidentally writing an entire book. For all German schoolchildren, the Saxony story hinges around the Stealing of the Princes, an upbeat version of the Princes in the Tower, when in 1455 the fiendish (and brilliantly named) Kunz von Kaufungen and his confederates infiltrated the great Schloss at Altenburg, snatched Ernst and Albrecht, the two little heirs of the mighty Wettin family, Electors of Saxony, and rushed away with them. The plan had been to barter with their father the Elector from the safety of the highly unstable Saxon–Bohemian borderlands to right the ancient wrongs felt by Kunz, but it all went wrong: the princes were recovered and Kunz was beheaded. Nine years later the Elector, Frederick the Gentle, died and Ernst and Albrecht ruled Saxony jointly until 1485, reabsorbing during this time western territories lost through earlier disputes.

In 1485 a crucial decision was taken. The two brothers agreed to split their country, with Ernst becoming the Elector of Saxony, based at the soon-to-be-famous Wittenberg, and Albrecht becoming Margrave of Meissen and ruling over the cities of Leipzig and Dresden. Ernst died at Colditz only a year later after an accident, making the whole split superfluous – but in the way of such dynastic decisions it now had its own momentum, rapidly generating a multi-branch tree of descent as the Ernestine Wettin and Albertine Wettin lines went their separate ways. As a consequence of Ernestine support for Luther (including, famously, the Elector's hiding

Luther in his great Eisenach castle, the Wartburg) and military defeat by the Emperor's forces at the Battle of Mühlberg (with loaned Spanish troops filling Wittenberg), the Electoral vote was moved by the Emperor to the Albertine line. Indeed historically at this point the Ernestines' great work was done – without the Electors' support for Luther it is quite possible that the Catholics could have hunted down and extirpated him and his followers as they had done with the Cathars and Hussites.

Ownership of the Electorate tended to keep territories together, as a substantial country was necessary for the dignity of the role. By contrast the Ernestine line, now restricted to the jumbled hills and valleys of Thuringia, tended to split lands between sons, resulting in a chaotic jumble of tiny states, all prefaced (in English and French) with Saxe-. These little places were economically insignificant but sometimes culturally and dynastically amazingly important – most obviously Saxe-Weimar but also (for many royal families) Saxe-Coburg and even somewhere hardly traceable on a map like Saxe-Hildburghausen could make its mark (it was the marriage of a princess of Saxe-Hildburghausen to the Crown Prince of Bavaria in 1810 that instituted the Oktoberfest, now attended by some six million people a year).

As can be imagined there was gloom and ill feeling between the Ernestine and Albertine Wettins, despite a long, distinguished shared medieval heritage. A strong sense of this can still be felt in the magnificent, if daft, Victorian decorations to the Albrechtsburg in Meissen, in any event one of the world's best castles but capped off by zany statues of all the often rather made-up-sounding ancient Wettin ancestors: 'the Oppressed', 'the Strict', 'the Warlike', 'the Degenerate' and so on, all frowning from their pedestals and accompanied by a genealogical table mapping the subsequent fates of all the Wettins, a document so complex that its designer must have gone mad.

The Albertines, once they had the Elector's title, remained for many years aware that their hold on it remained precarious and it became a sort of enjoyable pastime for the Ernestines to scheme and undermine the Elector using any means to hand. It has to be said

that the Electors were not a very admirable or interesting bunch –
cruel, heavy-drinking, indecisive. The indecision was what made
Saxony so hated by Protestants. In the end ownership of the title
of Elector was based on the Emperor's favour and so, while Saxony
remained the quintessential Protestant state, this meant it was
useless as an ally to other Protestants. This problem – and the fundamental headache of not being big enough to be able to defend
itself properly and yet big enough to be worth invading – tortured
the Electors (when they weren't drinking or having immense numbers of children). After the Thirty Years War the territory gradually
recovered and, as it was rebuilt after a great fire in 1685, Dresden
started to take on its current appearance, with its oddly encrusted
towers and domes.

Saxony immediately generates an atmosphere of ease – a step
away from the great issues generated by being in Berlin and Vienna.
I even spent some happy days in Meissen under the pathetic delusion that I could learn to draw everything I saw in coloured pencil,
sitting by the Elbe sketching the Albrechtsburg, hoping that my
lack of talent could be balanced out by buying really expensive pencils and paper. Having spent so much time seeing the sometimes
startling out-of-doors work of other amateur artists I was more than
happy sitting there, putting in little touches on the intricate townscape conjured from my fingers, before I realized that passers-by, in
the very body language of their walk, thought I was on day-release
from some mental asylum, and I sadly set aside my wonky and lurid
little pictures.

Saxony's great invention was porcelain. Created in around 1704
by a mathematician and an alchemist in the pay of Augustus the
Strong, Meissen porcelain allowed Europeans to make their own
rather than import it from China. The porcelain factory in Meissen
is still there: simpering shepherdesses, a fox playing a piano, a
drunken goat in glasses with a drunken Saxon official on his back
– just terrible. I knew it was a mistake walking in, but I had not
realized that for some three hundred years consistently awful
objects had streamed out of Meissen. Other rulers copied Augustus
and soon there were several loss-making imitations scattered around

Germany. For many years, as an ingeniously nasty way of reducing royal losses slightly, Jews wishing to get married in Brandenburg were obliged, in return for royal permission, to buy an ornate and hideous set of Berlin porcelain.

Saxony as a whole has an oddly porcelain air, with Dresden itself seemingly made out of buildings which have the same sort of fragile crispness. Its great wealth came from agriculture and mining and it always offered an odd contrast to its bleak northern neighbour in Brandenburg. But while the main cities of Saxony remain extremely civilized places, they also show the limits of incompetence. The rulers of Saxony had a strange inability to rule intelligently. After the reasonably successful military career of Johann Georg III, who died of plague in 1691 and initiated the rebuilding of Dresden, a pathetic sequence followed. His son Johann Georg IV had a brief and deranged reign during which, obsessed with his teenage mistress (who was also quite possibly his half-sister), he tried to murder his wife only to be prevented by his younger brother Friedrich August, whose hand was permanently damaged in the struggle. Johann Georg and his mistress shortly thereafter both died of smallpox and Friedrich August quite unexpectedly came to the throne. Here there was a potential glimpse of greatness: a young, rich and motivated ruler. The Hohenzollerns in Brandenburg managed in the seventeenth and eighteenth centuries to convert themselves into a major power by picking up territories across Northern Europe; the Habsburgs did the same, taking Hungary and Transylvania from the Turks.

The Wettin opportunity came with Friedrich August being elected King of Poland (after huge bribes and a breathtaking switch to Catholicism) as August II the Strong. He spent and spent on making Dresden into a great centre of patronage and courtly life (including the babyish gesture, which still dominates the complex today, of featuring a giant stone version of the Polish crown as a decorative feature in the new Zwinger palace). The result was ruinous. He embroiled Poland in disastrous wars, frittered his money away on bits of amber and ivory, fathered over three hundred children, did a party-piece involving tearing apart a horseshoe with his bare hands, and left Saxony helpless and indebted to an eye-watering degree. In 1700 or so Prussia and Saxony had equal-sized armies – by the 1740s, when Prussia set out to destroy Saxony's pretensions, the former's army was three times the size. August the Strong's son, August III the Fat, was a helpless and catastrophic figure who in his long reign oversaw the dismantling of Saxony–Poland as a major power. The Wettins were never able to make the Polish crown hereditary and were ultimately swamped by the greater intelligence and voracity of Prussia, Austria and Russia – indeed it was the sheer uselessness of the Wettins that contributed so much to the destruction of Poland, a country which August III could hardly be bothered to visit and which was finally partitioned and disappeared in the last part of the century. Understandably the memory of the Saxon kings of Poland is much execrated by the Poles. August III's grandson followed in a rich tradition by managing during the wars with Napoleon to play his hand so poorly that he wound up losing over half his country to Prussia in 1815, including Wittenberg, the home of Lutheranism, the faith the Wettins had so creepily betrayed in their grab at becoming kings of Poland.

August III the Fat was a pitiful king and Elector but he did enjoy paintings and it was his commissions to the great Venetian painter Bernardo Bellotto that have left the most striking images of Saxony, both its buildings and its people. Many of these paintings are of palaces and residential castles, all rendered in an oddly photographic black and brown. Bellotto's greatest work, though, is his quite unintentionally resonant 1765 painting *The Demolition of the Church of the Crucifixion*. Here in the Old Market is a sea of rubble, workmen and planks with only a single, devastated wall from the old church still standing, a permanent monument to a moment in time before the building of the current church began. Its eerie link with 1945 hardly needs to be pointed out and the picture appears as an appalling premonition of Dresden itself as a sea of ruins (indeed the successor church was itself burned out). The political infantilism of the eighteenth-century Saxon electors ended up destroying Poland and reducing their own country to a nullity. It has always been easy to feel unease at the sheer predatory cynicism of Frederick the Great and see in this the seeds of later German disasters, but after a while Saxony's behaviour also starts to become more curious and interesting. After all, Germany's twentieth-century fate was *not* as Wilhelm II and Hitler believed it to be: to follow in the footsteps of Frederick the Great. Instead Germany followed in the footsteps of August III the Fat and his successors and was beaten, devastated, occupied and partitioned, having twice entirely misunderstood the forces and resources arrayed against it. Perhaps Saxony is a more striking model for the anxious appraisal of German behaviour in the modern era and a much less harmless one than first seemed the case.

CHAPTER NINE

Little Sophie Zerbst

Until the wars with Napoleon – and to a degree still even after them – the fundamental clock that ruled German life was always dynastic. Any national, patriotic feelings that might be felt by an individual living in, say, Saxony would be less important than the plans and wishes of his rulers. It was entirely possible for these rulers to swap territories, amalgamate them through marriage or conquest, split them between obstreperous brothers. Like some absurdly long-term game of cards, with each generation inheriting the previous generation's hand at irregular intervals, each duke, elector or king would play either a stronger or a weaker hand depending on geography, wealth, luck or personal brilliance/idiocy. Sometimes the game would move at a glacial pace – entire decades went by waiting for Carlos II of Spain to die without children and thereby provoke the War of the Spanish Succession; most of the Emperor Karl VI's long reign was spent pleading, with little dignity, for everyone to accept, against the entire course of imperial custom, that his daughter Maria Theresa should succeed him. Germany is littered with foolhardy building projects based around short-lived possibilities of immense inheritance, whereas equally there were states such as Prussia and Austria who, although they were fundamentally fighting states, gained far more through luck and marriage.

One real oddity was the continuing attractiveness of the little German states as sources of marriage partners. For much of the time really big partners were more trouble than they were worth (most famously perhaps Louis XVI's marriage to Maria Theresa's daughter Maria Antonia). In a pre-industrial era when quite tiny states could potentially be more than rich enough to bring in jewels and some nice hunting territory, there was much to be gained for one of the major rulers in tracking down some broad-minded, micro-state-bred creature who could proceed to fill a Schloss fairly reliably with children without causing serious diplomatic damage.

The Hanoverians, once they had become rulers of Britain, were brilliant at this and indeed have, with only two exceptions, followed an unvarying rule of provoking squeaks of baffled delight from princesses and their imperious mothers in tiny states up to the present day. In order, from George I onwards they have married a duchess of the Braunschweig-Celle family, a margravine of Brandenburg-Ansbach, a princess of Saxe-Gotha, a duchess of Mecklenburg-Strelitz, a duchess of Braunschweig-Wolfenbüttel (the unfortunate Caroline, beating fruitlessly on the doors of Westminster Abbey to be allowed in to attend her estranged husband's coronation), a princess of Saxe-Meiningen, a prince of Saxe-Coburg and Gotha, a princess of Schleswig-Holstein-Sonderburg-Glücksburg and a princess of Teck. This unvaryingly German choice partly came from the important role that the British royal family had in German life, a link that only frayed with the First World War, but also from the peculiarly narrow requirement that the bride had to be Protestant as well as upper class, thereby cutting out great swathes of potentially less frosty and more enjoyable Mediterranean partners. The kaleidoscope of small German states however always meant that there was plenty of choice, that is until the kaleidoscope was put away in 1918 with the German revolution and all the princesses vanished into dodgy coastal hotels around Europe. This was part of the backdrop to Edward VIII's disastrous decision to marry a Maryland divorcée and his younger brother's cleverer choice of the steely youngest daughter of a Scottish aristocrat. The current queen took us back to the good old days by marrying another member of the Schleswig-Holstein-Sonderburg-Glücksburg family, much to everyone's relief.

I go on about this, partly because it is funny and curious (both the facts and the names), but also because these little territories had potentially very considerable power and prestige and the most bashful beginnings could end in glory. In a sort of asteroid belt of low-grade German princesses and narrow, petty, moustachioed princes, there was enough room for something really surprising to happen. Most absolutely alarming in this respect was pretty little Sophie Augusta Frederica of the laughable territory of Anhalt-Zerbst, a place so small it could hardly breathe. Her father was a Prussian field marshal and as a helpless pawn in plans to boost Prussian–Russian relations in the 1740s Sophie was shunted off to Russia where, after several ups and downs, she married the Grand Duke Peter, learned Russian, became Russian Orthodox, had Peter killed and wound up as Catherine the Great, devastating the Ottomans, the Swedes and the Poles and carving out immense new territories from Latvia to the Crimea. Indeed, a case could be made for her being the single most successful German ruler of all time, albeit not one ruling Germany. Oddly, but appropriately, she sits in Ludwig I's hall of German heroes, one of the handful of female marble busts. She probably did more than anyone to make Russia into the totally unmanageable super-nation that was to prove such a mixed blessing to Germany over the coming two centuries.

Shoving contemptuously to one side the countless rather stiff and uninvolving paintings of Catherine made in her lifetime, the delirious, dream-come-true 1934 movie *The Scarlet Empress* remains the definitive account of how she came to power – albeit one with a loose hold on historical detail. Perhaps the greatest collaboration between the Berliner Marlene Dietrich and the Austro-Hungarian-American Josef von Sternberg, *The Scarlet Empress* manages to compress into an hour and a half a riot of German anti-Russian loathing, with Hollywood footing the bill for the demented production, which includes a superb, one-minute summary of Russian history as a carnival of iron maidens, mass beheadings, conveniently nude girls burned at the stake, humans used as bell-clappers, etc. A battle-hardened performer, Dietrich has some difficulty playing Little Sophie as a girlish thing in ringlets but once she gets into the saddle as 'the ill-famed Messalina of the North' it's all wigs, furs and crazy Russian cruelty, stalking about among von Sternberg's astonishing expressionist sets (huge, pain-wracked statues, doors of inhuman size). The final tableau of a grinning Dietrich in a devastating snow-white Cossack outfit, surrounded by flying flags and cheering troops, is one of the strangest 1930s fantasies about German greatness and Russian barbarity. The movie is so vivid and brutal that it almost blocks out completely the real Catherine, but it would be a gloomy pedant who did not revel in *The Scarlet Empress* and admit that watching Dietrich dressed in a sort of satellite dish covered in pompoms eying up her strapping troopers brings history to life.

Little Sophie of Anhalt-Zerbst's fate is so ridiculous that it shows there was no limit to the dreams available to marginal German princesses. But how many turrets must have remained filled with the unrequited sighs of the remaining marginals, to balance out all the jewelled dresses, Turkish conquests and Baltic palace horse sex? (I know, I know – but who else attracts such anecdotes, even if untrue?) Long-term marriage planning really did set the tone for the eighteenth century – it would decide who would rule over you, whose army you would fight in, who would nick your crops. Entire states could ruin themselves in pursuit of mad dynastic ambition – Bavaria tore itself to bits at frequent intervals in its futile attempts to break out of middle-rank status; Hannover hit pay dirt; Saxony crashed and burned. The loss-making computer game *Liege Lord* could be run showing the total numbers of German princesses coming onto the market and the changing opportunities available to rulers in specific years (the throne of Poland, alliance with the Habsburgs, immediate invasion).

Parks and follies

I have spent so many days clumping around German parks that they now form a substantial, happy region of my memory – a sort of collective burst of pleasure which can be drawn on at any time. To be able to drift into a reverie and think about these magical spaces is as good a way of meditating on the nature of civilization as any. I have dealt with these parks under all conditions, at all times of day and all times of year and this process of cheerful drift – both actual and recollected – could perhaps be seen as taking the place of drugs or music in some lives. I could almost imagine having total recall of the bridges and paths of the park at Weimar if I could only concentrate hard enough: the path out to Liszt's house, the Soviet cemetery, the rock with an inscription of friendship from the Duke of Anhalt-Dessau, Goethe's summer house (in itself a little dull, but transformed by a postcard showing an elderly, uneasy yet compelling Thomas Mann posing outside it in a long coat and bow tie), the ridge with its line of grand villas, including one of the very first Bauhaus buildings – the original Bauhaus being on the other side of the park. Admittedly, the park at Weimar is almost madly fecund – a concentrated essence of German pleasures – but there are none that are boring and many hide small but startling things.

As with so many aspects of German life, the great parks are a side-effect of the broken-up, fragmentary nature of German politics. Each ruler of however small a state expressed his rule through parks. These parks had practical purposes – for hunting, growing things for the palace, recreation, drill, exercising horses, major festivals. The Schloss was always the main focus of the town with the park as an important and exclusively royal element of that, whereas things like squares and boulevards always had tense overlaps with merchants and other potentially awkward townspeople. Some rulers had parks with wide access, others kept most of their subjects out. In many ways they are an expression of the joys of cheap labour, with the tinkly fountains and green contours being simply an eighteenth-century version of pyramids, temples or ziggurats – expressions of power over the lives of the veritable armies who worked to create them, albeit less violent and more daisy-strewn.

Being English it is impossible for me not to notice how aggressively English these parks are. The English style of park, always contrasted with the geometric, gravelly French park, early on became a symbol in Germany not for liberalism as such, but at least for thinking vaguely about liberalism (and for being anti-French). It became an easy indication of their reasonableness for German rulers to order large percentages of their local populations to labour entire seasons on carving out little dells, irregular lakes, bosky knolls and intimate tea-houses. The Princes of Reuss-Gera never showed specific symptoms of liberalism, aside from an undying hatred of Bismarck, but down by Gera's little river there is a perfect English park tucked into the foothills of eastern Thuringia, closing in on the Czech border, with weeping willows, artfully laid-out flowerbeds and gangs of coots pigging out on nematodes. In the nineteenth century such places were, as in Britain, generally thrown open to the public before passing into public ownership entirely when their royal owners were chased away in 1918. They remain both as workaday lungs for each town and as strange reminders of a quite recent feudal past.

This Englishness was not by any means the only outcome. Perhaps Europe's most disturbing park is in Kassel, where the repulsively absolutist idea came to one of the Landgraves of Hesse-Kassel that a single straight line should be drawn from the top of a hillside outside Kassel down to the far end of the town. At the top of the hill is a peculiarly massive yet uninteresting Italian statue of Hercules, then, following the line, a series of waterfalls drop down the hillside, eventually mutating into a road that cuts through the whole town. This image of total ducal control was matched by elaborate gardens flanking the cascades. This hideous work, patently comparable to the pyramids in its cruel pointlessness (and paid for by the duke's selling his subjects as mercenary soldiers to other countries), was subverted by a later duke who messed up the geometric gardens by making them more English and liberal, but the damage had been done. Kassel has a headachy quality, like being trapped in a De Chirico painting: a quality not helped by so much of the town being rebuilt after devastating bombing, but more fundamentally arising from the gloomy, controlling legacy of the dukes.

There are also of course the great Prussian parks in Berlin and Potsdam, again both very English in flavour. I worked out how to write my first book wandering about through the high grass of Potsdam's vast park with its somewhat theme-park ambience, offering sites of exceptional beauty and leisure (the Sanssouci Palace, the Chinese tea-house) and whip-crack authoritarianism (the New Palace), Prussia's schizophrenia all laid out in these rolling acres.

Changing tastes could provoke wholesale changes to each park – the current layouts being simply the point at which the parks passed into static, custodial public ownership, as in the end of a round of musical chairs. All over Germany, the two models of Versailles and Blenheim battled it out: a brawl between Le Nôtre and Capability Brown, both requiring immense numbers of workers, formidable hydraulics, paid-by-length-or-weight sculptures and decorators and a willingness to rearrange nature on a scale now perhaps only practised with new airports or shopping centres. In the end English ideas won, not only because aristocratic design in England offered an interesting and seemingly valid model for innumerable princelings, but because once the initial work had been done it was easier to keep up – absolutism having as its Achilles heel the need endlessly to rake around gravel, board up unloved statues of Venus in winter and have elaborate fountain systems of a kind to defy cheap repair.

This tension between open artifice and a hard-won but specious naturalness is celebrated at Wörlitz, the set of burstingly fecund gardens along the Elbe built by the Duke of Anhalt-Dessau, the Duke of Weimar's friend, described at the time as a great gardener but an indifferent ruler. My time there was a bit scarred by my very odd hotel, which featured in its dining room one table occupied by eight human-size toy rabbits eating plastic food and a selection of gentle orchestral pop hits such as 'Tie a Yellow Ribbon' emanating from an old record player, a waiter having the job of moving the needle back to the start of the LP the moment the side finished, all under the owner's beady eye. I felt ever more anxious that the corpses of previous guests in the thinly populated hotel were inside the rabbit suits, a trickle of blood from one paw slowly engulfing the plastic ice-cream in a ghastly sort of sauce. This rather blots out my memory of the gardens themselves, beyond a lingering sense that they were very beautiful.

In the footsteps of Goethe

In the parts of Germany not historically under some faintly rational large-scale management, the landscape becomes so thickly dotted with palaces and castles that it is possible to feel ever more jaded and irritable as yet another oversized pile with its banqueting hall, podgy statues representing virtue and clemency, shady walks, gift shop and heavily signposted toilets heaves into view. I once arrived in the Bavarian town of Ansbach late in the afternoon and still feel a guilty sense of relief that I had just missed the final guided tour and would never have to enjoy the splendours of the usual ho-hum mirrored state room, dowager's bedchamber and so on. As these buildings with each passing second move further and further away from the era of their true functions there must surely come a time when they are at least heavily culled. Ansbach was made memorable not by its stiff-looking and now shut palace but by a caretaker who gleefully undid for me a gloomy, padlocked door under the church to show me the last resting place of the Margraves of Brandenburg-Ansbach, a crypt of utter desolation, partly filled with water and with a miscellany of stark lead tombs scattered around, the whole place having the air of an abandoned car-repair shop. It was very cold and wet and the general neglect gave a strong sense of the futile oldness of palatial rule in Germany. Ansbach itself when independent was a bizarre scattering of bits of territory, some pieces literally consisting of single fields, to the west and south-west of Nuremberg. Its inhabitants had the peculiar ignominy of simply being sold to Prussia by the last margrave, who in 1791 pocketed the money, married his mistress and capered off to Newbury (to add to the local total lack of Ansbacher self-respect, Prussia after Napoleon's defeat did a quick swap with the Bavarians, giving them Ansbach in return for the lovely Duchy of Berg). It is perhaps unsurprising that the margraves' tombs appear so forlorn, with the entire, mildly distinguished history of independent Ansbach so humiliatingly ended: a key player in the Reformation but also home of the fiendish Wolf of Ansbach which gorged on the locals in the late seventeenth century before being caught, killed and – its corpse dressed in a wig and coat – paraded through the streets before being hanged as a werewolf. These are, in all honesty, slim pickings and perhaps the margrave was right to sell up when he did. In any event Napoleon would put a bullet into hundreds of places like Ansbach.

Another footling German state would have to be the Duchy of Saxe-Weimar-Eisenach, tucked away in Thuringia, and in the late eighteenth century a classic example of the limits of what could be done in this highly constrained world. Duke Karl August clearly enjoyed his reign hugely, with his specially uniformed hunting staff, his mistresses and charming park (this last already described). In love with military life, he insisted on having his own light cavalry-men (with a specially designed uniform) but could only afford a very few of them. He briefly created a fair-sized miniature army until the state debts forced him down to a mere thirty-eight cavalry and a hundred and thirty-six infantry. This amiable and enthusiastic man was assisted for many years by Goethe and clearly there was something about the atmosphere at this tiny court that attracted the most extraordinary literary talents.

Goethe in Weimar is a richly comic but also poignant subject. There is something about his earnest and thoughtful attempts to bring some order to the priorities and money of this little state that makes it hard not to cry. There is simply such a large gap between Goethe's solid application and his master's zany attempts, for example, to reintroduce wild boar to his land because it would be funny to hunt them, or his insistence on keeping his dogs with him at all times, meaning that they could howl and snarl with impunity during concerts. That his enthusiasm for hunting dogs resulted in the creation of the pretty Weimaraner is some compensation.

There is a sensational walk through the Thuringian Woods west of Weimar, outside the town of Ilmenau where Goethe used to go on totally doomed trips to try to get the local copper mines going again in the hope this might at least pay for a little Weimaraner food. In a spirit both of frustration and pleasure, Goethe would walk up into the almost ridiculously beautiful hills and you can still see the immense battered rock which he studied, the views he could see and the site (with a commemorative repro hut) on Kickelhahn Mountain where he wrote his tiny lyric 'Wanderer's Night Song II'. I had probably been primed on too many Grimms' stories at this point. Each turn of the Goethe trail implied the sudden appearance of a mysterious charcoal-burner's hut or of a tiny grey man who you really, really must be polite to. The atmosphere generated by Goethe's presence for generations of hikers and the exciting extra provided by the outside chance of a gnome or two make it a walk with a unique atmosphere.

Of course, what this most appealing, reasonable and great individual actually thought about as he wandered through these hills is unrecoverable (he conceivably worried mostly about the derisive laughter of the peculiarly inept copper-miners of Ilmenau), but one feels that the entire spirit of the walk (and indeed of so much of Thuringia) and this 'small state' Germany was essential to Goethe and the other figures who made Weimar so exceptional – from Schiller to Herder to Liszt to Wagner to Nietzsche to the Bauhaus. When the Napoleonic Wars broke out the duke marched off with his tiny army (he and Goethe were both at the siege of Mainz) as a tiny contingent in the Prussian army, which was dissolved almost without being noticed, fighting for both sides as fate helplessly dictated. Managing to steer himself sufficiently towards the Allies, Karl August ensured Saxe-Weimar-Eisenach's independence or semi-independence right through to the end of the Second Reich, the much-loathed, sadistic last duke being kicked out with everyone else in 1918. The national assembly that met in Weimar inaugurated its constitution there as a symbolic alternative to the militarism of Berlin – sadly and unfairly making 'Weimar' in the twentieth century a synonym for failure and disaster.

A glass pyramid filled with robin eggs

The Franconian city of Bamberg is somewhere I find myself in my imagination coming back to over and over again. Almost undamaged in the war, it sprawls over seven small hills and is jammed with amazing buildings and atmosphere, as well as being the home of a 'smoked beer' that deserves patience and respect.

I cannot stand not mentioning just in passing the lovely Michaelsberg, one of Bamberg's seven hills, with a group of monastic buildings on its summit in a sort of unified fantasy of medieval excellence, now turned appropriately into an old people's home and therefore carrying on the site's ancient hospital function. Not only would I like to live in Bamberg, but I'd cash in my next couple of decades out of sheer impatience to launch myself into the planet's most fortunate old people's home. The sheer variety and pleasure of constant access to the Bamberg roofscape of spires and red tiles would be enough, but beyond that is the monastic garden, filled with every plant mentioned in the Bible: aloe, box, mint, hyssop, wormwood, gourds – there are a lot. It is an even better biblical garden than the superb one in Bremen, only with similar issues about flowers and trees finding themselves marooned in some cases perhaps unhappily in a non-Palestinian environment of steady drizzle. The inside of the monastic chapel roof is made up of dozens and dozens of panels, each depicting a beautiful painting of a medicinal plant, so that in the long round of daily masses the monks could spend spare moments remembering what cured what. But then, setting aside some astounding tombs, in a side chapel: the piece of resistance. This is a monstrous sculpture of the sacred heart, designed to be admired candle-lit and with singing monks and which has much of the air of an old movie special effect which is no longer convincing. Even better is the side chapel's ceiling, made in blue and white stucco as a rococo Dance of Death, with little paintings of a proud artist finishing the picture on his easel and Death as a mocking, cloaked, skeleton connoisseur laughing behind his back – or Death as a skeleton wrapped in a toga painting a final stucco air-bubble onto the ceiling. Germany is filled with derisive skeletons, but these are the best – both satanic and camp – and they would be enough to keep me cheerful even as my decrepit frame gives out.

This must all be understood to be in brackets (indeed, there could be an argument that this entire book should be understood to be in brackets). The real reason for mentioning Bamberg is that it contains perhaps the most wonderful room in the world. There are many grander, more original or more powerful rooms, but in the admittedly implausible context of being forced for no conceivable reason to choose only one, it would have to be the prince-bishop's Natural History Museum in Bamberg. In an act of very late restitution, as though realizing that the whole idea of a prince-bishop was at an end with the French Revolution, Franz Ludwig von Erthal (also Prince-Bishop of Würzburg) decided that he needed to educate his flock. Therefore, among other initiatives, he decided to build a museum specifically to teach the beauties and use of Franconian flora and fauna. After his death in 1795 (he had only one successor before independent Bamberg was swept away) work carried on until the little museum took its current form in 1810. I do not really know how it has survived without being ruined – inertia (an unsung friend to many German things) must have been involved, beyond the sheer beauty of the place, a beauty which could always have fallen to changes in fashion.

This room may be an eccentric love of mine. I have a limitless tolerance for even the most static, moth-ravaged natural-history displays and can squat up near the roof of the epic Natural History Museum in London for hours just for the view down on the diplodocus-filled hall; I have spent entire days in the library there leafing through old volumes of engravings of animals, plants and native peoples. Alexander von Humboldt is my God, so in many ways I was already pre-programmed to a fatalistic degree to like the bishop's museum. It is also – another happy piece of continuity in many of the best places in Germany – virtually deserted, giving a strange, time-travel quality to the experience which would be denied if it was carrying on more effectively its original educational function.

The room is painted, including all the display cabinets, entirely in white and gold aside from a prominent portrait of the prince-bishop. The cases themselves are a monument to a specific, pretty neo-classical moment in design that enjoyed pyramids, bobbles and high little galleries. Everywhere there are stuffed animals, skeletons, piles of hedgerow birds' eggs. As usual in such places there is an attempt to impose some sort of order – principally this is meant to be a practical museum giving descriptions and examples of Franconian wildlife. But of course, this stolid purpose is undermined by fun extras – an orangutan, a glass obelisk of hummingbirds, an entirely arbitrary whale jaw. The room requires no soundtrack: so many historical spaces need sprucing up with some mental Bach or Mozart, but the stuffed creatures and the delicate architecture chase off that kind of extra, as though you have come through to the exact, silent heart of Enlightenment idealism. One small cabinet contains wax models of all the edible fruits of Franconia (accidentally preserving just how *small* fruit used to be). These strange masterpieces were designed to cut through the wilderness of folk names for different kinds of plum and pear and establish a definitive name and definitive appearance. Some of the fruit are somewhat damaged, with holes in the thin wax both destroying and enhancing the illusion of exact ripeness and desirability.

The sometime Bamberg residents who may have enjoyed the museum were a mixed bag – on the one hand the leader of the July Plot, Colonel von Stauffenberg, on the other Willy Messerschmitt. But one very strange inhabitant of Bamberg was there while the museum was being built and the Napoleonic Wars were tearing Germany to pieces: the Prussian master-magician E. T. A. Hoffmann. I can't really remember when I first read Hoffmann but since adolescence I've always felt wrapped in his cloak. Standing in the rain outside his old house in Bamberg and realizing it was shut (much to my relief, of course, as writer's house museums are invariably a let-down) seemed, in a very tiny way, to allow me to share the pain of my hero, who seemed to spend much of his time socially and intellectually locked out and wet. A caricaturist, theatre manager, essayist, composer, civil servant, short-story writer and playwright, Hoffmann flailed from post to post, chased by amazing bad luck (including a spell as a civil servant in Prussia's recently stolen chunk of Poland). Wherever he went, from Berlin to Warsaw, he was, like many other Germans, pursued by Napoleon's troops, in the humiliating mayhem which warped and traumatized German nationalism for generations. But in Bamberg, futilely trying to run the theatre there in the face of an orgy of backbiting, not helped by his falling in helpless love with one of his young music pupils, Hoffmann at last found his true metier, starting to write, both under psychological pressure but also through sheer imaginative verve, stories which changed European literature.

Hoffmann's vision of the world, with its Sandman scooping out children's eyes, its clockwork dolls, grinning door-knockers, glass face masks and magic snakes, seems to me to mark so much of Germany. He makes crooked alleys and wonky houses alive and frightening – populating with his imagination entire small blameless towns. What is so startling is how oddly his stories hang together, indeed often hardly make sense – and he definitely took some disastrous wrong turns such as the achingly boring Venetian fantasia 'Princess Brambilla'. Perhaps what is so appealing about Hoffmann is that he cannot be categorized and is completely unuseful – he leads nowhere and is entirely self-sufficient. His work can be illustrated, it has been made into ballets and films, but none of these come close to the odd atmosphere that makes each of his paragraphs so unstable and hair-raising. It is impossible to imagine Kafka, say, or Grass without Hoffmann, and yet in the end he is just himself, mysteriously polluting everything around him, with eyes looking out through windows, figures glimpsed in the street, absolute malice creeping up the stairs.

So while Napoleon was remoulding Europe, as many thousands of elegantly uniformed men were being mown down on battlefields, as Prussia teetered on the verge of extinction and hundreds of German knights, counts, bishops and dukes packed their bags, in one small town a small white-and-gold shrine to Enlightenment benevolence was being completed and, down the road, the way was being prepared for the residence of the man who would dream up 'The Mines of Falun'.

A surprise appearance by sea cow

If Hoffmann shows some of the most freakish side of Prussia, then the most rational but also romantic side is shown in his contemporary Alexander von Humboldt. Both Hoffmann and Humboldt are strikingly unmilitary figures, and although their lives were shaped by Napoleon's wars, they did what they were famous for despite the events around them. Humboldt spent five years in the New World, before coming back to Europe in 1804 shortly after Napoleon had declared the French empire, to find that most of the German states with which he had been familiar had completely disappeared.

There does not seem to have been a downside to Humboldt and he remains one of those entirely admirable figures who both greatly extended our knowledge of the world and through their work helped create a new model both for scientific application and inter-national adventure tourism. He drew on Germany's interesting but thin thread of global science, unsurprisingly thin given Germany's unoceanic place in the world. His most direct predecessor was Georg Wilhelm Steller, a Nuremberger who in the 1730s and 1740s had worked for the Danish-Russian explorer Vitus Bering in charting and investigating the northern Pacific. He described for Europeans countless new creatures, such as sea otters and northern sea lions. I spend a lot of time with my wife's family in America's Pacific North-west and, having flown around from England I always feel I am meeting up with Steller from the other direction as I sit in a garden frequented by the big, violent, noisy but very startlingly blue Steller's jay. He also discovered Steller's sea cows (as they were now named), huge but helpless manatees that had survived human hunt-ing as a residual population in some Siberian coves but which were then, thanks to the discovery, all killed off in about thirty years. He also left the mystery of the 'sea ape', a weird animal that sported around his ship in the north Pacific but which has never been satis-factorily linked up to any real creature.

There were also Johann and Georg Forster, father and son, the descendants of Scottish emigrants who had settled in the Polish-ruled section of Prussia in the seventeenth century. The Forsters, through a series of bizarre chances, found themselves as the scientists on James Cook's second great voyage (1772–75), and so became the first Europeans ever to see the Antarctic (a miserable disappointment, as the hope had been it would prove to be a new Australia). The younger Forster's *A Voyage around the World* is still a venerated classic in Germany and it is hard not to feel intense envy for this man in his early twenties living a life of contrasting icebergs and palm islands, lost in a sort of wonderland of small tropical civilizations, many thousands of miles from the blustering and cabbagy North German Plain.

Georg Forster taught in Kassel and Vilnius before settling as head librarian at the University of Mainz. Here he was swept up in the excitements of the early 1790s, declaring for the revolutionary Republic of Mainz. When this was crushed by Prussian troops he fled to Paris where he died of illness, still aged only thirty-nine. Forster was the young Humboldt's great hero and example and, setting out to make his own mark in the world, Humboldt left for South America – an expedition that he would spend a large chunk of his adult life then writing about, an epic that would result in twenty-one volumes of scientific and personal material and transform the study of tropical America. Reading Humboldt's *Personal Narrative* it is impossible not to cheer at every turn. He is simply so *interested* in everything, from the details of the Venezuelan voting franchise to the nature of riverbeds to the diversity of mountain plants. He is great on piranhas, jaguars and caimans, childhood enthusiasms I have never managed (or wanted) to shake off. He also gives a sensational account of his attempts to capture some electric eels, with harpoon-armed Indian cowboys herding horses and mules into a bend in the river where the eels counterattacked, electrocuting their persecutors so that the river became a mass of stunned and dead animals before some exhausted and by now low-powered eels are hauled ashore. Characteristically Humboldt both studies the eels and then tries cooking them: 'their flesh is not bad, although most of the body consists of the electric apparatus, which is slimy and disagreeable to eat'. Who can ask for more?

In a rich and marvellous life Humboldt spread his ideas on biology, meteorology, physical geography and anthropology (he popularized the term 'Aztec') all over Europe. He split his time between Paris and Berlin and, aged sixty, travelled across Russia as far as the Yenisei River, in the footsteps of Georg Wilhelm Steller. Reading about Humboldt's achievements he must be seen both as one of the most appealing figures of the nineteenth century, and also one who, only a month younger than Napoleon, perhaps shaped the world in more profound ways than the Great Man himself.

German victimhood

The ducal palace in Gotha is the proud owner of one of Napoleon's hats. It is undoubtedly the hat we all know from pictures, sitting there in its glass case, now nearly two hundred years old. Looking at these sorts of musty objects reminds me of the scene in W. G. Sebald's novel *Vertigo*, set in the high Alpine valleys of Bavaria, where an aunt of the narrator has a Habsburg Tyrolean soldier's uniform of the Napoleonic era in her attic, draped on a tailor's dummy. It has been undisturbed for many decades, and when the narrator goes up to inspect it, his attempt to feel the cloth ends in disaster as it falls into flakes of dust between his fingers. Surely Napoleon's hat must be under a similar threat – a constant battle between curators armed with temperature-control gadgets and insecticide and the ceaseless grind of passing minutes, hours and years.

Presumably the hat must always have been on display and for many years most of its observers would have felt it to be thrilling or alarming to see the hat of the great man, who had passed through Gotha only two or twenty or fifty years previously. Given his contemptuous reordering of Germany and overall Frenchness he was a hard figure to admire for most Germans, but as a general and as a man of action his only rival was Frederick the Great. And for Germans the Napoleonic Wars were a providential story, much as the Second World War has been for the British: defeat, humiliation, helplessness, and then a gradual recovery of spirit, new allies and the final, absolute destruction of a generation-long nightmare at Leipzig and Waterloo. The difference was that the compromises and humiliations for Germans were so much greater (enemy occupation, the loss of many thousands of lives fighting alongside Napoleon in Russia) and the end result was a world utterly unrecognizable from that of 1792, when a Prussian army under the command of the

Duke of Braunschweig had so confidently and, as it proved, fool-
ishly lumbered across the French frontier to end the Revolution.
The Germans in 1815 had absolutely no choice but to come up
with something quite new.

The great reorganization of Germany in 1803, the last act of the
Holy Roman Empire before its abolition, is often seen as the traumatic result of Napoleon's overwhelming defeat of various German
armies and his gobbling-up of the Rhine. But the damage had in
many ways been done much earlier with the partitions of Poland.
Looked at now, these seem pieces of insanity. It had been clear, if surprising, since the early eighteenth century and the victories of Peter
the Great that Russia was to be as big a factor in European politics as
Britain (both countries flanking Europe and, in their different ways,
impervious to normal attack). It should have been in everyone's
interest to keep Poland as a cheerful, thriving buffer, but instead, for
careless, short-term reasons the Prussians, Austrians and Russians
carved Poland into non-existence. Aside from the rights of the Poles
to an ancient and, for centuries, highly successful state, this international piracy meant that Germans and Russians now shared a border
– an issue that was to define international politics until Soviet tanks
arrived in Berlin in 1945. The 1772 partition gave Prussia Danzig/
Gdańsk, Austria Lemberg/Lvov/Lviv and Russia a chunk of Belarus
and Ukraine; the second, in 1793 gave Prussia Posen/Poznań and
Russia Minsk and most of Ukraine; the third, in 1795, quickly finishing the job in the face of a despairing Polish rebellion, gave Austria Lublin and Krakau/Kraków, Russia Lithuania and Prussia a
fleetingly existent province of South Prussia based around Warsaw.

This carve-up implied that aggressive violence and the cold
fixing of boundaries would be the future. The whole of Germany
was racked with fear as to who would eat and who be eaten. The
guarantor of the entire system was meant to be the Holy Roman
Emperor, Joseph II, but he was always bored by his pan-German
duties, and having taken his lump of Poland looked around for
other improvements. Oddly the great defender of these hundreds of
timorous states turned out to be Frederick the Great who, having
digested both Silesia and western Poland, enjoyed winding up the

Austrians by posing as the little man's true champion. Each time Joseph tried some further plan of rationalization, swapping territories or absorbing monasteries, Frederick expressed shock and dismay, wrapping himself in Imperial virtue and even going to war with Joseph over his plans to take over Bavaria. But if a state as ancient and central to the Empire as Bavaria could potentially be messed around with by the Emperor, then it was all up for the Abbess of Quedlinburg or the Count of Quadt-Isny. Before dying of exhaustion in 1790, Joseph II spent much of his feverishly busy reign attacking and shutting down religious institutions of exactly the kind on which, on a larger scale, Napoleon was to ring the dinner bell in the following decade. If the Holy Roman Emperor was not the friend of funny little indefensible territories, some quite rich, then nobody else would be.

Napoleon marched therefore into an older, rotten environment filled with greedy and often incompetent petty monarchs, many of whom flocked to his colours in the hope of an abbey or two. The basis for resisting Napoleon was always a bit unclear. There had been only limited interest in helping Louis XVI, and for some years after the Revolution there was a gleeful if wrong belief that the France which had been such a misery for much of Europe was now permanently in the bin. Prominent among those who would have stared at Napoleon's hat in Gotha over the years were many senior members of the Prussian military, who may have hated Napoleon as a foreigner but were entranced by the ease with which he beat army after army, surrounded initially by a group of ardent young officers of genius and surrounded ultimately by a group of jaded, overweight fuss-pots with failed marriages and piles. It did not seem to matter what the conditions were or the odds, Napoleon always devastated yet another painfully assembled Austrian army. Just as British naval commanders spent the rest of the nineteenth century oppressed by dreams of a second Trafalgar that never happened, so Prussian generals such as Moltke dreamt of emulating one of Napoleon's battles which, in a century otherwise notable for ill-managed, grotesque mutual slaughterhouses, they actually managed to do, defeating Austria in 1866 and France in 1870. These victories in turn set a

fresh level of Napoleonic brilliance for the unhappy successors of
Moltke (including his nephew) in 1914, which they were – at least
in the west – unable to match at all.

This frantic change of sides during the Napoleonic era can be
seen in all its confusion in the small but wealthy state of Hesse-
Darmstadt. Landgrave Ludwig X is portrayed before the Revolution
in conventional short wig, sash and lovely fabrics – but with
Napoleon's headlong charge into Germany he played his cards perfectly, becoming Grand Duke Ludwig I, losing the wig, sash and
lovely fabrics and suddenly appearing in portraits looking remarkably like Napoleon, with sensible hair and dark, vaguely military
clothing. In Napoleon's carving-up of Germany, Ludwig was
handed out startling amounts of land along the Rhine and in Westphalia. After Napoleon's defeat some clever footwork was required
to avoid being ploughed under like the King of Saxony, but in
return for losing his lightly acquired north-west German lands
Ludwig nonetheless kept a sizeable chunk, including Mainz, and
the odd new title of Grand Duke of Hesse and by Rhine.

The price paid by his subjects can be seen in the monument to
the Napoleonic Wars which stands in one of Darmstadt's terrific
parks – a giant, nude sort of Viking with a horned helmet, his
shield covering his penis, standing in a vaguely church-like tower
festooned with the names of the countless battles fought by the
Hessians on the side of whoever was in the saddle at that time.
Most accounts of these battles do not even mention the Hessians'
presence: as a minor element in vast campaigns, they were killed
in Spain, Russia, Germany and France to very little purpose. The
monument was built in the 1840s and therefore shares the charm of
other early nationalist structures, in happy contrast to the mature
absurdity of the neo-Olmec piles that were to litter the German
landscape later in the century. It is impossible not to think that the
veterans standing around at the opening ceremony must have been
a confused lot – fighting first for reaction, then for Napoleonic
empire, then back to reaction again. For the smaller states the threats
and opportunities offered by Napoleon were in every way deeply
perplexing. The Frenchmen scattered all over Germany had a simi-

lar effect to the Americans in the later 1940s – spreading new ideas, upsetting existing hierarchies, remaking the German world in ways that quickly made the old Holy Roman Empire look staggeringly antique. Hundreds of states vanished for good and those that survived, such as Hesse-Darmstadt, Baden or Württemberg, may have offered constitutional continuity in their monarchs, but nobody can have been unaware of the often grotesque compromises that had allowed them to cling on and ingest their neighbours.

Without Napoleon's decision to invade Russia in 1812 and his failure (killing in the process many thousands of Germans, in a sneak preview of 1941) it is impossible to begin to speculate on how Germany would have developed. Effectively the whole of Central and Western Europe briefly existed only to supply the needs of this immense invasion force – and when this force collapsed, the region was in turn invaded by Russia. Austrian perseverance in fighting Napoleon is one of the key aspects of the war, often underplayed. Drawing on an even bigger hinterland than France, Austria was fiendishly hard to attack and tended to be defeated only when it entered the main part of Germany, at least allowing it to retreat and regroup. In the end it was an Austrian as well as a Russian army that spearheaded and commanded the first successful foreign attack on Paris since some ridiculous point in the Dark Ages. Prussia survived through the patronage of the Russian tsar, whose loyalty to the undeserving Frederick William III prevented Napoleon from dispersing Prussia altogether. A substantial element in Berlin's bullying neurosis in the nineteenth century can be seen to stem not from the final victories over Napoleon in which Prussia was so prominent, but from a strong sense of having been within an ace of being expunged – Prussia as an ex-state with the same curiosity value as the defunct Electorate of Cologne.

Napoleon's inventions, such as the Kingdom of Westphalia (with its capital in Kassel) or the new French *départements* that gave a makeover to the Rhineland and north Germany, lasted only a few years, but bewildered the minds of later generations hypnotized by fear of a repeat humiliation. That one Frenchman could wipe out so much history, reorganize states more or less at will, make up fun new names for them, give them to relatives to run, fill them when he fancied with French troops: this was a nightmare of helplessness with strong echoes of the Thirty Years War, generating a longing for self-sufficiency and a justified hatred of France that was to shape Europe's future.

As the whole enterprise came to such a feeble end, Napoleon's project inevitably feels melancholy and futile, but at the time there must have been a high-rolling excitement. One melancholy and futile indicator of this is the monument to Marshal Berthier in Bamberg. Berthier had spent some thirty-five years washed along in the excitement of French military life – fighting the British in America, protecting the French royal family, capturing the Pope, fighting in Egypt, deeply engaged in the elaborate, world-changing (as it turned out) Louisiana Purchase. He fought at Austerlitz, Jena, Friedland, in Spain and in Russia. But in the giddy months when Napoleon returned from exile to re-found his Empire before going down under wave after wave of Allied armies (with Prussian troops going on to occupy Normandy, in an anticipation of 1870–71), Berthier, who had experienced so much and lived so vigorously, found himself marooned in Bamberg at the bishop's fortified palace. Not knowing what to do and unable to reach Napoleon he fell to his death from a dizzyingly high window a fortnight before Waterloo. It will never be established if this was an accident or deliberate, but the place where his body was found is still marked and generally adds a not unpleasant sense of gloom. If this can still be felt now, then it is easy to imagine just how widespread that gloom was at the time – whether as loser or winner (and all of Germany had been faced with political extinction at one point or another), a complex and strange adventure which had engulfed an entire generation had finally come to an end, leaving a peculiar and friable new world in its place.

Good-value chicken

Wandering through a street market in Hannover one evening, I re-visited my happy sense that this was simply an updated version of a picture by Breughel. The same world of credulity bumping into low cunning, a world of higglers and mountebanks, with everyone vying to sell their plastic dolls, coconut water, strange wall ornaments – and with only the trader's skill making any of these things faintly plausible as purchases. I spent ages watching one man stalking back and forth on a platform, a microphone strapped to his head, his patter entrancing a huge crowd as he presented metal trays crammed with chicken pieces which had an air of having been circulating within the restaurant trade for quite some while. His waggling eyebrows, lewd gestures and virtuoso range of comic accents made even me – who could hardly understand a word – want to press forward waving my money and walk off with whole bin bags of old thighs.

This sort of core German skill is beautifully preserved in one of the happiest memorials to the Napoleonic Wars, Johann Peter Hebel's little book *The Treasure Chest*, first published in 1811. In dozens of tiny stories, moral tales or helpful bits of information, Hebel (a teacher and poet who lived much of his life in Karlsruhe) describes a world of larrikins and ne'er-do-wells, clever servants, cunning hussars, put-upon inn-keepers and stalwart hangmen. Many of the stories have a market-day atmosphere to them, where twisters of all kinds flummox town guards and fleece idiotic townsfolk. Quack medicines, hidden stashes of coins, dubious strangers wandering into marketplace pubs, these are all Breughel's standbys; they are just as at home in Hebel's world and seem remarkably close to the world of the modern Hannover market and countless others like it.

These German markets have a quite different atmosphere from the sunnier and more cheerful ones in more southern countries. There is a perhaps more frantic edge to German markets, dictated by the way the weather can whip in and chase off a day's entire customer base. The range of local produce can also be extremely restricted – one blustery, autumn Saturday market in Darmstadt seemed to be limited almost entirely to pumpkins and honey, local demand for which could presumably be sated quite quickly. But this seasonality continues to make itself felt in ways more or less alien to Britain, say, or the United States. The stalls that spring up along

the Rhine in October selling generally really awful cider, for example, or the white asparagus that dominates menus in May sometimes
give me the feeling, over some years, of being trapped inside a complicated astrological clock filled with symbols dictating that *now*
you can eat goose (pride of the Altenburg Ratskeller) and *now* the
shopkeepers can take the little ghost and witch models out of their
boxes and decorate their windows with them. This rhythm is cute,
but also a bit maddening, as though the same year has to be lived
over and over again.

Enormous annual fairs add to the sense of seasonal clockwork.
Far more than many other countries, Germany continues to thrive
with giant fairs – from the terrifyingly pseudo-jolly Christmas markets in places such as Nuremberg, Esslingen and Vienna to the trade
fairs in Cologne, Frankfurt and Leipzig. These fairs give concrete
form to Germany as the place that needs to be crossed to get to
other places – the Leipzig fairs were where for centuries German,
Italian, Dutch and French goods were exchanged for Polish and
Russian. A network of dizzying complexity linked barges, mules
and wagons to town markets, individual shops and chapmen,
spreading furs and horses, barometers and swords, nails and music-
boxes wherever they were required. The huge Leipzig fairgrounds
have been through a lot in the twentieth century, but they remained
under the communists the key trade fair grounds within the Eastern Bloc and now carry on with their crazily diverse portfolios, the
staff presumably rolling their eyes with bafflement as they clean up
after a prize chicken show, the ophthalmology convention, an expo
about new sewage techniques, garden furniture, frozen food, the
Baptist World Conference and so on and so on.

My own most direct and consistent experience of this process
has been the Frankfurt Book Fair each October where people from
around the world gather to buy and sell the rights to publish books,
many of us quite closely related in spirit to the Hannover chicken-
higgler. The scale of the Fair is inspiring or depressing depending
on whether you find the commerce in books funny or not. Over a
quarter of a million people from every conceivable nation wander
in a daze through a seeming infinity of stands trying to work out

what the next international bestseller will be. For myself I can think of nothing more fun than going from booth to booth, not least because the spirit of *The Treasure Chest* is so alive and well. The larrikins and mountebanks might now be wearing poorly fitted international business clothing, but they are still the same men and women on the lookout for the unwary or poorly informed. Myriad almost unrelated worlds are tangled up, united only by their products being expressed in paper – photo-books of toddlers dressed as flowers, calendars of baby-oiled, semi-nude firemen, entire booths devoted only to cute animals or Che Guevara or manga or a complete new critical edition of the works of Thomas Mann or vintage motorbikes or models with their pubic hair shaved off or really cheap-looking and depressing nursery-rhyme collections. Booth after booth is filled with stuff which can only make sense financially if someone else in another country can be tricked into taking it on. By the end of the fair many thousands of deals will be done, with pointless books on knitting with dog hair or cooking with insects now just as pointlessly being translated into Spanish or Korean. And lurking in the background: those discreet men who can arrange for the whole print-run to be tipped into the sea off the docks at Lagos with the insurance money split 50:50. In a fever of credulity and suspicion the publishers carry out their dreadful work, spreading printed things around the planet and using the seemingly antique form of the medieval trade fair to do so.

CHAPTER TEN

Marches militaires » Karl and Albrecht » Girls in turrets »
Heroic acorns » Victory columns

Marches militaires

The period between the defeat of Napoleon and the revolutions of 1848 has always been despised by writers of both left and right – from the left because of its creeping atmosphere of cosy apoliticism and from the right because Germany appears to settle into a determined effort at being non-heroic and local. Once the German empire was underway the 'Biedermeier' generation appeared as a sort of farce of genteel idiocy. The heroic young students with their swords and special hats swearing to make a united Germany were seen as the lost prophets of the era – swamped by the general atmosphere of fine tea-sets, frilly napkins and tinkling pianos. Of course twentieth-century events have long undermined that contempt, but there is still something smashable and tiresome about so much of the sort of physical material that tends to survive from the period (spindly tables, ladies' fans, wanly pretty plates) that it does require an effort not to fall in with nationalist ideas that this was all a wrong turn, a shameful drift away from manifest destiny. What was being created – in London, Paris, Leipzig and Munich – was the first timid attempt at bourgeois civil society, a sort of limbering up for us all now just sitting in a happy pile watching television, but of course there were many horrible twists and turns before that point was reached.

It was a period when throughout Central Europe huge amounts of effort went into creating plausible new states from the rubble left by Napoleon. The Revolutionary interlude had caused such political and geographical havoc – and killed such immense numbers of people – that a time of quiet consolidation seemed inevitable and appealing. Just as most Europeans after the Second World War were, if given the chance, quite happy sitting around in family groups and buying consumer goods, so the new rulers were able to preside over a generally rather dozy population. Indeed, a parallel history of Europe could be written which viewed family life and regular work as the essential Continental motor of civilization. Then war and revolution would need to be seen by historians as startling, sick departures from that norm of a kind that require serious explanation, rather than viewing periods of gentle introversy as mere tiresome interludes before the next thrill-packed bloodbath.

The unquestionable heart of this world was Vienna. The Habsburgs, with only a few humiliating wobbles, had been implacable opponents of Napoleon and they found their reward in 1815 with a complete endorsement of their immense territories, their special position in German-speaking Europe confirmed (despite the disappearance of the Holy Roman Empire) and a cultural power with no equals. An era which starts with Beethoven's Ninth and Schubert's songs and sonatas and ends with Johann Strauss I's 'Radetzky March' cannot be all bad. The last of these was – an accidental discovery – the only piece of music that would calm down our eldest child when he was a baby, a fact perhaps more odd than interesting. In many ways the era can be summed up by Schubert's *Marches militaires* for piano four-hands, with their drawing-room, decorative, comically unmilitary flavour: they could not be softer or less threatening and come from a time when it was possible to wear really lovely uniforms without having to fight too much.

Austrian confidence in the future was expressed most forcibly by the country's new role in Italy. Having been shaken apart by Napoleon, the Habsburg grip on Italy and the Adriatic was greatly expanded, most splashily by picking up the old territories of Venice – the city itself, the mainland north-eastern block of Italy and the Dalmatian coast (plus the old Republic of Ragusa, which tried and failed to re-establish its independence). This all proved in the longer run to be a disaster. Rather like the British acquisition of Middle Eastern colonies after the First World War, what had appeared to be a dream come true soon turned into an insoluble problem and sap on resources. Austrian soldiers and administrators loved Venice and the top army posts tended to become Italian ones – fulfilling beautifully long-held German fantasies of sunshine, grappa, special girls and soft living. The Habsburgs had always had a small area of the northern Adriatic (ultimately known as the Austrian Littoral) under their control, focused on Trieste, but this had long been a backwater. Their wider hold over the Adriatic now forced them to become a more serious Mediterranean presence. These delightful schemes – a mass of fortifications, special uniforms, navies – had almost as much effect in draining Austria's otherwise preeminent role within Germany as any mean actions taken by Prussia. It became one of the pleasures of Austrian life to defeat the Italians in battle (indeed the 'Radetzky March' celebrated Field Marshal Radetzky's victory at Custoza), but this misdirected effort led nowhere as Austria was still prised out of Italy by Italy's more powerful sponsors, particularly France.

Austria's role in the Adriatic was to have all kinds of implications. Italian nationalists viewed the territories of Venice as part of Italy and so once the Austrians, following their defeat by the Prussians in 1866, were kicked out of the rest of Venetia, the coast of what had been Venetian Dalmatia remained a highly unstable zone of nationalist desire, despite its having only a very few Italian speakers. This was to have disastrous and destabilizing consequences in both world wars. And Austrian ownership of the coast gave logic to imperialistic interest in the interior: Bosnia and Herzegovina. The eventual annexation of this land in 1908 was meant to imply a greedy robustness in the Empire, but in practice it disposed of a useful barrier between the Habsburgs and the Serbians and became one of the causes of the First World War.

But, as with so many aspects of Central European history, there is such an amazing spread of unintended consequences that only a form of political paralysis can substitute for the actual kaleidoscope of decisions which generate the oddness of European history – a small, bitter and crowded landscape somehow incapable of (indeed allergic to) the broad-ranging uniformity of the Chinese Empire or the United States. It is unfortunate that what seems in many lights so fascinating about Europe should also, as a spin-off, be the basis for so much rage and death. There seems to be no would-be European superpower whose existence does not almost at once generate a reaction of a sort that ultimately humiliates and crushes the aspirant. In this period Napoleon's fate had been the most obvious example, but within a somewhat smaller compass, the Habsburgs (who, of course, could point to many ancestors similarly brought low) would also see their amazing prizes of 1815 rapidly turn into depressing liabilities.

An unresolvable problem for the new political philosophy following Napoleon's defeat remained the issue of legitimacy. If the point of Napoleon's reordering of Europe had been to create some sense, however cynical, that talent should rule, then the various emperors, kings and grand dukes of 1815 were meant to chase away for good any such idea. Legitimacy – rule by monarchs following in strict family succession – was the new (old) order. Historically, there had been a great diversity of types of rule across Europe, from republics to elective monarchs to absolute monarchs, and 1815 saw this diversity collapse. Most of the Free Imperial Cities with their local merchant oligarchies had vanished and were not brought back, nor were the welter of funny Church lands, some of which had been very aristocratic and others more egalitarian, but almost all of which had been employed in a genuine, serious and almost exclusive focus on devotional life rather than power politics. Such oddities as the Imperial Abbey of Quedlinburg, however much its real independence had been circumscribed and threatened, had been killed off by Napoleon and now they just became minor bits of Prussia or lurched forward into a doubtful new greatness: the old Imperial Abbey of Essen, for example, now under Prussian rule, turning out to be the home of the inventive Krupp family.

So what was odd in the 'Biedermeier' period was the uneasy combination of a claim by rulers of legitimacy based on ancient right being imposed on a landscape filled with people fully aware of what a joke such claims really were. The Dukes of Württemberg, for example, had long been derided for their powerlessness, entangled in a mass of legalism both by their own subjects and by the inhabitants of the dozens of often prosperous enclaves buried in their territory. The Napoleonic Wars had been one long round of humiliation for the duke. At last he had got hold of all the irritating enclaves like Heilbronn, Esslingen, Gmünd, Ravensburg and Hall, but in return had to support Napoleon – the nadir being the army of some sixteen thousand Württembergers sent to Moscow, of whom only a few hundred returned. The duke might now become King of Württemberg but he ruled over a depopulated, wrecked landscape and had betrayed his people. Luckily the scoundrel now known as King Frederick I (who incidentally weighed over thirty stone) died shortly after the Congress of Vienna, allowing for a fresh start. But essentially it was hard to see what legitimacy really meant under such unpromising circumstances.

Even if the new German Confederation consisted only of thirty-nine states rather than the hundreds before Napoleon, this still allowed for an impressive variety of legitimacy-backed rulers to come forward and make a case for their continuing existence. Unfortunately many were peculiarly dreadful or useless people, throwing up in their every action questions for even the most passive intellectual or the most hidebound local politician. The King of Hannover, Ernst August I, for example, was a genuinely horrible man. The younger brother of George IV of Great Britain, he inherited Hannover once Victoria's succession to the British throne meant that the link through the male line connecting Britain and Hannover was broken. A reactionary of an almost demented kind, Ernst had been ironically cheered by the British press as he left London (where he had been known as the Duke of Cumberland and was tainted with possible murder and incest). A founder of the Orange Order in Ireland, a violent opponent of Catholicism and reform of any kind, Ernst fought against any timid attempt by the inhabitants of Hannover to hang on to their political rights, even, in a moment of irreparable swinishness, expelling a Brother Grimm. Ernst's every gesture implied the problems and limits of legitimacy.

So too did the awful Duke of Brunswick, Karl II, who despite the welter of good will created by both his father (the Black Duke) and grandfather dying fighting Napoleon, managed to get thrown out by an enraged mob by 1830, his palace burnt to the ground.

The Prussian run of luck was clearly over with two vacillating mediocrities in a row (five in a row, depending on one's mood, which takes you up to the end of the entire dynasty in 1918). And in Vienna itself the colourless, mean and dreary Franz I eked out his suspicious and uninspiring existence (conveyed so beautifully in even the most obsequious court portraiture), handing over on his death to Ferdinand I, an epileptic simpleton hardly seen in public, a further parody of legitimacy's shortcomings. By all accounts an amiable man, Ferdinand was quietly set aside during the 1848 revolutions and lived out the rest of his long life surrounded by doctors in Prague Castle.

This pattern of hopelessness could be partly balanced out by more worthwhile figures such as Leopold I, the Grand Duke of Baden, or Ludwig I of Bavaria, who was brought low by his extensive and clearly fun sex life. But there was always a problem of inbreeding or bad luck lurking in every corner and the Badenese and Bavarian royal families were haunted by madness even if they avoided the violence and crudity of Hannover.

Karl and Albrecht

Born less than eighteen months apart, in prosperous circumstances, two of the quintessential nineteenth-century Germans could not have had more different fates, although they shared many interests, not least in science and progress, and both wound up spending the bulk of their lives in London. Both were educated at the University of Bonn and both were Lutherans. They never met but could probably have found some neutral ground in leadenly amusing stories about the limits and irritating tics of the English.

Karl Marx's pretty if heavily rebuilt home in Trier has been through some ups and downs. The most tiresomely symbolic humiliation must have been its use as a local Nazi headquarters under the Third Reich, gleefully festooned in swastikas. The West German state was created almost as much as an anti-communist citadel as an anti-Fascist one, but Karl Marx's House was always a place of heavy pilgrimage for Western Leftists even if many from the Eastern Bloc were frustratingly unable to get there. Of course this high tide has long gone out and the days when Chilean Trotskyists and Italian Stalinists would hiss at each other on the rather narrow staircase are long over. And unrestricted travel for those in the former Eastern Bloc unfortunately (at least from the narrow perspective of those running the Karl Marx House) coincided with the collapse of the ideology that would make a coach outing to Trier seem a high priority. A continuing wild card remains the People's Republic of China, whose fervent tour groups swamp the hotel facilities of Trier at random intervals. I would be curious to know what happens to these groups once they have trampled around the perhaps rather thin pleasures of the Karl Marx House: it is a long way to come just to see the old *haut bourgeois* home of a Prussian lawyer with a cafe attached. Even with the relative relaxation of Chinese life, it seems hard to see what positive enforcement for the Party could be given by touring nearby vineyards or wandering around the Black Gate of the Roman empire, except perhaps to think about shipping it back for inclusion in some future 'Failed Empires of the Past' exhibition in a *Flash Gordon*-like New Beijing of the later twenty-first century.

My own woeful inability to absorb abstract ideas would make me a flailing, threadbare guide to philosophy, a crucially important strand in German life, so I intend to avoid humiliation just by dodging the entire area. I am happy to read knock-about material like the more epigrammatic bits of Schopenhauer and Nietzsche, but can progress no further. Marx's theories of the function of the state and economy therefore drop from my crudely materialist fingers, but simply as a journalist, polemicist and commentator he remains the most caustic, sneering and enjoyable of writers for all the European events he observed from his North London exile. It could be – although I confess that this is unlikely – that Napoleon III was a creative, thoughtful and progressive figure dedicated to improving France (which he really did in various ways), but Marx's derision has to win the day. Marx's entire reputation hangs on the importance granted to ideas and we can never know what shape the major and minor revolutions of the twentieth century might have taken without his writing. Presumably the upheavals themselves would have happened anyway (Russia would always have collapsed in 1917), but Marx provided the ideology that opened the door for a strong central state of a kind the nineteenth century could not have even dreamed of.

The Germans did many parochial and stupid things in the First World War, but the breathtakingly decayed decision to put Lenin onto a sealed train and transfer him from Switzerland to Sweden (and thence on to St Petersburg) probably takes the biscuit. Their wish to whip up unrest in Russia by injecting such a famous revolutionary into the mix had consequences which shaped the whole twentieth century, and comes as close historically as we are likely to get to laboratory conditions for releasing the power of ideas into the world. Without straying too far from the subject, Lenin certainly believed he was enacting (with a few little embellishments of his own) the ideas of the chain-smoking sage of Highgate. The nature, ambition and horizons of these ideas changed the possibilities of government and made the most foam-flecked golden-uniformed, execution-obsessed absolutist seem overnight like a genially ineffective pub quiz-master. Marx's father was a Jewish convert to Lutheranism, and religion – as one would hope for consistency's sake – played little part in Karl's own life. But the perception that Marx's ideas were in a sense Jewish ideas sunk into German life and had consequences. These chilling certainties make the Karl Marx House still fairly funny, with its gift shop and its place in a row of stores selling vacuum-cleaner parts and children's shoes, but not *that* funny.

Marx's Thuringian contemporary, Albrecht (or Albert as he was to be hastily retooled later on), was the second son of Ernst I, Duke of Saxe-Coburg-Gotha. Traditionally girls of the minor courts tended to be picked off by members of the British royal family, but because Princess Victoria was limbering up for the big job, Albrecht had to play the girl and found himself whisked off to Britain to marry his first cousin and become her consort. The peculiarly uninteresting court portraiture of this period and the need to stay still for photographs have tended to make Albert look like a pompous waxwork. Every now and then though, in unguarded moments, photos have by accident preserved images of the tough, clever and arrogant German operator behind this facade. He was much disliked by many during his lifetime, though the cult that developed around his memory after his death of typhoid in 1861 obscures this. Britain's German wives of the past had stayed out of the way or become tabloid disgraces like George IV's Caroline of Braunschweig-Wolfenbüttel (whose sad little red-velvet-covered coffin lies in the gloomy confines of the Braunschweig Cathedral crypt). Albert's activism and German accent, on the other hand, seemed politically unclear – on what authority was he reforming the army or writing to his foreign relations or setting up the Great Exhibition? Albert's enthusiasm for natural science and museums makes him dear to my heart. His crucial role in both creating the Great Exhibition (what a paradise it must have been to visit it!) and the museums of South Kensington tapped into deep and existing British enthusiasms, but they were also an expression of the kinds of German trade fairs and cabinets of curiosities which I at any rate am unable to get enough of. The whole area for the museums was bought with the profits from the Great Exhibition and although substantially developed after Albert's death, it is still fair to say that the museums would not exist without him. It is some measure of Albert's intelligence that after *On the Origin of Species* was published in 1859 he proposed a knighthood for Darwin (an idea that was rejected).

Albert's interests seem thoroughly genial, a relief in the stony desert that is the intellectual life of the British royal family, but in other senses he was a dynast of an old-fashioned kind. He married off his teenage daughter Victoria to the Prussian Crown Prince, Friedrich Wilhelm, and thereby initiated one of the great tragedies of German royal life. Victoria and Friedrich waited for decades for the latter's fantastically old father, Wilhelm I, to die so that they could sack Bismarck and liberalize the German empire, but Wilhelm held on long enough for Friedrich himself to be dying, of throat cancer, by the time he became Kaiser Friedrich III. He ruled for three months – speechless, in despair and communicating through little bits of paper – before clearing the way prematurely for his and Victoria's unappetizing child, who ruled as Kaiser Wilhelm II. Ultimately Friedrich III and Victoria's only real legacies were a cranky and hysterical heir and a completely superb marble monument in their mausoleum in Potsdam. Albert's dynastic scheme therefore misfired sadly and indeed Kaiser Wilhelm II's being Queen Victoria's grandson only gave him a further, unfortunate sense of debility, stoked by the patronizing grandeur of his uncle, the bulky womanizer Edward VII.

Albert is also famous in the English-speaking world as the man who transmitted the idea of the Christmas tree beyond Germany. The British royal family had put up Christmas trees in the eighteenth century through the desires of George III's wife from Mecklenburg-Strelitz, but it was the publicity for Britain's own 'Biedermeier' idyll Victoria and Albert and the young royal family having Christmas at home which really made a tree an increasingly crucial aspect of life for prosperous people. This has always struck me as a mixed blessing. One of my own festive tasks tends to be to go to get our Christmas tree and the car-park traders I frequent have an uncanny ability to offload on me a pine with some hidden and deathly sickness. By Christmas morning the front windows of all the houses on our street will be shining with piny good cheer while our own tree looks as though it has been hit with Agent Orange. The effect is not helped by the miscellaneous and home-made nature of our ornaments. These crude lumps of papier-mâché and wrinkled oblongs of card covered in cotton wool and poster paint, made in the children's nursery schools of yesteryear, are allied to odd mementoes from trips to the Pacific North-west, such as a little Seattle ferryboat or a toy elk, now with no legs or antlers but which still swings ghoulishly from the tree's spectral branches. The overall effect – with a few inexpertly added bits of old tinsel and some malfunctioning lights – is of a blackened, loosely pyramidal object on which the Christmas Monster has thrown up. And so, even our humble home can offer an allegorical parallel for Prince Albert's attempts to mould the future of the Prussian royal family.

The historic year 1848 saw very different priorities for Karl

Marx and for Prince Albert, with the former embroiled in the destruction of autocracy and writing *The Communist Manifesto* and the latter looking to buy land in Balmoral for a new Scottish royal palace suitable for a growing family.

The vast scope of the Revolutions of 1848 encompassed in one form or another everywhere from Ireland to Sweden, albeit with often different roots and with an increasing element of copycatism as the year progressed. The failure of the revolutions almost everywhere has meant that they have tended to be patronized and dismissed both from left and right. It is certainly easy to deride such insurrectionaries as the young opera-composer Wagner (entirely a by-product of court culture) on the barricades in Dresden. There is a very funny 'Wanted' poster for Wagner issued by the Saxon government and with a sketched likeness unlikely to single him out from the crowd with any confidence. But the stakes were in practice very high with a tremendous fizz of excitement and possibility, although few were able to articulate a consistent definition of these stakes. Beyond a revulsion at the cold grind of repression instituted by regimes such as Metternich's in the Austrian Empire after 1815, there was no real agreement as to what should come next. This was allied to a middle-class timorousness that wanted political representation but was acutely anxious, on the whole, to exclude the working class.

All sides in 1848 felt an often crippling self-consciousness. Few events have occurred with more of a sense of acting out a historical script, of making gestures all waiting to be immortalized in the period's innumerable cheap prints. In Germany, everything followed behind France – both an obsession with interpreting correctly what had gone right or wrong there in 1789 and the fact that in February 1848 the French had got the ball rolling again by easily throwing out their own monarch, Louis-Philippe, thereby serving notice on other monarchies across Europe. Just as the kings themselves all had the ghoulish image of a beheaded Louis XVI and Marie Antoinette dangling before their eyes, so many middle-class insurgents felt sick with anxiety that they would be torn apart by brutalized proles, who they nonetheless needed to bulk out barricades and offer a sense of real threat. The working class in turn was constantly braced against the inevitable middle-class betrayal. This mix of excitement and hesitancy gave a dream-like quality to 1848 – with the forces of reaction not appreciating how strong a hand they had to play and the middle class not clear just how few concessions from their rulers might cause it to switch sides and lick the hand that fed it. This nervousness in the end provided the basis for royalist and militarist forces to fight back, headed by such hate figures as the Prince of Windisch-Grätz, who gunned down rebels in Prague and Vienna and generally reimposed order.

The decision to try to create a united German parliament in Frankfurt dramatized the problem that was to tear Germany and therefore Europe into pieces until the imposition of order after 1945: if there was to be a united Germany rather than lots of smaller countries some of which happened to have German speakers in them, then how was that Germany to be defined? German insurrectionaries in Prague thought Bohemia should be part of a united Germany because they were politically dominant there, even though most of Bohemia's inhabitants were Slav. German nationalists in Vienna wanted Austria to be included, but were viewed with almost as much loathing by the Habsburgs as were the revolutionary Hungarians: the Habsburgs might themselves have been originally Germans but the whole point of their Empire was that Germans, Croats and Romanians were equally subservient elements within it and German nationalism could only (as it ultimately did) destroy that Empire. St Paul's Church in Frankfurt where the parliament met was flattened during the Second World War and inevitably its rebuilt incarnation has none of the atmosphere which must have stuck to the old building, but that atmosphere, for all its idealism and democratic potential, was also not entirely admirable. Anti-Semitism, tirades in favour of war with Danes and Poles, urgent calls for 'Germanization' of any number of minority groups, all filled it. The attempt to ask the King of Prussia to become King of a united Germany was doomed by the King's contempt but also by the shaky legitimacy of the whole institution. When Friedrich Wilhelm IV turned down the 'shit crown' offered to him by 'bakers and butchers' this was hardly a surprising result. As soon as the rulers realized the timid and confused nature of the revolutions' representatives they operated with ferocity, first using the loyal armies to strike them down and then using the fervent excitement of nationalism to distract and suborn them. The last, sad attempt at insurrection took place in June 1849 in the Baden hills where a tiny revolutionary army was effortlessly taken apart by Prussian and Badenese troops – every tenth surrendered soldier was shot and the rest spent much of their lives in jail.

1848 has always been an intensely serious and painful subject for German democrats – the flag proposed by the Frankfurt Parliament became the flag of the Weimar Republic and of the West German state. St Paul's Church was one of the first buildings in Frankfurt to be resurrected after 1945. The implication that Germany could have taken a democratic, inclusive and peaceful turn in 1848, and that this opportunity was lost by the selfishness and bigotry of a ruling elite who were themselves swept to perdition in 1918 leaving Germany prey to far worse forces, is surely a delusion. There is nothing in the French example, where there was plenty of experience with regime change, to imply some golden uplands that Germany was denied – and in any event it could be argued that Germany was a remarkably peaceful place after the suppression of the revolutions, unengaged in any serious fighting outside Bismarck's brief wars for several generations. But the questions raised – both good and bad – were to bristle for many Germans on left and on right.

Marx was to prove in the rest of his long life a crucial figure in articulating these questions, particularly as the unexpected primacy of the Ruhr turned first Prussia and then the German empire into a considerably more powerful place than it had previously been. Prince Albert died too early to see the astounding changes to Germany later in the decade of his death. He would have been pleased to see his elder brother, Ernst II, finesse it so that Saxe-Coburg-Gotha became a proper if tiny part of Bismarck's new German empire and not absorbed into Prussia. The childless Ernst was then succeeded by Prince Albert's second son, Alfred, Duke of

Edinburgh who – having spent much of his life travelling to places
like Australia, India and Africa, playing the violin and collecting
glassware, picking up a Russian wife and turning down the Greek
throne – found himself in the gloomy confines of Coburg for the
last nine years of his life. Albert would have been less pleased with
the grandson, Charles Edward, who succeeded Alfred following the
suicide of Alfred's son and the busy renunciation of the title by
everybody with a better claim than Charles Edward who, still a
schoolboy at Eton, was suddenly packed off to his little throne. In
an extremely unfair series of events, following his perfectly reasonable decision to side with his adopted country during the First
World War, Karl Eduard (as he now was) had his British titles
stripped from him. He was then thrown out in the 1918 revolutions, ultimately becoming a convinced supporter of Hitler and
attending George V's funeral in London in Nazi uniform. His record
during the Second World War was contemptible and he was probably well aware at the very least of the Nazi euthanasia programme.

But all this family shame lay in the future and only resulted from
the twists and turns of unimaginable cataclysms really *not* rooted in
the failure of the 1848 revolutions. In 1848 Victoria and Albert
moved as a precaution to the Isle of Wight in case insurrection
broke out in London, but it never did. Albert's English family lived
on in prosperous peace, in a dynamic, wealthy and inventive Britain,
as did Karl Marx.

Girls in turrets

I was once placidly standing outside a kebab shop in Regensburg
when a sharp flash of pain crossed the inside of my head, accompanied by a horrible, almost electric fizzing noise. In the moments
before I realized that the fizzing came from a malfunctioning neon
sign rather than my brain I suddenly felt very alone and panicked.
Nobody I knew was even aware of the name of the town I was in
and my mobile was, as ever, stone dead. My happy isolation seemed
suddenly threatened and stupid – but I soon got over it.

Solitary tourism is something that everybody should indulge in. Of course it is a fraudulent solitude because its enjoyment comes from its limited duration and having a cheerful, only very temporarily abandoned main base area. I am paid at work to be a sort of grotesque Mr Chatterbox, in a chaotic welter of talking about books and their virtues. There are similar volumes of sound at home, with everyone shouting and mucking about, and every decision reached on the basis of almost UN-like levels of frayed consultation. And then, suddenly, I am in Vienna, standing in the shadow of a monstrous, derelict flak tower, and completely alone. The virtue of solitary tourism is its infinite ability to absorb boredom. I often find myself almost crippled with anxiety that the companion or companions on a journey might be finding everything wholly without interest, would rather be eating somewhere else, are secretly angry that we have wound up walking down this street rather than that, are contemptuous of my own interests. Solitary tourism cauterizes all this: if a museum is boring beyond all measure there is no pressure to feign interest, you just leave. I am perfectly happy, in a zoned-out way, to crisscross a town, walking for hours, just for the off-chance something curious might be round the next corner – indeed in the confidence that there will *always* be something curious (there always is). But for each street, each bar, each folklore museum to be converted into an inter-human negotiation creates an entirely different dynamic.

One pleasure of solitude is a heightened awareness of animals. A decision simply to stand still and not make a noise, if in the borderline tedious company of oneself, is easy. I remember in Lübeck sheltering from rain under a blossoming crab-apple tree crowded with blue tits tumbling about above my head; or spending ages watching a shrew working its way up a slope of the Dragon's Rock, a modest Rhineland hill, but a sort of larvae-packed Annapurna from the shrew's point of view. I once walked the length of a sunny street in Hildesheim accompanied by a light-scared bat, which flittered about, scooted under a car, panicked again and shot back over my head, as though I was a wizard with an admittedly rather incompetent familiar.

That is quite enough *Nature Notes*, but these moments and many others seemed to validate in the happiest form a simple wish to be left alone. The constant need to entertain myself meant spinning out endless rough topics for this book, so many of which wound up knocked on the head: astrology and decoration, the fear of bears, ice in German culture, unbuilt statues, magic and alchemy, the cult of the Landsknecht, rogue taxidermy and the hideous Bavarian Wolpertinger, Viennese novels between the wars, Altenburg and its playing-card factory, the paintings of Albrecht Altdorfer and so on and so on, generating an infinite, crushing shambles of topics, but also a small handful of real ideas.

Quite possibly the pleasure of this way of life would be much reduced in some other countries, particularly more insistently gregarious places such as Italy. German culture puts a high value on temporary solitude of a stagey kind. Perhaps this is its great gift. In some moods I think there is no need to do anything other than read German writers from the first half of the nineteenth century – a sort of inexhaustible storehouse of attitudes flattering to those who just like sometimes to be left alone. Everyone must have at least a part of them that wants to live in a stairless, doorless tower as a sort of intellectual Rapunzel, setting aside, at least in part, the complicated sexual frisson laid out by such an idea. Germany really *is* thick with ivy-covered turrets and the promise of solitude (Kepler staring at the planets above Prague, Faust conjuring demons) – the great majority presumably built in the nineteenth century in response to the whole literature devoted to the subject. There is one turret in Lübeck, built onto a city guard tower of just outrageous fakeness, which would do me for life.

The figures such ideas draw on do not really feature in English literature – the independent scholar in his tower, the journeyman going from town to town, the maiden in the castle, the wandering freebooter trying to win his spurs. These all sprang from the strange political structure of hundreds of different little countries and cities. Germany was made up of the circulation of people through the infinite arteries of broad roads, dirt tracks, mountain passes (such as the ones so frighteningly described in Adalbert Stifter's *Rock*

Crystal) and scarcely marked paths: labourers, merchants, mendicants, quacks, troops, drifting across a landscape that could range from the most populous and benign to the most dangerous and isolated. Grimms' fairy tales, mostly drawn from the relatively settled and safe world of Hesse, can in some moods just seem too horrifying, with their isolated protagonists the victims of magical powers, lost in trackless forests. But on balance I could not be happier than falling in with the German love of the lonely woods. A walk in an English forest is associated with brevity and teatime treats – if you throw a stone you are almost certain to hit somewhere selling coffee and walnut cake. A walk in the German forest, however manicured and signposted, is to plunge into a tradition of infinite richness. 'A king once went hunting in a great forest, and he went in such eager pursuit of one deer that none of his huntsmen could follow him. As evening drew near he stopped and looked about him, and saw that he was lost' (the Grimms' 'The Six Swans'). What else can compete with such opening sentences? Or from Friedrich de la Motte Fouqué's definitive *Undine* (1811): 'The Black Valley lies deep in the mountains. What they call it nowadays is impossible to tell. In those days, the country folk named it after the impenetrable darkness cast by the shadows of the high pine trees. Even the stream that trickled between the rocks looked quite black . . .' The reader just has to sit back and wait for a single, questing knight to gallop into such a landscape.

The poetry on this subject stretches out to the most hazy, distant horizon and fed a century of German songs, culminating perhaps in one of the greatest of all them all: Mahler's setting of a Rückert poem, 'I have lost track of the world with which I used to waste much time', a work of such richness that it can only be listened to under highly controlled circumstances. The idea, whether in Goethe, Mörike, Rückert or Heine, is to be alone, in a wood, on a mountain, in some overpoweringly verdant garden, or just inside one's head, almost always as a moment's pause before plunging back into a world of love and normal human decisions. This tic is of course a bit unpolitical and some writers have seen it as passive in a way that implies a German malleability and failure to engage with disastrous implications for the future. But equally it is an anti-political, fiercely private stance, with a built-in resistance to fanaticism or mass manipulation. It seems hard on Schubert's songs for them to be viewed as early danger signs of a failure to stand up to Nazism.

I need to move on – I want to write page after page about stories in impossibly remote castles, or old women or little men found by the roadside who may or may not be benign. Or the musical representation of the lonely forests – particularly Schumann's astounding summary of all woodland music, 'A Place of Evil Reputation' from *Forest Scenes* (1848), which manages to be pretty, menacing, uneasy and mournful in about three minutes. But I really have to stop before this book stalls completely.

An exception though must be made for a brief mention of Joseph von Eichendorff's *Life of a Good-for-nothing*, published in 1826. Eichendorff is yet another friendly Prussian who can be called into service to trump all the clinking-spurred, *en brosse* military men, although unlike Humboldt or Hoffmann he did in fact fight in the Napoleonic Wars. He wrote an immense amount, not least poems which further fuelled the needs of song composers from Mendelssohn to Richard Strauss – indeed perhaps marking the absolute end of the tradition, as Eichendorff's 'At Sunset' (set to music in 1948) is played as the last of the *Four Last Songs*.

Life of a Good-for-nothing is a tall tale and a narrative wonder, where the reader is hurtled along through the miscellaneous adventures of the chaotic, underachieving narrator. The story is thick with coaches, palaces, beautiful yet mysterious women, rascals, gardens, forests – a sort of omnium gatherum of Romanticism. 'So I went into the house and took off the wall the fiddle I played so well, and my father gave me a few coppers to help me on my way, and off I strolled down the long street and out of the village . . . ' The palace scenes immortalize the whole pre-Napoleonic world of the little court (as does Mörike's equally sunny and nostalgic *Mozart's Journey to Prague* written a generation later), with its tiny concerns, its beauties and love affairs. And then, in an astonishing turn, Eichendorff sends his hero to Italy, thereby making almost a parody of German attitudes of longing for the land where 'raisins just drop into one's mouth'. The tone is often of an unbearably brightly coloured dream, crammed with songbirds with gaudy feathers, obscurely threatening strangers, unexplained chases through deserted city streets. Every paragraph seems to contain a further reason to be happy, with the narrator rolling about like a puppy in the pleasure of his own wanderlust.

Strolling along the banks of the Danube or up in the Harz Mountains, I've never been whisked up into a coach, encountered a mysterious charcoal-burner's hut or had to decide whether or not to be polite to a roadside gnome, but it hardly matters. It is impossible to take a step without feeling very slightly like a journeyman larrikin embarking on his wandering years or a knight on some unfeasible errand. A simple walk in the woods is invariably accompanied by an ineptly hummed *Siegfried* 'Prelude', no matter how undragon-filled the walk might be. But then, just getting a bus outside Cologne to get to the magical wooded valley of Cloister Altenberg you can't, while punching your ticket, not whistle a bar or two from 'Siegfried's Rhine Journey' (indeed, commuters taking the tram into Bonn must routinely at the very least hum it, rocking from side to side, making the whole journey quite noisy). Such choking clouds of musical, visual (Caspar David Friedrich!) and written material swathe themselves around anyone – however unyouthful or unheroic – to such an extent that it is impossible to talk of this being a genuinely solitary experience at all.

Heroic acorns

A contrasting strand to the doomed wish for solitude is the exaggerated German enthusiasm for group activity. Towns can become almost unnegotiable as their historic cores silt up with tour groups; cathedrals choke on the numbers of little singing clubs and parish coach outings; a simple walk in some mountains will find the solitary hiker almost swept from the path by gnu-like herds of specially equipped, hiking Germans. It is always possible to join a group at a Ratskeller, to find space at a table, with everyone moving up and smiling, in an open and welcoming manner prone to make English people pass out with horror. There is a sort of semi-genial tyranny in these groups with their matching tops and their little medals stamped onto their walking sticks and they always make me a bit skittish – as though one moment they could all be chatting and swapping anecdotes about long-haul vacation packages and the next going berserk in a *Clockwork Orange* sort of way.

One odd manifestation of this communal behaviour is the seemingly limitless enthusiasm for sitting in boats going up and down rivers. On bits of the Rhine or the Danube flotillas of glass-roofed vessels will drift pointlessly back and forth past very slightly interesting crags or mildly appealing ruined castles (the sheer numbers of the last rapidly devalue their currency). Of course the point of these jaunts is not really to do more than glimpse at these low-grade sites, which really are just the thinnest of pretexts. The real goal is to sit in groups around tables, eating astonishing amounts of sausage and cake, drinking massive glasses of lager and smoking furiously. I've often been struck by the delicate chemical balance within these boats – the flame from the cigarettes glowing bright in the methane-rich atmosphere, mercifully burning off the dangerous edge to the inevitable human by-product generated by the sausage, lager and cake combo. I almost come to expect to see in the twilight, dotted along the river, sudden, brilliant vermilion flares as boats detonate from an unlucky, fatal combination of build-up and a solitary smoker's delay in lighting up.

It was on one of these unstable experiments in human living that I went to see the Walhalla. As part of that great wave of early nineteenth-century love of everything Greek, Prince Ludwig of Bavaria decided that when he became king he would build a copy of the Parthenon on a hill above the Danube and make it into a hall for heroes, a Walhalla, filled with busts sculpted by the greatest sculptors of the greatest Germans in German history, as judged by himself and some of his friends.

The building looked completely odd from inside the fuggy boat – its lush deciduous surroundings an odd substitute for parched and blistered Athens. It is appealing enough, though – with the enormous advantage over the original of not looking all sad, bust-up and broken. The boat moored and some of us got off, leaving others to clear the display cases of strudel and generally enjoy themselves. The walk to the Walhalla was arduous, a struggle alongside a great mass of burping, heaving leisure clothing across paths choked with millions of acorns from the heroic oak trees planted everywhere. But once inside, having registered the mildly interesting view and noted with approval the underfloor heating system (another clear improvement on the Greek original), all jokes are off.

The interior is about two-thirds Enlightenment magic and about a third everything that's freaky about Germany. Light pours in on a neo-Greek cuboid, stern caryatids, sumptuous marbles, a ridiculous statue of King Ludwig. Only after a few moments of mental stabilization is it possible then to focus on the point of the place, the row upon row of white-marble busts, like some classicizing science-fiction vision of cryogenically frozen geniuses awaiting the signal for their brains to reactivate. When Ludwig came up with his original list he must have had great fun, chucking in blood-soaked Dark Age nonsense like Totila and Hengist, some generals he admired, lots of kings (Heinrich the Fowler, Otto the Great, Charlemagne, Frederick the Great). Ludwig understood 'German' to mean 'Germanic' or even 'kind of Germanic', so Swiss, Dutch and even Belgian heroes can get in (Rubens looks particularly implausible). Ever since its inception new busts have been added at intervals, each one having a Nobel Prize-like quality of enshrinement, however bogus, and since it first opened every visitor has complained about obvious, sinister or incompetent omissions – no Schumann, no Daimler, no Heine (finally allowed in in 2009), neither Mann brother and so on and so on. The pleasure lies in the arbitrary arrangement, with scientists and composers blissfully entangled in the Bismarcks and medieval fruitcakes. There are hardly any women, but one that *is* included more or less counterbalances the totality of all the other Germans there, as surely the most successful and powerful German of all: Catherine the Great. The modern era has to intrude and the whole project's fresh-faced, early nineteenth-century pottiness is at the very least under question. But as usual it is crucial to concentrate a bit and not witlessly track everything back. It is eerie, but it is also bracing and happy – a version of Top Trumps, albeit an unwieldy one.

Uneasy attempts have been made in recent decades to balance out the sea of kings and generals, including an almost unrecognizable Einstein. But the great, genuinely moving coup of 2003 was to install a bust of Sophie Scholl, the remarkable Munich student beheaded by the Nazis in 1943. As a member of the White Rose movement, recklessly distributing anti-Nazi pamphlets, she is one of the handful of figures within Germany at the time who can be pointed to with pride. The bust itself as sculpture is hopeless (she looks like a Tiny Tears doll) but it doesn't matter. Her presence, undifferentiated from the Kants and the Gneisenaus, the van Dycks and the Strausses, seems to revalidate the whole idea of German forms of cultural and moral greatness. In Scholl's final statement ('Such a fine, sunny day, and I have to go, but what does my death matter, if through us thousands of people are awakened and stirred to action?') there is a sense that she and her colleagues knew exactly what they were doing, knew that they were *literally* saving their country through the moral courage of their actions. Her bust in this bizarre time-capsule of two centuries of German nationalism makes it again into a real hall of heroes, subjugating and denying the power of the 'Hitler time'.

As I reeled and staggered back down the hill, on a sort of avalanche of heroic, ball-bearing-like old acorns, I felt moved by the strange outcome of Ludwig's eccentric vision. There are, however, other nineteenth-century German monuments which have not broken free in the same way.

Some hundred and twenty miles north of Ludwig's strange 1830s temple lies something far worse and which, however hedged around with qualifications, has to stand for what went wrong with Germany in the following sixty years or so. If much of the point of this book is to lament the widespread lack of engagement with German places, people and things, then by contrast we should all be grateful to be shielded from the Battle of the Nations monument

outside Leipzig. Anyone who through sheer, foolish bad luck types
into Google Image the word *Völkerschlachtdenkmal* will find their
screen filled with photos of Europe's largest, heaviest and nastiest
memorial. This historicist monster was built to mark the centenary
of the 1813 Battle of Leipzig – the largest battle in Europe's history to that point, with over half a million troops involved and a
key event in the destruction of Napoleon's empire. The monument's
inauguration in 1913 was attended by the usual ostrich-plumed
crowd of soldiers and royals. That it was built entirely through
private initiative makes everything even worse. Leipzig is a musical
and mercantile city and it is strange that only a tram-ride from
Schumann's rather funny-smelling favourite restaurant an object of
such immense, humourless, Aztec gloom should be languishing.

The monument has been through a lot and is one of the most
historically charged sights in Germany – for the battle it commemorated, for the values it suggests, for its status as a last hurrah for
the peacetime Kaiser, for Hitler's enjoying giving speeches in front
of it and for its role in the passing-out parades of the East German
army. It is the work of Bruno Schmitz, the world's worst architect,
who unleashed his wretched talents on ruining several previously
charming sites (the Kyffhäuser mountain, the point where the Rhine
and Mosel join) and smothering them in industrialized pseudo-
mythology.

The contrast between the pretty landscaping of the park and the
monstrous memorial of rough, blackened granite that lurks in it is
really disturbing. Something that should be found in the heart of a
jungle, lying half strewn about and choked with jungle creepers,
bats, snakes and poisonous flowers, has been set down in what looks
like a quiet bit of Central Park. The sheer mass is strangely needless – it is a bulk rather than a definite architectural shape and even
walking towards it there is an uneasy sense of resignation that you
are about to be in the presence of a whole lot of ludicrous allegoric
carving. Once inside you are threatened by immense stone figures
– the worst being the medieval madness of the eighteen-foot-high
'Guards of the Dead' in full armour, awaiting activation in some
pathetic horror film. The only pleasure it gives (a not small one) is

the atmosphere of decay and neglect – the bits of old scaffolding and sheeting, the steady drip of water. After 1945 the communists decided that although the memorial was an imperialist one it should be kept going as during the Battle of Leipzig the Russians and at least some Germans had fought on the same side. The united German authorities have, with their usual bludgeoning seriousness, decided that they have a duty to later generations (who might just possibly have so degraded an aesthetic sense as to not find the memorial hideous) to restore it at a cost of millions of euros. One local priest made the happy suggestion that a fraction of the money should be spent on a cafe overlooking the site where, over the course of the coming century, lucky drinkers might witness a really big piece of the monument crashing to the ground as the whole thing fell to bits – the edifice itself becoming a powerful symbol for the futility of war rather than merely a pricey kitsch misfire. But this idea was ignored and dozens of stonemasons must now be employed in toning up the beard or pecs on the huge statue of Strength Through Belief and fixing up the sword of a Guard of the Dead.

Across the German world the period before the First World War threw up all kinds of ghastly monuments and buildings in a similar vein to this one – from the appalling Berlin Cathedral to the Neu Burg in Vienna. The only thing that saves these buildings is that they stand as monuments to failure – the civilization that built them was destroyed. The Neu Burg is doomed to forever face onto a Heroes' Square which will never be completed, a place famous only as the setting for Hitler's announcement of the destruction of independent Austria. As for Berlin Cathedral – perhaps figures such as Wilhelm II are underestimated and in fact one of their secret, never-to-be-spoken-of pleasures was the carrying out of dull, ugly but very expensive building projects knowing that they would rapidly become synonymous with dynastic futility. The Hohenzollern crypt, bringing together the sarcophagi of some eighty Prussian royals, has the cramped and uninvolving atmosphere of an underground car park, with dozens and dozens of near identical coffins laid out in rows like vehicles, all assembled just in time, after half a millennium of power, for the whole enterprise to pack up: only one family member (a child) was ever interned there and Wilhelm himself was buried in exile in the Netherlands. This monstrousness is absolutely palpable – these were dynasts of a highly traditional frame of mind wanting to express their ideas using modern financing, materials and size. There is something very similar in such awful mistakes as the Hamburg or Hannover town halls – buildings so huge and nasty that they appear only to have been put there (let alone remade after war damage) to confound later generations. But there is no direct line between such bad taste and Armageddon – everywhere in Europe large, dull, backward-looking structures were going up shortly before 1914: they deface Rome or Brussels, they could include such lumpish objects as Buckingham Palace (one of Europe's most banal rather than most frightening structures). What is attractive when surrounded by such horrors is the knowledge that, like small mammals that scampered around while triceratops lurched across the plains, the architects who were to end all this madness were hidden away throughout the German and Austro-Hungarian Empires, in Weimar and Vienna.

Victory columns

With such a welter of rulers, the different bits of Germany were always bound to be richly peppered with monuments to the greatness of individuals and families. Made from stone or bronze, these monuments are meant to last forever and some have had serious longevity. The eerie lion statue in Braunschweig has been there since 1166, albeit now in its third identical casting, the first free-standing statue in Northern Europe since the Roman empire. The Bamberg Rider and the Magdeburg Rider from the following century also survive. The meaning of the lion statue remains opaque: it clearly refers to Henry the Lion and to the power of the Welf family but we no longer have any idea of what occasion it was created for. The two horseback statues are also reinventions: in turn, these are the first northern figures on horseback to be sculpted since the Roman empire. This is either impressive, or shows how entirely derivative of Italian models medieval Germany really was, depending on your prejudices. Although some guesses can be made there is no evidence at all as to the identity of either Rider or why they were made: somehow, at some point, through disaster or accident or indifference, the names of these no doubt very significant figures were lost.

I have spent far too much time staring at monuments such as these, peering into crypts, battling to understand inscriptions. My favourite piece of prose is Sir Thomas Browne's magnificently resigned and gloomy *Urne-Burial*, one of the wonders of the seventeenth century, in which Browne meditates on the futility of all human monuments in a language of suffocating and dusty richness. Looking at so many battered, neglected columns, carved tablets and war memorials, Browne's reflections beckon at every turn. 'Pyramids, Arches, Obelisks, were but the irregularities of vainglory, and wilde enormities of ancient magnanimity', or 'But the iniquity of oblivion blindely scattereth her poppy, and deals with the memory of men without distinction to merit of perpetuity. Who can but pity the founder of the Pyramids?' Of course the damage done to so many memorials adds immeasurably to their own message of human frailty, the beau ideal perhaps being those tablets in churches where the lettering has completely worn away, leaving only a skull or an hourglass decoration, the inscription's disappearance making a more aggressive *Vanitas* than the dead person's family had intended.

These monuments have two purposes. Their overwhelmingly more important one was during the lifetime of those who built them. The materials used are meant to be for all futurity, but in effect this is always a knowing bluff. What really matters is to mark the present, whether it is the survivors of a war or the immediate descendants of a recently dead ruler. In this sense we are all poorly informed interlopers, relishing the irony but missing the point. No better example of this is the rash of monuments put up to bolster the new kingdoms after Napoleon's defeat. As these kingdoms were only genuinely independent for a couple of reigns each and during that time were weak and on the whole unloved, these victory or memorial columns seem rather vulnerable, but their real value lay in the grief of those who lived through the events marked. The huge Waterloo column in Hannover or the black-and-gold column in Braunschweig marking the deaths in battle of two successive dukes fighting Napoleon had a double weight of marking, in the traditional nationalist manner, the blood-price foundation stone of new states, but also providing a focus for the thousands of individuals who had lost relatives or friends. We can see the same process now with British memorials to the world wars: events around these monuments which in my childhood brought together rank upon rank of elderly veterans of the First World War are now filled with comparably elderly veterans of the Second, who in turn will soon peter out, leaving behind a relatively hollow and static meaning for those who, thanks to the durable materials used to make the objects, will encounter them in the future.

Perhaps the strangest of these surviving monuments – surviving with fragments gouged out from the base by Soviet shrapnel – is the Victory Column in Berlin. This ugly and unengaging thing was for many years the focus of all sorts of hopes and fears. It was started to commemorate the Second Schleswig War of 1864 and the Prussian defeat of Denmark. The war marked the first really serious engagement by the Prussian army since 1815 and an appropriately grandiose monument was required. While this was still being designed the Prussians and Austrians fell out (not least over Schleswig-Holstein, but more generally over who would be the dominant force in Germany) and, following Austria's crushing defeat in 1866, the column was given further meaning. But again, this was too soon, the column was not finished and war with France in 1870–71 and the unification of Germany meant that the column had to bear the weight, not of a minor police action in Denmark, but of events of boggling world-historical importance. These led to the already very clumsy and dour column having a bulky bronze statue put on top. The Nazis moved it, added a bit more and put in subways under the roads to reach the column. It was further messed around by the French taking advantage of being among the occupying authorities in Berlin in 1945 and gleefully removing some of

the more gloating reliefs on the base marking their earlier humiliating defeat. The Victory Column has been kicked about so much
that it floats entirely free of its chauvinist origins, or indeed of the
original commemorations once held around its base where the great
figures of the era, Bismarck, Moltke, Wilhelm I, Roon, the Crown
Prince, would gather, thinking about events that they had themselves carved out. A plaintive exhibition inside points out that the
Column is comparable to similarly grandiose projects of the era
such as the Statue of Liberty or Tower Bridge in London, but of
course it is infinitely more scary and on its own circuit entirely –
not because of the events it commemorated, but because of its
mutation through so many years of German-initiated disaster. It
still stands as a grim, battered reminder of human folly, waste
and delusion – the exact opposite of its architect's and sponsors'
intent. It is also, in a quintessential act of Berlin subversion, now
the focus of an annual gay pride march, which in a way that so often
is the case in modern Germany, cauterizes the damage reflected in
the memorial in a beautifully appropriate way.

CHAPTER ELEVEN

The grandeur and misery of nationalism »
Snow-shake particularism » A surprise trip to Mexico

The grandeur and misery of nationalism

Of course, I am as ravaged by nationalism as anyone else. All I have
to do is listen to the quiet, intensely noble part of Sibelius' *Finlandia*
and I start to fall apart – appreciating the short season for picking
cloudberries, grateful for the cooling summer wind that comes off
uncountable Finnish lakes, the taste of cured reindeer meat on my
tongue, shoulder to shoulder in epic defence of a country which,
actually, I've never visited.

Nationalism is one of the most confusing subjects of the nineteenth century, with the added bonus of becoming worse and worse
the more anyone thinks about it. The central problem lies in the con-
viction that it was something specifically dynamic and *new* in Europe
which crystallized there and then sped around the rest of the world
in the twentieth century. Even under the briefest scrutiny this does
not work very well. Reading *Simplicissimus*, the seventeenth-century
German novel about the Thirty Years War, there can be no doubt that
the characters are aware of nationalism – that they are proud to be
sociable, comradely, fair-minded Badenese or Swedish or French,
that they are equally contemptuous of the small-minded, miserly,
vicious Badenese or Swedish or French. While it is true that ruling
dynasties had ownership over their territories in a way which did not
imply for a moment that their subjects could have national views,
this does not seem to have in practice prevented them from doing so.
To imagine that a Brunswick army facing off against a Bavarian army
was *not* filled with a welter of religious, social, linguistic and moral
views on its opponent, but was instead only doing its duty as a mass
of grovelling subjects, is to condescend towards the past much too
heavily.

The nationalist argument was extremely useful to the Prussians and their allies scattered across Germany (both liberal and reactionary) because it implied a sort of inevitability in the creation of a single Germany (which nonetheless somehow missed out German-speaking parts of the Habsburg Empire). The chaos, ill feeling and, ultimately, murder carried out in the name of nationalism makes it an intensely serious subject in Germany, but it is difficult not to feel derisive about its claims. The most successful of nineteenth-century European states was undoubtedly Britain, which was to the core of its self-definition multi-national, both in itself and in its colonial empire, with the English, however overweaning and ghastly, always using and even admiring collaborators among other groups. Portugal and Spain started off the nineteenth century as ancient nationalist states, but with enormous empires of many races which shaped and defined their sense of national sentiment. France might, after centuries of fighting, be moving slowly towards being a linguistically coherent place, but it seemed to have an insatiable need to attack bits of the Rhineland without the faintest claim to Frenchness. The Habsburg Empire was far more wholeheartedly multi-national even than Britain, Russia was a shambles of irredeemable national chaos and Italy had been in fragments since the end of the Roman empire. Germany was split into tiny bits for centuries and had sometimes thrived and sometimes been miserable, but it was hard to say that the amazing achievements of a disunited Germany were all irrelevant. The country best poised to take advantage of German nationalism, Prussia, ruled over millions of Poles and was split into a jigsaw of purely dynastic chunks.

With the high tide of frightening, activist nationalism now ebbed from Europe and the Cold War that froze it up equally vanished, it seems clearer that a united Germany came from forces way beyond the imaginative projects of specific intellectuals or politicians. The black-red-gold flag used by some of the Freikorps fighting Napoleon and embraced by the student fraternities and others who met at the Wartburg Schloss in Eisenach in 1817 on the fourth anniversary of the Battle of Leipzig traditionally marks the beginning of serious German nationalism. But these students were really only cranky and rather sad. Their views were at the time either ignored or disapproved of by an immense cross-section of opinion. They can get no credit – and indeed hardly any blame – for turning out after dozens of twists to be 'right', much to everyone's loss.

What is curious about German nationalism is its slowness and indeed incompleteness. As a linguistically defined entity it only began to function with the very brief incorporation of Austria from 1938 to 1945 and always included chaotic mutations and exceptions, with the Kaiser's Reich still filled with many autonomous kings and dukes. In an extreme form it is possible to say that German nationalism only had coherence between the incorporation of Austria in March 1938 and the takeover of the remains of western Czechoslovakia a year and two days later, when linguistic nationalism became once more a chaotic and disgusting imperialism. By the time such German-speaking areas as Danzig and Posen had been 'brought home' following the invasion of Poland, Germany was onto a track which made a mockery of the language-defined state. Clearly it is possible to say that the normal run of life for the roughly German-speaking areas of Europe has been, in the many centuries from the end of the Ottonian Empire to the present day, to live in a tangle of political arrangements – with the exception of these 367 days. Oh, and I've forgotten about Switzerland again – a standing affront to nineteenth-century nationalist dreamers: federal, multilingual and completely uninterested in invading people.

The reasons for the unification of some Germans into a single entity were peculiar and specific. Some of the new states carved out after Napoleon's defeat, such as Baden, could easily have stabilized and become countries not dissimilar to Switzerland. Others, such as an enhanced Bavaria, were entirely plausible – Bavaria's wealth has always been a given, however misused by its rulers, and in the early twenty-first-century world of European states such as Latvia and Slovenia, Bavaria could easily exist on its own. The smaller surviving early-nineteenth-century bits and pieces, such as the lands of the Reuss princes or (my favourite) Schaumburg-Lippe, were always going to be vulnerable to the slightest breeze, but equally these could have become harmless anomalies like Liechtenstein or Andorra or Monaco – daft but not inherently impossible.

Prussia had benefited more than anybody from Napoleon's demise. From being a state teetering on the verge of extinction and a gloomy, French-occupied satellite, it had jumped clear of its dependence during Napoleon's defeat in Russia and got lucky, since Berlin was far enough away from Paris to avoid immediate retribution. The decision by specific Prussian army officers to throw away the alliance with France and force the dithering monarch's hand was both heroic and dangerous, but it was also only successful because of forces very far beyond Prussia's control. In the final phases of the fighting Prussia was significant but in various configurations always less so than Russia or Austria or Britain.

Where Prussia cashed in enormously, in ways which would dominate the nineteenth century despite severe setbacks, was in the division of the spoils. Everyone assumed after Napoleon's eventual, final and exhausting defeat that France had only been thrown back into a temporary prison and that the nineteenth century would be dominated, as the previous nearly two centuries had been, by aggressive French expansionism. (Interestingly, a similar assumption was made about Germany in 1919. Only in that case the assumption was not properly enforced, and turned out to be true.) The British therefore disposed of the old Austrian Netherlands, Belgium, adding it onto the Netherlands to make a single, substantial country to the north of France, guaranteed by Britain against future French incursion. To match this to the east of France, Prussia, which had previously only owned bits and pieces in western Germany, was given huge, valuable chunks to allow it a permanent policeman's role.

The difficulties this produced were invisible to the Congress of Vienna but boiled down to the very slow realization that, although Paris became, if anything, even more enjoyable to visit as the century wore on, France had had her fun geopolitically and was no longer an overwhelming threat. Further, the strong northern state of the United Netherlands was ruined by the insurrection that created a separate Belgium, thus creating a small, tempting, vulnerable state that was to cause such headaches in two world wars. Further than this, it turned out that, more or less by accident, Prussia had been given the Ruhr Valley (previously split up between harmless little states such as the Vest Recklinghausen lands of Cologne and the Lordship of Limburg-Styrum-Styrum). Some of this had been handed to Prussia by Napoleon in happier days, the rest agreed at the Congress of Vienna, but unfortunately with nobody realizing that the inhabitants of a somewhat under-resourced but militarily excitable bit of land up near Poland had accidentally been given *the heart of the coal and steel Industrial Revolution!*

It is an odd accident that Mary Shelley should have been writing *Frankenstein* just as Prussia was settling into its new territories – a similar tale of unrelated chunks being stitched together. Her book was in large part inspired by a visit to the medical faculty at Ingolstadt with its state-of-the-art preserved cadavers, the corpses threaded with coloured wiring to show veins and nerves – plus the usual bottled horrors suspended in pickle. These are still there and unbeatably sinister and fun (together with a simply amazing display of models of the diseased human eye, discoloured, distended, leaking, clouded, according to type of illness). But this is to stray off the subject. There was nothing on the face of it *inherently* bad about Prussia now being constructed of bits and pieces from such disparate cultures – other states had managed this, not least Austria, which had ruled places from Ostend to Dubrovnik. The old Prussia had owned some very small but valuable western lands, such as the County of Mark, for many years. It was not programmed to be a Frankenstein's monster – it could have simply become a genial, schizophrenic mess. There was also always an influential, and rather moving, element within Prussian life that was scornful of or anxious about Prussia's preponderant weight inside Germany. Frederick William III and his son Frederick William IV may have been poor kings, but their weakness left its mark on Prussia until the latter's stroke in 1857. Both in their different ways were highly suspicious of a united Germany, rightly feeling that such an organization might swamp the country they valued. They were also admiring of and deferential towards the Habsburg Empire and would have been appalled by the events supervised by their successor.

Unfortunately nationalism was not trundling along at the whim of monarchs, but through industrialization that crushed everything before it. Canals and railways and rivers, but particularly railways, made a mockery of the often very local customs and dues which paid for each small state. These innovations hated localism and demanded instead as big a customs-free zone as possible. This zone, joined by most German states by 1852, became a political weapon. Initially it reinforced individual countries as it increased customs revenue overall and let sovereigns fritter the money on the new palaces and funny, self-serving statues and columns that litter the era. But once it had settled in it tended to make financiers and merchants think nationally.

But just as potent was the continuing fear of the French who, despite suffering what in retrospect is clearly a sort of wasting illness, looked to still have designs on the Rhineland. The new German Confederation which allowed military cooperation between the different states should have been guarantee enough. But with much crucial Rhineland territory ruled by small places like Baden and the Grand Duchy of Hesse it was inevitable that in any emergency Prussian troops would be the only serious guarantor. The territorial tidying away of old Austrian lands such as Belgium and the Black Forest enclaves had the entirely accidental effect, allied to new Austrian responsibilities in the Balkans and Italy, of making the Rhine 'front line' of limited further interest to the Habsburgs, who had always been one of France's most unthinking enemies. Tons of resources were poured into such Confederal fortresses as Luxembourg, Mainz and Rastatt, but in the event of a serious French attack everyone knew they would run screaming to the Prussians for help.

Much of the period was spent preparing for wars that never happened. The British and the Americans were convinced that they would fight each other again after the Treaty of Ghent in 1814 and used most of the century planning for it. The British and the French spent immense sums, both sick with anxiety that some naval innovation would give the other a crushing superiority that would annihilate the other in some second Trafalgar – an anxiety that in the event never came to anything. Equally, much of German history was based on terror of a fresh French incursion, perhaps most strikingly in 1840 when the French government incautiously and incorrigibly stated that it viewed the Rhine as France's natural eastern border. This provoked a frenzy of German-wide indignation, including the song sung by so many million German soldiers over the coming century, 'The Watch on the Rhine' ('As rich in water is your flood/ Is Germany in heroes' blood', &c). It was sometimes as though the French were goading the Germans into unification, as announcements such as this had places like Württemberg and Hesse-Darmstadt bleating with fright. This meant that when war did at last break out in 1870, the British were neutral, assuming despondently that the French would win, but hoping that the Prussians might at least damage them severely in the process. This British attitude of seeing the Germans as a sort of thermostat that could be regulated to keep France at the right temperature now spectacularly malfunctioned as Prussian troops marauded across Normandy (leaving a trail of excellent Guy de Maupassant short stories behind them). But this was a surprising outcome – and surprising to many Germans too, until then hostile and sceptical towards what was happening.

Snow-shake particularism

Tucked away in a corner of north-west Germany lies the former Principality of Schaumburg-Lippe, an absurd Plutoid with fewer than fifty thousand inhabitants that through cunning and luck managed to survive until the German Revolution of 1918, and where the ruling family has clung on to their palace in the lovely if undeniably tiny town of Bückeburg right up to the present. As with other German princely families, such as the amazingly wealthy Thurn und Taxis family in Regensburg (I am *not* visiting any more museums with displays of mouldering old coaches and sleighs *ever*

again), the Princes of Schaumburg-Lippe make it clear just how
boring it would be if any of these families had actually retained real
power into the present day. We are lucky that they were all kicked
out in 1918, thereby preserving forever their image as pop-eyed,
moustachioed uniform-obsessives. The modern Schaumburg-Lippes
in their beautiful Schloss – complete with duck-packed moat, ugly
late-nineteenth-century ballroom and intimate salon filled with
mythological statues – have photos of themselves enjoying a joke
with King Hussein of Jordan or sitting regally with their adorable
Labrador, but all with that same air of plain-suited dullness that
curses too other, more significant European ruling families. The
shop sells Schaumburg-Lippe chocolate, CDs of music played in the
ugly ballroom, and a Christmas-at-Schloss-Bückeburg snow-shake
dome which never leaves my computer table (made, dare we dream,
by the Prince himself?).

Outside the station at Bückeburg (and the town is so small that
if you lose concentration for a moment you have already walked
past the palace) is a lumpy and untalented statue commemorating
the Franco-Prussian War, in which some five of the Prince's subjects
were killed. I have to admit here that I am absolutely obsessed with
the way Germany has commemorated its wars and it is a constant
struggle not to write an entire book about these monuments, so any
reference to them must be read against an implied background of a
writer fighting to hold back a sort of brain-explosion of carefully
scribbled but, alas, unused material. This monument in Bückeburg
(a town which, to be honest, also deserves an entire book) is interesting because on the smallest possible scale it shows the oddity of
German unification. This was not a simple *town* war memorial, but
the expression of the sacrifice of a constituent principality in the
German empire. The ruler, Adolf I, had in the 1860s played his
cards so well that rather than being devoured without a thought by
a Prussia thousands of times his size he managed at just the right
moment to become their military ally, while his mighty neighbour,
the Kingdom of Hannover, under its blind, autocratic ruler George
V, got everything wrong and disappeared forever.

The 1860s were a time of exhilarating, precarious change in

Germany. The Prussians had gained a total ascendancy over the much smaller remaining north German states, and had designs too on the substantial southern German kingdoms and their protectors Austria and France. The decision by the overbearing, brutal Prussian Minister-President Otto von Bismarck to achieve German unification through war seems a fearful precursor in retrospect to all that went wrong in the twentieth century, but at the time was far less controversial. Countries routinely switched alliances, went to war and generally were quite happy to do the most outrageous things to each other. Grotesque land grabs were going on everywhere. An amazing example from the 1840s was the Mexican War (as it is known in the USA) or the United States Invasion (as it is known in Mexico). The US carved out for itself immense new territories at gunpoint – for example, uh, California and, uh, Texas – simply stolen from Mexico in a spirit of stuffy and ludicrous Protestant rectitude. The British hardly allowed a year to go by without shooting up a pile of individuals somewhere in the interests of free trade and British decency. And the multinational force of British, French and Sardinian troops who had invaded southern Russia and Kamchatka in the 1850s exhibited no greater or lesser frivolity of purpose than Bismarck did in his wars of the 1860s.

Warfare was therefore, it is reasonable to say, an acceptable if risky aspect of nineteenth-century European life. The elites were military elites – a fact shielded from the British only by the odd chance of their being ruled then by a woman who spent much of her reign in mourning dress: her now less historically visible male children were utterly drenched in medals, spurs, sashes and sabres. War was not embarked on lightly (except in Africa and Asia) but it was always a card to play and most of the point of the revenue-raising power of the state was to come up with money for ever more elaborate armaments. The sheer, delirious inventiveness of the nineteenth century meant that this became very expensive, with obsolescence always threatened for any weapons system within a decade. Some states could simply not keep up. The Habsburg Empire remained a dynamic, brilliant and (in the light of later events) admirable part of Europe, but its dominance crumbled rapidly as it did not have the depth of industry or tax base (thanks not least to a lot of unhelpful and obscurantist Hungarian noblemen) to compete with France or Prussia.

These hidden strengths and weaknesses – how quickly could an army mobilize, did it have secret weapons, would morale hold up? – meant that each of the mid-century wars was a complete surprise. The military manoeuvres which, alongside hunting, occupied so much of Europe's rulers' time and money could never answer these questions, and in all the major conflicts both sides would face war with similar levels of self-confidence: with the result showing one side's self-confidence to have been misguided. There were some baffling military culs-de-sac. One great oddity was the Battle of Lissa, a naval struggle in 1866 off the Dalmatian coast between units of the Habsburg and Italian navies (with neither opponent drawing on a glowing naval tradition). This chaotic melee resulted in a Habsburg victory because the Austrians used their ships to *ram* the Italians (a technique previously resorted to back in the days of Mediterranean oared galleys). This meant that for some years ships were fitted (at considerable expense and with much futile training) with rams – which as it turned out were never used. The wider war of 1866, in which the Habsburg Empire defeated the Italians but was crushed by the Prussians, ended in humiliation for the Habsburgs. But the Battle of Lissa was also interesting because it ensured that the Dalmatian coast would remain – unlike the rest of the old Venetian territories but now handed over, at Prussian insistence, to the Italians – under Habsburg rule. The side-effect of a captain's fluky decision to use a ram therefore entirely changed what would become the histories of Yugoslavia and Croatia.

The three wars fought by Prussia – with Denmark; with Austria and her ineffective German allies; and with France and one last batch of ineffective German allies – made her synonymous with military brilliance. But this was, it must be remembered, a new reputation. Everybody understood that the Danes could not win their war, but most observers assumed that Austria and then France would crush the Prussians and, indeed, with a little more luck, intelligence and planning that could well have happened. The Prussian military machine – the work of Roon and Moltke – was drawing from weak roots. Frederick the Great's defensive battles of the mid-eighteenth century were a long time ago and for stakes that now look paltry. It had never faintly been plausible that he could bring the Habsburgs to their knees – his only aim was simply to prevent them from getting back Silesia. He was incapable of, say, attacking Vienna itself, let alone Paris or St Petersburg. And the Prussian performance in the wars with Napoleon had been initially unremarkable – defeated and humiliated both in fighting the French and then in fighting the Russians alongside the French, the Prussians ended the war, having extensively reformed their state, as a striking and brave but patently less important element in the coalition. Indeed a wider point could be made that the oddity of the modern German military experience – including the two world wars – has been the catastrophic *inability* of its strategists ever to win a war outside this delusive little seven-year period in the 1860s. If the point of a war was to create a more favourable political and economic environment for its winner then there was a sickness at the heart of German military-political planning that made it uniquely *unable* to achieve a result, ultimately with the most terrible consequences imaginable.

The 1860s wars were retrospectively called 'cabinet wars' because they were so brief: operations against Denmark took nine months, against Austria less than two months and against France ten months. The first of these was fought by Prussia alongside Austria to prevent the Danes absorbing fully the region of Schleswig-Holstein, a territory which had always had a mongrel, semi-Danish, semi-German political status now unacceptable to rising Danish and German nationalism. The other two wars were more significant, indeed central to the story of Germany, because between them they wrapped up all the remaining independent German states. The wars asked every constituent country whether they were for or against Prussia, with rulers from the King of Bavaria to the Prince of Schaumburg-Lippe having to take extremely fast decisions. Militarily none of the minor states had the resources (particularly given the speed of the wars) to make much difference, although substantial

Prussian resources went into defeating them. The Catholic south, particularly Bavaria and Baden, had every reason to loathe the idea of being absorbed into Prussia. Not just the elites, but absolutely everyone had been raised on a traditional hatred for Prussia (a small example: Frederick the Great's comment that 'Bavaria was a paradise inhabited by animals'). But there was also nowhere which did not have tucked away a pro-Prussian party or, more significantly, a pro-united-Germany party.

As it turned out the forces of particularism crumbled to bits in the face of the Prussian military (aided by minor allies such as Brunswick and Oldenburg, who thereby preserved their futures cheerily). The independent city of Frankfurt refused to back Prussia; it was occupied by Prussian troops and turned into part of Prussia. The Kingdom of Hannover backed the Austrians and was destroyed (George V's immense treasury was privately snaffled by Bismarck, who spent many years using it as his secret 'Reptile Fund' for buying off journalists). Liechtenstein suddenly declared its neutral independence and somehow got away with it. All over Germany panicked decisions were taken in the shadow of the world-changing defeats of the smaller states' great power sponsors. At the immense Battle of Königgrätz in 1866, Austria and her ally Saxony were crushed and at the Battle of Sedan in 1870 the French army was attacked so brilliantly that it was in part destroyed but also so completely outmanoeuvred that its remaining large units remained intact but paralysed.

In the wars with Austria and France, the Prussians were as surprised as anybody that the fighting was so brief – and this became another poisonous legacy. The idea of the lightning strike which, in a single strategic gesture, could end a conflict became something that entranced Europe's militaries. In contrast to the miseries of the Crimean War or the American Civil War, perhaps a more Napoleonic model could be retrieved, where the sheer brilliance of the Prussian–German military could prevail. Generations of German generals would lie crushed beneath the reputation of Moltke and his staff – but for over forty years after the defeat of France their services saw no further fighting. Paul von Hindenburg had fought as a teenager at Königgrätz and was hauled out of retirement in his late sixties to fight the Russians in 1914. Graf von Schlieffen spent most of his life planning for and dreaming of a further war yet died aged almost eighty before the First World War broke out, on which he had such a profound and – as it proved – useless and damaging influence.

These were 'cabinet wars' therefore only in as much as they happened to end quite quickly and with the disastrous suggestion that this might be true of future wars. Far from being a militaristic barracks state, Germany was in practice simply in love with the idea of cheap victory. An all-encompassing cult of volunteer units, veterans' associations, shooting clubs and special privileges for anyone in uniform grew up from a relatively trivial real military experience of a few weeks of lopsided fighting. More pleasantly, most of these associations were just fronts for colossal drinking bouts and the paunchy reservist became a standard satirical figure. Bismarck himself, who had never really fought anybody, and Kaiser Wilhelm II, who had not even been a cadet, set the pace in a laughable scrapyard of breastplates, ornamental sword pommels and ever sillier helmets. Perhaps a micro-history of the German empire could be written from the point of view of the networks of perhaps quite amusing individuals who actually designed this stuff, or just of the merchants who dealt in ostrich feathers.

These were also wars in which a surprising number of people had been killed, but over such a brief period and in such a swirl of patriotic euphoria that, however much devastated private grief the deaths might have generated, it was viewed as an acceptable 'blood-price' for unification. In my pan-German fossicking for curious memorials to the Second Reich, I found in a dark corner of a church in Mühlhausen, propped mouldering against the wall, a large wooden board covered in white Gothic script listing the names of local men who had died in the Austro-Prussian War. For such a small town it had an alarming number of names. This was, as far as I could find, a unique survival, but every town had its memorial to the Franco-Prussian War and – again a brief conflict – the names really stacked up: fifty for this town, a hundred for that.

In several battles of the war the Prussians had been massacred even if they had ultimately won. There was a clear implication that modern weapons (which were being revoltingly refined every year) in a war which proved less one-sided could have a quite new effect. This was to be found out by the grandchildren of the victors of Königgrätz and Sedan and the children of the harmlessly posturing, beer-enhanced military clubbers of the 1880s. What would happen in a long war and what the point of such a ghastly investment of lives might be was not something which military or civilian leaders had to think through after the astonishing victories of their newly mighty armies in the 1860s.

Already however in the Franco-Prussian War itself there were disturbing signs of how hard it was for the military rulers of Prussia and then Germany (as it became at the end of the war) to separate political and military questions. The Battle of Sedan was so brilliantly handled that this should have marked the point at which a treaty was signed. Instead, the army pointlessly besieged Paris and began to suffer from guerrilla warfare from an increasingly enraged French population. The war ultimately ended with France an insurrectionary, bitter disaster area and with the fateful decision to annexe Alsace-Lorraine, partly for the usual specious strategic-security reasons (Hitler wound up annexing most of Europe without improving his strategic position) but also because of the curse of history: too many nationalist medievalist obsessives wanted to welcome home this ancient part of the Holy Roman Empire, despoiled by Louis XIII, XIV and XV. The Austrians had in 1866 been almost happy to be defeated and soon became Germany's key ally. This was impossible for the French and set both sides on a specific, disastrous course for the following eighty years. Whatever damage was done by jingoistic soldier-worship in creating united Germany, it was nothing compared to the original sin of grabbing Alsace-Lorraine.

The aftermath of the wars was the declaration of the German empire in the Palace of Versailles in 1871. The oddness of this ceremony has often been commented on. It partly came from the continuing war and the degree to which most German princes were hanging around in France anyway, but it also came from a genuine problem that there would have been no location within Germany in which such a ceremony would have been acceptable. Everyone going red in the face and waving their swords around in fealty would for the Badenese or Saxons or Bavarians have been totally impossible in Berlin, the inner sanctum of Prussianism.

Huge efforts were made to ensure that although the emperor just *happened* to be also the King of Prussia, it was understood that at a royal level at least the new empire was still a bit federal and evasive – if you were a royal who had come through the chaos of the 1860s with your territory intact then you could just keep going. Ambassadors continued to be exchanged within Germany as though Bavaria or indeed Schwarzburg-Rudolstadt was still independent. Leipzig railway station, now stuffed with some two hundred shops, is the world's largest simply because of the farcical need to make it both a Reich and a Saxon terminus, with separate grand entrance ways for the Kaiser and for the King. No German emperor (well, there were only three anyway) was ever crowned because such a ceremony would have been so ersatz, but also so confusing. So even at a point when Germany had 'united' it still kept the stubborn obscurantism and federalism which makes it such an attractive place today. Only the brief twelve-year interlude of Nazism ever forced Germany into a pseudo-coherent frame, albeit by bringing back the medieval term 'Gau' – comparable to 'shire' – as the seemingly rational new administrative unit, but these as it proved temporary arrangements did nothing to erase older localist habits.

This brings everything back to thinking about Schaumburg-Lippe. Dozy and absurd, the principality is now just a small area of a neither-here-nor-there corner of Lower Saxony. Through the guile of Adolf I it came through the traumas of unification intact, and Adolf could stand shoulder to shoulder with Kaiser Wilhelm or enjoy a joke with Ludwig II of Bavaria. But the tiny memorial to the dead of the Franco-Prussian War, with its little statue of Victory so shoddy that it might just be a cheaply recycled decoration from some dilapidated orangery, has wound up carrying far more weight than it intended. Becoming entangled in the German empire was, for even its most rural and minor elements, going to prove to be an unlimited liability.

A surprise trip to Mexico

The broad area outside St Stephen's Cathedral in Vienna is one of those terrible tourist zones – like Covent Garden in London or the Place Georges Pompidou in Paris – which raise real questions about the nature of humanity. A sort of chimps' tea-party of baffled tour groups, petty criminals and people dressed as Mozart drift listlessly about in a fog of mutual incomprehension and boredom. I do not say this from any lofty position, having just dropped chocolate ice-cream all over my shoes. Italians seemed to be the majority of the tour groups, drawn perhaps by the unhappy historical tangle which has so often pitted Austrians and Italians against each other, and expressing through their gestures and the angles of their heads their sense of dismay at the reality of life in the ill-kempt heart of the old enemy.

I had flattered myself that I had been pretty hardened by the street performers of Covent Garden, but an amazing new level of stupidity was introduced outside St Stephen's Cathedral by a man break-dancing on his head while pretending to fart at his audience while also singing snatches of Puccini. I later saw him in a drunken row with someone painted entirely silver, presumably an off-duty Mozart statue. As part of this farrago, but far more worth watching, there was a troupe of bulky Mexican Indians dressed only in extravagant feathers, leather and shells, there to protest over Austria's continuing ownership of 'Montezuma's Head Dress'. This object may or may not have belonged to Montezuma but is undoubtedly a very ancient and beautiful Mexican artefact in Habsburg hands at least since the days of Archduke Ferdinand II at Schloss Ambras, who had thought it was a 'Moorish' head-dress. (Oh, *why* are old rulers so ethnographically disappointing? James I of England owned a suit of Japanese armour which he thought belonged to 'the Great Mogul'.) An interesting history of the world could be written entirely consisting of accounts of total mutual incomprehension and ignorance. In any event, these Mexicans dance a bit and then berate the dazed crowd with a fervour that puts the juggling fire-eater and the Emperor Joseph II singing statue to shame.

The Habsburg engagement in Mexico may have been a longstanding one, but the Austrian branch of the family, even if many of its members were raised in Spain, bailed out from any serious interest in the New World very early on, leaving the money and the headaches to their Spanish cousins. This changed in the 1860s when Napoleon III came up with the ingenious idea of setting up Franz Joseph's younger brother, Maximilian, as emperor there. The more anyone reads about Napoleon III the more horrifying he becomes – his sheer *childishness* and role as a sort of Lord of Misrule in the mid-nineteenth century caused quite as much damage as Bismarck. Indeed it could be argued that the chaotic, hyperactive yet ineffectual nature of France in this period made Bismarck possible and necessary.

In any event, the Mexican adventure was a Napoleon III classic: it stemmed from what seemed a fair certainty that the United States was breaking apart. While quietly pleased about this, most European countries remained neutral, but Napoleon III saw an opportunity to carve out a French empire in Mexico and cut a deal with the Confederate States of America which would give him an entirely new and grand field of operations. The frivolity of packing off thousands of baffled rural conscripts to fight and get killed in Mexico now seems breathtaking, but we have the advantage of knowing that Napoleon misjudged every aspect of the situation, a French-backed Mexican monarchy being almost the single most offensive thing possible if you happened to be a rapidly recovering, angry and reunited United States. Prussia's increasingly threatening stance meant that Napoleon had to withdraw most of his troops so that they could be beaten at home at the end of the decade, leaving Maximilian with almost no support and eventual execution.

Maximilian does seem to have been a rare example of a smart Habsburg (indeed there was a persistent rumour that his real father was Napoleon I's son, the short-lived Duke of Reichstadt – which would explain it) and he had carved out a pleasant life for himself developing the port of Trieste, ruling bits of Italy, running the Habsburg navy and designing a palace on the Adriatic which he never lived to see completed. Still only in his late twenties and fresh from a fun trip to Brazil, it must have seemed at least plausible that he could make his own empire, even if he must have been in part aware that Napoleon III only saw him as a bit of class with which to dress up some inept piracy. His reign lasted three years, political disturbance meaning that he was never crowned, and by any stretch it was all a fiasco. All that remains of his reign is Mexico City's Paseo de la Reforma, built by an Austrian engineer at Maximilian's instigation – and formerly if briefly known, in honour of Maximilian's wife Charlotte (briefly Carlota), as the Paseo de la Emperatriz, plus some superb uniforms and (an unintended by-product) Manet's famous paintings of his execution. In the matchless History of the Army Museum in Vienna, there is a set of Prussian-style metal helmets for Maximilian's bodyguard, but with the spikes replaced by the Mexican eagle-snake-cactus combination and the whole lot given a coating of gold-plate. These gorgeous objects (together with a genuine Imperial sombrero) make it appear, perhaps rightly, that more time was spent designing Habsburg gewgaws than in working out how to rule an enormous, fractured and ancient country with no interest in an Austrian emperor with a Belgian wife backed by French troops.

This regrettable and needless incident robbed Franz Joseph of a useful brother, drove their mother, Sophie of Bavaria, into a depression from which she never recovered and tipped Maximilian's widow into lunacy. At the time Franz Joseph was recovering from the humiliation of his armies by the Prussians at Königgrätz and the loss of Italy, but Maximilian's execution began the long, strange process by which Franz Joseph found himself through bad luck, longevity and his own dreary personality shedding entire generations of Habsburg support as his endless reign lumbered along. Close relatives shot themselves, became transvestites, were assassinated or died of typhoid, while the droningly diligent uniform-obsessive continued his decades upon decades of bureaucratic routine at the Schönbrunn and Hofburg palaces, a routine varied by equally boring hunting trips, all the way to the middle of the First World War.

Possibly the tedium of Franz Joseph was a clever response to the intractable issues that surrounded him. Maximilian's exploits at least had a freshness to them, whereas Franz Joseph was doomed to spend his life dealing with a mass of nationality issues which could never be resolved but only kept in play. If he had spent more time trying to get to grips with the Wallachians' burgeoning sense of Daco-Romanian romanticism it is not clear how helpful this would have been. The obscurantism and almost gleeful provinciality of the Hungarian gentry had been an annoying constant in Habsburg life ever since they had been unwisely released from Turkish bondage in the wars after the relief of the siege of Vienna. But it was only a limited help to Franz Joseph that Slovak, Romanian, Croat and Serbian hatred for the Hungarians meant that he never had to deal with a united front against himself. As the empire was only held together by the existence of the monarch, wearing a variety of different crowns, Franz Joseph and his ever more ankylosed regime had to be just as suspicious of German nationalism as Romanian, leaving German-speaking Bohemians and Austrians in positions of exposed and doubtful privilege.

It has been endlessly argued whether the sheer length of Franz Joseph's reign held the empire together – much like wallpaper holding together an otherwise shot and mouldering plaster wall – or whether a more normal change of regime, with Franz Ferdinand taking over in 1900 or so, could have saved it. This is unknowable, but just as Wilhelm I's long and latterly dotard reign can be seen as a disaster for Prussia (Bismarck's semi-dictatorship would patently have ended the moment Wilhelm's son had been allowed to take over), it is hard not to think that Franz Joseph's very existence, supervising Central Europe from early railway-building to the invention of the aerial bomber, was unhelpful. His reign saw the amazing process whereby cities such as Prague and Pressburg (Bratislava) became filled by a new, non-German-speaking working class. Literacy no longer meant writing in German (or Latin in Hungary) but instead in the local and increasingly national language, with figures such as Smetana and even Dvořák having through sheer will-power to make themselves capable of writing in Czech. These are among the most dramatic events of the nineteenth century – a process which continues to unravel unpredictably and sometimes violently today. In the light of the many disasters lying in wait for the descendants of these first nationalists, it is hard not to feel that the Habsburg empire was, right up to its very end, a worthwhile organization, smashed to pieces by a world war it did not want.

I enjoy Austro-Hungarian nostalgia as much as anyone and have had great flurries of reading Joseph Roth and Stefan Zweig, mentally putting away my hussar's uniform for the last time while humming a melancholy air, my tears dropping with tiny plops into an espresso. When I first visited Vienna in the early 1990s it was still a time-warped cul-de-sac, an ageing and bitter place only just beginning to feel the implications of the Iron Curtain's disappearance. By 2009 it had become again what its geographical location naturally made it – the point at which German, Italian, Hungarian and Slav criminals intersect, with the European Union as a soft, unmoustachioed version of the empire. This seems in the end a very happy development with enough historical twists and turns to make the Habsburgs seem very distant rather than regretted. Walking around outside St Stephen's Cathedral, though, it was hard not to imagine the pleasure of seeing troops in really beautiful uniforms (approved by Franz Joseph) using canister shot to clear a path through the tour groups and farting breakdancers.

CHAPTER TWELVE

Lambs and ladybirds » Jigsaw country »
Hunting masters » Ruritania, Syldavia and their friends »
An absence

Lambs and ladybirds

The doubtful pleasures of German unification were symbiotically linked to the explosion in German *things* – objects and drinks of previously only local interest which could now be spread through new transport systems to create a network of tastes and brands which we still have to live with today.

My least favourite example of these is marzipan – a highly specialized material which I can just about manage under the controlled circumstances of an English Christmas cake, but which otherwise has some of the untouchable qualities of cat faeces. This is all just unacceptable personal prejudice, of course, but there seem to be a number of uses of sugar that waste everyone's time and money and warp the lives of those obliged to make them. But setting aside such grim materials as nougat and Edinburgh rock, and the horrors of dragées, the real disaster is Lübeck marzipan and its high temple, the Neideregger shop. Neideregger is a classic example of a business that used simply to be a local problem, but which as the nineteenth century progressed was able to manipulate railways and press advertising to pump its products into a far wider world. My already vexed relationship with Thomas Mann took a further bad turn when I read one of his letters from after his family's move from Lübeck to Munich, where he excitedly recounts the arrival of a box of Neideregger marzipan to brighten his Christmas.

The shop is a temple to a particular kind of kitsch, perhaps one-third jokey and two-thirds felt to be artistic. Giant models of the Brandenburg Gate, the Eiffel Tower, the Houses of Parliament, all made of hundredweights of marzipan, crowd the windows, while inside there are row upon row of miniaturized marzipan fruit, farm animals, lobsters and so on. I have a robust capacity for sugar but the idea of even the smallest taste of marzipan potato makes me feel on the verge of some systemic shutdown. I feel a mad pleasure in handling the marzipan cauliflowers or tiny baskets of marzipan fish, while feeling the erratic throbs and lurches of my internal organs keenly aware of nearby danger.

In the end, after a surprise encounter in a Lüneberg sweetshop, convulsed with self-hatred, I bought a marzipan lamb with a facial expression of such happy imbecility that it had to be brought home. Here, in the manner of W. G. Sebald, is a photo of him admiring a little matchbox portrait of Kaiser Wilhelm II:

For the past few months the children have taken turns hiding him in ludicrous locations around the house (on the toilet, in the fridge, inside a cereal packet – he had a long stint on the car dashboard where he went sort of melty). He has had some family educational value though as an example of evolution in action – through a brilliant genetic stroke a lamb avoids all risk of being eaten by being born made of marzipan.

Anyway, marzipan is just one of the many unwanted objects that leaked through the arteries of Germany's new markets. There were so many of these: the absolutely impossible card-game of Skat, invented in the early nineteenth century in Altenburg and making that appealing town oddly prosperous ever since; the flood of nut-cracker dolls and garden gnomes from Thuringia which had only ever been a local menace before; the almost inedible Nuremberg gingerbread (although I may have, to be fair, been unlucky in my encounters with it). This spread has not led to uniformity; for example, there remains today a clear demarcation line between wine and non-wine Germany. Equally you can tell when you move away from the Worms-focused pretzel belt, or the central zone from Saxony to Hesse where you can be confident of decent street bratwurst. This irrepressible localism is, of course, one of the keys to Germany's charm – the marzipan and gingerbread might be universal but there is in parallel always an insistence on local beer, local wine, a specific kind of cake. The evolutionary model works for all kinds of things and some thrive and go national, but some never get anywhere. Bremen, for example, has a very odd black-and-white sort of cake which seems to have been made up in the hope of emulating the stranglehold of Nuremberg gingerbread, but which has been justly shunned, outside a handful of desperate-looking bakeries east of the cathedral.

The innumerable different forms of high-intensity alcohol were also for the most part an industrial creation of the nineteenth century – previously small and local and suddenly able to be made on a national scale, making schnapps as characteristic a mass German product as pianos or guns. As a timorous but insistent enthusiast for these sorts of drinks I have tried so many that I have really lost track, beyond noticing whether they leave a burning or a sticky sensation. Long evenings have gone by in one of the snug bars at the Kaiser Friedrich III in Bremen working through the landlord's astonishing selection, most startling perhaps the little-known but enjoyably named Prussian Mouthful, which at that point in the evening struck me as so hilarious that I wanted immediately to change the name of this book to *A Prussian Mouthful*, before being dissuaded, perhaps wrongly. It tastes like something that might be used to clean rust from girders and can be recommended to nobody.

Many years ago I triumphantly returned from then Soviet-ruled Latvia with a bottle of Riga Black Balsam, the unwanted invention of a German chemist in the eighteenth century and a rather cursed gift to my parents (who were hardened and happy Scotch, Calvados and Cointreau drinkers). We would occasionally tip out a bit into a small glass (it looks rather like medium heavy crude) while we discussed whether or not it needed to be mixed with something else, or whether or not its unalluring viscosity meant it had gone off and was now actively dangerous. My own kitchen is now littered with briefly opened then shut bottles of Korn, Kummel, Aquavit and so on and it is understood that it would be unwelcome if I were to rub my hands together and suggest we unbend with a spot of some horror leeched from plums. The last straw in what I had thought of as a harmless, high-proof drinking adventure was a Bavarian Obstler (in a salt-fired stone bottle) which when opened filled the air with an unbearable smell exactly like the fluid ladybirds squirt everywhere when frightened.

What is curious about all these drinks is that they are so nationally specific. They have in many cases moved from being a local problem into a national one, but have gone no further. This is partly of course to do with twentieth-century history – it would be very odd if any of Germany's neighbours chose to mark a special occasion with the help of a swift Prince Bismarck. But the rest of the world is not needed, given the enthusiasm with which Germans themselves drink the products of a simple industrial process involving doing things to grain and perhaps a few unlucky fruit. Proudest of all German liqueur brands is Jägermeister (Hunting Master), an alcoholic herb and root drink emitted by factories in Wolfenbüttel, where there is also a richly comic corporate shop where you can buy Jägermeister sports clothing, camping equipment, bathrobes and so on. Jägermeister was a relative late-comer, having only been sold since 1934. New drinks can be invented any time, but it adds an extra layer of oddity that something so gormless should have a quite accidentally Nazi element – a curious example of ordinary things happening at less than ordinary times.

Jägermeister is the only German liqueur ever found in airport shops, which will be stuffed with rubbish like raspberry-flavoured Bacardi or Wild African Cream, a sort of Bailey's in a fake leopard-skin bottle, but shuns such classics as Prince Bismarck, suggesting that even Germans going abroad want to leave this stuff behind. As so often, I sometimes wonder whether, just as Germans are all in fact happily tucking into dishes loaded with nam pla or vindaloo paste while I'm the one left with the sausages, so Germans are washing down their baltis with glasses of Chilean shiraz or a Nastro Azzuro while I'm the one left choking on the Prussian Mouthful.

Jigsaw country

I have never found mountains particularly interesting. Through various accidents they have not really featured much in my life. I once climbed Scafell Pike – England's very own highest mountain – via an indirect and rather remote and challenging route and, my lungs burning, cheeks heaving and so on, I scrambled to the summit and found my momentary be-the-best-that-you-can-be mood fatally undermined by uncontrollable swarms of children, some of them virtual toddlers, the elderly, abandoned supermarket trolleys, the sick and the infirm who crowded the top ('summit' seems too strong a term here). It then struck me that it might have been a more intelligent use of life to have simply stayed true to the family creed and stayed in the attractive hotel with a book and a few drinks – that civilization lies in libraries and bars rather than on some shale-heaped lump with a culturally null view.

This feeling was reinforced after taking a steam train up the Brocken, a mountain outcrop in Saxony-Anhalt. With the whistle blowing and the smell of burning coal and the chugging of the engine and the merry waves of passers-by this was certainly enjoyable (for about four minutes) but as we approached the top the same sense of futility overwhelmed me. Surely mountains are the enemy: the dreary, semi-sterile protrusions which dot the landscape and make it uninhabitable. This is particularly stark in the case of the Brocken because it looks something like a hideous tumour covered in dirty ice, while from the peak you can look down on a happy landscape of farms and small towns, which are admittedly helped

out by the water pouring down the Brocken's sides. The Brocken
has always had an association with witchcraft and the uncanny, but
these are the enjoyable fantasies of people sitting in pubs down on
the distant plain. The only real pleasures of the peak were trying to
work out why people would want to stay in the hotel there and
admiring the enormous battery of electronic equipment perched on
the original 1930s transmission tower. The German obsession with
ensuring that all road signs be pure pictograms has resulted in a
unique red-edged monstrosity here that had to convey the information in a single image: that it was dangerous to get too close to
the transmission tower as under specific conditions huge, oddly
shaped blocks of ice clinging to the tower might come loose and
crash on top of you causing hideous maiming or death. Wandering
around the freezing footpaths, tensed against flying, irregular yet
lethal ice-shapes, and admiring the foxes rooting in the hotel bins,
I felt an absolute wish not to bother with mountains any more.

Unfortunately in Germany this is not really an option as, while
much of the country manages to avoid them (and I am excluding
here of course the delightful foothills of the non-Brocken Harz and
the Thuringian Forest), they are central to the existence of southern Bavaria and the Tyrol. I put off going anywhere near these
places for some years. This decision was reinforced by people
brightly suggesting that I should go to Berchtesgaden to see the
remains of Hitler's Alpine palace, an idea which both confirmed
my feeling that mountains are aesthetically pathetic (Hitler liked
them) and that places built for Nazi recreation should be very low
on any list.

One summer while we were growing up, my sister, slightly
younger than I, was given by some vicious relative an enormous
Ravensburger jigsaw of the usual Alpine kind: an onion-domed
church surrounded by dense, sunlit, uniformly green trees with, set
further back, a jagged white mountain and acres of blue sky. These
things were then reflected in an absolutely still pool of water which
filled the lower half the picture. This exercise in sadism almost ate
my sister's brain. An entire summer seemed to go by with this
cursed object filling the table as day by day she crazily mulled over

each of the thousands of pieces. It was like watching a mental version of the queen who danced herself to death in red-hot shoes. This pointless jigsaw-related tragedy did not help my view of the Alps. Indeed, pieces of music such as Strauss's *Alpine Symphony* or the more excitably fresh-air, pantheistic bits of Mahler's *Third Symphony* always seem to me to be music versions of a Ravensburger jigsaw and are completely spoilt as a result. Should one of the more minor bits of business transacted at the Potsdam conference in 1945 have been to send some troops down to Ravensburg (a little town in the Swabian Alps) and make sure the jigsaw factory never functioned again?

Ultimately I had no choice but to confront these inner demons and head off into the mountains as it seemed implausible to try to write a book about Germany without at the very least visiting Neuschwanstein and Innsbruck. Most of the train journey was spent wreathed in thick mist, which meant that the Alps more or less disappeared and it was not unlike taking a train through the Chilterns. The Allgäu region is stuffed with immense numbers of very pretty cows with clonking bells and lovely eyes – but after a while it becomes clear that this is a monoculture as sinister in its way as the vines of the Mosel Valley, only with hooves substituting for trellises and with a great, burping Nestlé factory lurking at the heart of it. But as I like milk chocolate as much as I like wine I am happy to turn a blind eye to this ferocious industrialization masquerading as loveable upland.

Neuschwanstein is famous both as Ludwig II's most spectacular homage to Wagner and as the castle the expense of which broke the patience of the Bavarian treasury. Ludwig was forced to abdicate and then died mysteriously, perhaps by throwing himself in humiliation and despair into a lake and drowning both himself and his doctor in the process. Nobody ever lived in Neuschwanstein, it was never finished and it was opened to the public only weeks after Ludwig's possible suicide. It was an inspiration for Disney's castle and through an enjoyable reverse-loop feed its owners now copy Disney techniques of timed entry tickets and super-saturation tchotchkes. Ludwig's relationship with Wagner was clearly a very important one and the Bayreuth Festival Hall only exists at all thanks to Ludwig's or rather Bavaria's money. But one thing I absolutely refused to research for this book is Wagner's own feelings about Ludwig. Wandering around Neuschwanstein it is clear that what he took from Wagner was something really very tacky – a world of simpering maidens and bovine heroes painted in immense almost talent-free frescoes all over the castle walls. Each room has a different opera as its theme and the momentary pleasure of the place comes only from trying to work out which is what. Is this immense, completely stifling and unengaging woodland scene from *Siegfried*? Or from *Parzifal*? Who is that dim-looking girl in a wimple (too many options!)? I have never been an obsessive fan of Wagner, but I certainly like him well enough not to want to have answered the question: did Wagner like these wall paintings? If the composer himself felt that his music – which seems sometimes to achieve an almost unique level of stifling imaginative pressure – was accurately portrayed in Ludwig's journeyman vision then it is all over. My sneaking anxiety is that he *did* like them – sketches of the original sets for *Lohengrin* look suspiciously dopey. Perhaps it is inevitable that stagecraft dates as cruelly as special effects in the movies, but I would like to think of Wagner's musical mental picture streaming light years ahead of what could actually be achieved on stage. I just don't want to know unless the news is good.

In any event Ludwig's homage to Wagner at Neuschwanstein has proved to be a desperate failure. Even though you wade through Ludwig-related rubbish almost up to your mouth (mouse mats, tea-towels, lushly written biographies, fridge magnets, ashtrays, all coated in his creepy features), the castle shop has almost nothing on Wagner at all. The cult of this puerile loony continues to flourish, fed by coach after coach of generally rather odd people. (What are they doing in the Allgäu at all? How can they be interested in this sad figure? I guess the romantic cult of Ludwig never really reached Britain.) Wagner himself remains completely sidelined, leaving the notional shrine as merely a residue posh excess – the thousands of pieces of mosaic in the forever unfinished throne-room of an extinct dynasty, the yet further turrets that will never be built, the completely ugly wood-carved room in which Ludwig was reading when he received the news that he was at last being fired.

The only thing to be said in Ludwig's favour was that once he had signed the paper ending Bavaria's independent existence he refused to go to Versailles for the gross hailing of the Kaiser. He was also interesting simply because he showed in perhaps its most horrible form the degree to which some Germans had become absolutely worm-eaten with medievalism. The idea that he built at Linderhof (which I absolutely refuse to visit) a fantasy of Hunding's Hut from *The Valkyrie* in which he would hold Germanic oath feasts seems just beyond idiocy.

The Wittelsbach dynasty lurched along, past Ludwig's sad, institutionalized brother Otto, through Regent Luitpold, a sort of Kris Kringle lookalike, who kept a commendably cold distance from Prussia, particularly during the absurdities of Bismarck's anti-Catholic agitation, and then, very briefly, Ludwig III, who was similarly elderly and also looked like Kris Kringle, before the whole lot fizzled out in 1918, ending a rule over Bavaria that could be traced back to the twelfth century – or in madder moods to the ninth. They had ups and downs and at various points were a faithless or incompetent lot, but it seems sad that ultimately they should be remembered for these infantile Alpine fantasies.

Hunting masters

Growing up in south-east England, we used occasionally to go on family walks through the countryside, sometimes just rambling aimlessly and sometimes with a specific goal, such as finding various wildflowers. One of my father's many cheerful habits was to give these on the face of it slightly dull outings excitement by suddenly freezing still and gesturing to us all to be silent whenever a bush rustled. We would then hold our breaths, waiting to see what came out. Of course, it being England, it could never be anything even faintly galvanizing – indeed almost always it was a questing thrush. But just for a moment (I was fairly young) my father's gesture would suggest a real chance that a feared Gila monster might lurch from the little hawthorn.

I can only blame these outings for a continuing sense, as an adult, of the terrifying possibilities implied by going on a walk. In Germany, all my woodland and mountain meanderings have been tinged by a bogus sense of slight danger. The big signs in the Harz Mountains promising lynx and wild boar always set my heart racing, puffing along quite alone and without even a walking stick to fend off these killing-machines. Indeed, given how much time I have spent fruitlessly looking for boar, wading up to my ankles in beech mast (the boar's favourite food!) strewn like giant breakfast cereal over the forest floor, staring between the trunks looking for boar, it would be a bit love–death if one did actually kill me. Even as I was being disembowelled I would simply have to laugh at the irony that I had finally, finally encountered that tusky lord of the deciduous woods.

The huge scale of even the central German forests where you can, albeit with a certain amount of artistry, get views of tens of thousands of trees reaching into the haze, does imply a closer relationship to ancient European megafauna than in Britain, where by the Middle Ages everything bigger than a badger or a deer had been wiped out. Wolves and bears remained a potent element in many lives until the seventeenth century. There is a sad little stone memorial kept in the Darmstadt provincial museum commemorating the last wolf to be killed in Hesse and in Sigmaringen there is the actual, stuffed last ever Upper Danube wolf, albeit much repaired with what looks like low-grade industrial teddy-bear fur. Further east and south-east, wolves remained a serious problem into the nineteenth century, particularly after major wars. After the Austro-Ottoman war which ended in 1718, in the brutally depopulated regions beyond the Military Zone (in what would now be Serbia) there are descriptions of packs a thousand strong forcing the very few travellers to take substantial military escorts. Any long-term war would see wolf populations rapidly soar, with a matching campaign in the war's aftermath to exterminate them. The availability of more or less uninhabited woods in central Germany,

Austria and Bohemia allowed wolf packs to melt away for some generations and resurge quickly when the chance showed itself. For most Germans, though, wolves became by the seventeenth century at latest merely a folk memory – but an important one that was to spill into nineteenth-century legends and stories in heaps of ways, impinging just enough even now to allow for some slight thrill in the midst of the Thuringian Woods, with their sombre glades, stifling silences and carefully marked hiking paths.

The serious access enjoyed by Germans to megafauna used to be in East Prussia, particularly in the Rominten Wilderness (a region now split between Poland and the Russian exclave of Kaliningrad, based around the formerly German city of Königsberg). This was the very area over which for centuries the Teutonic Knights and the Lithuanians had fought – a remorseless tangle of misty forest and swamp of no value in itself but providing a neutral zone in which raiding parties could get lost, go mad and starve. It was forests like this and similar, seemingly endless tracts further south which sheltered amazing creatures – occasionally interrupted by baffled people in chainmail – such as tarpan, aurochs and bison, with stuff like wolves, lynx and boar almost on the defensive.

By the time East Prussia was coalescing into a reasonably peaceful and straightforward piece of German land in the seventeenth century it was already too late for the tarpan: the ancestral wild horse was last recorded there in 1627 (the very last one in existence, probably itself cross-bred hopelessly with domestic stock, died in a Ukrainian zoo in 1918). The aurochs, the ancestral wild cattle, a creature of dazing size preserved in a handful of skeletal remains, disappeared from Prussia even earlier, with a handful of final reports from Poland coming in during the early seventeenth century. The last Prussian bison was spotted in 1755.

The memory of these huge animals continued to stalk Rominten and nineteenth-century illustrators loved to do drawings of aurochs fighting off wolf packs. Kaiser Wilhelm II was obsessed with Rominten, built himself an extravagant lodge there and spent as much time as he could gunning down elk and other big-antlered objects in a pathetically one-sided and pointless contest. As usual with Wilhelm everything seemed frenetic and a bit depressing – the atmosphere of gun-oil, hipflasks, special feathered hats and hour upon hour of male badinage cannot have made Rominten a fun spot. But what Wilhelm saw there was an image of a murky, feudal, mythical Germany, of Teutonic Knights and the forest scenes from *Siegfried*, with a dragon hidden in some impossibly distant cave.

As usual with German medievalism, the fact that access came thanks to telephones, electricity, internal combustion engines and a massive tax base was not allowed to intrude. Indeed, perhaps one of the reasons Wilhelm is so odd a figure is that his reign so precisely marks the point when the iconography of horses, special costumes and deference is swept away by inventions which – while they find their apotheosis in the First World War – are already changing everything in the previous decade. Whereas in the 1880s the bulk of Europe's population would be dealing routinely with horses (the breeding of which was an East Prussian speciality), by 1918 everything pointed to the Stuttgart-invented future of cars and motorcycles. Hitler barely touched a horse and lived a petrol-based fantasy, with the Third Reich's iconography entirely horseless, even when, in practice, the Eastern Front required astronomical numbers of pack animals. Certainly nobody would have dreamt of commemorating any of Hitler's actions in a statue of him on horseback – a problem that has indeed more generally plagued military sculpture throughout the twentieth century as a bronze staff car and driver obviously would not work.

But the Kaiser, with his gun and his toadies, creeping through the Rominten bogs would not have imagined that as he royally shot stag after stag he was ending a regal tradition as old as the idea of kingship itself. Indeed, for many German princes it has been argued that they spent more time hunting than ruling, raising unmanageable questions about what royalty was really for. Many mid-range eighteenth-century German princes, in heavy obeisance to the example of Louis XIV, would do little else but hunt, leaving large parts of the country still dotted with pretty lodges but rather denuded of animals. In case we should imagine that the Kaiser, with his mega-rifle, was uniquely unbalancing the man–animal relationship, these baroque hunts were no less ridiculous. Often the royal involved, with favoured guests, would stand on the edge of a pen and as deer were released into the pen, would kill them with a bow and arrow. There were also bizarre, vanished variants such as the baffling Saxon royal sport of fox-tossing where, in front of hundreds of happy onlookers, dozens of foxes would be chucked up and down in blankets in the courtyard of the Dresden palace until they died.

Of course Rominten came to a bad end. The First World War had seen the area briefly threatened by an invading Russian army and, in a horrible parody of traditional Prussia, bored and hungry German troops in the Polish forests gunned down many of the surviving bison there with their howitzers – the idea of modern artillery and lumbering, snuffly herbivores intersecting in this way is peculiarly distressing.

Herman Göring among the Nazis most directly inherited the Prussian lust for hunting and declared himself Reich Hunting Master. From his bitter exile in Holland (where he spent much of his time shooting every living thing on his estate there), the Kaiser refused to sell his hunting lodge to Göring, who was obliged to build his own. The rather sinister, if compelling, East Prussia provincial museum in Lüneburg, a town some six hundred miles away from East Prussia where many East Prussian refugees settled after their flight from their homeland in 1945, has colossal sets of antlers from deer killed by Göring's favoured guests quite late in the war (including the antlers of 'The Mammoth', a fabled whopper shot in 1942). Göring was obsessed with the missing megafauna (and had hunting costumes quite as daft as the Kaiser's) and became involved with the quixotic project of the Heck brothers in Munich, begun in the 1920s, to try to 'reverse engineer' tarpans and aurochs through selective breeding. This resulted in some slightly odd-looking horses and large bulls but was genetically, of course, a joke.

Attached to the Kaiser's hunting lodge was a royal chapel dedicated to St Hubertus, patron of hunters – a typically inane Wilhelmine gesture. This featured a bronze statue of a stag which, after many unguessable wartime adventures, wound up decorating a children's playground in Smolensk, a happy ending for at least one aspect of a strange German inheritance. The exiled Kaiser died in the summer of 1941, three years before the historical German presence in Rominten (where a hunting lodge had first been built for his great-great-great-great-granduncle, Frederick William I of Brandenburg-Prussia) was erased by defeat and disaster in the Second World War – a war fought by the Nazis imbued with many of the more disgusting and weird ideas that had been floating around these forests for many years.

Ruritania, Syldavia and their friends

There are many dozens of towns scattered across Germany which immediately make the word 'Ruritanian' spring into your brain. Ruritania was the invention of Anthony Hope, a cheerful and clever English barrister, who enjoyed writing stories set in made-up places. Invented countries were not new of course (Utopia, Lilliput; even California began as a fictional country), but *The Prisoner of Zenda*, published in 1894, was the sensation that gave the fantasy of a time-warped little country a fresh impetus. It made Hope extremely rich and crystallized a particular idea of German political organiza-tion shortly after the nineteenth century had effectively rubbed out such places. Of course, Ruritania's location is in practice rather unclear and its political rough-and-tumble unlikely in the painfully overregulated and somnolent world of the real German micro-state. In many ways Hope is making fun not so much of Germany (although the cultural milieu is undoubtedly German) as of the new states of south-east Europe – the details sometimes seem as much Serbian or Greek as purely German.

The overwhelming success of *The Prisoner of Zenda* led to numer-ous stage plays and movies and a rash of imitators, who enjoyed a nutty framework which allows an infinity of ridiculous castles, archaic, lovingly described customs and scheming queen-mothers, all floating happily free of actual historical events. Everyone will have their own lists – Hergé's Tintin stories *The Calculus Affair* and

King Ottakar's Sceptre ('Even at this moment those scoundrels may be trying to steal your sceptre!') are glowing riffs on Ruritania, with Syldavia a zany mass of clicking heels, aides-de-camp, lemon-yellow uniforms, monocles and big-shirted revolutionaries fighting it out against a backdrop of (as revealed in *Destination Moon*) disturbingly enormous deposits of uranium. The evil republic of Borduria (khaki, cropped hair, big statues, secret police, a generalized gloom) makes repeated but fruitless attempts to destabilize Syldavia, a country entirely reliant on a quiffed Belgian journalist of an uncertain age for its defence.

Thomas Mann's *Royal Highness* is an uncharacteristically relaxed novel for him and a classic Ruritanian work, with the book's pleasure lying in the breathless elaboration of his Grand Duchy's Schloss, the Grimmburg, not to be confused with the 'formal, gracious beauty' of the summer palace at Hollerbrunn, and the panoply of advisers, customs, special rooms and so on, all being derided yet also rather revered, simply as an enjoyable stream of invention. In the same breath one could mention Captain W. E. Johns' *Biggles Goes to War*, where the redoubtable British pilot supports the plucky inhabitants of Maltovia against the double-dyed fiends of Lovitzna, possibly the only context in which the crusty captain and the Master of Lübeck slightly intersect. Examples of Ruritanian fiction indeed close in from all sides, with even Winston Churchill having a go with Laurania, subject of his only published novel, *Savrola*. I should probably stop just by mentioning the funniest, George Macdonald Fraser's magnificent Victorian pastiche *Royal Flash* (1970), set in the too plausible Duchy of Strackenz ('"Don't dare to order me about, you cabbage-eating bastard," says I. "I am a British officer"') and the most amiable, Antal Szerb's *Oliver VII* (1942), with its sardine- and wine-exporting little state of Alturia, packed with the usual panoply of enjoyments ('. . . his hair, which was unusually straight for an Alturian') and a cheerless neighbour in Norlandia, with its gloomy skies and obsession with money.

The wobbling location of Ruritania and its variants reflects the numerous opportunities for Ruritanian behaviour among German princes, of which there were so many that they could be packed off to deal with the royal needs of many of Europe's nineteenth-century monarchies. A quintessential petty German state, Hohenzollern-Sigmaringen is scattered along the banks of a little bit of the Upper Danube. Its rulers were maddened with humiliation at being just the junior branch of the same family that was otherwise in charge of *the whole of Prussia* and they successfully grabbed at the chance to become the royal family for Romania. A junior prince of Hesse tried to start an abortive royal family for Bulgaria, while the tiny Wettin territory of Saxe-Coburg-Gotha generated royal families for Portugal, Bulgaria and Belgium as well as a husband for Queen Victoria. Indeed by descent Wettins have utterly outclassed their long-time, now crash-and-burn Prussian Hohenzollern rivals by being rulers to the present day of places as diverse as Barbados and Australia – not to mention their Bulgarian branch office managing to pull off the astonishing coup of getting their last king (Simeon II), at one time humiliated and forced into exile by the communists, elected as the country's prime minister, under the name Simeon Saxe-Coburg-Gotha.

Otto, second son of the madly pro-Greek king of Bavaria Ludwig I, was packed off to newly independent Greece in 1832, in a quintessentially Ruritanian move. His long reign was a disaster in all kinds of ways and a curious example of pre-German unification semi-imperialism, with Bavaria attempting in a highly constrained way to run Greece, albeit very unsuccessfully. Eventually Otto and his wife (a feisty daughter of the Grand Duke of Oldenburg) were kicked out and replaced by a teenage member of the Danish royal family (sometimes the past looks just odder and odder). One of the great Ruritanian shrines is the suite of rooms where the couple spent their gloomy exile back in the old and neglected palace of the Bishops of Bamberg. There they practised speaking Greek to each other every day and insisted on wearing forms of Greek dress of an archaic kind, waiting futilely to be called back. It must have been an extraordinary adventure for them to be packed off from Catholic, landlocked Bavaria to Orthodox, island-and-seawater-oriented Greece, spend thirty years in the sunshine alienating everybody, and then wind up back again in a draughty Bavarian palace.

There is a magnificent white marble bust of Otto in Greek costume which is perhaps poignant, and yet as so often with royals Otto clearly emits a general sense of not taking full advantage of what was on offer. For every dashing, clever, brave and artistic royal there are dozens of total blanks: imperious, not very bright, symbolic fodder staring drearily from official portraits and photos, floundering in a sea of acrimonious politics. Rudolph V of Ruritania and his British doppelganger in *The Prisoner of Zenda*, whether played by Stewart Grainger or Ronald Coleman or Christopher Plummer, have the lovely advantage over their real-life equivalents of being frozen in time, of always being dashing, always looking super in close-fitting uniforms, of always being about to get the girl. It is impossible not to think that the reign itself could only be a disappointment, a slough of weight-gain, infertility, querulous younger brothers, degrading sexual temptation, anarchist daggers and bourgeois agitation. Perhaps an unwatchably harsh sequel could be made with Rudolph sharing the fate of the real Otto, pacing up and down in Bamberg, declaiming to his now phantom subjects. *The Prisoner of Zenda* is so wonderful because it is such a chronologically constrained historical slice, shutting out the hidden trajectory of heroism which ends so many once glamorous careers: in a seedy, burned-out Robin Hood, in a prolix, cadging and elderly Hannibal.

An absence

In the Lower Saxon city of Brunswick (Braunschweig) there is a small museum built into the monastery behind the battered church of St Giles. The museum has a selection of objects illustrating Jewish life in Germany down the centuries, its origins lying in the nineteenth-century Braunschweig Patriotic Museum, whose probably very curious contents have been otherwise destroyed, stored or passed on. The centrepiece of the museum, which survived the Third Reich, is a series of painted wood panels and pieces of furniture from the nearby town of Hornburg. These were the most important fittings (ark, lamp, reader's platform) from a disused synagogue which was dismantled in 1925 and brought to Braunschweig.

This is a book about things that can now be seen in Germany, and what cannot be seen is anything much to do with Germany's Jews. The accidental rescue of the old Hornburg synagogue preserves it as a gloomy and isolated oddity. The unmanageably distressing Worms burial ground remains, and the much grander one in the Pankow district cemetery in Berlin, but (except in Prague, where Nazi plans to create a Museum of an Extinct Race preserved far more) otherwise many centuries of Jewish life have left horribly little trace. A range of post-war monuments, markers and symbolic pieces of rebuilding help, but in effect they all merely emphasize absence. At the other end of the German lands, in the Austrian-Hungarian border town of Eisenstadt, a small synagogue survives. This is only because the authorities moved so aggressively to expel the ancient Jewish population on the Nazi takeover of Austria (unfurling the traditional 'Free of Jews' banner across the main road) that by the time of the mass destruction of synagogues in the pogrom of 9 November 1938 it was already government property and therefore protected. There is a certain satisfaction in knowing that it was heavily used by Soviet Jewish troops until they evacuated Austria in 1955, but not much. In the museum next to the synagogue there are displays about different festivals. Purim features a large photo of Holocaust survivors in a refugee camp in 1946 celebrating by wearing their old camp clothing and with one of their number dressed in Nazi costume and made up to look like Hitler. The idea of the masquerade, the way the photo is taken, the expressions of those involved, make it a masterpiece of uneasiness, defiance and pain, living in the absolute outer reaches of black humour.

These fragments and the fate of the Jews under Nazism make it very difficult to focus on earlier German history without seeing it as a sort of prelude or fools' paradise. If this book has a serious point then it is as a record of the constant but necessary effort required to resist such backdating. To say that we deal with the Nazis too earnestly might sound frivolous, but I think it is true. The

killing of Europe's Jews stemmed from the pitiful ideas of a handful of inadequate cranks. Through a series of devastating military
and economic events, so many echelons of Germany's normal
leadership (albeit itself often anti-Semitic in a 'traditional' way)
were killed or discredited that these pitiful figures came to power.
Virulent anti-Semitism was a vital glue in making Nazism, but its
mass support came from Hitler's promise to make Germany great
again, with anti-Semitism only a minor element. It was a measure
of the despair and confusion of the time that so many Germans
were willing to concede the idea that defeat in 1918 and the
rise of communism was somehow to do with 'the Jews', but this
was thousands of miles from any endorsement of what became
Auschwitz. The process by which so many Germans came to par-
ticipate in or turn a blind eye to the Holocaust is a terrifying
example of how any group of humans can be led and misled, but
it is hard (albeit flattering to other nationalities who therefore get
off the hook) to see this as a specific, pre-programmed, exclusive
and inevitable *German* frame of mind.

I mention this now, in a section of this book dedicated to the
nineteenth century, because I will end in 1933 and it remains for
very obvious reasons not possible to write about Germany in any
form without addressing this issue. But the Jews of nineteenth-
century Germany and Austria have their own story and, despite
continuing discrimination, for the most part it is a very happy one.
It is extremely tempting to see this as delusive, carrying the seeds
of destruction within it, and so on – but it is simply not the case.
Germany had to be warped, torn and beaten, a generation killed
and its economy so ruined that its moral, political and social
fabric disintegrated and something terrible stepped in. Without
the wholly unlooked-for curse of a stalemated war in 1914 these
events would not have happened. The nineteenth-century world has
to be allowed its autonomy, with its events and views uncontami-
nated by the hideous ironies that seem to lie to hand from our own
post-Holocaust vantage point.

An immediate example of this is the 'Hep, hep' anti-Jewish
rioting that convulsed many German cities in the aftermath of the

Napoleonic Wars. These horrible events have never really been understood – contemporaries were baffled by them and they were not repeated as the century progressed. No Prussian cities were affected and this spasm of mob hatred died out for no better reason than it suddenly emerged. Starting in Würzburg in the summer of 1819 the riots spread south to Frankfurt and Darmstadt and then up and down the Rhine, engulfing notionally liberal cities such as Karlsruhe and Cologne and spreading as far north as Hamburg, where many Jews fled for safety to Denmark. Shops and houses were burnt down, Jews were killed, many more were severely beaten up and generally terrorized into leaving. Order was rapidly restored by the army and in most places the authorities seem to have been shocked and revolted by what had happened. The riots showed how odd the role of Jews in German society remained. The terrible chant of 'Hep! Hep! Slaughter all Jews!' which accompanied the street mobs everywhere seems to have been an acronym for 'Hierosolyma est perdita', 'Jerusalem is lost', apparently the cry of the crusaders in the Rhineland pogroms seven hundred years earlier. If ever there was a good example of how creepy an interest in history can be then this must be it – and it has a strong whiff of the sort of violent, right-wing pseudo-medieval pedantry of the contemporaneous students swearing undying brotherhood in the Wartburg.

The riots seem to have in part been a reaction to the chaotic status of Jews in Germany. Napoleon emancipated them but his defeat meant that many of the German states rolled out a fresh array of disabilities, in some cases (such as Frankfurt) attempting to recreate medieval levels of discrimination. This association between Napoleon and emancipation meant that many rulers tended to ignore the way that so much discrimination had in fact been removed by enlightened monarchs well before the Revolution. German states which still defined themselves by their Christianity (traditionally, but also in contrast to the godless French revolutionaries) battled to work out how to deal with this awkward non-Christian minority in their midst. The unimpressive but devout Prussian king Frederick William III refused to promote a Jewish soldier, not because he doubted his bravery or patriotism, but because he felt in his heart that the soldier should first convert to Christianity. Indeed this idea so obsessed him that he quashed all attempts by Berlin Jews to reform observances, abusing his role as their rather notional protector out of fear that lessening what he saw as the obscurantism and backwardness of Judaism would make the Jews less likely to convert. Frederick William's on the face of it deranged if internally consistent thinking would have a long history.

This highly complex swirl of motives, slights and confusion propelled the German–Jewish relationship until 1933. Until final emancipation in 1871, Jews continued to be torn between the wish to maintain their separate identity and their wish to overcome the mass of major and petty disabilities that governed their lives. Despite centuries of anti-Semitic fantasy, most German Jews were extremely poor in the early nineteenth century. The astonishing exception of the Rothschilds, who had escaped the rigours of the Frankfurt ghetto, could not hide the fact that most Jews worked in rough and marginal jobs, legally shut out from much of German society. The gradual and then quite rapid shaking-off of these disabilities is one of the nineteenth century's great stories, but it is one too often seen in isolation. The century was for many Germans regardless of religion a time of extraordinary excitement, with a sort of tidal wave of opportunities creating prosperity and mobility unimaginable in the crumbled, introvert, local planet in which almost everyone had lived. Towns which had hardly grown in size in centuries became unrecognizable, education was transformed. Professions such as banking, medicine, science, soldiering and the law became immense concerns – anyone in these roles in the 1870s would have had only the tiniest connection to what, in retrospect, seemed their obscurantist, dust-covered and ignorant equivalents from the 1770s. The Jews who entered these professions and became famous were only ever participating in a German-wide phenomenon and were, by definition, heavily outnumbered in everything they did. What came to be seen as their 'prominence' was always niche or local.

As the nineteenth century progresses it becomes ever more difficult even to see Jews as a coherent group. Traditionalists would have little to do with those eager to assimilate to the mainstream – both strands would join in dismay at the Eastern European Jews who at the end of the century were taken in sealed trains across Germany to Hamburg and Bremen to emigrate to the United States. For many Jews it was simply not problematic to be both Jewish and German, particularly as, in common with other European countries, confession became ever more adrift from government. Jews were, after all, used to being Jews and the agonies of how to deal with them were created not by Jews themselves but by the chaotic anxieties of rulers who felt they ruled at the behest of and under the critical eye of Baby Jesus. If you had little time for such stuff (whether you were Napoleon or Bismarck) then the pressure was off. It was only if nationalism itself became a religion (and only then once it had been injected with some truly pathetic ideas about race on top of the pathetic ones about language) that there could be any serious question about Jews not being as German as Lutherans.

One of the culminations of this German Jewishness was the famous engraving of Jewish officers and men commemorating Yom Kippur on a battlefield outside Metz during the Franco-Prussian War. Once a common sight in German Jewish homes, this allegory (based on a real, but much smaller-scale event) shows a huge ark of the law surrounded by many Jewish troops with, in the distance, German Christian soldiers guarding the service. With many thousands of Jewish combatants (three hundred and seventy-three receiving the Iron Cross), the war and the entire process of German unification seemed to show that there was nothing about being Jewish which prevented anyone from being German.

There was, though, widespread anti-Semitism within German society. The term itself was invented by the deeply confused and pathetic figure of Wilhelm Marr in his 1879 pamphlet *The Way to Victory for Germanness over Judaism*. Originally from Magdeburg, Marr had variously bummed around Austria, Switzerland, Frankfurt, Hamburg and Costa Rica (oddly), claiming at different times to be an anarchist or a communist or a nationalist. He had been a delegate at the 1848 parliament and in a very uncomfortable way he does show himself to be an heir to the Wartburg students. His ideas and his Anti-Semitic League had little impact and late in life he renounced anti-Semitism as, on further reflection, patently untrue, but he had established a poisonous if very small stream to which others would contribute.

Despite both casual and official anti-Semitism, German Jews found that they could create a sufficiently robust reality that it simply did not matter. Indeed, much as late-nineteenth-century Prussia was diverse and vigorous enough to turn out both the best militant German nationalists and the most articulate and derisive critics of that tradition, so German Jews adopted every imaginable position from pop-eyed king-and-country to doctrinaire communism, with the great unnoticed majority simply leading quiet German lives. So confusing and capacious is this world that it even throws out the invention of Zionism – the Austrian Theodor Herzl's astonishing, strange insight that the Jews should have their own home. This idea, which seems in so many ways to be steeped in traditional German particularism, began with the hope, again in some ways traditional (the emperor as the Jews' doubtful protector), that the Kaiser could carve out a protectorate for the Jews in Palestine.

Wilhelm II became keen on this idea but from very mixed motives, not least the dreamy perception that he could then wave goodbye to loads of the Jewish communists, satirists and intellectuals who thought he was so wicked/hilarious. The Kaiser's involvement came to nothing and the idea of Zionism was widely mocked within Germany, although it found an immediate echo among hideously persecuted Eastern European Jews. Herzl held the First Zionist Congress in the Basel Municipal Casino in 1897 and in effect created there a virtual Israel complete with national anthem. The speed with which the idea spread and developed can be seen in the career of Herzl's radical successor, the East Prussian Jew Kurt Blumenfeld, who became Secretary-General of the World Zionist Organization in 1911. Future events should have doomed to him to death or expulsion as an East Prussian by the Soviets or death by the Nazis, but instead he died in Israel in 1963: a country which owes its existence both to the most creative and imaginative aspects of the Germans and to the very worst.

Some families converted to Christianity or simply dropped serious observance and there is a point at which it becomes too odd to insist on figures such as Karl Marx, Gustav Mahler, Fritz Haber and Ludwig Wittgenstein – who in quite different ways and to quite different extents were Jewish – only being explicable through a lens they themselves were bored by or spurned. It becomes an almost impossible struggle to work out whether or not it is even faintly relevant to someone's success that they were Jewish – and whether being too curious on this subject runs the risk of falling into an odd form of anti-Semitism. What is incontrovertible is that by the early twentieth century, individuals who to a greater or lesser extent had a Jewish background formed a remarkable part in a brilliant culture, whether literary, philosophical, medical, musical or scientific, one of the most dynamic and creative in European history, as much in the new German empire as in the Habsburg Empire. It could be seen as a joint German and Jewish project, but it sometimes seems to me more important just to pay no attention – that people from an immense variety of backgrounds were using the German language to revolutionary effect to change the world. The almost over-whelming blow that world received in 1914–18 left German culture devastated but still turning out extraordinary ideas – but then came the Great Depression and the arrival of an autodidact fantasist who loathed that culture, wished to destroy modernism in all its non-military forms, and who had specific ideas about how Germany had gone wrong.

Sitting in the cold, dusty Braunschweig museum and looking at the abandoned remains of the old Hornburg synagogue the sadness comes in so many waves. I have myself no serious links to Judaism – I am staring at something I do not understand except in an arid, unengaged way and the people who might explain it to me are long gone.

CHAPTER THIRTEEN

Beside the seaside

For many foreigners Germany is associated with a sort of special bleakness and indeed there are parts of Pomerania or Brandenburg that could usefully be twinned with Saskatchewan or Caithness for sheer undesirability. For me the real punishment unit though has to be Wilhelmshaven. This eye-achingly desolate, helpless place is where, in effect, Germany began to go badly wrong, setting itself on a ruinous course with its own disastrous logic.

Wilhelmshaven stemmed from a sense that a proper navy was needed if Prussia was to be taken seriously by the other great powers. In the 1850s Prussia's rulers were thinking about how to nurture what they increasingly felt to be their mission to unite Germany. At that point there seemed numerous obstacles, all of which were in fact to be disposed of in less than twenty years. One was Prussian vulnerability to naval blockade: however excellent its army, much of its growing overseas trade could be stopped by France threatening a handful of river mouths. Prussia's ports were all the wrong side of Denmark and Danish hostility (which was to be fixed in the two Schleswig Wars) could easily bottle up Prussian ships in the Baltic. And so the building of a specifically Prussian North Sea base started to make sense. A classic map-obsessive's project, it had a certain plausibility. Jade Bay, the future site of Wilhelmshaven, is a huge semi-circle of land on the North Sea which, just to look at for a few moments from a blustery esplanade, would make most people lose the will to live, particularly once they have had to get there by walking through a haggard shopping centre featuring a man in Bavarian dress playing 'The Sheik of Araby' on his saxophone. Jade Bay was owned by the torpid micro-state of Oldenburg.

The only real German North Sea ports were in the hands of the semi-independent states of Bremen and Hamburg, who could not be relied on at all for military purposes. In a fine example of the sort of nonsense which made liberals tend to favour German unification, Prussian plans to create a port required baffling, tortured negotiations, leasing the land from Oldenburg and then building a special road to supply it through the territory of the substantial Kingdom of Hannover.

Oldenburg took the money but then Hannover just to be tiresome refused permission for the road, meaning the entire port had to be built stone by stone and worker by worker by sea – a project that took many years to complete. In the meantime Denmark had been defeated in the Second Schleswig War of 1864, allowing the Prussians, after a brief interlude of joint Austrian occupation, to purloin the excellent Baltic port of Kiel. Hannover belatedly backed Austria in her 1866 war with Prussia and went down to defeat and extinction, allowing Prussia to take Hannover over and *at last have a proper road* from which to build its naval port. But in 1871 the specifically Prussian port became futile, as Germany unified and Bremen and Hamburg came on board.

This was all too late, as the new port had finally been built and unimaginatively named after King Wilhelm. Walking around the town now, with its neat rows of administrators' houses, garrison church and old statues, it is possible to get a sense of the pride and value felt for this new Prussian city. It all however proved to be one enormous mistake. Once the framework for a navy existed then a navy needed to be built, and to justify the immense novel German expenditure on modern ships a plausible enemy was needed. International relations shifted about with such violent speed around the time of the port's inauguration that it is hard to know what a rational policy would have been for Wilhelmshaven's use. In the interval between its inauguration and its second birthday all three of Prussia's major enemies – Denmark, Austria, then France – had been easily defeated. Changes in naval technology from the 1870s onwards were almost as giddying as the chaos of international relations: ships were rapidly obsolete and yet soaked up huge funds.

One of the reasons Germany acquired its oddly marginal and point-less overseas empire was then to provide its navy with something a quarter-way rational to do, and the Wilhelmshaven garrison church is filled with monuments to nasty wars in Namibia and China.

Wilhelmshaven became the focus of ever-madder dreams. As ships got bigger the otherwise miraculous new Kiel Canal became harder to use and Wilhelmshaven built up ever further. By 1900 naval fantasists began to feel that Britain must be the enemy – not for any very specific reason as British and German interests were on the whole complementary, but because an ocean-going navy only made sense in relation to Britain being the enemy, all the more usual enemies being easily dealt with by a traditional army.

And so a port built from scratch on a gloomy stretch of a shunned coast became the focus of a naval arms race, which did more than anything else to alienate Britain – a country that had stood by benignly through all Germany's wars of unification. The enormous casualty lists tell the rest of the story. Essentially the German navy was always an expensive and stupid failure. There was simply never enough money or steel or men to take on Britain, a country which entirely defined itself by its global naval presence, whatever theories oddly bearded visionary nutcases like Grand Admiral von Tirpitz conjured up.

There was also the almost comic problem with Wilhelmshaven's total unsuitability as a naval port by the early twentieth century. Its sand bar made the entrance to the port impassable for big ships except at high tide, meaning that for the entire fleet to leave Wilhelmshaven it took two tides, theoretically allowing the British to blow to pieces the first half while waiting for the second half. This nightmare scenario never came to pass, but essentially the German fleet was too fragile to be used. One serious attempt was made at the Battle of Jutland in 1916, but to the rage of the German commanders it was immediately clear that while they had a clear technical superiority over the British, the latter were simply too numerous. The closeness to which the German fleet came to massacre on that occasion, massacre averted only through timidity and confusion among the British, meant that it was unthinkable to try again. As one historian recently and gleefully pointed out, the investment of so many millions of marks in an ocean-going fleet simply meant that the Kaiser had vaingloriously and expensively created the organization that would destroy him. As Germany faced defeat in 1918 a typically deranged plan to send out the entire navy on an honourable suicide mission resulted in the bored-to-tears sailors rebelling. There are splendid photos of the whole of official Wilhelmshaven packed with angry sailors, the statues and the administrators' houses seemingly afloat on a sea of mutineers. The sailors' actions implied a possible general breakdown and the grandson of Wilhelmshaven's founder had to resign and head off to exile in the Netherlands.

So the port that had seemed to signal a new beginning at its opening had killed off the Prussian crown less than fifty years into its existence. Of course, there were huge aftershocks – most notably the Wilhelmshaven shipyards building the Nazi super-ship *Tirpitz* (appropriately enough), but again the Second World War showed that the Germans simply didn't have the economy or the geography to have a navy. The U-boats were a terrible weapon, but a weapon based on weakness, with anything German above water sunk or marginalized by swarms of British ships in the first two years of the conflict. Wilhelmshaven's clear coastal position meant that for the duration of the war it became the stop-off of choice for Bomber Command, who dropped things on it whenever they had a spare moment. The shattered remnant of the town (with three-quarters of its buildings destroyed) surrendered to an Allied Polish army at the end of the war. In a further ignominy, what was left of the docks was dismantled by German prisoners-of-war and packed off to the USSR as reparations (a job supervised by the very young John Harvey-Jones, the future head of Imperial Chemical Industries, curiously).

Wilhelmshaven is now a large port again, helped by the oddities of German geography in the Cold War, but really it just should not be there at all. It is very peculiar to walk around an entire town whose origins lie in such a ruinous mistake and which should really just be salt-raddled marginal farmland. The Wilhelmshaven story is a very unhappy one – but then, as the twentieth century progressed, this was to become true for many other towns too.

Texan Wends

The impulse to build a glum place like Wilhelmshaven came in part from a need for an empire, and first Prussia and then Germany's sense that German-speaking lands were ill-equipped with this key nineteenth-century accessory. One of the very major facts in Germany's history which speak in its favour is its lack of an empire: the degree to which it was a country that, for geographical rather than ethical reasons, did relatively little harm. A group of Augsburg bankers had attempted in the sixteenth century to settle Venezuela (Klein Venedig) but with total lack of success. There had also been a short-lived Prussian slave-shipping fort (proudly called Gross-Friedrichsburg) on the West African coast in the late seventeenth century but it was always a money-losing fiasco, reliant on a handful of leased warehouses in the Danish Virgin Islands and attacked by the Dutch whenever they fancied. The vast bulk of the slave trade's moral nightmare ends in Spain's and then England's laps. Germany's orientation was in the end just too squarely directed towards the concerns of Central Europe, with more exotic goods arriving second-hand via London or Amsterdam.

Like so many European countries, however, Germany and its predecessors had various forms of internal empire, with the Poles, Czechs and Slovenes having much the same role as the Irish had within the British empire: patronized, discriminated against, confusing to the dominant grouping, but also a critical cultural, intellectual and military source of strength. These minorities had mainly been a Prussian and Austrian (and Swiss) issue though, and did not impact on most German states. It is not as though Germans were unaware of the wider world – they were just poorly positioned to take political or economic advantage of it. Georg Forster may have written his *Journey Around the World*, a classic of German scientific travel literature, but he wrote it as a guest of Captain Cook,

whose journeys scooped Australia, New Zealand and much of the
Pacific for Britain rather than for Hesse-Kassel, where Forster settled
on his return – a dreary contrast to all the breadfruit, bare breasts
and roasted flying-fish that must have continued to fill his mind.

Everyone's favourite Prussian, Alexander von Humboldt, travelled throughout South and Central America in the 1800s, had a
marvellous time with piranha fish and electric eels, wallowed about
in the icy horrors of the northern Pacific, but had no political
impact of any kind, however grateful we might be for his marvellous account of his adventures. The Royal Bavarian expedition to
Brazil (1817) meant the sensational Spix's macaw was named after
Johann Baptist von Spix, the appealing-sounding expedition leader,
and the Royal Prussian expedition to Egypt (1842) resulted in the
Great Pyramid getting its only hieroglyphs, put there by Profes-
sor Karl Richard Lepsius to extol the Prussian king ('All hail to
the Eagle, *The Protector of the Cross*, to the King, *The Sun and Rock
of Prussia*, to the Sun of the Sun, who freed his native country,
Friedrich Wilhelm the Fourth, & c.') but, while fun, these trips did
not notably extend Bavarian or Prussian global reach. The Austrians, in a rich parody of colonial futility, explored part of the
Arctic Ocean in the 1870s (an expedition reimagined in Christoph
Ransmayr's remarkable novel *The Terrors of Ice and Darkness*), and
fully mapped and named what is still called Franz Joseph Land, a
deathly, uninhabited nightmare. But still, Germans tended to avoid
anything more than the most tentative of non-political trading outposts – such as the Hamburg-initiated port of Douala in Cameroon
in the 1870s.

This colonial blamelessness was caused by political weakness
rather than German virtue. It would never be plausible for somewhere like Hesse-Kassel to have an empire, and Hamburg and
Bremen's independence from the rest of Germany until 1871 meant
that the two states with a genuinely global outlook were committed to free trade and a close relationship with Britain quite
at odds with nutty nationalist imaginings. This was the era of
ever greater Hamburg trade with the world and of beautifully
cartographed German maps featuring San Franzisko, Kalkutta,

Kapstadt, Neu-Orleans, Sansibar, Singapur and Schanghai (well, that was gratuitous!). The huge and fascinating exception to this imperial sidelining was the degree to which Germans themselves as individuals were of course great emigrants. They might not own the countries they were leaving for, but they were crucial nonetheless to these countries' success.

This settler drift was expressed in tiny communities – of Prussians in South Australia, or Westphalians in central Jamaica (a community which still does a traditional German pork roast on special occasions, even though two hundred and fifty years of intermarriage have made it black). But it was also expressed in great mass movements. George Washington and his friends had fun offering the most outrageous blandishments of money and land to confused Hessian mercenaries fighting for the British, several thousand of whom took the hint and headed off to help build Pittsburgh and Detroit. As in England, special religious communities shifted en masse to America, hoping to find space in which they would be left alone to pursue the full gamut of cranky revelation. They were often successful, with their descendants still tucked away in bits of Pennsylvania or Manitoba, testaments to a specific form of single-mindedness. But more broadly millions of ordinary Germans poured into North America – a minority always conceding political power to English-speakers but often wealthy and powerful in its own sphere, filling Yorktown in Manhattan, Germantown in Cincinnati and so on. Sometimes there were quite conscious attempts to plant an abiding Germanness. Prince Carl of Solms-Braunfels, 'Texas-Carl', in 1845, in the year Texas traded in its independence to become part of the United States, went over to found New Braunfels (or Neu-Braunfels) in eastern Texas, a town which to this day carries an industrial load of Teutonic folksiness.

It was common for millions of Americans to speak German at home or among friends and English to a wider world. Given the difficulty of maintaining a fierce attachment to the memory of, say, Schwarzburg-Rudolstadt it is unsurprising that German-Americans were so unconditionally loyal to the USA. But these communities were devastated by the First World War, which provoked a general sense that German was no longer publicly acceptable and a collapse in German-language newspapers. This was rapidly followed by a second disaster in Prohibition. A social group that organized itself around beer and wine festivals and the ownership of giant breweries was devastated. The names live on: Miller (or rather Müller), Pabst, Schlitz, Anheuser and Busch, but the forms of sociability that made them become rich first disappeared and then re-emerged with the end of Prohibition as more generally American, losing any real German flavour. The Germans therefore share with the English the odd non-achievement of being one of the very few ethnic groups not to get annual parades in New York. I blanch when I think about the amount of time wasted when I lived there in discussions with friends, coming up with themes for the ridiculous floats that would decorate an English Pride parade, but possibly it is as well too that during the course of the twentieth century it never struck anyone as a smart idea to have celebrations of German ethnicity trundling downtown, coldly lacking in the merry spontaneity worked on so hard by so many other national groups.

One painful story is told at the Institute of Texan Cultures in San Antonio, a miraculous museum that manages with a minimum of folksiness to convey the full diversity of Texan settlement. This was where I learned about the Texan Wends. The Wends are a Sorb-speaking Slav group living on the upper Spree, now mainly in Saxony, in the lignite-mining region of Lusatia. In the nineteenth century they were partly under Prussian and partly under Saxon rule and subject to ever greater interference with their language and religion in a gust of German nationalism that predated unification by two decades, in moves of similar intolerance to those experienced by Welsh- or Breton-speakers. Under a charismatic pastor, Jan Kilian, they decided to save their culture by moving en masse to Texas in the 1850s. A group of six hundred had already been devastated by cholera by the time they reached Liverpool. More contracted yellow fever when they finally reached Galveston, but the survivors set up a small town inland, near New Braunfels, called Serbin and settled down to protect their culture. Of course, this was completely ineffective as the community leaked away into the surrounding immensity of English- and Spanish-speakers. The last Sorb newspaper packed up in 1921 (its Gothic script having in 1917 ironically attracted the same opprobrium as if it were being used to convey German words).

Wends ended up as a tiny strand in the new inter-war Gulf of Mexico boomtowns down in the Golden Triangle on the border with Louisiana – an alarming region I once visited, with hurricane-ravaged beaches thick with smashed up Portuguese-men-o'-war and dollops of tar, water that reeked of sulphur and cockroaches of a huge, meaty, glistening and imperturbable kind. The Wends who had remained back in the sparse and temperate woods of Lusatia had a grim time under all forms of German nationalism, from Second Reich to Third Reich to German Democratic Republic, with their villages ripped up to make way for open-cast mines. Wends within the new post-1945 Polish borders were all expelled into the fledgling GDR. But, unlike Jan Kilian's congregation, they have somehow survived and now have to make their way in the first genuinely unantagonistic regime in generations – in the end as much a threat to Wendish solidarity as the strange temptations of Texas.

The Texan Wends may have not thrived as a specific cultural community but like millions of other Germans – making the crossing first via British ports and then later direct from Bremen via North German Lloyd or from Hamburg via the colossal Hapag – they found potentially enjoyable and straightforward lives in America. Indeed, so many left that by the time Hitler came up with his pitiful ideas for somehow reigniting – after quite a break – Germans' medieval eastward colonization, there were almost no 'spare' Germans with which to do it, as they were almost all safe in America, having taken a decision that spared them and their descendants from the moral disaster about to be inflicted by those who had stayed at home.

Pidgin German

A new and unfortunate global German era was hustled in during the chaotic struggle for minor colonial territories in the 1880s. If the French could be described as having an empire made up of the bits the British didn't want, then the newly united Germans got hold of places shunned even by the French. This strange, wholly uncharacteristic bid for empire was in its way as disturbing a sign as the building of Wilhelmshaven that there was something magniloquent and parodic about the new German state – a state bent on acquiring remote, harsh pieces of land for the sheer wish to point at them on a map.

In the inimitable Bavarian Army Museum in Ingolstadt there is, among many other treasures, a ridiculous tin clock with crude, tiny paintings of palm trees and beaches on it. Painted on the clock is the little heading to the effect: the German empire on which the sun never sets. It would be easy to come up with a conspiracy theory that it was the manufacturers of this clock who secretly bribed Bismarck to purchase and swap into existence a German empire, as they may have been the only people to have really benefited. To make the sun never set (and it really *must* have set anyway quite a bit of the time) can have been the only reason to have snatched so crazily a remote territory as Western Samoa which now, to Samoan bafflement, found itself reporting to Kaiser Wilhelm.

The power projection required to rule Samoa and cut a reasonable figure in the South Pacific in itself provided a rationale for the German navy, a rationale which could have been avoided simply by not being involved in the first place. From Yap to New Pomerania all that Bismarck could promise from the German Pacific Empire was a certain amount of coffee and an infinity of coconut matting. The people actually living in these islands probably did no worse under the Germans than under anybody else, and had in most cases already been devastated by fatal illnesses from other Europeans. One should give a few seconds' thought to the more or less blameless colonial administrators; men who had presumably planned to shine in local administration in Münster or Wuppertal, perhaps settling down and marrying a local girl, who now suddenly found themselves wading ashore, already seriously ill, on Truk or Blup Blup with mule-loads of ineffective medicines, crates of tinned sausages and a hastily designed, hard-to-clean white uniform.

The one exception, and the real if evanescent lynch-pin of Prussia-in-the-Pacific, was the concession port of Tsingtao on the coast of eastern China. This is still a baffling place. For many years I had a crudely coloured postcard by my desk showing the monstrous governor's mansion, the Lutheran church and the brewery that introduced Bavarian beer to China and which still exports Tsingtao lager, despite some thin periods since the Germans left. This could have become the German Hong Kong, but it would only ever remain a liability and piece of window-dressing unless Germany could make itself into a genuinely global power. This seemed plausible in 1900 with the launch of the nastiest (in a crowded field) of all colonial outings – the International Expedition to destroy the Boxer Rebellion in China and impose foreign order on the rulers in Peking. This expedition was an extraordinary mix of British, Japanese, American, Russian, French, Italian, German and Austrian marines, a prominent member of the last group being the future Captain von Trapp of *The Sound of Music* fame. This provoked the Kaiser's speech about how German troops should behave in China mercilessly, 'like Huns' (which they duly did, like everyone else) – one of the most clear-cut examples of a German worldview which was patently becoming toxic. This brutal walkover and looting raid was commemorated feverishly in Germany, with parades and memorials and exotic postcards: I saw one showing German cavalry on the Great Wall of China – a curious high-water mark in European self-aggrandisement.

However, this spirited agreement by Europeans to all join together in mowing down helpless Chinese peasant troops with machine guns did not last and, through chaotic and incompetent diplomacy, Germany had no Pacific allies at all by 1914, allowing Britain and its very many allies easily to mop up these expensive outposts and never give them back. Indeed the fundamental derangement at the heart of German strategic thinking can be seen in the loopiness of its empire, an empire which could only be serviced by ships tiptoeing past innumerable British bases. Even a hint of British hostility made German pretensions in the Far East (hedged in by, for instance, the whole of India and Australia) completely bizarre. The tragedy for the western Pacific was that through the frivolous disregard of every political actor in the region, many of the old German islands wound up in Japanese hands – thereby helping to put the Japanese Empire on its own disastrous, delusive trajectory: one of Bismarck's regime's many parting gifts to the twentieth century.

The German presence in Africa was more substantial and part of a wider and more inexorable European pressure to exploit economic and technological discoveries, dress these up as racial supremacy, and impose a brittle, short-lived hegemony over Africa. The German parts were far from prime real estate and it is hard not to feel that the Kaiser's fury over Britain's sickeningly self-serving and ferocious absorption of the Boer republics (and with it the cornering of most of the world's gold and diamonds) was fair enough. His own imperial trailblazers died of malaria or gradually sank into the swamps of scattered, prostrate African territories, turning out nothing that could justify the investment required by actual ownership, when a far cheaper option would have been simply to trade with their inhabitants. Throughout the nineteenth century Germans had traded in a minor way along the coast, fitting in with the sort of creepy transactions still dominated by the British. One striking humiliation was the Germans' lack of sugar islands in the Caribbean, obliging them to trade in 'rum' which was in fact tinted Prussian potato schnapps. Specific companies dominated each coast, with Bremen linked to Togo, Hamburg to Cameroon and Rhineland missionaries to Namibia, but with none penetrating beyond a tiny coastal strip. Bismarck's decision to annex these regions was hardly influenced by the existence of these peripheral concerns: he was simply aware that these were areas not yet snapped up by colonial rivals, making it a cheery way to wave the flag – but a cheery way that was to have a disastrous impact on many thousands of Africans.

If shooting Chinese was a clear indication that something had gone wrong with Germany, and indeed with Europe, then events in the barren German territory of South-West Africa in 1904 took things a step further. Lothar von Trotha was born in Prussian-ruled Magdeburg, joined the Prussian army and in a quintessential German career fought in both the Austro-Prussian and Franco-Prussian wars before encountering the conventional problem: that Bismarck then lost all interest in warfare. This gave the army a long period with few opportunities and generated some of the peculiar frustrations which would emerge so horribly in the twentieth century. Indeed, although it would be impossible in practice to analyse this, could the long period of almost total unemployment for the German army between 1871 and 1914 be the heart of the disaster? This combination of very high prestige, an ever more burdensome and mythic legacy of heady, startling achievement in three quickly won wars and then an absolute doldrums for forty-three years must certainly have played its part.

In any event von Trotha scraped together the opportunities still left – first killing those protesting against German rule in East Africa (Tanganyika), then joining in the fun in China. In South-West Africa he was taken off the leash entirely and crushed Herero and Nama resistance to German rule with a savagery that even the British in the Transvaal would have baulked at, driving thousands of Africans into the desert to die in what has a reasonable claim to be seen as genocide. The only things that can be said in the Germans' defence is that once it was clear what had happened there was outrage in Berlin, but this had no effect on the frame of mind that thought in such terms. It can also be pointed out that the Herero and Nama massacres in retrospect became a convenient shorthand, woven into what seemed a uniquely German pattern of viciousness, when in so many ways it mirrored European behaviour elsewhere in Africa. Everywhere, a truly poisonous technological and moral atmosphere seems to have driven Europeans mad; whether in the Transvaal or the Congo or Morocco or Sudan there was a sort of frenzy of violence, bolstered by a contemptible religious and patriotic high-mindedness. This ferocity, this strange formula that allowed the takeover of other people's land to be followed by speechless outrage when those people had the gall to resist, is a phenomenon not sufficiently thought through. This telegraph, gunboat and machine-gun hysteria that racked so many places in the run-up to the First World War formed a generalized European nadir, a sickness within much of the continent which would end up being turned on Europe itself.

There are such a lot of odd things about the German empire. Two will have to be enough here. One of the many enraging facts for sweating administrators on the African west coast was that centuries of British slaving and trading meant that the German territories of Togo and Kamerun used an English pidgin. In a classic piece of German absurdity, painful and sustained labour went into creating a synthetic German pidgin which was going to be enforced along the German coastal sections. The brainchild of a Munich lawyer, 'colonial German' was reduced to a thousand or so words and was meant to counter the slap in the face of the status quo. Of course the only value of pidgin is its usefulness and the idea that all German colonial administrators were going to be taught a simplified version of German and then have to teach it to traders and illiterate fishermen is so hilarious that it is a big shame the First World War intervened. Just before 'colonial German' was due to be rolled out the Allies took over the whole of German South-West Africa and German West Africa and the Germans never came back. The enterprising British explorer Mary Kingsley, when setting out in 1895 to become the first European to climb Mount Cameroon, noted (in her immortal *Travels in West Africa*) several fair-haired Germans toiling away on roads in the jungle, which seemed to lead nowhere. This very temporary German presence ends up as a parody of the equally quixotic and sometimes lethal attempt by all Europeans to 'rule' such places, with the British, French and Belgian inheritors of the German empire themselves shrugged off just a generation later.

Another oddity was the island swap organized between Germany and Britain in 1890. The Germans had vague claims to Zanzibar, off the coast of what had just become German East Africa.

The British also thought they as good as owned Zanzibar because of their hold over its far-off notional real owner in Muscat. Indeed they so valued Zanzibar that to secure it (and its useful nutmeg crop) they gave the Germans the island of Heligoland in the North Sea, a piece of loot the British had stolen from Denmark during the Napoleonic Wars. Heligoland was in fact a rather vexed spot of land of limited use as a naval base, but its possession in the First World War would have drastically threatened the Germans. Of course nobody in 1890 could have imagined how events would unfold in the twentieth century (not least none of the peculiarly luckless inhabitants of Heligoland, a place which ended up by 1945 as a sort of giant ashtray, a probable result whether under either British or German ownership). Every year odd decisions are taken with incalculable results. Too much time thinking about them can result in madness.

Thomas and Ernie

In a constant hunt for cheap but interesting lodgings I have spent a lot of time crisscrossing German suburbs, or rather the late-nineteenth-century ring of housing which, for many towns, showed that after sometimes centuries of inanition they were once more economically on the move. These houses were built for the locally wealthy and have a mass and stolidity matched perhaps only in the Midwest of the same period: homes for lawyers, bankers, managers of substantial factories. The variety in these homes is enormous, but it is variety only of ornament — folkloric rhymes, industrial Jugendstil decoration, monstrous pillars and lots of coloured glass. Even walking past these houses I feel as though I am becoming a German banker of the 1900s, in a burstingly tight swallow-tail coat, mopping the bulges of fat at the back of my shaved head with a fine linen handkerchief, studs about to explode from my collar as I inwardly boil about Social Democrat traitors, whether my wife would benefit from a little electro-convulsion therapy and why my daughter has cut her hair so short and started smoking cigarettes.

There is a uniform atmosphere of sadness about these homes, the product of such a brief period of aggressively confident prosperity, but since then filled with terrible political ideas, telegrams with unmanageable news, endless demands for public action of a kind that destroyed private life. This is not helped too by the German fondness for small cactuses which, in their tumescent gloom, press themselves against the windows of a hundred thousand suburban windows, like a toytown, sadistically confined version of Saguaro National Park. The old suburbs of eastern Germany have a further layer of distress to deal with and it is perhaps in the smaller towns, such as Eisenach or Eisleben or Meissen, that the full measure of the German disaster becomes clear, a feeling that what has been achieved since the 1900s has simply been a sequence of private nightmares building on each other until, at last, the Wall was brought down. At regular intervals these eastern suburbs still have abandoned homes – and industrial Jugendstil looks very grotty with amazing speed – put into limbo by legal uncertainties and mocking all the busy restoration work on the rest of the street.

The era of these houses can also be seen in the shops, where a large proportion of the surviving buildings come from the same mad wave of prosperity, even the most quaint and hand-painted old apothecaries turning out to be the remaining flotsam of some 1890s bout of historicism. The years of blockade in the First World War, Depression, Total War and communism offered few opportunities to replace or even maintain anything at all – beyond the often understandably utilitarian response to bomb damage.

This pre-war Germany now seems an almost intolerably poignant place, expressed in the building stock that still keeps indifferently going despite the terrors of its owners. There is a sort of confident innocence too about the major chancellors of the period, Caprivi and Bülow, who between them spent some thirteen years under Kaiser Wilhelm certainly making an aggressive and overweening Germany, but not a place of unique or awful dysfunction.

This atmosphere is perfectly preserved in Thomas Mann's early novels. I've always had a rather mixed relation with Mann. I remember reading *The Magic Mountain*, ill-advisedly, on the south-eastern edge of the Gobi Desert where the rival attractions of Bactrian camels, mutton stew, yurts and a genial Han guide who spoke excellent French but no English rather swamped Mann's beautifully modulated philosophical discussions. The most serious Mann setback was undoubtedly during a period when I commuted daily on a train across a dull bit of south-central England and decided to use the opportunity to read the whole of Mann's *Joseph and His Brothers*, his immense tetralogy dramatizing the world of Genesis. I remember with mixed shame and triumph, as my train pulled into Woking station, jumping out, impelled by some inner necessity, dumping *Joseph and His Brothers* in a platform waste bin (a satisfying clang) and leaping back onto the train.

These setbacks aside, I have always come back to Mann (but not to *Joseph*) and particularly to *Buddenbrooks* and *Royal Highness* and the pre-war short stories which in their different ways exemplify the pleasures and tensions of an era which had so much going for it and which, in the light of what happened in the next thirty years, seemed so painfully hopeful and appealing. These books are a world away from the spiked-helmet, scarlet-faced Germany of the parade ground, as indeed were so very many aspects of German life.

There can be no doubt though that the scarlet-faced Germany does have a strong presence in the run-up to the First World War. Spurred on by the example of Bismarck's own heroic physique, a style of total excess married to ever more outlandish decoration makes German leaders of this period thoroughly distinctive. A sort of sexual dimorphism comparable to that seen among sea-elephants kicks in – with women tending to be little, gaunt, corseted, sickly and prone to hanging around in spas, while the men, stuffed with course upon course of beer and venison at ever-grosser regimental reunions took on a monstrous bulk, festooned in vast moustaches and beards, ostrich-plumed hats, and medievally inflected uniforms. There must have been myriad grimly boisterous occasions when these characters bloviated interminably about Germany's greatness, its unique mission, the disgustingness of Jews, Poles, etc. So large do these monsters loom (Tirpitz's whiskers, Moltke the Younger's stomach) that it is tempting to see them as the quintessence of the era. Certainly Hitler very self-consciously made himself into their exact opposite – a tiny moustache, a raincoat, vegetarianism. For people used to having the Kaiser's moustache in their faces, Hitler's radicalism must have been immediately visible before he even spoke.

But while these figures were both important and as it turned out disastrous for Germany, they only represented one strand in a country which in other ways could not have been more admirable or exciting. Everywhere Germany bristles with reminders of this world, however haggard from later devastation. There are so many examples, but Darmstadt really sticks in my mind. I first went there after the Frankfurt Book Fair many years ago because it was nearby and because I thought it would be funny to go to the Wella Hair Care Museum. As it turned out I never went to the museum as the rest of the city was fascinating enough. Darmstadt is the old capital of Hesse-Darmstadt, the southern enemy of Hesse-Kassel (Hesse had been split between the children of Phillip I of Hesse in 1567). Outrageous attempts to do each other down were mixed with other periods of cooperation or indifference, but in the end it was Darmstadt that won: Hesse-Kassel battled through amazing setbacks to survive the Napoleonic Wars (in the process playing a crucial part in bringing the Rothschild family from nearby Frankfurt to prominence), but blew it by supporting the Austrians in 1866 and being swallowed up as a Prussian state. Hesse-Darmstadt was nimbler and survived as a political unit into the Weimar Republic.

Kassel and Darmstadt were reunited, however, in the devastation of Allied bombing – in one hideous raid sixteen thousand people were killed in Darmstadt in a few minutes and the old city destroyed. Darmstadt had as many reasons to be destroyed as any German town, but at least in its pre-1914 incarnation it had stood for some of the sort of slightly daffy introversy which Mann had celebrated in *Royal Highness*. The vexed, death-obsessed, gay Grand Duke Ernst Louis ('Ernie') is one of those fabulous if rare figures who make being interested in modern royalty actually worthwhile. I can't overload this book with much detail on his cursed upbringing, but it is fair to mention just as a start that he believed himself responsible for the death of his mother and had survived the deaths of a brother (a horrible accident) and a sister (diphtheria). He married a granddaughter of Queen Victoria, known as 'Ducky', who had a nightmarish time battling for Ernie's attention under the impact of his numerous affairs and bitter melancholy. They had two children, one stillborn and one who – shortly after Ducky finally divorced Ernie – died of typhoid (she is still commemorated in a Darmstadt park with a moving if strange little relief showing her as Snow White in the midst of grieving dwarves).

This sequence of depressing domestic events filled in the 1890s, but as usual the personal gets buried and all that is left is the buildings – or in this case a handful of mainly reconstructed buildings. Ernst Louis's great claim to everyone's time was his enthusiasm for Jugendstil and his founding of the Darmstadt Artists' Colony, an entirely adorable initiative which makes Darmstadt the wonderland of pre-1914 modern design, just as the strongly linked later Bauhaus fulfils the same role for the post-1918 era. Of course, this role makes both initiatives at many levels unbearable. The sheer pleasure that the artists took in working across madly different media and their commissions dotted across the German landscape (often for patrons who were made to suffer financially for their enthusiasm) is so at odds with what Germany is more generally known for in the first half of the twentieth century that in some moods their jaunty clocks, typefaces, statues, cupboards and tapestries seem almost too much. And these designs and their creators cannot be completely corralled off from the rise of the Nazis, whose aesthetic was deeply indebted to their work. Someone like Joseph Maria Olrich seems now so lucky to have died young and unimplicated, having created first the Vienna Secession Building and then some of the happiest and strangest Darmstadt buildings, including the Wedding Tower with its wondrous sun-dial by the great typeface designer and graphic artist Friedrich Wilhelm Kleukens. Peter Behrens built a house in Darmstadt designed down to the last towel (what a marvellous thing to be able to do!) and then went on to design the AEG Turbine Hall in Berlin and invent the idea of corporate design and logos, teach Le Corbusier, Gropius and Mies van der Rohe, and live just long enough to become tangled in Nazism before mercifully dying in 1940. It is impossible even to conceive of the modern world without these figures and so much was kick-started by 'Ernie'. Most late-Victorian royals seem to be merely freakish soldiers awaiting their own extinction while either eating and drinking themselves sick or shooting the sorts of animals that children like. But 'Ernie' is an appealing throwback to Archduke Ferdinand II in Innsbruck three centuries earlier, however much emotional wreckage he left around him.

Indeed the more I mull over this subject, the more difficult it becomes to leave it: there is almost no upper limit to the achievements of this slightly marginal Germany, as it is this Germany which has survived, while the political and historical Germany destroyed itself. I have to stop, but must mention at least in passing figures as various as Alfred Ballin, the millionaire Jewish owner of Hamburg America, the world's largest shipping line, who ferried to America a large proportion of the five and a half million Germans who left in the century before 1914 and thereby absolutely revolutionized the fates of their children and grandchildren – perhaps not something that can be dwelt on too much: what seemingly sensible decisions are any of us taking today which might have as drastically a happy or unhappy result? Or Paula Modersohn-Becker, a painter who lived as part of the Worpswede community outside Bremen, and created a wonderful sequence of self-portraits, landscapes, pictures of little girls and images of rural life before dying aged thirty-one of complications after giving birth to her first child. Her painting of herself naked, heavily pregnant, proud and anxious, is one of the great modern self-portraits, but of course for us informed by her fate shortly afterwards. Or Albert Einstein from Ulm. Or Gustav Mahler, a Jewish, German-speaking Moravian employed by the Habsburg court who died in 1911, fortunate to avoid any knowledge of the destruction of the Jews, the end of the Habsburg court and the expulsion of the German Moravians. Indeed so many aspects of Mahler's existence were swept away after his death that we could really just be flattering ourselves to think of ourselves as living in a culture which is connected to him, much as the inhabitants of the Renaissance were severed from the Middle Ages by the

Black Death. But if the point of this section is to show the vigour
and pleasure of the pre-1914 world this can be summed up by the
image of Mahler and Strauss in 1905 happily playing through the
score of the latter's forthcoming opera *Salome* in a piano shop in
Straßburg, a reminder that magical events could occur even in the
occupied Reich Territory of Alsace. Or there is my favourite German
painter, August Macke, who I would have liked to devote an entire
chapter to. Under the pressures of such a pointless question, if I *had*
to choose a single, favourite painting it would have to be Macke's
Little Walter's Playthings in the Städel Museum in Frankfurt: a series
of simple colour shapes to create a table corner, a mat and its surroundings and a group of objects – a matryoshka, two balls, flowers
in a pot, a toy rabbit and a little rodent pet. There are thousands of
grander, more powerful and more brilliant pictures in the world, but
I'd settle for *Little Walter's Playthings*, not least for its revolutionary
role in making guinea pigs an acceptable subject for portraiture.
Macke spent his entire, short life creating paintings of happiness –
shops, souks, parks, parrots, beautiful hats, all in the most surprising and lovely colours. He was killed in Champagne a few weeks
into the war, which of course is where the problem begins.

Podsnap in Berlin

Originally built in a village some way outside Berlin, the Charlottenburg Palace continues somehow to feel rural despite streets,
houses and factories having long since chewed up to and around it.
As so often in Germany its 'English Park' manages to be more successfully of its type than most of those in England itself, with little
buildings and statues tucked away, proliferating, richly smelling
undergrowth, plus such exotics (to English eyes) as macabre hooded
crows and almost tame red squirrels, with straggling tufts of
unkempt hair and hectic eyes that give them something of the air
of traditional Berlin squatters.

    The Palace holds all kinds of pleasures and since it was built in
the late seventeenth century it has represented the cheerful, normal

side of Prussia. The tombs of several Prussian monarchs, none too mad or flashy, are in the mausoleum. Karl Friedrich Schinkel worked on the buildings in the early nineteenth century and his whole career (he died in 1841) is a reminder of the civilized, eclectic and charming aspects of Prussia, just as much as figures such as Kleist, Humboldt or Hoffmann. His legacy has taken a beating from high explosives, but every one of his surviving works is likeable and still surprising. Perhaps even more enjoyable (as with the work of his older English contemporary Sir John Soane) is stepping into the fantasy world of unbuilt projects, such as his delirious plans for a massive royal palace for Otto, the Wittelsbach king of newly independent Greece, which would have incorporated the Parthenon as almost a minor decorative feature. Schinkel also happened to be a marvellous if part-time painter, and his *Gothic Church on a Cliff by the Sea* (in the Old National Gallery in Berlin) is a sort of encyclopaedia of mad German enthusiasm for the Middle Ages, with brave knights, mighty banners, a Schloss, a rainbow, ancient German woods and the most amazing lighting effects. Painted in 1815 it all seems a world away from the infantile and obscene medieval world imagined by Himmler but, as with Caspar David Friedrich, one can see worrying, if blameless, flashes of what became so curdled in later German nationalism.

Schinkel's work at Charlottenburg sets the tone for the whole place – particularly a pavilion built for Friedrich Wilhelm III in an Italian style, which, almost uniquely among German-Italian buildings, does not look suicidally glum and displaced. Wandering around the palace itself there is the happy surprise of one of David's heroic paintings of Napoleon crossing the Alps, which Marshal Blücher picked up as war loot and which ended up here on a wall far too small for its demented size. But all the fun comes to an end with a stifling room devoted to a monstrous set of silver, given as a wedding present to Crown Prince Wilhelm and his wife on their marriage in 1905. Seeing this infinite expanse of heavy, dreary, unusable and pointless cutlery is to land heavily in the noxious world of Mr Podsnap from *Our Mutual Friend*, with his inhumanly heavy silver dinner-table centrepieces, his spoons too wide for normal mouths, his insufferably self-righteous opinions about his nation's superiority to all others and about the evils of the poor.

It is perhaps putting too much weight on some knives and forks, but the atmosphere of almost weary grossness in that room is truly startling and can be linked to a wider unease with how official Germany saw itself in this period. The most enormous example of the same tendency remains Berlin Cathedral, built at the orders of Wilhelm II as a showcase for Hohenzollern religiosity, and as a last resting place for numerous Hohenzollern lead coffins which had formerly been scattered about. This truly awful historicist stoneyard can of course be enjoyed very briefly for the irony of the royal family it extols being kicked out in the decade following its completion, but this only gets you as far as the front steps. Some trouble was taken in dropping bombs on the cathedral during the war and the communist authorities should have honoured this by dynamiting the rest, but somehow it survived and was lavishly restored after reunification.

All this is really just to say that Wilhelm II's Berlin is miles away from the wonders of Schinkel's imagination, or the baroque cheeriness of the main Charlottenburg complex. There is something absolutely arid and cheerless about this official Prussian world which also infects so much of the photography of the period. The Kaiser himself might have been enthusiastic about inventions – Zeppelins, dreadnoughts, cinema – but he and his entourage seem caught, much like the Romanovs and the Habsburgs, in a clotted aesthetic almost unrelated to the modern world springing up all around them, adrift from Germany's vigorous consumerism, its social democracy, its arts and science. The Prussian rulers and their military had no monopoly on unstable and disturbing nationalism, but there is something definitely hectic and extremely unattractive about official Germany, with its relentless obsession with uniforms, grandiloquent, talentless building projects, unfeasible cutlery, ceaseless ceremonial, speeches, stuffiness and chauvinism.

Varieties of militarism

The causes of the First World War is a despairing essay topic. For the British generation who fought that war, and for those who had to deal with its even worse successor, the Great War was the result of German militarism. It was essential to any worthwhile narrative that there should be a villain in 1914 because it would be self-evidently too horrible to imagine killing on such a scale as a result of mere accident. The famous American poster showing Germany as a huge gorilla in a spiked helmet, standing in a devastated landscape with the corpse of a girl in one hand and a blood-caked club with 'Kultur' written on it, has haunted me ever since I saw it in a history book as a child. The Kaiser himself, in fact a rather depressive and marginal figure during the war, is shown in hundreds of cartoons exulting in death, attempting to eat the world, and so on.

With the cooling of the hatreds of the time this view seems odder and odder. There can be no doubt about the disastrous *result* of the war – the destruction of the world economy and the incubation of dozens of sick and creepy forms of nationalism that resulted in a further world war orchestrated by the pitiful and malign figure of Hitler. When writing this book I had to decide when I would bale out – and that would clearly be when most of the Germans I most admire also baled out if they could, about 1933. Germany enters a genuine and horrifying dark age at that point, but this was still a long way off in 1914.

What now seems strange is the fake nature of German militarism. It was not expressed in fighting anybody – since its inception in 1871 the German empire had fought nobody at all outside small but disgusting colonial wars, on which it shared a level playing field with Britain and France. By contrast the Russians had fought two very serious wars – one in 1876–7 against the Ottoman empire in conjunction with the Serbs, Romanians and Bulgarians and one against the Japanese in 1904–5. Both these conflicts were on a huge scale and strained all the countries involved to their limit: the strain even of success on the societies that fought them was hard to sustain, the casualties huge and the damage horrifying. The total destruction of a Russian fleet by the Japanese in a few minutes made admirals around the world sick with fear. As a gesture of solidarity with Russia, Montenegro had also declared war on Japan. While this in practical terms achieved little, it could have been a little warning – which went unregarded – about the mystical and irrational links between Russia and the small Balkan states. In the same period Russia carved out a Central Asian empire for itself of over half a million square miles and industrialized on an increasingly startling scale, not least through French investment. The army lay at the heart of the Russian ruling class and was the principal focus of state expenditure.

The point of discussing Russia is not to launch into yet another grand summary of the causes of the war but to provide some context for Germany's own undoubted militarism. Compared to Russia, Germany was a state that venerated its army, poured money into it, and dressed it up, but did not use it. Britain is another interesting contrast. Her key needs were for a navy and she had the largest in the world. In order to secure much of the world's gold and diamond production she had provoked a conflict with the Boer-ruled, independent republics of the Orange Free State and the South African Republic (Transvaal). Some seventy-five thousand people were killed in the fighting, including a huge number of Boer civilians put into concentration camps to end the guerrilla warfare that followed the defeat of the main Boer armies. The Germans had invested heavily in the Boer states, but had been told by a British emissary before the war broke out that if they interfered the British would declare war on Germany, destroy all German shipping and blockade Hamburg and Bremen so that Germany would choke. This was an interesting and tactful preview of British behaviour in 1914. In that single threat was all the argument that figures such as Admiral von Tirpitz needed to build Germany's own navy to prevent this happening (which, after colossal expenditure, it didn't).

However clean-limbed and magnificent this fresh surge of British might and main appeared to repulsive figures such as Cecil Rhodes and the imperial grandee Lord Milner (himself, very oddly,

German in fact, from Hesse-Darmstadt), the effect elsewhere was less than happy, allowing politicians around the world to take out of the cupboard and give a polish to the standard figure of the violent and hypocritical Englishman. Kaiser Wilhelm and many others gagged with rage and disgust at this sort of piracy which they would themselves love to have engaged in but which British power ruled out.

I won't talk about French fighting in Morocco or south-east Asia, or the Italian invasion of Libya or the British revenge expedition to Sudan (where Mahdist prisoners were summarily executed and the Mahdi's tomb dynamited) or the British invasion of Tibet. I have already talked about the International Expedition to lay waste to parts of China. These are all only interesting here because it is clear that European states were more than happy to use their armies and continued to see them as legitimate instruments of state will in a variety of circumstances which we would find surprising – or we would like to think of ourselves as finding surprising.

In this context Germany certainly has a worrying enthusiasm for soldiers, but not to an excessive degree – a larger percentage of Frenchmen were in uniform, the British had a larger navy, the Russian rearmament plans after the defeat by Japan threatened to dwarf everyone. Only the Austrians, because of political division and their weak industrial basis, were unable to keep up, giving their stumbling pre-1914 presence a sort of poignancy celebrated by writers such as Joseph Roth. But as usual with incompetence, its pleasures only get you so far: if the Austrians *could* have been militarily more vicious then they undoubtedly would have been – indeed during the Second World War the German Austrians who briefly moved back to administer parts of their old empire showed no feebleness at all. All these were societies that worshipped uniforms, fawned on the reminiscences of those who had been in battle and taught their children about military glory and sacrifice. They expressed this with different emphases but not on any visible moral sliding scale that would put any specific country, like, say, Britain, higher. Nobody entered the war in 1914 with anything other than a strong sense of the seriousness of the situation – it was not a frivolous throw of the dice. But none, of course, had the remotest sense of the night-mare outcome and all viewed military conflict as a state's highest test rather than as something which might destroy Europe.

This is a personally humiliating story, but I may as well wade in all the way at this point. Aged nineteen I went on a walking holiday in the Lake District with some friends. An odd mixture of *The Famous Five* and sexual tension, we went up various hills and then came down them again before wandering into a newsagent for some snacks. There we were greeted with the news that Argentina had invaded the Falkland Islands. I had hardly heard of the Falklands but — and I am not exaggerating — I wanted to volunteer to fight! Quite unknown to my outwardly scornful persona, a little Lord Milner had been nurtured within. Those years of sleeping in school dormitories named after Wellington and Churchill, those *Commando* comics, those history books, had been making me into a ludicrous sort of nationalist. I wanted Buenos Aires to be reduced to acres of smouldering and irradiated rubble — a lesson to the world for future generations that *nobody* but *nobody* could defy Great Britain, take over a small piece of sub-Antarctic scrub and get away with it.

Now, separately I should say that I am not making light of what was a grotesque defiance of international law — the resulting war turned out to be in almost everyone's best interests. But my more narrow point is that whenever I read about the opening of the First World War I tend to think of myself standing in the Lake District, trying to find a recruiting station. The cause there was remote and irrelevant, my desirability as a recruit zero and the possibility of signing up non-existent. The competitive imperial European framework which channelled and was channelled by such urges had disappeared years before, and yet as a feebleminded footnote, at just the right age to be recruited, here I was crazily chewing on nationalist uppers. This sort of response and the degree to which it could be fed by newspapers became something almost out of the control of European leaders as the nineteenth century progressed. It was something politicians were intimately aware of and which they manipulated but which created a substantial, patriotic public sphere of a kind that was fickle and powerful. The hysteria in Germany that greeted the battles of the 1860s was a mere taster for the public appetite by the 1910s. The political system was based around an emperor and a hierarchical military on one side and a restive but patriotic set of civilian politicians on the other. This arrangement had endured, at peace for a generation and with figures such as Wilhelm II or Moltke the Younger only dimly aware of the forces which too much stress on the existing system could unleash.

A taste of the excitement felt in Germany at the outbreak of war (and there are comparable pictures for all the major belligerents) can be found in Heinrich Hoffmann's famous photograph of the Odeonsplatz in Munich. This great public space was even at that time already so freighted with meaning as to invite total personal collapse. Along one side of the square is the Bavarian Electors' palace from which so many generally ill-advised wars had been launched and so many dynastic deals scrooged over. Opposite is the Theatine Church, built in the late seventeenth century in thanks for the long-awaited birth of an heir to the Electorate, who turned out to be Maximilian II Emanuel – a great fighter of the Turks and patron of the arts, but famous in Britain as the Bavarian ruler crushingly defeated by the Duke of Marlborough at the battles of Blenheim and then Ramillies. The church built to celebrate his birth also proved to be the church in which he was buried, along with a mixed crew of often equally unfortunate descendants. The other, enclosed south wall of the Odeonsplatz holds the Field Marshals' Hall, built as one of King Ludwig I's enjoyable monuments of the 1840s. Only two field marshals are in fact featured, scraped together from Bavaria's awkward history: Tilly (actually from Belgium), the unappealing 'Monk in Armour', hammer of Protestantism in the Thirty Years War, and Karl Philipp von Wrede (actually from Heidelberg), who in the Napoleonic Wars managed to fight first against the French, then for the French and then against the French again (when he was beaten one last time by Napoleon at the Battle of Hanau).

At the centre of the Field Marshals' Hall was one further monument – a striking group of statues commemorating the Franco-

Prussian War, which would have been stared at by everyone in the frenzied crowd in Hoffmann's remarkable photo, a sea of waving hands and hats. To have been in that crowd, cheering the most exciting historical moment in generations, surrounded by reverent symbols of the Thirty Years War, the War of the Spanish Succession, the Napoleonic Wars and the mythic war which had a generation before destroyed France and created the Second Reich: it must have been quite extraordinary. The photo is famous both as a quintessential image of the nationalistic derangement that swept Europe, but also because of a conversation after the war between Hoffmann and the local Munich agitator Adolf Hitler, who said that he had himself been in the Odeonsplatz on that day. After meticulously combing through each face in the picture Hoffmann indeed found Hitler — and there he is, with a long moustache, a dark hat and an ecstatic expression.

CHAPTER FOURTEEN

Nr. 598₁₃   Stuttgart den 22. Juni   1909

DER WAHRE JACOB

∘∘∘ Abonnementspreis pro Jahr Mk. 2.60 ∘∘∘ | ∘∘∘∘∘∘ Erscheint alle vierzehn Tage. ∘∘∘∘∘∘ | Verantwortlich für die Redaktion: B. Heymann in Stuttgart.
Anzeigen pro 4 gespaltene Nonpareille-Zeile Mk. 1.50 | Preis bei Postbezug vierteljährlich 65 Pfg. (ohne Bestellgeld). | ∘∘ Verlag und Druck von Paul Singer in Stuttgart. ∘∘

Im Dreadnougth-Fieber.

Failure

Franz Ferdinand spent some twenty-five years of his adult life waiting for the Emperor Franz Josef to die. As with Crown Prince Friedrich in Germany (or less dramatically Britain's very own Prince Charles) he was cursed by the pampered longevity of the reigning monarch. Franz Ferdinand worked on elaborate and quite possibly successful plans for a United States of Austria to replace the existing chaos of the Habsburg Empire, using federalism to defuse nationalism. Through Franz Josef's incredible staying power (ineffectually on the throne since 1848), Franz Ferdinand was reduced to doing such time-filling things as visiting Sarajevo, the chief city of Austria-Hungary's newest colony, the former Ottoman territory of Bosnia-Hercegovina. It turned out that, through incredible bad luck (the Serbia-backed assassins were barely competent), all Franz Ferdinand's years of preparation turned out only to be for his own death.

The outrage among other monarchs was immediate and genuine – many had known Franz Ferdinand well and shared his impatience with the dotard Franz Joseph. He was a serious and important figure and his death the single clearest outrage since the assassinations of King Umberto I of Italy and President McKinley of the USA well over a decade before, but with far more profound international implications. From the German point of view the killing had everyone excitedly brushing off military planning charts. The risk was that if the Austrians took military reprisals against Serbia then this would force the Russians to come to the latter's assistance. This would then require France to honour its alliance with Russia and either the Germans could sit by and watch their major European ally get torn apart or they could face the inevitable and mobilize.

The curse that hung over the German empire was that it was relatively less important than its neighbours. No matter how many giant smelting plants, dreadnoughts, chemical works or monstrous statues of Bismarck it built, Germany's essential provincialism remained. The motor that ruined European culture was not the overbearing might of Germany but its relative marginality. France, Russia and Britain all had enormous overseas empires which they valued highly and were very sensitive about: Russia and Britain had settled their differences over Central Asia and Britain and France over Africa, and while Germany was slightly involved in some of these discussions she was never more than a fun extra. After years of mutual hostility Britain had also finally decided she could never realistically fight the United States and – in perhaps one of the twentieth century's key decisions – downgraded her Canadian naval bases and thereby freed up many ships and staff for a future war elsewhere. This decision, among others, allowed for ever closer cooperation between Britain and America of a kind which Germany could not even start to interfere with. France could never work with Germany as long as Alsace-Lorraine remained in German hands and therefore took a great pleasure in its ostentatious alliance with Russia in the sure knowledge that this was Germany's worst night-mare. Massive French investment in Russia oriented Russia under all circumstances away from Germany (with whom the Russians had often been entirely friendly in the past). So, far from being the mon-ster of legend, Germany was left with an army that had not been used properly in most Germans' living memory and which was aggressively encircled, with only Austria-Hungary and perhaps Italy and Turkey (another focus of German investment) as possible allies. Undoubtedly the Germans' cheerless and futile diplomatic aggres-siveness played a part in making the atmosphere worse in the years running up to 1914, but all these manoeuvres had gained for them was a cementing of all their European enemies' relationships, and the cession to them by the French of a small area of the Congo basin (New Kamerun – a political entity even shorter lived than the French Revolutionary-era South Prussia).

All the mainland European countries could see circumstances

emerging when it would make sense to use their armies and they all ran through elaborate military plans to destroy their opponents. These would use resources swollen dropsically by industrialization to a level unimagined when Western European fighting had ended in 1871. But as to who would prevail, it was really anybody's guess – nobody, except perhaps some of the Austrians, declared war thinking they would actually lose.

The Germans had created a plan that would allow them to defeat France quickly, as they had done in 1870, but on a much grander scale – and then switch to defeat Russia in turn. What had not been planned for was how Britain might feel in the event of such a war. The Germans worked on the basis that British declarations of neutrality were genuine. They were aware that Britain was not obliged by treaty to assist France, that Britain had been benignly neutral in the 1860s and 1870s and that the numerous links between the British and German royal families implied a community of interest. This assumption was shared by many British too, but neither side fully realized just how much damage Tirpitz's naval arms race had done and how, in a serious crisis, this corrosive sense of German hostility had brought Britain and France very close. A universal recklessness and a specifically German itch to take on Russia and France before they became even more powerful lies at the centre of 1914, but Britain's failure to show her hand until too late was also fatal. It is probably fair to say that with British involvement the German battle plans simply made no sense. Germany was stuck in the middle of Central Europe and indeed among the first British hostile acts of the war was cutting the Germans' cable links to the rest of the world and the effortless destruction of their global radio network, leaving the planet's communication system in British hands. Germany had managed to antagonize Britain through her naval and colonial ambitions but never had a serious plan to deal with the result of such – as it turned out – futile posturing. Military planning for a British intervention was a sub-set of the plan to defeat France and Russia: and the hope that this latter could be done so fast that Britain's ability over the long-term to use its navy to starve Germany to death would prove irrelevant.

The endlessly interesting Museum of the First World War, a sub-museum of the immortal Bavarian Army Museum in Ingolstadt, dramatizes the autumn of 1914 in an appealing contemporary map, not as the story of the Schlieffen Plan (by which the Germans failed to defeat the French army), but as the story of the successful defence of Germany against simultaneous French and Russian invasion. This Looking-Glass Land epic is deeply confusing to those such as me, brought up on the *Look & Learn Book of the First World War*. As soon as war was declared, the French hurled themselves into Alsace-Lorraine and the Russians into East Prussia – the exact situation which the Germans had been having kittens over for a generation. As it turned out the Russians were able to mobilize armies with such speed that the whole German idea of defeating first France and then Russia was reduced to rubbish within days. The small bits of German territory held by the French and Russians proved delusive (although mass panics in East Prussia had Germans in wagons streaming down the roads in a sneak preview of 1944). The French managed to spend a couple of days in the Alsatian town of Mul-house/Mühlhausen, provoking hysterical scenes of joy in Paris, but were then pushed out again. The total failure of the French inva-sion (the unconfident, havering-sounding 'Plan XVII') in practice doomed the German army, as the French survivors (who might with success have otherwise carried on marching off into a fairly point-less corner of Germany) were then redeployed back into France to contribute to the Battle of the Marne. The series of devastating encounters in the east known as the Battle of Tannenberg, after early anxieties, wound up destroying two entire Russian armies, removing any threat of invasion from the east. The battle made the reputation of the two commanders, Hindenburg and Ludendorff, who were ultimately to become the military dictators of the latter part of the war and at different points crucial, both unwillingly and willingly, in easing Hitler's path to power.

In a fit of the medievalism that makes Germany so unappealing it was called Tannenberg, despite that town not really featuring in the fighting, to match the titanic Battle of Tannenberg fought between the Teutonic Knights and the Polish-Lithuanians in the early fifteenth century and which broke the power of the Knights. Through some insane logic this battle was therefore seen as righting an ancient wrong, as the Germans at last conquered the Slav hordes. Tannenberg implied to the Germans that they were living in a new heroic age – that annihilatory battles of the old Königgrätz/Sedan type were still possible and that everyone could buy into a war which promised further such heroics. It also fatally distracted many Germans from the full meaning of the Battle of the Marne in the following week, which in practice ended any such prospect of future heroism and aborted the invasion of France. Tannenberg lived on in all kinds of ways – as an event marked with fervour by East Prussians as their deliverance from Russian slavery, as a key piece of the Nazis' mythology on the Eastern Front (soon overlain by their own victories) and in all kinds of nooks and corners – from a beautiful but disturbingly Nazi 'Tannenberg' typeface designed after Hitler came to power to the Tannenberg Street in Berlin where Nabokov forced the Russian émigré protagonist of his novel *The Gift* to live.

Ultimately, as the First World War progressed, Russia was devastated, humiliated and cut apart by German troops before falling under communist dictatorship. Russia therefore appeared to be a long way from the superpower envisaged by German military planners before 1914, although on the way down she did manage to destroy the Habsburg Empire. If the First World War wound up being lost by the Germans, it had not been lost in the east and the temporary appearance of immense German-run colonies in places such as Ukraine in 1917 implied a might-have-been future which was to have a delusive and misleading effect on Nazi planners who, on the basis of what seemed like good evidence, felt they could achieve the same or better in 1941.

The British–German divorce

The alienation between Britain and Germany turned out, to everybody's surprise, to be the disastrous main theme of the first half of

twentieth-century European history. Nobody involved in any of
the fighting from 1914 onwards was in a position to think like this,
so it is a useless supposition: but nonetheless if Britain *had* been
neutral in 1914 it is hard to see how Germany could not have won
the war in a fairly conventional way in a couple of years, thereby
sparing Europe the unlimited disasters that followed. After all, in
the aftermath of the Franco-Prussian War almost everyone just got
on with their lives, buying stuff and having families – and a Europe
dominated by the Germany of 1914 would have been infinitely
preferable to a Europe dominated by the Germany of 1939.

British planners had spent generations planning a war with
France, just as Germany had in substantial part become united out
of fear of France. It took only a superficial interest in history to
notice that at regular intervals France appeared to go crazy and
attack everyone. The British continued to pour resources into a
navy specifically aimed at France. As had been the case in previous
wars, Britain's natural allies were Prussia and Austria (ideally both
of them if they were not at each other's throats). In the nineteenth
century this relationship remained a complex and almost unthinking tangle of assumptions. These were fed by the great Allied
moments of the past – the British and Austrians crushing the French
at Blenheim in 1704, the British and Prussians crushing the
French at Waterloo in 1815. The establishment of a new European
order after Waterloo was mainly the work of British and Austrian
negotiators – and indeed an interesting and little-examined issue is
why, by the outbreak of the First World War, Britain and Austria
seemed to be living in such different and unrelated worlds after
such a long partnership. As already discussed, the British were both
instrumental in building Prussian power in Western Europe and
benevolent neutrals in the German wars of unification. There was
also a shared monarchical, ideological disgust with France – with
its fake kings and emperors, turbulence, revolutions and implied
continual affronts to the legitimist (and closely intermarried) British
and German royal families.

The speed of the alienation was breathtaking. Neither side had a
convincing strategy for fighting the other. Britain's main naval

stations at Plymouth and Portsmouth had developed over centuries to fight France, and the new North Sea bases needed to fight Germany were always provisional, half-hearted and vulnerable. Even Britain's continuing commitment to defend Belgian neutrality had always been meant to be a tripwire against some future French eruption – a tediously traditional strategy for over two centuries, left over in part from when Belgium had been ruled by Austria. Nobody had really thought through the mad implausibility that Belgium might be invaded from the east, as now happened. Within moments of war existing between Britain and Germany both sides became utterly invested in the destruction of the other. The British public was appalled by the German 'rape' of Belgium and was fed a diet of bizarre stories of Belgian nuns being tied to the clappers of church bells and squelched to death when these were rung. The German army was undoubtedly brutal in Belgium, but only to a degree the British should have found familiar from their own behaviour in, say, China or South Africa. The German public (and leadership) felt that they had gone to war confident of British neutrality and that they were now being stabbed in the back by repulsive and hypocritical 'shopkeepers', using the excuse of Belgium's neutrality to try to destroy their patent successors as Europe's leaders. This confidence was reckless and almost infantile – a feeling that if you could only wish hard enough Britain would not stand by France and German war plans might work; therefore it was necessary to assume Britain would stay neutral. But Britain gave out chaotic, dithery signals and its tiny army did not seem relevant to even a year-long war.

This is a fiendishly difficult issue, but Britain's global preponderance was undoubtedly an element in creating the pressure-cooker atmosphere that resulted in 1914. Some over-perceptive Russian officers in the latter stages of the Napoleonic Wars had suggested that Russia should stop fighting, as every fresh Russian victory over Napoleon simply opened up the world even further to the British. This had also been the case with the Seven Years War, when Prussia had done the really hard fighting while Britain wildly snatched up chunks of the rest of the planet. Victorian Britain had therefore managed, despite the loss of the United States, to become an imperial

power like no other. However, Britain's range of 'holdings' was
always vulnerable to some fresh predator. The whole nineteenth
century was spent in a maze of complex negotiations and threats in
order to keep it all together. In 1900, as Britain took over the rest of
South Africa, it was an interesting question how the British empire
(and therefore much of the world) would evolve and whether or
not this process would involve British decline. Many British leaders
were appalled by the South African War – how isolated it had made
them from scornful world opinion, how expensive and violent it
was, given what was supposed to be weak opposition, how many
people had been killed. Would the future involve endless fighting
of this kind? These anxieties led to the colonial agreements with
Russia and France – a wish to settle the futures of Africa and Asia
without further bloodshed, but which turned out to draw together
the three allies in ways which resulted in far worse bloodshed in
Europe.

The Germans were bitterly resentful of this British preponderance and became ever more deeply prey to a sense that they were
being shut out of the world. Something of the same effect can be
seen today in, for example, the nature of French anti-Americanism,
in which so many of the discontents of French culture are mysteriously the fault of the United States. In Germany's case this began
to take on pathological proportions. This has tended to be portrayed as the result of the Kaiser's feeling of inferiority and dislike
over his mother's British family and their (admittedly) patronizing
attitude. Wilhelm II was an important element and a more genial,
tubby and self-indulgent figure on the throne could have led Germany in a different direction, but he was also reflecting a mass of
seething, wonky German nationalist opinion.

Without fighting anybody, Germany was dominating Europe
before 1914 – its factories were creating goods sold all over the
world. A marvellous sense of this can be found in the old Free Port
area of Hamburg. As part of the negotiation for Hamburg joining
the German empire, Hamburg's rulers insisted on maintaining a
separate Free Port which would allow the city to continue its preeminent role as mainland Europe's great entrepôt: a tax-free island

where goods could be warehoused and released into the market as price and demand dictated. The enormous zone built to achieve this – cut off from the mainland by its own canals, bridges and police force (yet again a united Germany manages to wind up with enclaves, exceptions and oddities) – could not be more painfully atmospheric of the Germany that could have been. Stinking of low-tide mudflats, the great warehouses (some of which are still used, particularly for Persian carpets) are a warren of narrow corridors and steel anti-fire doors. I have a vulnerable sort of interest in commodities and so was a pig-in-clover at the warehouse museum, with its displays of sacks of coffee, crates of tea, sheets of raw rubber. There is even a diagram, from a later date, showing the loading of a German merchant ship as it headed to the Far East (mechanical equipment, fencing, processed goods) and the loading for the return trip (bauxite, copra, ball rubber). Weights and measures, pulleys, ladders, cranes, stevedores' hooks, dollies, hessian – these should have been the basis for Germany's future rather than troop trains and siege artillery. Much of the history of the world could be described through ship manifests and warehousing. The old Hamburg free port is a sort of concentrated essence of what most people value and Germany by 1900 lay at its heart. It slurped in immense quantities of tropical goods, squirting them into an infinite range of specialized factories and then selling them back across the world – and doing all this through an infinity of middlemen and normal mercantile behaviour, with only a tiny element contributed by the German colonial empire itself.

Unfortunately tangled up with this was a feeling of intense competitiveness with Britain. Germany was winning that competition – its industries *were* overtaking Britain's, but in a rapidly expanding global market this need hardly be viewed as a problem. But a mutually reinforcing ideology grew in some circles in Britain and Germany that their futures were becoming incompatible. This was expressed most famously in the 'naval race', with Germany building huge new battleships of a kind which could only be seen as taking on Britain militarily. The British poured about a quarter of all government revenues into making sure that they won this

race, which they did. But it stoked a powerful, mutually reinforcing paranoia. If anyone had carried out opinion polls in 1890 the
idea of an Anglo-German war would in both countries have seemed
ludicrous – by 1910 it would have appeared very plausible.

The outbreak of war pushed into hyper-drive this British sense
of Germany as a sort of illegitimate horror. It required some rapid
retooling by the royal family, who had been until very recently
more than happy intimates with many Germans. Photographs of
George V wearing a spiked helmet tended to disappear and the
House of Saxe-Coburg-Gotha suddenly became the House of
Windsor. When Kaiser Wilhelm heard this he proposed, in a rare
moment of wit, that the German translation of Shakespeare's play
should be altered to *The Merry Wives of Saxe-Coburg-Gotha*. His
Serene Highness Prince Louis of Battenberg (after whom the odd
yet addictive bright yellow and pink British cake is named), a clever
and capable royal adventurer who had spent most of his career in
the Royal Navy and was First Sea Lord in 1914, suddenly found
himself having to retire and change his name to Mountbatten.
Nobody could have been more British – he had become naturalized
aged fourteen and was married to Queen Victoria's granddaughter,
but suddenly he was unacceptably German.

War may have broken out in 1914 through recklessness and
mismanagement, but its justification at once became monolithic and
adamant. The Germans, as it turned out, were intensely militaristic
(despite having a smaller proportion of citizens under arms than the
French), despotic (despite being strikingly less so than Russia) and
materialistic (despite the Allies being far richer than the Central
Powers). Germany's previously admired philosophers became the
prophets of zombie unthink; its widely drunk wines grossly infe-
rior to those of France and swept from the table; its beautiful
language the gargled jackboot voice of a parade-ground culture.
It's as inevitable a part of fighting as putting on uniforms, but it
doesn't make it any less depressing. This exhaustive intellectual and
cultural boarding-up of all the windows and locking all the doors
we have lived with ever since – attitudes which still make Germany
a sort of dead zone. The course of Nazism confirmed these attitudes

in every way: what could (if the result had not been so serious) be seen almost as a parody of British ideas from 1914 of German loathsomeness.

It was what turned out to be the unwinnable nature of the war that destroyed everything. The 'Hamburg future' was tragically deferred for Western Europe until the normal consumer world of early 1914 re-emerged for survivors after 1945 and after Hamburg itself had been razed to the ground. But even in the depths of the First World War, a relentlessly narrow and exclusively military struggle, at least on the Western and Italian fronts, nobody could imagine the specifically German evil that would ultimately be unleashed.

The Germans saw themselves in the Great War as sitting at the heart of European heritage, fighting against a bunch of vulgar materialists (the British), pants-down revanchists (the French) and drunken savages (the Russians). This was expressed by the Germans in Wagnerian and medievalist terms – the German soldier as a knight errant, as the cultured and thoughtful man obliged to arm himself for national defence. Until 1914 most British intellectuals would have denied being vulgar materialists, but would have been happy to agree with the descriptions of their new allies and have conceded Germany's central place in European culture. In 1914 this was knocked on the head with an immediate campaign across British universities to expunge 'German' thinking and block out any sense at all of Germany as a major culture, except perhaps in the far-distant past. It became, for obvious reasons, suspect to have any interest in Germany at all. The British and later the Americans mocked the idea of German 'Kultur', contrasting these appeals to ancient epics and chivalry with the sort of baby-eating, nun-violating reality. This infuriated the Germans and drove them to produce a deranged poster (on view in the Ingolstadt museum) comparing the output of literate schoolchildren, graduating students and publication of new books in Germany and Britain and showing (with suitable decorative trimmings such as the wise owl of Minerva) how Germany was miles more literate, innovative and sensitive – which was probably true. But it is striking now, when the passions of 1914 are broadly spent, just how much damage was done by this process. Decisions taken by sweating military men and tense politicians for specific – and as it turned out grotesquely wrong – reasons spilt out into every aspect of life in a sort of total mobilization with which in some measure we still live.

Disaster

The horrible military surprises piled up hour by hour. Only the most complacent elements in various high commands thought that the war would be brief, but everyone had assumed a serious victory followed by a further campaigning season to finish everything off. It turned out that the technology, particularly artillery, had run out of control and could kill off astonishing numbers of troops. Everyone's offensives, however frenzied, seized up in a disgusting hail of shell.

Every element in the war had failed within weeks to comply with the military leaders' plans – even Austria-Hungary's invasion of Serbia had gone completely wrong. It is at this point that the issue of Germany having a uniquely malign role in modern history becomes acute. After the French had won the Battle of the Marne, the Germans never developed a new plan that would have allowed them to prevail: even if the French could somehow be defeated there was now the promise of effectively infinite British and British empire resources backed potentially by American resources too. Everyone was stunned by the hundreds of thousands of casualties that had piled up. Germany's rulers *should* have sued for peace at that point. They had a substantial chunk of French territory to bargain with, but the failure to do this doomed everybody. Public opinion made an end to the war impossible for all sides and the way that the Germans failed even to discuss something which became self-evident later on—that the odds were hopelessly against them—is trivial and frightening. Both German defensive excellence and revolting haemorrhages such as the Battle of Verdun killed people in a way that made a mockery of the old Prussian élan that all German commanders swore by. Like the Emperor Ferdinand II in the Thirty Years War, the German General Staff held a delusive hope that the following campaigning season would make a major difference, whereas it simply radicalized and decayed the war further.

It is impossible to say much more about the Great War without overbalancing this whole book yet again. It is striking that the whole thrust of German 'world strategy' before the war (which had been the reason Britain was now fighting alongside France) proved entirely futile. The German empire wound up having no value at all. One of the few guilty pleasures available to the British was the swift destruction of this empire. Britain's Japanese allies took over the German concession in China and many Pacific islands; the cruelties and viciousness of the Germans all over Africa were replaced by a different layer of cruelties and viciousness. The only exception was a brilliant guerrilla campaign in German East Africa which had no wider meaning beyond misery and death for countless Africans.

One of the surprises proved to be the German surface navy, which had soaked up huge resources of steel, men and ingenuity but which effectively played no serious part in the war. The British blockaded Germany with ease, using their immense Grand Fleet to hold the two choke points of the English Channel and northern approaches to the North Sea; the Germans blockaded Britain in turn with U-boats. But however much damage the U-boats did they were a weapon of extreme weakness. The world's oceans crawled with British ships but all roving German surface units had been wiped out by the end of 1914 and U-boats could not reach most of Britain's global commerce. As it turned out, the British blockade was far more effective and Central Europe was starving by the third winter of the war, whereas the British just had to be frugal. The North Sea block-ade was matched by an amazing line of boats across the bottom of the Adriatic between Italy and Corfu which penned in the Austro-Hungarian navy, essentially making it inoperative for the whole war: U-boats slipped through but the ships built at such huge and futile cost by the Habsburgs stayed impotent. This was of course a rela-tively minor aspect of the war, but it sums up the problem faced by the Central Powers: the point of their history had been a constant argument for many centuries over who ruled which bit of a broadly landlocked part of the world. The Hungarians, as rulers of Fiume (now Rijeka), had spent a fortune on building their own dread-nought, the *Saint Stephen*, which was then sunk by an Italian torpedo-boat. The only fruit of all this was the commander of that navy, Admiral Horthy, after Hungary became reduced to a residual land-locked state after 1918, became its ruler for almost twenty-five years, with mixed results. Essentially the First World War did not earn that name because of Germany or Austria-Hungary, who could hardly move out of their small chunk of Central Europe, but because of the Allies, who ruled most of the world.

This parochialism doomed the Germans at repeated intervals. The Battle of Jutland in 1916 should have been a crushing British fleet victory, but what turned out for the British, after a century of having no serious opponents, to have been a mishandled mess proved to be irrelevant: the German ships' retreat to port ended the challenge. It was in effect a British victory because the German surface fleet conceded it could never get out of the North Sea. The navy which had done so much to ruin international relations before 1914 and alienate Germany from Britain had only one further role. It sat sullenly in Wilhelmshaven and Kiel waiting to bring down through mutiny the imperial regime which had lavished so much money on it. In the end, some fifty of the ships, including monsters like the *Crown Prince*, after being interned by the British in the Orkney Islands were scuttled by their German commander in June 1919 – the last futile act of a German empire that had imagined itself a global sea-power despite centuries of experience that implied otherwise. Most hair-raising is the suggestion that with the resources frittered on its navy it could easily have used the metal to make an almost infinite amount of artillery (how many field weapons could be made out of a floating town of steel like the *Crown Prince*?) with which the Battle of the Marne might even have been won.

Defeat and revolution

The war ended after more than four years of the most wearying and horrible fighting with a German defeat which structurally had been built in by the autumn of 1914. The conflict made a mockery of earlier wars, where the fighting had generally been a means of gaining political points. The Germans never had a coherent vision of what they wanted from the war beyond an ill-defined Mitteleuropa power-bloc, whereas for the British and the French the objective was clearly just to defeat the Germans and liberate northern France and Belgium. Kaiser Wilhelm was sidelined early in the war and never recovered. Germany converted itself into a military bureaucracy dedicated to promoting victory, channelling millions of young men to the different fronts with the right training and equipment. Because of the circumstances of the initial fighting and the static nature of the trenches the conflict was entirely different from traditional European wars in which at the first provocation armies from all over the Continent marched across a German landscape. In this sense unification proved a success – after the defeat of the French and Russian invasions the country itself remained safe throughout the war. The only clues that most Germans had to the war's progress was their own progressive weakening from lack of food and a horrible rain of telegrams reaching into even the most dopey former princely towns with news of yet more deaths. Eventual German casualties came to some six and a half million, in other words every ten days or so they had as many dead or wounded as in the whole Franco-Prussian War.

The Austro-Hungarians suffered around five million casualties before their Empire fell to pieces. The idea that the Habsburg Empire had been a rotten entity in 1914 has little basis in truth – it was clearly heading for a heavy rearrangement on Franz Joseph's death (which finally occurred, way too late, in 1916) but there was nothing to imply that it would become a mass of poisonous micro-states. It is probably fair to say that among the million and a half actual combat dead, in an Empire which had always had as much a military as a dynastic rationale, were many who had really valued the Empire and these could not be replaced. With the destruction of the army there was nothing left and it broke into some of its constituent fiefs – albeit with internal colonization in turn, so the Bohemian Czechs soaked up the Moravians, Slovaks

and Ruthenes, and the Serbs soaked up Slovenes, Croats and
Bosnians. The original late-medieval German-speaking base of
the Habsburg empire became by default a new Austrian state, a
subdued and potentially vicious little German nationalist dream
come true with its instantaneously parochialized minor capital in
Vienna. Some of the pre-war cultural life continued, but there was,
even before the Nazi takeover, an unmistakable sense of everyone
shutting up shop. Ludwig Wittgenstein had fought with heroism
and distinction in the Austro-Hungarian army on the Russian and
Italian fronts. On the latter he was fighting only a little west of the
young Erwin Rommel and Friedrich Paulus, who would be so
involved in the next war, and just missed Robert Musil, whose
essays on fighting there (in *Posthumous Papers of a Living Author*) are
some of the great miniaturist pieces of writing on the war. Wittgenstein wasted little time before heading to England; Schoenberg and
Roth moved to Berlin; Loos lived a sad, isolated existence; Klimt
and Schiele were dead. Some attempts were made to create a viable
Austrian state, but it was always racked with political dysfunction
and there was a German nationalist logic to joining the main
German state – a logic which the Habsburgs had fought for so long
to prevent.

The revolutions that engulfed Central Europe with the end of
fighting on the Western and Italian fronts were little understood in
Britain but played a disastrous role in explaining the unfolding of
events over the following two decades.

Aside from a few, quickly killed French and Russian soldiers in
1914, the odd spy and some prisoners-of-war, nobody in the Allied
military during the entire course of the Great War had stepped onto
German soil. The Armistice of November 1918 was in effect an
admission that this would always be too difficult – the Germans had
undoubtedly been defeated and their army was falling to pieces, but
there was to be no invasion of the kind that had previously marked
failure in war (most obviously after the Napoleonic Wars or the
Franco-Prussian War). This had a profound effect in turn on British
and French military commanders in 1939–40, almost all of whom
had fought in 1918, and who found the idea of successfully invad-

ing Germany with now far smaller armies psychologically quite impossible. In the short term this ambiguity – an armistice being a grand-sounding term for a ceasefire rather than a surrender – was to instil a catastrophic narrative into German life. Ludendorff had washed his hands of the war, assumed social revolution would follow defeat and headed off to Sweden to read detective novels in tranquillity. The hunt for traitors was almost immediate. Clearly the German ruling class had failed and they were swept away, with the Kaiser panicking and fleeing into exile in the Netherlands (perhaps needlessly; it is curious to think what might have happened if he had chosen to fight it out – he still had considerable resources, and the revolutionaries in Berlin were quickly and brutally defeated). All the other German royals fled or cut deals to allow them to live quietly in the countryside – an astonishingly speedy and total collapse for a system which had seemed so robust in 1914.

The blockaded, entrenched, sealed space of Germany which gradually became accessible again in 1919 was scarcely recognizable. Ravaged by influenza, much of the population half starving and with millions of dead and wounded, there should have been no doubt that Germany had been defeated. Instead the idea grew up, propagated not least by the Kaiser from exile, that there had been a 'stab in the back': that the army had *not* been defeated, but had instead been betrayed by communists, profiteers and civilian parasites – and not by 'true' Germans (as this would have complicated the idea of who was betraying whom), but by the Jews. With horrible speed a small group, among whom there were so many individuals who had been, despite routine discrimination, among the most magical and innovative figures in the German empire, became singled out as *un*-German.

Chaotic fighting now broke out in many major cities, most emblematically in Berlin and in Munich. The fighting that broke out across Munich could not have been more shocking. A city that took pride in its hierarchical, orderly, Catholic and legalistic heritage, beautiful shops and civic spaces became a disaster area. Already ravaged by the blockade and with many thousands of its citizens dead, Munich now succumbed to street-fighting in the chaotic week leading up to the Armistice as Ludwig III dissolved the monarchy and fled abroad. The terror that Munich would now fall to Bolshevism (seen by many, including many of those who did not support it, as the unstoppable wave of the future) led to mayhem. Before 1914 genuinely insurrectionary groups in Central Europe had been almost irrelevant. It had just been fun for conservatives to frighten themselves with the idea. If anything anarchism had then been a more striking movement. Its inbuilt ineffectiveness had at least spun off the odd, unexpected success, such as the killing of the Empress Elizabeth. Joseph Roth's derisive novel *The Silent Prophet* (written in the late 1920s) sums up the non-existent drama of the pre-1914 revolutionary in the figure of the hectic Galician communist Chaikin who, in his tiny Habsburg border town, tries to foment violent change, hectoring the municipal watchmen as 'capitalist lackeys' and stirring up the 'proletarian masses', in this case some hundred and twenty brushmakers. In Roth's crushing formulation: 'Nothing would have made him happier than to be arrested. But no one regarded him as dangerous.' Until the collapse of the winter of 1918 the most significant revolutionary act had in fact been carried out by the German imperial authorities themselves, with the decision to allow Lenin out of Switzerland and on to his remarkable destiny in Petrograd (the same ministerial group—a cornucopia of smart thinking – had recently come up with a plan to contact the Mexicans to ask if they could attack the USA, and get Texas, Arizona and New Mexico back as their reward – a low-comedy telegram gleefully intercepted by the British and shown to the enraged and ever less neutral United States).

But now the social revolution that broke out across Germany was genuine and nowhere more so than in Munich, where, after months of violence, the Soviet Republic of Bavaria was declared in the spring of 1919. It lasted less than a month and had almost no authority outside a tiny area (it impotently declared war on Switzerland) and was suppressed with 1914–1918-inherited brutality, with a thousand or so supporters of the Soviet Republic being killed in action and several hundred executed after capture. Disastrously, there were a striking number of Jews supporting the Soviet Republic (as there had been in the failed Spartacist uprising in Berlin that January) and this provided a lot of chapter-and-verse for those trying to shape a plausible narrative to explain to a traumatized population why the German empire had lost the war and collapsed into anarchy. Of course, it could also have been emphasized that however many Jews were involved, the great majority had been non-Jews, but somehow this was missed.

Munich has now so completely recovered its self-satisfied facade that it is very hard to see it as this irredeemably poisoned city – a poison only finally removed with its destruction and the arrival of the Americans in 1945. It has rebuilt itself as a pleasurable, student-filled and wealthy place – and now seems a twenty-first-century version of the city described in Thomas Mann's pre-1914 fiction (even down to the shops selling talent-free paintings). But, far more than Berlin, Munich was the laboratory experiment that destroyed Europe – a polarized, violence-obsessed society completely adrift from its old roots in the opportunistic but enjoyably unsuccessful world of the Kingdom of Bavaria, but with no plan for how it should comport itself as simply a regional German city.

The violence which periodically convulsed Germany and Austria in the 1920s and 1930s (and indeed other former Habsburg states) can perhaps best be seen as a series of civil wars which, unlike the one that eventually broke out in Spain, were overwhelmingly heavily weighted in favour of the right. Attempts to copy the Soviet Union failed dismally, with only weeks needed for the 'forces of order' to destroy the left. Munich was a perfect example – both in the left's futility and in the lesson it provided for a huge swathe of middle- and working-class people that it was better to connive with illegality and street violence than risk Bolshevism. Despite all its efforts the Weimar Republic could never compete with this visceral fear, a yearning for military protection against the monster that had been briefly unleashed in Munich. Many Germans still thought of themselves as standing by the law-abiding, polite and stratified pre-war society that they grew up in, but in practice this was often merely empty habit and wishfulness.

The British had set up the blockade in 1914 despite its illegality, simply because it was a clear way to damage Germany and a means of bringing Britain's main weapon, sea-power, to bear. As a purely military expedient it was meant to add to the difficulties Germany faced in fighting the war. As with everything else to do with the war, what started off as clever became something absolutely out of control. By 1918 the principal champion of free trade had destroyed free trade. Germany, which had been such a vital factor in global trade before 1914, was now just a mass of run-down factories dedicated to churning out ersatz foods and trench weapons (the Freikorps and the new Central European states could live off these stockpiles for years). Its main markets were now either an impoverished shambles (the former Habsburg Empire) or unhelpful enemies such as Britain, France and Italy who had switched to the United States as their supplier of comparable goods. World trade was also confronted by the USSR as a new autarky – another huge market for many countries now permanently shut.

This catastrophe was not really resolved until 1989 and the collapse of the Eastern Bloc – since then most of the world has traded normally with countries vying for position in the traditional way, as before 1914. In 1919, however, the situation was new and many among the Allies saw it as an amazing opportunity that so formidable a competitor had been knocked out, apparently forever. This was reflected in the Treaty of Versailles, which among many other things, saddled Germany with dizzying 'reparations', a hugely inflated version of what the Germans had done to France in 1871. The justification was based around German 'war guilt' – a disastrous piece of victor's justice which both absolved the Allies for all responsibility for 1914 and which rang completely untrue within Germany, thereby fermenting further a sense of almost overwhelming grievance across an alarming cross-section of society.

The links between reparations and the hyper-inflation of 1921–3 are confused, but the twin pressures of having to pay, for example, a quarter of all export earnings to the Allied commission and trying to restabilize a country ravaged by layer upon layer of economic headaches combined to generate a two-year horror movie which overlaid the war dead, the influenza and the revolutionary fighting to sever for many Germans any sense of belonging to a coherent political entity. There is no little local museum that does not have an exhibition on the appalling local effects of the inflation. Like the layer of iridium which marks the boundary between the Cretaceous and Tertiary eras, hyper-inflation marks perhaps a change even more fundamental than the war itself. If defeat had shown that Germany's leaders were worthless and if the failed revolutions had given the country's social fabric a disturbingly provisional pattern, then hyper-inflation trashed the bases on which families and individuals planned their lives – pensions disappeared, savings became a mockery, an entire German tradition of thrift and the authority of the country's banks dissolved. Behind the famous photos of people keeping themselves warm with stoves burning banknotes as a cheaper alternative to wood, or using banknotes as wallpaper, lay an absolutely traumatic event that scars Germany even today. It shows the inadequacy of historical narrative that propels events forward into the later 1920s, then into the 1930s, when what stayed stuck uppermost in many minds remained the memory of hyper-inflation.

The merciless quest for reparations meant that French and Belgian troops occupied the Ruhr in January 1923, so that instead of waiting for the German economy to recover, physical goods and supplies could simply be put on trains and diverted west. This occupation, which had been successfully fended off in 1918, was a humiliation which both radicalized a generally liberal part of Germany and reawakened historical nightmares of German weakness in the face of French predation. This anxiety was also stoked by French rule over the Saarland, a small chip of coal-rich territory which – through various twists and turns – only finally returned to Germany in 1957. Added to French attempts to foster a separate Rhineland state independent of the rest of Germany (this was not a success), it implied to many that the era in which Germany was not frightened of the French had lasted less than a lifetime.

When Germany's currency was finally fixed at the end of 1923 the damage had been done. Many individuals' lives had been ruined by the hyper-inflation, but others had prospered and, as with the revolutions of 1918–19, *some* of those had been Jews. Among extremist circles both on right and left, but also casually in conversation and in newspaper cartoons, a terrible set of assumptions about the Jews as puppet-masters, aliens, plotters, as the root of Germany's humiliation became plausible. Despite forming a mass movement the left turned out to remain feeble and vulnerable. The communists were easily disposed of in Germany in 1933 and in Austria in 1934. It was therefore right-wing anti-Semitism that proved so significant – with Nazism absorbing much of the left's old fantasies about Jews and capitalism.

Remembering the dead

I always feel compelled when turning up in any new German town to track down at once its First World War memorial. For very obvious reasons there are almost none to the Second World War beyond general expressions of distress and regret. The shame after 1918 lay in defeat rather than a level of moral dismay not previously experienced by a beaten power. Some Austrian war memorials (such as the one in the town of Rust, in the Burgenland) disconcertingly follow the British pattern of a memorial of a soldier statue with a list of names, with a further list of Second World War names tacked on, as though this was a straightforward matter. In Germany the only comparable example I could find was a beautiful snarling lion statue in Darmstadt, a broken spear stuck in its chest (a stab in the front, at least). This monument is irretrievably soiled by the bizarre decision to add on the battlefields of 1939–45 – the mutual, almost exclusively military disaster of the earlier conflict now tangled up in the civilian massacres and genocide of the second. The unimaginable level of private grief within Germany after 1945 was otherwise rightly expressed in private memorials, remembrance books, lists tucked away in town halls, church services – but not by major public memorials.

The bitter atmosphere after 1918 meant that each town came

up with its own solution as to how to memorialize its appalling numbers of dead. This resulted in extraordinarily interesting, or banal, or sometimes lastingly brilliant works in stone, wood, glass and metal which began as focuses for deep distress but rapidly became highly political and vexed and then neglected after the even greater disaster after 1939. With none of the national memorial guidelines issued in Britain and France, German responses were fascinatingly various. They respond to the existing genre of monuments to the Franco-Prussian War (which tended to use extravagant amounts of bronze and feature annoying allegorical figures plus reliefs of Wilhelm I and Bismarck) but in the very different atmosphere of national crisis and failure. Some are enjoyably backward – cavalrymen on horseback; some are madly historicist – such as a sort of neo-Assyrian bowl in Lübeck. Others attempt to follow in the great tradition of civic decoration – such as a beautiful but oddly overtangential fountain in Speyer. For many years I felt the greatest of these monuments was the memorial garden and statues in Worms – three stone figures in greatcoats and helmets. What was so moving was that under the ledge provided by the fronts of the statues' stone helmets a form of black moss had grown, covering the figures' eyes. I was, as an editor, once very involved in the publication of a new translation of Ernst Jünger's *Storm of Steel*, and made frantic and unsuccessful attempts to find photos of these moss-blinded statues for the jacket, even though their mournful message was quite at odds with the text. On a recent visit to Worms I found to my dismay that the statues had been cleaned up and without the moss were merely clunky and unoriginal.

Accidental decisions could have a major effect on the durability of a memorial. A huge list of dead inside Wolfenbüttel's principal church keeps all its power, whereas one outside the church in Augsburg is so weatherworn it is missing many names. It has its own power, however, because inside is a photo of King Ludwig III of Bavaria arriving in the summer of 1914 to dedicate the new regiment, many of whose troops, present in the church on that day, would have shortly thereafter contributed their names to the list on the fading marble outside. As with all such monuments there is a sense that even taking a slight interest makes one an interloper. It is unlikely that the memorials ever took on a constant meaning. Most were put up in the early 1920s once order had been reimposed, often after local civil wars. Fresh events were piling up so rapidly that the atmosphere of the dedication ceremonies is unimaginable. It was the constant wish of politicians in the Weimar Republic that people would move on – but they didn't. The millions of dead, the influenza epidemic, the loss of national territory, the hyper-inflation crushed any sense of a future. Each year the inhabitants of whole towns would gather around their memorial and reflect on Germany's, their town's, their family's disaster. In due course the memorials were richly Nazified and then set aside by later events.

The greatest German memorial remains the first one I encountered, on my first visit to Germany in 1991. For reasons that I simply cannot recall I spent some time in Hamburg but then went to spend several days in the haggard East German town of Magdeburg. This was at a point of very superficial reunification – empty, Stalinist squares lined with shops selling only cans of meat. Magdeburg was one of the most unrelievedly grim of these towns, but I enjoyed it endlessly – the layers of history seemed so thick and reunification held such promise (mainly fulfilled as it turned out) that Germany's dark years were finally coming to an end. The new authorities had made some tiny efforts to perk things up, but as yet these appeared merely ghoulish. The soot-caked, suicidally gloomy old Wilhelmine post office, with its rotting statues of Otto the Great and friends, had been decorated with stickers featuring a cheerful yellow cartoon glove with eyes, exhorting Germans to enjoy their postal services.

Through almost unbelievable setbacks the much battered and repatched cathedral has survived and so, despite years of controversy and hiding, does Ernst Barlach's Magdeburg Cenotaph. Barlach is one of the many highly attractive Weimar figures who, much like the Darmstadt artists before 1914, give Germany a completely different direction – but one which comes to nothing, flattened by a mass militarism which has had such uniquely terrible consequences. Barlach had been happily swept up in the fervour of

1914 but ended his service as a convinced pacifist. The cenotaph does not for a moment glorify war, but instead, in a set of monumental wooden figures, shows mournful, frightened or dead troops clinging to a cross. At night, in the darkened cathedral, with an area filled with candles in front of it, the cenotaph seems to sum up the shocked, fearful response to the Great War in a German equivalent to Robert Graves' *Goodbye to All That* (published in 1929 – the year that Barlach's memorial was unveiled). In the ever more threatening, polarized atmosphere of Germany the monument caused outrage and was, of course, dismantled after the Nazi seizure of power in 1933. Hidden, the monument re-emerged in East Germany and was reinstated, becoming in due course a focus for pro-unification sentiments in 1989. Like so many of Germany's great monuments, it implies a road not travelled – and takes on an almost unbearable additional layer of meaning.

Some royal aftershocks

Stepping off the train at yet another tiny railway station, swinging my ballsy pigskin grip filled with heaps of books and underwear, it became after a while almost second nature to orient myself deftly to the geography of small princely towns. The main street from the railway would be surprisingly far away from the town square – a reflection on the local lord wanting to keep the threat, noise and indignity of trains at a distance. A spire or tower would quickly mark the main town church, which would be near the principal (or indeed only) square, with the Schloss set back several streets. As I whistled a tune and swung my grip (or, latterly, as I pulled along a little wheelie-bag, having damaged my lower back with that initial, ill-judged piece of luggage), I could not help feeling the sheer pleasure of harmlessness. These daft little towns, even if individual princes might have been in practice Prussian commanders, offered such a welcome affront to the more brutal currents in German history. If Saxony was a lesson in the limits of political incompetence, then the small towns seemed to celebrate a pure and genuine irrelevance, a crucial trait underestimated by historians. These places are like potato crisps in that there seems to be no upper limit to how many it is enjoyable to consume. Indeed, this entire book could have been filled with evasive and marginal material on an infinity of loopy backwaters, none without value or some unique oddness.

I cannot prevent myself, for example, from returning to that old favourite Bückeburg, former capital of the doll's handkerchief state of Schaumburg-Lippe. Almost nothing ever happened here, for the understandable reason that there were too few people for anything other than a minor argument. But, as usual, it contains something strange – a Mannerist chapel inside the Schloss coated in painted flowers, fruit and cupids, the best, maddest heraldic decorations conceivable and an altar held up by enormous gold angels, sheltering the buried hearts of the counts and princes of Schaumburg-Lippe. The tours of such places are always tense as, however boring any given room, there is always the chance for something grotesque around the next corner and it is hard not to skip ahead in the hope of finding a treat – a stuffed wolf, a miniature cannon, an arbitrary tusk or some unsuccessful piece of locally produced classical allegory. Bückeburg's glory is its run of portraits of the counts (who became princes with the end of the Holy Roman Empire) which allows an incredibly quick fast-forward of the entire experience of minor absolutist fashion from the seventeenth to the early twentieth centuries, as a full dark wig gives way to a short white wig; sensible hair and a high collar to a manly beard and military uniform; and in turn to monocle, moustache and evening wear – and over and out! Bückeburg's entirely disturbing feature is a series of chairs, each with its seat pattern stitched by the new bride of the count/prince – an assembly with a Duke Bluebeard-like atmosphere, implying a whole world of panicked and incompetent young stitching fingers now long reduced to dust.

I mention these places now because it is striking how recently they were at the heart of each small town, indeed much of the economic point. The people who lived in places like Bückeburg or Sigmaringen or Altenburg were there to service the family, economically and deferentially. Sometimes the late nineteenth century brought local or even quite substantial industries and at the latest real power drained away from these minor figures with the German empire's creation in 1871. But if they could survive dynastic twists and deaths many of the rulers lasted to 1918. Wandering around these immense piles it is impossible not to notice how many of them took on new wealth and improvements right up to the First World War. The deal done with the surviving rulers in 1871 suggested that they would be frozen in place in an uneasy subserviency to the new emperor indefinitely and they behaved as such, continuing to lay down fresh layers of dynastic tat for their sons and their sons' sons. In old photos the principal hall at the astonishingly large and magniloquent Schloss Altenburg is sensible, dull and neo-classical. Following a fire in 1900 or so it was rebuilt in an industrial neo-Renaissance style with riots of carved woodwork, elaborate fireplaces and leering wildmen. If the Dukes of Saxe-Altenburg had enjoyed a bit more use of the hall before being kicked out it might have looked by now, with a century of scuffs and kippering, fairly realistic. Or at Schloss Sigmaringen, also rebuilt after a fire, there is a gentlemen's games room with a revolutionary black-graphite ceiling to absorb tobacco smoke, the whole place redolent of a sort of broad-arsed and side-whiskered Edwardian bonhomie of a very unappealing kind. The highlight of any of these, almost but not quite interchangeable tours is always the royal/princely/comital bathroom, permanently frozen with the style of toilet installed in the 1890s or 1900s.

I need to stop here before I am reduced to sketching in details of the Empress Zita's shower facilities, put into the Schonbrünn Palace during the First World War. The point is that in the chaotic, terrifying weeks of the Emperor Wilhelm II and the Emperor Karl I's resignations, the whole lot fell to bits. Without the legitimacy of the main monarch, dynasties which had lasted centuries suddenly stopped. Many of these rulers, particularly the larger ones, had flattered themselves that they maintained a sort of autonomy, but in practice none did. They were as much part of the failed, loathed system which had brought the Central Powers to ruin as the more ostensibly powerful emperors. Some fled abroad acknowledging no change, some resigned in brief pedantic ceremonies, some managed to negotiate reasonable deals to retire. This Central Europe-wide spasm, straddling the announcement of the actual Armistice, was both positively revolutionary and oddly null. There seems to have been almost no interest in preserving these figures, flicking idly through their bathroom-fixture magazines, and the entire skein of symbolism and inter-marriage in many ways quite unexpectedly disintegrated. This generated some temporary oddities, such as the People's Republic of Reuss, a Thumbelina-sized nest of Bolshevism created on the abdication of the last Reuss princes which was crushed and incorporated into the Weimar Republic by 1920.

Some families managed after 1918 to twist and find fresh public roles for themselves – Prince Charles Frederick of Hesse managed to become King of Finland for a couple of months, his son Prince Philipp of Hesse had a horrible role in the Third Reich. Many retired into wealthy private life. Others had a strange, continuing dynastic half-life. The Hohenzollern-Sigmaringen family, in their guiltily appealing Schloss on the Upper Danube, had suffered the indignity of seeing the other, Protestant branch of their family become Kings of Prussia. They lost control over their own territory in the aftermath of the 1848 revolutions, being absorbed by Prussia almost without anyone commenting. They retained their Schloss and honours as Hohenzollern princes and played their cards shrewdly (latterly, under that revolutionary black-graphite ceiling). Prince Karl Anton managed to have one child married to the King of Portugal and another to a son of the King of Belgium; another died fighting in the Austro-Prussian War and another was offered the Spanish throne, the action that sparked the Franco-Prussian War. There can hardly have been a dull week for the postman in Sigmaringen from the 1840s to the 1870s. And in a superb dynastic coup which made the others relatively paltry, a further son, Karl, became first Prince and then King of Romania, as Carol I. Quirkily, the Romanian Hohenzollerns found themselves fighting the Prussian Hohenzollerns when Romania joined the Allies in the

First World War. Despite a disastrous war, the Romanians were rewarded for this, as Kaiser Wilhelm sloped off into exile, by being given piles of old Habsburg and Russian territory in a final, mad efflorescence of Hohenzollern–Sigmaringen power on the Black Sea. King Carol's birth at Sigmaringen is proudly marked on a slate tablet in one of the upper courtyards of the Schloss (just after a quite matchless arquebus display), placed there to mark its centenary in 1939, immediately before the outbreak of the war that would finally destroy the dynasty.

Sigmaringen is also famous for the unwanted reason that the Nazis used it as the final home of the Vichy government, after D-Day had made it unsafe for them to remain in the country they were supposed to govern. The remaining members of the Hohenzollern family were themselves kicked out and lodged in a nearby Schloss of the Stauffenberg family, which had been confiscated following Claus von Stauffenberg's involvement in the July 1944 plot to kill Hitler. There can be few better examples of the futility and terror of political power than the slow months spent by the Vichy government, pacing back and forth in the gentlemen's games room or under heavy chandeliers of industrial Bohemian glass pretending to rule France and snarling at each other over whose fault it all was, with Pétain having as his medical attendant (by a happy stroke of luck) the collaborationist novelist of genius Céline, who wrote a brilliant, albeit impenetrable, novel, *Castle to Castle*, around his experiences.

Rather as the Taiwanese government would solemnly debate dam-building projects in Sichuan as though it still ruled mainland China, so the Vichy government was obliged to behave as though it still had a role in the life of France. Instead its members had now to suffer the exquisite torture of an endless, nightmarish, permanent Schloss tour: here is the yellow drawing room, so named after the canary-coloured furnishings, here is the dowager's room, where she used to take chocolate with her friends, here yet again is the gentlemen's games room, please note the revolutionary black-graphite ceiling, back and forth, back and forth for month after month waiting for the Allies to arrive and to be exiled or shot.

   Indeed as ever more time goes by and with their real functions
lying in an ever remoter and less plausible past, these places might
all merge together into a single tour, an awful continuum before the
final disaster: a slurry of fly-blown glass, hand-stitched cushions,
paintings of men in sashes, unflushable toilets, rotten bed-frames,
ridiculous old weapons, worm-eaten mounted elk heads, with the
whole lot – following a final cry of 'And through the next door is
the yellow drawing room' – slowly lurching to one side and crashing into the moat/river/formal gardens below.

CHAPTER FIFTEEN

An unattractive lake

Having felt sorry for Europeans obliged to holiday on the shores of the brackish and unengaging Baltic, I felt my sympathies being recalibrated further at the sight of families clustered on the shores of the reed-choked, biting-insect haven of the Neusiedler See. This surreal lake on the border between Austria and Hungary is very shallow (indeed so shallow that it occasionally just vanishes) and its water, as you chug across it in a lugubrious boat, takes on the appearance of lightly slopping and shiny chicken stock. In an intensely inland world, this haven of liquid, however duff, is so sought after that the little towns around it have hacked their way through the reeds and mud to build concrete vacation platforms which allow holidaymakers to encounter the lake's quite narrowly definable pleasures. Suddenly the Baltic seems on a par with Waikiki.

The southern end of the lake is controlled by Hungary, and while it may be a somewhat depressing place to swim, the whole area is from almost every other point of view completely fascinating. An old piece of Royal Hungary (the small chunk held by the Habsburgs after the Ottoman annihilation of the Hungarian monarch and aristocracy in 1526), the lake and its shores were one of countless casualties in the shattering of the Empire in 1918. It is now the most eastern spot where German is spoken and forms one of the great linguistic frontiers. It is hard to convey to anyone not besotted with Central European culture *just* how tough it has been for me over the past few years to maintain mental military discipline and not spin off into thinly justified trips outside the core German zone. I so want to see Roth's Galicia, von Rezzori's Bukovina, Kiš's

Voivodina, Handke's Karst, the countryside that inspired Bartók's 'night music'. Once down in the German-speaking far south-east it seemed unfair and mad that I had decided to saddle myself with a linguistic circumference which now – I hectically felt, with the cunning of an addict – simply made *no sense*. Sitting in the little Austrian village of Rust, eating pumpkin soup, watching countless tiny insects mating on my shirt, listening to the freakish rattle of storks clacking their beaks from their chimney-top nests, I could almost feel the gravitational pull of Hungary – only a short walk down the road to Fertörákos! I had deliberately left my passport in Vienna to prevent myself from taking that walk and this confusion and self-loathing probably contributed a lot to my antagonism towards the blamelessly slopping Neusiedler See.

The inhabitants of Royal Hungary had generally been ruled by Hungarian aristocrats, but in many cases themselves spoke German. This was true from Pressburg in the north, through to Ödenburg and innumerable small towns, enough of which ended in the suffix burg to justify the newly invented, 1918 Austrian term Burgenland. At the end of the First World War the inhabitants of such places across Central Europe had only miserable options. Often dopey and agrarian regions which had been either internal to Austria-Hungary or, like the Sudetenland, been on a benign and unthreatening border, suddenly became key linguistic and ethnic fighting grounds. The point where German stops being spoken around the Neusiedler See could not be more dramatic – on the left bank was the small town of Eisenstadt with its old Hungarian aristocracy and German, Jewish and Croat inhabitants (including most famously, in much happier times, Haydn and Liszt), but once down off the hills and across the lake there are a handful of microscopic places before the prairie begins, crammed with grapes and sunflowers, and there can be no doubt you are heading into Hungary. In rough outline this was the point where medieval German settlers and Hungarian settlers crashed into each other, squeezing aside Slavs up to the north (who became Czechs and Slovaks) and Slavs down to the south (who became Croats and Slovenes).

As the Habsburg Empire imploded after the Armistice, the question of who ruled this area provoked serious fighting, upheaval and poverty as Allied forces tried to adjudicate between the puny new Austrian state and the equally demoralized and shorn Hungarian one. The Czechs pulled off the strange trick of appearing to have always been on the side of the Allies and secured the northern city of Pressburg, changing its name to Bratislava. A tense, brutal referendum in Ödenburg made it part of Hungary and turned it into Sopron. Posters and pamphlets from the time (1921) are a horrible reminder of just how quickly politics can sour. The Austrian and Hungarian relationship had always been a tense and awkward one, but between them they had defeated the Ottomans, played an incalculably important role in European culture for four centuries and just fought a world war alongside each other at huge, mutual sacrifice. The Empire's end tore this up in weeks. Pro-Austrian propaganda offered the voters of Ödenburg/Sopron a choice between Austrian 'Freedom, Nationhood, Prosperity' or Hungarian 'Brutality, War, Starvation'. Another pamphlet shows Hungary as a skeleton in gypsy clothing beguiling the innocent Ödenburgers with his violin music into voting for Hungarian loathsomeness. It is all a long way from the slightly dopey beauty of Schubert's *Hungarian Melody*. Thousands left their homes in scenes which were to be become gruellingly familiar over the coming decades, but which then had a shock of novelty for Germans. With the Cold War the inhabitants of Bratislava and Sopron had the unhappy experience of realizing that decisions taken by their parents and grandparents put them on the wrong side of the Iron Curtain while the rest of the Burgenland, once the Russians had gone in 1955, was left to muck around in expensive cars and enjoy, quite accidentally, the pleasures of post-war white-goods capitalism.

This was one of many disasters – a pre-1914 world in which language had been important but not fundamental was replaced by a set of nation states committed to a linguistically driven uniformity. Linguistic nationalism, once it had created some good operas, erected a few statues and changed some road names, tended to turn ferociously on anyone viewed as outside the ethnic pale. The only justification for the existence of, say, Czechoslovakia was a linguistic one – but in practice the new country remained linguistically a shambles. Even the relatively moderate Czechs were compelled by the logic of their own language nationalism to come down hard on 'their' Germans, Slovaks, Hungarians, Poles and Ruthenes. This toxicity was resolved with the most extreme violence: the nature of the disaster was dictated by Nazism, but none of the nationalists in their new nations could ever stabilize and legitimize their unhappy countries.

Austro-Hungarian officers had been obliged to speak a number of languages, at least in pidgin form, but this was not the future. Romanians forced Hungarians and Germans to speak Romanian, Czechs turned on their German-speakers, and so on. Regions or provinces reliant on other regions suddenly became countries surrounded by enemy countries and their economies, never strong and already wrecked by war, simply collapsed. The traditional responses to such failure (to move to the cities or emigrate to America) came to nothing as the cities themselves began to fail (Vienna lost some three hundred thousand inhabitants after 1918) and America shut down immigration.

Each small country had its own absolutist ideology of a kind which was both loathsome and highly dangerous. German-speakers went into a kind of shock – their own chauvinistic language of rule had become a badge of shame and a broad swath of Central Europe from Danzig down into what became Yugoslavia enclosed all sorts of marooned German communities under the orders of other linguistic groups who their own nationalist culture had raised them to despise. And tangled up in a poisonous situation were groups viewed as beyond simple nationalist categories – Jews and gypsies. German organizations held elaborate regular ceremonies at the new borders to express their contempt for them. The fate of cities felt to be German, such as Bratislava, Posen, Riga and Sopron, was viewed with a similar fetishistic tearfulness to that felt by the French when Alsace-Lorraine had been made German in 1871.

It is impossible, even at this distance in time, not to feel absolute despair at the result of the First World War. It is traditional to see Germany as tied to the rotting hulk of the Habsburg Empire, but in terms of the impact of the war it is more plausible to see the

Habsburg Empire tied to the cretinous and wholly unrealistic goals of the Germans. All the Habsburgs wanted to do was punish Serbia for killing their heir and attempting to destabilize Bosnia. Their attempts to do this might in 1914 have provoked a Russian intervention which would have resulted in the Habsburgs losing and a treaty being drawn up with various changes of a traditional kind, but Germany's irrational attempts to defeat much of the world (including large and important bits its army could not even reach) doomed the Habsburgs to disaster. The Habsburgs' own epics of terrible defeat, ranging from the Siege of Przemyśl (a hundred and fifty thousand dead or captured) to the Brusilov Offensive (a million and a half dead, wounded and captured) could, despite regularly beating the Italians, have no effect on a war whose decision was being reached elsewhere.

The Empire would have broken up anyway at some point, but there was little indication in 1914 that this was going to happen in the ruinous way it did. Vienna had pointed to a fabulous future and was in no sense an anachronistic city. It had even created its own 'luxury modernism', expressed variously through Klimt, Freud, Berg, Hoffmann, Loos and so many others and which could easily have defined European style and ideas for decades. It seems more rational to be angry than mournful that a war of such a peculiar kind would end all this. The final movement of Berg's extraordinary *Three Orchestral Pieces*, with its lurching, macabre military march, written in the spring and summer of 1914, is generally seen as a brilliant premonition of the conflict to come – but nobody could foresee such a thing. It would be as plausible to criticize Klimt because his paintings incorrectly presaged a future mostly filled with half-nude society hostesses. Most of the great works of Central Europe after the war would have happened in some form regardless of the political arrangements. Just in terms of music, figures such as Bartók, Szymanowski, Janáček and Schoenberg were clearly set on their marvellous paths before or during the war and the subsequent political arrangements of their countries were an accident, however celebrated by nationalists. Without the fracturing of the Empire (and the Russian Civil War and its results) they could have been perhaps just more happy and productive – and certainly not ended up with Bartók struggling with American breakfast cereal in New York or Schoenberg watering his garden plants in Los Angeles.

Putsches and suspenders

Berlin in the 1920s is one of the modern era's great clichés. What had been the starchy heart of the Prussian barracks became almost overnight a lubricious wonderland. The sheer violent energy of Grosz's, Dix's and Beckmann's paintings, with their robot-like profiteers, porcine streetwalkers and mutilated beggars, define the period so vividly that any suggestion that this may not have been the common experience has almost no meaning. For myself, I am anxious that, dressed in suspenders, an old Freikorps helmet and clumsily applied blusher, lying in the corner of some chaotic squat, I would probably not have been able to keep up. But I doubt that I would have been alone. A more characteristic picture of the 1920s might have been one of an impoverished family whose high hopes in 1913 had been turned to garbage and whose wan lives were dominated by the deaths of several members through the trenches, civil war, epidemic or starvation and by having no work. Berlin was in the 1920s a city of ghosts, both at a private level and at a public one, with the military and imperial heart of the city ripped out and thrown away. The orgiastic feeling of the city, so enjoyed by foreigners, was based on a void.

1920s Berlin keeps an astonishing glamour now in large part because what followed was so horrible that this one decade can be seen as a delusive but pleasurable bubble, rather than as an incubator for subsequent events. There is no doubt that some of the era's cultural achievements were extremely alluring, but they stemmed from the strange vacuum in Berlin's moral code and were not characteristic of most of the rest of the country, which instead saw Berlin's vigour as a disgusting laxness and depravity that added to the sense the Weimar Republic was illegitimate.

Fritz Lang's spectacular and highly successful movies (*The Testament of Dr. Mabuse*, *M* and particularly perhaps the delirious *Spies*) all peddle Berlin and the Republic as display cases for the worship of criminals, drug use and promiscuity – a mix that perhaps drummed up as much support for Nazi discipline (albeit somewhat regretfully) among rural and small-town populations as the economic situation or fallen national pride. Equally the major artists of the period, with their emphasis on viciousness, prostitution and the distorted or murdered human form, appalled many Germans and made the Nazi 'Degenerate Art' exhibition and removal of Expressionist pictures and sculptures widely applauded. This tension, intolerance and rush to violence were as characteristic of the German avant-garde as of communist or Nazi street gangs. The room for manoeuvre among the thoughtful and genuinely democratic politicians remained painfully slight, even in the tiny period between Germany entering the League of Nations in 1926 and the Wall Street Crash three years later that ended any chance of the republic becoming 'normal'.

One of the most really uncomfortable 'Weimar' things to do remains walking the route taken by Hitler and his followers through central Munich in November 1923 at the end of their attempted putsch. The putsch was a joke, in as much as most of the country paid no attention and Hitler's announcement that the government in Bavaria and Berlin had ceased to exist had no currency outside the walls of the beer-cellar where he and his associates held several Bavarian officials hostage. Hitler, inspired by Mussolini's 'March on Rome' the previous year, in the face of which the Italian government had collapsed, felt he could achieve something similar. Extraordinarily, given that Hitler was still a marginal and ridiculous obsessive in a provincial town, Ludendorff (who had put down his detective novels and returned from Sweden when he thought it safe) was also a critical figure in the putsch. In the status-mad German world, a vegetarian ex-corporal plotting with a man who had only five years earlier been effective dictator of Germany shows how chaotic life had become, driven mad by military failure and economic implosion.

Aware that the putsch was being met in the wider world with indifference, Ludendorff attempted to dramatize events with a march through Munich. Some two thousand assorted Nazis tramped through the town centre – as you come to the narrowed road, lined with the palace to the right and pretty chocolate shops to the left, it becomes almost intolerable to share the same space. Here, before the street opened into Odeonsplatz and the Field Marshals' Hall, a cordon of police took advantage of the narrow street to bar the way. Both sides opened fire and the man linking arms with Hitler was killed. Given Hitler's unique and specific role in the death of millions, this gloomy, high-walled patch of road is one of the world's worst places. By a few inches an anonymous Bavarian policeman *just* managed to miss doing what it took an inconceivable level of worldwide violence to achieve.

The aftermath of the putsch was curious. Ludendorff, with a sort of loopy bravery, carried on marching until arrested, while Hitler ran away. Ludendorff despised Hitler from then on, was acquitted at the trial, and played no further part in the Nazi story. Even then, Hitler's range of offences was voluminous and he should have been in gaol until well into the 1950s, but the poison that had seeped into so many aspects of German life came to his rescue. An outrageously partial judge gave him a short sentence, patently out of admiration for a man of the right who was anti-communist, anti-Jewish and pro-military. The publicity around the trial gave Hitler a platform which he never relinquished and a near-comic failure became the basis for Europe's ruin.

The madly distant worlds of Berlin vaudeville and Munich militarist plotting were equally characteristic responses to the collapse of 1918. In Britain and America the great mass of millions of survivors of the war went home, and lived out their lives as veterans only at occasional beery reunions. A minority never recovered from their experience, remaining in vast purpose-built hospitals for the rest of their lives or distressingly at odds with the post-war world. But most were relieved that the fighting was over and had no further interest in the values of a terrible time, beyond a clipped and tidy manner much laughed at by later generations. These were countries which had suffered, but had also triumphed. Every country had its own reaction. Perhaps most disastrously many Italians felt their war dead (in proportion even worse than Britain's) an absolute and shameful exercise in futility. This resulted in the collapse of its government and the arrival of Mussolini – a figure who played a far more baleful wrecking role in Europe than Hitler did until 1938, a ruler as damaging to peace as Napoleon III had been in the 1850s and 1860s.

The German reaction to defeat was furious disbelief. The new government's decision to allow troops from the front to march through Berlin after the Armistice – like victors rather than the tail-end of a now permanently expunged military tradition – signified a disastrous confusion not resolved until 1945. There were, of course, plenty of beerily ineffective veterans' associations, but there were also repeats across Germany of the small group that formed around Hitler in Munich, constantly, acridly reliving the events of November 1918. Some consistently good economic news might have swept these groups away or a bit of luck might have killed or imprisoned Hitler (and it is striking that none of those around him could, in Hitler's absence, have ever been more than a brutal South American *caudillo* – the chaotic, very specific evangelical cocktail in Hitler's mind was crucial to what followed).

Far away from these bitter responses, there remained a quieter and more reflective Germany, albeit one that in the end proved completely useless. Most famously there was the 'Migrating Birds' (Wandervogel) movement, whereby hundreds of thousands of people hiked, sang songs and built camp-fires. Although its roots lay before the First World War its great expansion happened in the 1920s when every conceivable hiking trail must have been choked with uncontrollable defiles of whistling characters with special hiking sticks. (The aftershocks of this movement continue to make hiking a precarious activity today. In one of my ludicrous attempts to follow in Goethe's footsteps, this time in the hills above the Harz town of Thale, things started out perfectly enjoyably, but by mid-morning so many walkers in special fluorescent gear were pouring down the hillside, like a jolly version of an

orc army, that I had to press myself against the cliff face to get out
of the way.)

The 'Migrating Birds' movement was both a direct response to
the war and a further expression of popular romanticism, egged on
by better communication. The trains that had whisked millions of
soldiers to the Eastern and Western fronts now provided similar
super-saturated concentrations of cheerful hikers. Together with the
scouts, the 'Migrating Birds' were banned by the Nazis. Some of
their members enthusiastically switched to the outdoorsy values
of the Third Reich: others turned away and into themselves. As
so often in German history there was a strong pull towards the soft
or incompetent which tragically proved an insufficient response to
the aggression of others.

Forms of avant-garde life continued too, albeit with much
reduced resources. The vigour of German music had never relied
on the gormless Berlin court and so did not feel its loss. In 1921
Prince Max Egon von Fürstenberg founded the Donaueschingen
Festival in Germany's far south-west, which premiered in its first
season the perhaps quintessential piece of Weimar music, Paul
Hindemith's *Chamber Music Number One*, with its deliriously clatter-
ing xylophones, siren and tin can filled with sand – a vision of
somewhat frenetic happiness. The festival burst with remarkable
sounds until it collapsed in the Depression. It is a curious indication of how briefly the Nazis ruled that Prince Max was still
presiding over the revived festival in the 1950s, receiving on his
death memorial pieces by Stravinsky, Boulez and others. The effort
required to keep in mind these cultural currents without seeing
them as a naive interlude between wars is perhaps just too great, but
it remains crucial in the interests of sanity, proportion and self-
worth.

'5, 4, 3, 2, 1 . . .'

There is so much to be written about the popcorn-popper explosion of ideas out of Germany in this period, even if it was all within

a drastically narrower ambit than before 1914. The Bauhaus managed to invent most aspects of modern design in a mad flurry of excellence and to walk along the leafy street of the professors' houses in Dessau remains a thrilling experience. This continuing, light, stainless-steel version of Wagner's 'complete-work-of-art' approach to life had its schools in other countries too, but there was a wholeheartedness in Weimar Germany, inherited not least from the pre-war Darmstadt colony. It imprints an entire era, from writing paper to factories, and involved artists shuttling frantically between disciplines and ideas. Oskar Schlemmer is a perfect example – a painter and sculptor who used a sort of Bauhaus style in any number of media and who collaborated with Hindemith in making a 'Triadic Ballet' where dancers lurched about in semi-robotic costumes of great, colourful stylishness (and which can still be seen at the New State Gallery in Stuttgart). Schlemmer sums up a world of intensely experimental and curious ideas, linking the Bauhaus (where he taught) and many other practices and values, all feeding off each other.

The robot-like 'Triadic' dancers were part of a wider fascination with automata that also seems very characteristic of the period. Karel Čapek had introduced the word 'robot' in its modern sense in his 1921 Czech play *R.U.R.* and mechanical or jerkily moving people flit about in German culture in a way that makes the atmosphere new, alarming and very enjoyable. Nabokov's brilliant Berlin novel *King, Queen, Knave* enjoys itself with the invention of robot shop-window mannequins, artists such as Schlemmer or Klee portrayed humans as forms of dolls or automata, two of the most haunting German films, *The Golem* and *The Cabinet of Dr Caligari*, lumber and lurch and, of course, in one of the greatest pulp coups in all cinema, the atrocious Rotwang conjures up the Maria robot in *Metropolis*.

It is possible to see these as reflections of a reeling world heading for disaster, and there is definitely something unsettling, particularly in Fritz Lang's hectic movies. There is also a sense of despair that the tap of German film was about to be turned off – the period of good German sound films is even shorter than the

time spent by Germany in the League of Nations. But even before
the Nazis came to power the great directors were leaving for
Hollywood or were already dead. All of Lang's films remain hyp-
notically good, whether silent or with sound, but the most alarming
is definitely *The Woman in the Moon* (1929), his last silent picture.
A science-fiction film of daft solemnity, it was based on the ideas of
Hermann Oberth, a strange Transylvanian Saxon, who had come up
with the fundamental breakthroughs that to travel to the moon a
rocket would need to be made from a series of discardable stages
and that rocket flight would render astronauts weightless. The film
absorbs these ideas and suddenly becomes eerily modern (despite
such oddities as the Moon having an atmosphere and all the characters in the rocket wearing travelling tweeds and sensible shoes).
Lang lavished immense attention on his model rockets and had help
and advice from Oberth's Spaceflight Society, which had been
experimenting in fields outside Berlin with very small chemical-
filled projectiles.

As part of the marketing budget for *Woman in the Moon* money
was made available to the society to build something slightly more
ambitious. This plan came to nothing, but among society members
excited by *Woman in the Moon* was the teenage genius Wernher von
Braun, a refugee from what had become Poland (the prominence
of non-German Germans in rocket research is odd, but probably
meaningless) who now joined up with Oberth. *Woman in the Moon*
had echoes in von Braun's morally horrifying but quintessentially
twentieth-century career. This was perhaps most strangely expressed
in the spoken '5, 4, 3, 2, 1' blast-off sequence in the film, which
had been invented by Lang merely as a piece of 'business' but
which was carried over as a seemingly vital part of von Braun's
V-2, Gemini and Apollo programmes. There can be few more
complex cultural experiences than watching *Woman in the Moon* – a
film into which, far more than Lang's *Metropolis*, so much of the
modern world seems to fit: from the tomb of the Nordhausen V-2
slave-labour factory to the generational wonder of the real moon-
landings. In this one, in many ways very dopey movie, and in von
Braun's whole career, and indeed in so much of Weimar culture,

there seems to lurk a range of issues too complex and worrying ever to be untangled.

The death of science

Whatever the appeal some aspects of Weimar Germany might have, there is an undeniable sense of silting-up and failure – that this is a long way from the country of the late nineteenth century. A painful and clear-cut example was in what had been the magic world of German technical and scientific knowledge. To look back nostalgically, before 1914 a large part of modern existence was carved out by an engaging mixture of clever individuals and huge laboratories. Germans raced through piles of chemicals, machine-tools and bits of electrical equipment in a frenzy of inventiveness and ideas. My favourite example (aside from the most blindingly obvious such as Daimler and Benz inventing motorcycles and cars or Haber inventing nitrogen fertilizer or Diesel inventing his engine – or Einstein for goodness' sake!) is Ernst Haeckel. Haeckel spent his long and productive life as Darwin's principal German champion and ensured widespread acceptance of evolutionary theory there, his role being as important as Thomas Huxley's in Britain. He engaged in the same sort of scornful anti-religious bullying as Richard Dawkins today (indeed in Germany Dawkins is hailed as 'the new Haeckel') and popularized some extremely unattractive racial theories. Haeckel was also a microscope researcher of genius and his enthusiastic lectures and bestselling science books made legions of amateur and professional microscope obsessives. He could also claim to be perhaps the greatest German artist of the later nineteenth century – just as Maria Sibylla Merian had been the greatest at the end of the seventeenth century, if only the paintings and drawings of scientists were placed in the same mainstream as individuals painting, for example, landscapes. His mesmerizing pictures of protozoa, sponges and jellyfish were also a key inspiration for Jugendstil – a further reason for giving him an orthodox place in art history. It is fun to think of the ever more sclerotic military atmosphere in the German empire being invaded and undermined

by a drifting, wispy almost narcotic decorative atmosphere thanks
to unpoliticized wobbly objects scooped out of the sea off the
Canary Islands.

The strength of this science was its sense of being part of a
hugely complex and smoothly run machine, both national and
global. Experimentalists in places such as Jena could find enthusiastic students, amateur interest and industrial funding. The practical
implications of chemistry or lens-making would be seized on to fuel
ever more complex products which would then be sold everywhere.
Germany poured out a dizzying array of useful things to the rest of
the world, not unlike the United States. This highly interconnected
system was devastated by the First World War and in its nature left
little trace. It is only by looking back that one can see what goes
missing.

To carry on being nostalgic, one interesting survival (well,
marvellous survival to be honest) is the more or less untouched
range of galleries at the Natural History Museum in Vienna, one of
the great repositories of pre-1914 learning. As every reader must
have gathered by now I have a shaky-handed weakness for cabinets
of curiosities, and the Vienna museum is the dizzying pinnacle –
the natural-history equivalent of one of the great blast furnaces
of Essen. Setting aside its unimprovably bulky sea-elephant in the
entrance hall ('shot in the Falkland Islands in 1901') and what
must be the biggest and most threatening collection of crocodiles,
gharials and caimans anywhere, it is the decorative schemes in the
rooms which are the most surprising survivals. In all the heaving
late-Victorian decor there are some wonderful natural-history jokes
– none better than having the caryatids decorating the top of the
walls in the dinosaur section holding in their muscly arms wriggling
pterodactyls and plesiosaurs.

The centrepiece, however, is the mineral collection: case upon
case of every conceivable hard but surprising object that could be
dug from the earth. This labour was the work of many miners,
researchers and industrial scientists and in very solid, chunky form
it shows the sort of complex world which made German science
great. On the walls are a series of paintings celebrating the mineral

heritage of the Austro-Hungarian Empire – the Slovene karst, the Tatras mountains, a Galician salt mine, an 1866 meteorite strike on Hungary, all these different zones conjuring up different mineralogical excitements. Looking at these paintings it became clear that one of the real disasters of 1918 was the fracturing of this world – the arteries that had fed industries across Europe and which had grown up with the Industrial Revolution were now all choked up. The raw material now hid behind the borders of autarkic microstates in economic crisis. The sources throughout Central Europe, shown in these paintings, which had fuelled Austria-Hungary's industrial expansion had all gone and, even more seriously, the German motor, despite lopsided and febrile growth in the early 1920s, was fundamentally in ruins – its suppliers were gone, its old markets hostile or bankrupt. The scientific-industrial-commercial dream on the walls of the Vienna Natural History Museum had completely disappeared. The attempt to recreate it through depraved violence under the Nazis, helped by the machines and gases of the debased remnant of German science, ended in total defeat and a moral disaster. Under impossibly different conditions, the single market which had made Europe so inventive and prosperous before 1914, only drifted back into view after 1989.

Science was not completely moribund under Weimar and there were numerous expressions of goodwill and international conferences to try to kick-start what had once been there. Einstein himself engaged heavily with the Weimar Republic, despite having now been for many years a Swiss citizen – but the sense of decay, anti-Semitism and poisonous failure was in the end too much even for him, with a final move to the United States in 1932. Despite their protestations about modernity and their excitement with science, the Nazis had anti-Semitism as a far more core value, and the Jewish scientists and some of their more liberal colleagues who had maintained so much of what had made German science so brilliant and had kept this going despite chronic setbacks and economic convulsion now all left. This transplant to Britain and the United States was so important that the scientific histories of both countries changed direction.

Terminal throes

The Great Depression, which rapidly sucked out of Germany both the American credits which had kept it stable and any faltering sense of obligation by many citizens to the Weimar Republic, was the next stage in the disaster that turned Germany into the destroyer of Europe and of itself. The disaster unfolded under the baffled eyes of Paul von Hindenburg, since 1925 the President of Germany. Other countries have voted for men on their military record, without this being sinister – France voted for de Gaulle, Britain for Wellington, the USA for Jackson, Taylor, Grant and Eisenhower. Hindenburg was odd, however, in having, with Ludendorff, led his country into total disaster in the Great War – the duumvirate through the latter part of the war having had the authority if not the imagination to have salvaged a peace which would have been far preferable to the final result. While Ludendorff was instrumental in raising Hitler from Bavarian obscurity, Hindenburg's role was, however unwillingly, to provide the context for Hitler's eventual takeover. This reverence for Hindenburg showed how a dangerous and stupid view of the war was really hard-wired into the republic, further reinforcing the idea that Germany had not really lost. Hindenburg took his job seriously, distrusted and disliked Hitler and tried to keep some form of democratic government going – but exhausted, very old and ill he only stood for re-election at all in 1932 as the only person capable of holding Hitler off, a sure sign that before Hitler's actual seizure of power in early 1933 the republic was in ruins.

This layer upon layer of catastrophe – the war, the Versailles Treaty, hyper-inflation, the Depression – provided so many individual German families with reasons to have collective nervous breakdowns that there is no point in hunting for deeper roots. Germany in 1914 had been a normal country, espousing much of the same racism, military posturing and taste for ugly public architecture that bedevilled the rest of the Continent. It would be possible to pick out mystical, fatalistic or mad trends anywhere in Europe in the preceding decades. A curious game could be played imagining Britain as the leper state of 1918 with hordes of German writers shuddering in disgust at the solipsism, medievalism, arrogance and anti-democratic disgust of the Pre-Raphaelites and their followers, the astonishing disregard for human life, violence, hypocrisy and greed of the Boer War, the absolutely unacceptable signs and symbols to be found in the writing of Newbolt, Kipling, Churchill, Gilbert and Sullivan. In many ways Britain and Germany had been mad twins – the two big European Protestant countries, sharing many ideas, economically and scientifically obsessed, and with superiority complexes on a level with the Mongol hordes. They shared a profound sense of pity for non-British or non-German nations, a rampant sense of imperial mission (more deeply rooted among Austrians and Britons, but profound nonetheless) and a frightening and enraging (to those outside the charmed circle) obsession with military shibboleths – the Royal Navy for the former, the army for the latter.

The very different fates of the two countries can be pinned on the course and consequences of the Great War, not on some 'special path' trodden by German-speakers. Even as the appalling setbacks that devastated much of Europe from 1914 onwards played themselves out, there were always many Germans who resisted violence as a means of ending the ever more horrible impasse. Erich Maria Remarque's *All Quiet on the Western Front* is no less characteristic of German responses than Ernst Jünger's *Storm of Steel*. The brutality that became endemic to German society was recoiled from by a great percentage of the population. Once the war itself had ended, the return of millions of fighters, whether cheering on or crushing the post-war revolutions, always gave the option to Germany to become again a militaristic state – but most veterans' organizations were simply drinking clubs and even with the 'stab in the back' legend widely endorsed there was nothing *necessarily* sinister there.

A curious example would be Kurt von Schleicher, a scheming monarchist former general who became the last chancellor before Hitler, having been a powerful figure in the highly unstable

governments before his own. Schleicher could have been a traditional *caudillo* on the Central European or South American model,
and he would have been right at home in Chiang Kai-shek's China.
His uniform-obsessed rallies had a superficially Nazi atmosphere,
but in practice he tried to cooperate with the left and concluded
that Germany probably needed the return of the Hohenzollerns
for it to get back to normal. Schleicher's lack of followers and lack
of charisma meant, in Hindenburg's most terrible error, his being
sacked and, through several twists, replaced by Hitler – a figure
who the traditional right thought they could control. This, of course,
turned out not to be true. Schleicher's Germany (if such a thing
could ever have developed) would have been aggressive, would have
broken out of the Versailles Treaty and would have potentially
threatened its neighbours – but it seems an infinite distance away
from Barbarossa, slave labour, gas chambers and the whole path laid
out by a Nazi Party which had between the two elections of 1932,
separated by only three months, already lost some two million of
its voters and which could have ebbed away entirely without this
very specific set of circumstances. Schleicher was murdered in 1934
along with many other of Hitler's key enemies.

It is often pointed out that the tragedy of Germany in the 1930s
was the failure of the overwhelming majority to cooperate in facing
down Nazism, but this failure was so fundamental to the nature of
the republic that it is more of a weary given than material from
which a tragedy could be made. This could not be clearer than
in the work of John Heartfield. This remarkable communist artist
changed his name from Helmut Herzfeld in the middle of the Great
War to protest against the rabid nationalism and anti-British feeling
in Germany, an eccentric but endearing gesture that showed, even
in the midst of a sort of patriotic-bombastic maelstrom, that there
was more variety than at first appears. His photomontages for *AIZ*,
the *Workers' Illustrated Newspaper*, published first in Berlin and then,
after the Nazi seizure of power, in Prague, remain some of the most
painful and eloquent images of an alternative non-Hitler Germany:
Göring as mad butcher, a Christmas tree with its branches snapped
into swastika-shapes, Hitler stuffed with gold coins.

Many of the photomontages are great works of art, but it is hard not to notice how mistaken he is about virtually everything. Looking through all his *AIZ* work chronologically, the pattern that comes through is that the Social Democrats are no worse than the Nazis, that Hitler is simply the puppet of Big Business, that Hitler (the death's head moth) is the linear descendant of his Weimar predecessors Ebert (the caterpillar) and Hindenburg (the dozing pupa), and that Hitler will readily be brought down when the time comes by the anger of the workers. At the beginning of 1933 Heartfield wished *AIZ*'s half-million or so readers a facetious happy new year with a photomontage dream, showing the Social Democrat Theodor Leipart and Adolf Hitler both tumbling down the same mountainside This was only weeks before Hitler seized power, arrested Leipart, closed *AIZ* and crushed Social Democrat and communist opposition. The wishful thinking which imagined Leipart and Hitler as deserving and getting the same fate sums up a powerful yet useless strand in German life.

Germany's experience of communist revolution in 1919 and the terror felt by the propertied classes over the USSR meant that in practice German communists were pathetically vulnerable if the state were to be single-mindedly harnessed against them. Having established himself in power through wholly extra-legal means, Hitler became through expunging the communists and ending the disunity of Weimar the darling of millions who had never dreamed of voting for him. *AIZ*'s readership was arrested, fled or saw the Nazi light – some, through innumerable twists and turns, would find themselves under Soviet tutelage, in the surprising position of actually imposing their ideas in 1945, but this was in an almost unrecognizable country and continent.

Ending

This is the point where this book has to pack up, just as everybody who made Germany so remarkable a place packed up. The forces that took power in Germany in early 1933 were absolutely antithetical to what could be valued and mark a profound break. Nabokov's Berlin novel *Laughter in the Dark*, written in the spring of 1931, inadvertently provides one of the last looks at this old Germany, just as the films of the late 1920s and early 1930s now have an absolute value way beyond their creators' intentions. *Laughter in the Dark* is a cruel love story, but in the background can be glimpsed the Berlin of Weimar modernity – telephones, refrigerators, talkies, motorbikes, neon lighting, dance clubs. There is a constant wish to crane your neck and see round and behind the characters and enjoy more of the relatively benign Berlin they inhabit. When they visit the Berlin Sports Palace, it is just to see an ice-hockey game, not a Nazi rally. They are citizens still of a fractured, unhappy but plural Germany, run by Chancellor Brüning, Catholic, hard-working, contemptuous of the Nazis, but, like his contemporary Herbert Hoover (but with more fatal results) baffled and destroyed by the Great Depression. The Berlin Sports Palace at this time still held rallies for a wide range of political groups and the world of *Laughter in the Dark* seems a long way from the events which will in turn make the palace into one of Goebbels' principal stages, let alone the palace in which the bodies of countless air-raid dead would be laid out in rows. Indeed, in the common and disastrous error of the period the political threat in *Laughter in the Dark*, which is only treated briefly, is from angry communist gang members.

Nabokov clung on in Berlin until 1937 before continuing the enforced journey that would turn him into a great writer in another language. But very soon after Hitler came to power, the first wave of unwilling, frightened exiles had begun. Brecht headed for Scandinavia, Beckmann for Amsterdam, Gropius for London, Mann for Switzerland, Moholy-Nagy and Roth for Paris, Walter for Vienna, Heartfield for Prague. Some would end up with relatively easy new careers in the USA or Britain, others would be forced to move from country to country ahead of the Nazis, others were overtaken and destroyed. It is impossible not to focus on the absolute and terrible disasters – Stefan Zweig and his wife, his magical achievement in so many novels and stories now counting for nothing, killing themselves in southern Brazil in 1941; Walter Benjamin committing suicide on the Spanish border; Kurt Schwitters, creator of enchanting collages and Dadaist objects, forced apart from his wife, cut off from the whole world which had made him one of the most genial figures of the inter-war period, dying totally neglected in the English Lake District in 1948.

These figures are wholly unrepresentative, in as much as their fame and the nature of their work at least gave them mobility – but this is a personal book and I love what these people created so much, indeed cannot really imagine my own life without them, that I can only mark my own distress by stopping this book here. So many of the threads that run through modern German history – a creative irony, edginess, glee and oddness – are gone in a few weeks, wound up and replaced with messianic infantilism. The extreme violence of the regime is immediate and new and yet it is now hard to grasp because what followed once the regime had really settled in was so much worse, sorting all Germans (and then most Europeans) into perpetrators, bystanders and victims, categories which we will never cease agonizing over. Nazism's linking of a sort of historicist sickness to industrialism had no precedent. The terrible cruelties that had happened on German soil over the centuries, the pogroms, plagues and massacres had now given way to something far, far worse. Anecdotal facetiousness has to get out of the way and simply stop.

Conclusion

In the hills

There are so many places where this book could end. The ancient Harz city of Halberstadt might be one. In the closing days of the war this then beautiful place lay in the path of the American army. The fighting had almost ended and the Allies dropped leaflets instructing the town to put up a white flag on the city hall to indicate that it had surrendered. Halberstadt's Nazi ruler – in one of those thousands of German decisions in this period that now seem absolutely baffling – refused. The Allies sent over a plane to check and, when there was no flag, destroyed almost the entire town in a few minutes. The shattered remains were then handed over to the Soviets and became part of East Germany. It now feels like another of those eastern towns, like Halle, Köthen or Brandenburg, which will simply never recover. The inhabitants have gone through too much and too many just want to leave. Immense work has gone into rebuilding parts of the old city, but there is not enough money or energy left. One curious local initiative has been to hold an organ concert in one of the churches to play John Cage's piece *As Slow As Possible*, a performance which will end on 5 September 2640 and for which you have to book tickets years ahead to be present when the next key change is due. It should be pointed out that the notes are sustained mechanically rather than by employing several centuries' worth of under-achieving organists linked up to tubes and buckets. While Cage's piece is obviously a marvellous idea in itself, it does seem to act as a rather cruel theme-tune for modern Halberstadt.

To the south of the town there are some hills called the Spiegelsberge. The landscape is the usual lovely German woodland with the usual little animals scampering about, but it is also a sort of palimpsest of sad German themes. The woods are dotted with follies built by the eighteenth-century Prussian poet Ludwig Gleim, who wrote *The Grenadier's Prussian War Songs*, a once-famous collection sparked by the campaigns of Frederick the Great and initiating the great stream of German songs and lyrics that for two centuries punctuated and inspired nationalist events: some beautiful, some pompous and some loathsome, but almost all now completely sullied by later events. The follies have collapsed and are covered in soil, dead leaves and moss to a point where it has not been possible even to work out what some of them were meant to be. Gleim had been inspired by the endless, dream-like gardens at Wörlitz to make his own little version for the delight of his friends and, wandering around the remaining lumps and bumps, it is easy to sink into a general despondency about the cruelty of passing time and events.

Gleim's element in the Spiegelsberge is as nothing compared to Bismarck's. Abandoned, boarded-up and thoroughly unloved is one of the hundreds of Bismarck Towers which were put up all over Germany after the great man's death. They tend to look like a mixture of medieval keep and lighthouse and inevitably Bruno Schmitz, the World's Worst Architect, built many of them, when he was not busy creating ziggurats of rubbish like the Kaiser Wilhelm I Monument in Koblenz. Some of the towers were blown up and some fell over, but most are still around. The one over in Dessau has been attractively rebranded so that Bismarck's face and name were taken off and Schiller's put on instead. The Halberstadt tower is a standard-issue piece of bombast and on special occasions an immense flame used to be lit which would stream from its summit, visible for miles across the countryside and rich in runes/dwarfs/Wagner/fun-with-pagans meaning. The special-flame feature of course stopped working ages ago and the tower's only contemporary fans are occasional graffiti taggers. As a completely discredited symbol of local pride, something which on special occasions in the first half of the twentieth century all Halberstadters must have taken their excited children to see, the Bismarck Tower takes some beating.

By this point wading slowly through the sheer accumulation of gloomy symbolism in this wood, the rambler is then brought to a complete halt by a tucked-away Soviet cemetery. These cemeteries dot East Germany and it was an important part of the discussions when the Soviet empire collapsed that the German state would promise to protect and maintain them. They all fit the same pattern (aside from the massive set-piece monuments in places such as Vienna and Berlin), with row upon row of small headstones topped by a red star. Some of the cemeteries are in prominent places. Eisleben, for example, is notable for its strikingly unavoidable fields of Soviet war dead. Others are located with careful symbolism, such as the beautiful one in the ducal park in Weimar, a place which takes on rich additional layers of meaning with every passing year.

The Halberstadt cemetery is particularly melancholy because it is so hidden. Having had the town passed over to them by the Americans, these Soviet soldiers were killed in the final acrid days of mopping-up, of military accidents and countless almost private acts of Nazi fanaticism. The Soviets killed, raped and looted their way through the region in a riot of violence not seen since the Thirty Years War, in a vast act of retribution which it is impossible not to see as nearly legitimate and yet which also marks a point of final and absolute disaster from which Europe has been rebuilding slowly ever since. Now it has come to an end, East Germany itself seems part of that punishment – the taking of a large block of Germans, imprisoned for decades in a system of work and surveillance, a much less onerous version of the kind of punishment the Germans themselves had once wanted to impose on much of Europe.

Mendel's statue

Another town rich with conclusive possibilities is Schwäbisch Gmünd, a pretty, dozy place in the Stauferland, home for many years to an American missile regiment and the birthplace of Emanuel Leutze, painter of *Washington Crossing the Delaware*.

There is a particularly odd building in the hills behind the town

where a hermit once lived. After his death a chapel was built in the
seventeenth century around his cave, clinging to the cliff-side, part
Counter-Reformation standard issue and part living rock. It is a
dreary spot, damp with superstition and only enlivened by cats,
beetles and some aggressive redstarts, but the chapel has an accidentally Gaudí-like quality. There are some truly alarming life-size
stations-of-the-cross tableaux on the way up to the chapel which
offer a form of living folk religion that is a disturbing challenge
to the modern world. Gmünd's somnolence is absolute and the
hillside suggests there must be other caves, perhaps filled with
enchanted sleepers. Unlike Halberstadt, Gmünd's fabric was untouched by the war and it slipped, after some years of hard work,
into the same pleasant prosperity as the rest of West Germany.

Down in the town, I was wandering around one of the little
parks looking for surprising monuments when – as usual – I was
rewarded: this time with a bronze statue of Gregor Mendel. I knew
little about Mendel beyond the bare facts of his having been a
Moravian monk and the creator of modern genetics. I could not
understand why his statue would be in Gmünd, a world away from
the Habsburg north-east. It turned out the statue had been placed
there by Moravian Germans, some of the three million Germans
expelled from Czechoslovakia at the end of the war, partly out of
revenge and partly to ensure that no 'Sudetenland' issue would ever
arise again. Like other undamaged towns, Gmünd filled up with
expellees, in this case mainly from Brno (or Brünn). Mendel died
in 1884 (Janáček played the organ at his funeral) and his science
ultimately formed the basis of a system which made a mockery of
the Nazis' pathetic race concepts.

The world in which he had lived seemed impossibly distant from
the events which would have resulted in his statue coming to rest in
Swabia. The refugees from Brno are now very old and the whole
idea of Moravian Germans seems very remote, but Freud was born
in Moravia and Mahler spent his childhood there. This was not a
minor part of the world. The Iron Curtain blocked off the expelled
(who came from all over a huge belt, from Estonia to Yugoslavia)
and made maintaining a link with Central Europe impractical. In

any event the circumstances of expulsion had been themselves traumatic and shameful, with an unknown number of dead – at least half a million and probably many more. The Hitler issue of 'unjust' borders, of German minorities trapped and needing to be redeemed by the Fatherland, was decisively ended by the expulsions, but at a staggering cost.

Again, as with the ferocious actions of the Red Army, it is impossible to argue against the expulsions under the circumstances – there was a racial logic which the Nazis themselves would have approved of. But it was another act of European diminution, of a nationalist set of ideas which began in the nineteenth century and ended in the dementia of the Holocaust. When the German attempt to become the colonial rulers of Europe failed, the failure created its own momentum, no different from the expulsion of the French from Algeria or the Belgians from the Congo. The result was the shaking of Europeans into a dreary sequence of monoglot little states, none very creative, none very interesting, but at least no longer at each other's throats, aside from the unfinished Habsburg legacy of Yugoslavia.

I don't know quite why I found the Mendel statue so upsetting – there are plenty of other expellee monuments dotted around. His blamelessness perhaps, or the sense that his scientific importance sprang from a very complicated Habsburg universe which has been buried by layer after layer of later events. Is there in fact too great a break between modern Central Europe and the Jewish–Catholic–Protestant/German–Slav world which was the glory of the pre-1914 world? Just as historians now see Europe's civilization before the Great Famine and Black Death as in many ways distinct from its haggard successor, will we all retrospectively be seen as merely the provincial remnants of a great civilization that destroyed itself?

Death by oompah

That Zeppelin-shed of conviviality, the Hofbräuhaus in Munich, is one of those essential tests of Germanness which rapidly winnows out anyone who really cannot stand this particular model of civi-lization. For foreigners who dream of sun-dappled trattoria or sitting quietly with a pint of mild in the saloon bar of the Magpie and Stump, the sheer communal grossness of the Hofbräuhaus is a sort of hell on earth. The hundreds of mostly male drinkers are manipulated by the management through a clever use of folk cos-tume, breasts and an oompah band into a form of scarlet-faced hysteria. By late evening there is a clear and constant *roar* of aggres-sive conversation, the crash of dropped mugs and trays, screams of laughter as patrons fall backwards off their seats.

On balance I really cannot cope with Munich. Some places will always be ruined by Nazism and Munich is above all of them. If the Third Reich had survived, Munich would now be a sort of modern Bethlehem, linked to the other two great Bavarian Nazi sacred sites, Nuremberg and Berchtesgaden. Huge coach parties would be visiting the places that Hitler had created with such symbolic care: the 'Brown House', the national headquarters of the Party and last resting place of the 'Blood Banner' carried by the 1923 beer-hall putschists, the Bürgerbräukeller where that putsch began, the 'Honour Temples' built to house the bodies of the dead, the dif-ferent places around Munich where Hitler had stayed or given speeches. The Hofbräuhaus had an honoured place in this pantheon – in 1920 Hitler laid down the basic tenets of Nazi doctrine there and it remained a favourite destination for Hitler and his entourage (none of this is mentioned in the Hofbräuhaus's strikingly aphasic website).

Much of specifically Nazi Munich has been destroyed – the 'Brown House' by Allied bombing, the Bürgerbräukeller by a heroic and despairingly unlucky 1939 would-be Hitler assassin, the 'Honour Temples' by contemptuous American military administrators (weeds now attractively grow over the remains). The Hofbräuhaus was also wrecked but, unlike its fellows, was rebuilt and remains a vexed reminder of the culture that created Hitler. From the usual chaos of motives, I spent a long evening there and was, as it turned out, completely rewarded. As the hysteria mounted, conga-lines of foreign businessmen lurched past the frantic oompah band, deranged with laughter, and amid a general sense that the factory-scale toilets were now irreparably backed up and it was time for me to leave, something wonderful happened. A Japanese businessman or tourist tipped the band to allow him to pretend drunkenly to conduct a piece of music. This happened quite frequently – a few minutes previously an Australian with wild eyes and a cinnabar complexion managed to pretend to conduct the band through 'Waltzing Matilda'. But the Japanese man was a genius, as he asked them to play Shostakovich's *Waltz 2*. This piece was made famous as part of Stanley Kubrick's last film *Eyes Wide Shut*, an adaptation of Arthur Schnitzler's novella *Dream Story*. Hearing this marvellous, odd dance provoked initially very confused feelings. I had always loved Schnitzler and in my publishing job I had used the excuse of the Kubrick film to republish some of his work. This had not been a great success, falling victim to the – as it turned out – general contempt felt for the film. But then, at last, I realized what was truly startling. Here, in one of the birthplaces of Nazism, a traditional Bavarian band was playing an American jazz inflected piece by a Soviet composer, made famous by a Jewish-American adaptation of a Jewish-Austrian novella, the film's stars being a tiny Scientologist and a lovely Australian. It would be trivial to say that this music buried the past even for a second, but it was enjoyable to tot up the number of ways in which the famous pre-war frequenters of the Hofbräuhaus would have been struck dumb with rage by such a piece. Suddenly I felt aware of how much Germans had themselves put layer upon layer of work, culture and thought on top of their terrible past and that it was possible to sit in the chaos of the early twenty-first century and feel that actions are being taken every day – even by an oompah band and its drunken Japanese maestro – to build a replenished world in which Munich can be more than just the cradle of Nazism. But the band was now playing 'The Bonnie Banks o' Loch Lomond' and it was time to take the ill-judged decision to have another drink.

Bibliography

These are all books which have affected the way I have understood the subjects in this book. All the main sources are here plus a selection of novels and stories, some of which are mentioned in the text, while others lurk behind what I have written about. I have not included the piles of leaflets, CD notes, mini-guides and other scraps of paper that choke our house. Some of these have been very important (for example John Eliot Gardiner's superb essay on Schütz that accompanies his recording of the *Musikalische Exequien*).

There are many remarkable websites – every town and Schloss in Germany seems to have one, some just bits of Toytown vanity but others packed with interest. Photos of almost anything mentioned in this book can be found online. Perhaps the most remarkable website is Mark Hatlie's www.sites-of-memory.de, but there are also sites of fevered if enjoyable specificity such as www.bismarcktuerme.de or www.almanachdegotha.org. The ability to riffle quickly through generation after generation of royal and ducal family trees on www.wikipedia.org, often decorated with funny portraits, is an amazing technological improvement on horrible old printed family trees. Another great breakthrough is Thomas Höckmann's hypnotic *Germany 1789*, a series of electronic maps of the Holy Roman Empire which adds a sense of ease and pleasure to previously eye-watering microterritorial issues (www.hoeckmann.de). To be able to zoom in on the details of what the Dukes of Württemberg owned (and why these geographical constraints drove them mad) or investigate places like the Principality-Provosty of Ellwangen an der Jagst is both confidence-building and a way to waste oceans of time.

Easily the most important sources have been the various editions of Gordon McLachlan's *Rough Guide to Germany* (latest 6th edition, London, 2004), a perfect example of how a guide book can sometimes also be an exceptional piece of literature. I have never met McLachlan but worship him from afar, with an unhealthy closeness to the variants that emerge from each new edition's publication (the entry on Bernburg has been dropped from the sixth!). His enthusiasm can sometimes be borderline demented – no matter that a town's only focus of interest is a mildly odd fountain, the place is always worth a two-to-three-day stay – but the book is clever, enjoyable and encyclopaedic and my own book could not have been written without his guidance.

Place of publication and date given are for the editions I happen to have. In a spirit of personal truthfulness and consistency all books in German are here purely because they have nice pictures.

Uli Arnold et al., *Grünes Gewölbe Dresden* (Leipzig, 1986)

Ronald G. Asch, *The Thirty Years War: The Holy Roman Empire and Europe, 1618–48* (Basingstoke, 1997)

David Attenborough et al., *Amazing Rare Things: The Art of Natural History in the Age of Discovery* (London, 2007)

Erich Bachmann et al., *The Würzburg Residence and Court Gardens* (Munich, 1992)

Richard Barber, *The Penguin Guide to Medieval Europe* (Harmondsworth, 1984)

Robert Bartlett, *The Making of Europe: Conquest, Colonization and Cultural Change, 950–1350* (Princeton, 1993)

C .A. Bayley, *The Birth of the Modern World, 1780–1914* (Oxford, 2004)

Hans Belting, *The Germans and Their Art: A Troublesome Relationship* (New Haven and London, 1998)

John Berger, *Dürer* (Cologne, 1994)

Thomas Bernhard, *Concrete*, trans. David McLintock (London, 1989)

Thomas Bernhard, *Old Masters: A Comedy*, trans. Ewald Osers (London, 1989)

Thomas Bernhard, *Yes*, trans. Ewald Osers (Chicago, 1992)

David Blackbourn, *The Conquest of Nature: Water, Landscape and the Making of Modern Germany* (New York, 2006)

David Blackbourn, *History of Germany 1780–1918: The Long Nineteenth Century,* 2nd edition (Oxford, 2003)

T. M. W. Blanning, *The Culture of Power and the Power of Culture: Old Regime Europe 1660–1789* (Oxford, 2002)

T. M. W. Blanning, *Joseph II* (Harlow, 1994)

Tim [T. M. W.] Blanning, *The Pursuit of Glory: Europe 1648–1815* (London, 2007)

T. M. W. Blanning, *Reform and Revolution in Mainz, 1743–1803* (Cambridge, 1974)

Richard Bonney, *The European Dynastic States 1494–1660* (Oxford, 1991)

Douglas Botting, *In the Ruins of the Reich* (London, 1985)

Brian Boyd, *Vladimir Nabokov: The Russian Years* (Princeton, 1990)

Sir Thomas Browne, *Selected Writings,* ed. Sir Geoffrey Keynes (Chicago, 1968)

W. H. Bruford, *Germany in the Eighteenth Century: The Social Background of the Literary Revival* (Cambridge, 1959)

Elias Canetti, *Crowds and Power,* trans. Carol Stewart (London, 1962)

Eric Christiansen, *The Northern Crusades: The Baltic and the Catholic Frontier, 1100–1525* (Basingstoke, 1980)

Christopher Clark, *Iron Kingdom: The Rise and Downfall of Prussia, 1600–1947* (London, 2006)

Christopher Clark, *Wilhelm II* (Harlow, 2000)

Kenneth John Conant, *Carolingian and Romanesque Architecture, 800–1200* (Harmondsworth, 1959)

Kevin Cramer, *The Thirty Years' War and German Memory in the Nineteenth Century* (Lincoln and London, 2007)

Edward Crankshaw, *Bismarck* (London, 1981)

Matthew Craske, *Art in Europe 1700–1830* (Oxford, 1997)

Charles D. Cuttler, *Northern Painting: From Pucelle to Bruegel* (New York, 1968)

Sybille Ebert-Schifferer, *Hessisches Landesmuseum Darmstadt* (Fondation Paribas, 1996)

Mark Edmundson, *The Death of Sigmund Freud: Fascism, Psychoanalysis and the Rise of Fundamentalism* (London, 2007)

Erich Egg, *Hofkirche in Innsbruck. Das Grabmal Kaiser Maximilians I*
(Innsbruck, 1993)

Joseph von Eichendorff, *Life of a Good-for-Nothing*, trans. J. G. Nichols
(London, 2002)

Einhard and Notker the Stammerer, *Two Lives of Charlemagne*, trans.
Lewis Thorpe (Harmondsworth, 1969)

Amos Elon, *The Pity of It All: A History of Jews in Germany, 1743–1933*
(New York, 2002)

R. J. W. Evans, *Austria, Hungary and the Habsburgs: Central Europe
c. 1683–1867* (Oxford, 2006)

Richard J. Evans, *The Coming of the Third Reich* (London, 2003)

Niall Ferguson, *The Pity of War, 1914–1918* (London, 1998)

Theodor Fontane, *Before the Storm: A Novel of the Winter of 1812–13*,
trans. R. J. Hollingdale (Oxford, 1985)

Theodor Fontane, *Two Novellas: The Woman Taken in Adultery* and
The Poggenpuhl Family, trans. Gabriele Annan (Chicago, 1989)

George Macdonald Fraser, *Royal Flash. From* The Flashman Papers,
1842–43 and 1847–48 (London, 1970)

David Freedberg, *The Eye of the Lynx: Galileo, His Friends, and the
Beginnings of Modern Natural History* (Chicago, 2002)

Robert I. Frost, *The Northern Wars 1558–1721* (Harlow, 2000)

Horst Fuhrmann, *Germany in the High Middle Ages, c. 1050–1200*
(Cambridge, 1986)

Peter Gay, *Weimar Culture: The Outsider as Insider* (New York, 1968)

Johann Wolfgang von Goethe, *The Flight to Italy*, trans. T. J. Reed
(Oxford, 1999)

Johann Wolfgang von Goethe, *The Man of Fifty*, trans. Andrew Piper
(London, 2004)

Johann Wolfgang von Goethe et al., *Romantic Fairy Tales*, trans. Carol
Tully (Harmondsworth, 2000)

Günter Grass, *Cat and Mouse*, trans. Ralph Manheim (London, 1963)

Günter Grass, *Crabwalk*, trans. Krishna Winston (New York, 2002)

Günter Grass, *The Tin Drum*, trans. Ralph Manheim (London, 1962)

Jacob and Wilhelm Grimm, *Selected Tales*, trans. Joyce Crick (Oxford,
2005)

Johann Grimmelshausen, *Simplicissimus*, trans. Mike Mitchell (Sawtry, 1999)

Johann Peter Hebel, *The Treasure Chest*, trans. John Hibberd (London, 1994)

Heinrich Heine, *The Harz Journey and Selected Prose*, trans. Ritchie Robertson (Harmondsworth, 1993)

Heinrich Heine, *Selected Verse*, trans. Peter Branscombe (Harmondsworth, 1968)

Hermann Hesse, *Narziss and Goldmund*, trans. Geoffrey Dunlop (London, 1959)

E. T. A. Hoffmann, *The Golden Pot and Other Tales*, trans. Ritchie Robertson (Oxford, 1992)

E. T. A. Hoffmann, *Tales of Hoffmann*, trans. R. J. Hollingdale (Harmondsworth, 1982)

Charles Ingrao, *The Habsburg Monarchy 1618–1815*, 2nd edition (Cambridge, 2000)

Jan Jelínek, *Kutná Hora* (Prague, 1990)

Ernst Jünger, *Storm of Steel*, trans. Michael Hofmann (London, 2003)

Anton Kaes, *M* (London, 2000)

Ian Kershaw, *Hitler 1889–1933: Hubris* (Harmondsworth, 1998)

Rüdiger Klessmann et al., *Adam Elsheimer 1578–1610* (Edinburgh, 2006)

Michael Levey, *Giambattista Tiepolo: His Life and Art* (New Haven and London, 1986)

Dominic Lieven, *Russia Against Napoleon: The Battle for Europe, 1807 to 1814* (London, 2009)

Vejas Gabriel Liulevicius, *War Land on the Eastern Front: Culture, National Identity and German Occupation in World War I* (Cambridge, 2000)

Diarmaid MacCulloch, *Reformation: Europe's House Divided, 1490–1700* (London, 2003)

David McKay, *The Great Elector* (Harlow, 2001)

Claudio Magris, *Danube: A Journey Through the Landscape, History and Culture of Central Europe* (New York, 1989)

John Man, *Zwinger Palace, Dresden* (London, 1990)

Heinrich Mann, *Man of Straw*, no translator given (Harmondsworth, 1984)

Thomas Mann, *Buddenbrooks*, trans. H. T. Lowe-Porter (Harmondsworth, 1957)

Thomas Mann, *Death in Venice and Other Stories*, trans. David Luke (New York, 1988)

Thomas Mann, *Royal Highness*, trans. A. Cecil Curtis, rev. Constance McNab (Harmondsworth, 1975)

Peter Marshall, *The Magic Circle of Rudolf II: Alchemy and Astrology in Renaissance Prague* (New York, 2006)

Eduard Mörike, *Mozart's Journey to Prague*, trans. David Luke (London, 1997)

Thomas J. Müller-Bahlke, *Die Wunderkammer: Die Kunst- und Naturalienkammer der Franckeschen Stiftungen zu Halle (Saale)* (Halle, 1998)

Robert Musil, *The Man without Qualities*, 3 vols., trans. Eithne Wilkins and Ernst Kaiser (London, 1954)

Robert Musil, *The Posthumous Papers of a Living Author*, trans. Peter Wortsman (Hygiene, 1987)

Vladimir Nabokov, *The Gift*, trans. Michael Scammell in collaboration with the author (New York, 1963)

Vladimir Nabokov, *King, Queen, Knave*, trans. Dmitri Nabokov in collaboration with the author (New York, 1968)

Vladimir Nabokov, *Laughter in the Dark* (New York, 1938)

Thomas Pynchon, *Gravity's Rainbow* (New York, 1973)

Erich Maria Remarque, *All Quiet on the Western Front*, trans. Brian Murdoch (London, 1994)

Timothy Reuter, *Germany in the Early Middle Ages, 800–1056* (Harlow, 1991)

Gregor von Rezzori, *The Snows of Yesterday: Portraits for an Autobiography*, trans. H. F. Broch de Rothermann (New York, 1989)

Robert J. Richards, *The Tragic Sense of Life: Ernst Haeckel and the Struggle over Evolutionary Thought* (Chicago, 2008)

Alex Ross, *The Rest is Noise: Listening to the Twentieth Century* (New York, 2007)

Joseph Roth, *The Emperor's Tomb*, trans. John Hoare (London, 1984)

Joseph Roth, *Flight without End*, trans. David Le Vay (London, 1977)

Joseph Roth, *The Silent Prophet*, trans. David Le Vay (London, 1979)

Joseph Roth, *Three Novellas: Fallmerayer the Stationmaster, The Bust of the Emperor and The Legend of the Holy Drinker*, trans. John Hoare and Michael Hofmann (Woodstock, 2003)

Simon Schama, *Landscape and Memory* (London, 1995)

W. G. Sebald, *Vertigo*, trans. Michael Hulse (London, 1999)

James J. Sheehan, *German History 1770–1866* (Oxford, 1989)

Brendan Simms, *The Struggle for Mastery in Germany, 1779–1850* (Basingstoke, 1998)

Brendan Simms, *Three Victories and a Defeat: The Rise and Fall of the First British Empire, 1714–1783* (London, 2007)

Jeffrey Chipps Smith, *The Northern Renaissance* (London, 2004)

David Stevenson, *1914–1918: The History of the First World War* (London, 2004)

Adalbert Stifter, *Brigitta and Other Tales*, trans. Helen Watanabe-O'Kelly (London, 1994)

Adalbert Stifter, *Rock Crystal: A Christmas Tale*, trans. Elizabeth Mayer and Marianne Moore (London, 1999)

Helmut Stoecker, ed., *German Imperialism in Africa*, trans. Bernd Zöllner (London, 1986)

Richard Stokes (ed. and trans.), *The Book of Lieder* (London, 2005)

Norman Stone, *The Eastern Front, 1914–1917* (London, 1975)

Norman Stone, *World War One: A Short History* (London, 2007)

Hew Strachan, *The First World War, vol. 1: To Arms* (Oxford, 2001)

Michael Sußmann, *Der Dom zu Magdeburg* (Passau, 2002)

Antal Szerb, *Oliver VII*, trans. Len Rix (London, 2007)

Tacitus, *The Agricola* and *The Germania*, trans. H. Mattingly, revised S. A. Handford (Harmondsworth, 1970)

John Tincey, *Blenheim 1704* (Botley, 2004)

Adam Tooze, *The Wages of Destruction: The Making and Breaking of the Nazi Economy* (London, 2006)

Christopher Tyerman, *God's War: A New History of the Crusades*
(London, 2006)

David Rains Wallace, *Neptune's Ark: From Icthyosaurus to Orcas*
(Berkeley and Los Angeles, 2007)

Geoffrey Wawro, *The Austro-Prussian War: Austria's War with Prussia and
Italy in 1866* (Cambridge, 1996)

Geoffrey Wawro, *The Franco-Prussian War: The German Conquest of
France in 1870–1871* (Cambridge, 2003)

C. V. Wedgwood, *The Thirty Years War* (New York, 2005)

Peter H. Wilson, *Europe's Tragedy: A History of the Thirty Years War*
(London, 2009)

Peter H. Wilson, *The Holy Roman Empire 1495–1806* (Basingstoke,
1999)

Peter H. Wilson, *War, State and Society in Württemberg, 1677–1793*
(Cambridge, 1995)

Stefan Zweig, *The Invisible Collection* and *Buchmendel*, trans. Eden and
Cedar Paul (London, 1998)

Illustrations

The title page shows an Oktoberfest woodcut from the *Illustrierte Zeitung*, 18 October 1845 (*akg-images*). Chapter one: King Wilhelm I visiting the studio of Ernst van Bandel in 1869 to see the head of 'Hermann the German', part of the immense *Hermannsdenkmal* to be built in the Teutoburg Forest to mark the chieftain's defeat of the Romans. The monument took several decades to fund and build and was finally completed after German unification. Chapter two: a photo from 1879 of Cologne cathedral *still* unfinished with a railway now running past it (*Kölnisches Stadtmuseum/Rheinisches Bildarchiv, Köln*). Chapter three: a fourteenth-century miniature of the Wartburg under siege (*University of Heidelberg Library/akg-images/Erich Lessing*). Chapter four: to my frustration I ran out of space to talk about the Lübeck artist Bernt Notke, whose great sculpture of St George and the Dragon (the original in the Stockholm Great Church and a copy in St Catharine's church, Lübeck) is one of the last truly alarming flourishes of late medieval art. This is part of his once famous dance macabre for Lübeck's St Mary's church, showing a complacent Hansa merchant, his proud ships in the background (*akg-images*). The painting along with much of the town was destroyed in an RAF bombing raid. Chapter five: unfriendly Catholic image of Martin Luther from the early 1520s showing Luther as a Turk, a fanatic, a wildman, etc., referring to the seven-headed monster of the Apocalypse (*akg-images*). Chapter six: moving and heroic portrait of Gustavus Adolphus on a horse, coming to save Europe (*The Granger Collection/Topfoto*). Chapter seven: Mathaeus Greuter's engraving of bees from the *Melissographia* (Rome, 1625), after drawings made by Francesco Stelluti and members of the Academy of the Lynx (*The Trustees of the National Library of Scotland*). Chapter eight: dementia at the Saxon court: Johann Melchior Dinglinger's elephant, made from wood, silver, gilding, enamel, precious stones, beads and lacquer, just a tiny element in his budget-busting 'The Birthday of the Grand Mogul Aurangzeb', 1701–08 (*Grünes Gewölbe, Staatliche Kunstsammlung-en, Dresden/Jürgen Karpinski*). Chapter nine: a still from von Sternberg's immortal *The Scarlet Empress* (1934) (*akg-images*), with Marlene Dietrich as Catherine the Great and with John Lodge as the smouldering Slav love-animal Prince Alexei (Lodge went on in real life to become governor of Connecticut). Chapter ten: a typically mad and depressing photograph of the *Völkerschlachtdenkmal* under construction (*Deutsche Fotothek*). Chapter eleven: allegorical painting by Cesare dell'Acqua from the Miramare castle, Trieste, showing the Emperor Maximilian's apotheosis, surrounded by a helpfully clothing-free group of allegorical Mexican girls, c. 1865 (*Alinari Archive, Florence*). Chapter twelve: Neuschwanstein Castle under construction (view from the Heideck cliffs, based on a drawing by Robert Assmus, 1886) (*akg-images*). Chapter thirteen: Part of a German marine band with a Chinese man squatting mysteriously at their feet. Tsingtao, before 1914 (*Bundes-archiv Koblenz*). Chapter fourteen: an anonymous coloured print from a 1909 edition of *Der Wahre Jacob* showing the naval arms race between Germany and Britain, *Dreadnouht-Fieber* (sic), with a dance macabre pay-off (*akg-images*). Chapter fifteen: a panicked crowd racing through the streets of medieval Prague in Paul Wegener's German silent horror film *The Golem* (*1920*) – this unbelievably potent, beautiful and complex film brings together almost every theme from this book, but in a way that appeared to me in the end just too clunky to be spelled out. If you have got far enough in this book to be reading this paragraph then I can only urge you to go and watch it immediately (*Ullstein Bild/United Archives*).

Acknowledgements

I spend most of my time editing history books and have therefore had for some years the dreamy privilege of being able to talk at length with historians who, from a decision to stay civil to their publisher, have been both obliged to answer my sometimes confused German questions and at least mull over briefly some of my more obviously not true ideas. None of these beleaguered individuals have any responsibility for the content of this book, but I am indebted to them for conversations which, to me at any rate, were fascinating: Tim Blanning, Richard J. Evans, Niall Ferguson, Richard Overy, Mark Roseman, David Stevenson, Adam Tooze, Alex Watson and Peter Wilson. Adam Tooze will particularly appreciate the way I have misunderstood the ideas at the heart of his revolutionary book *The Wages of Destruction* and then misapplied them to other contexts. Alois Maderspacher generously shared his unpublished research on Kolonialdeutsch and John and Beth Romer were essential to solving my problem with Prussians in Egypt. I am very grateful to various friends who have read the text, much improved it with their suggestions and helped in important ways: Paul Baggaley, Nicholas Blake, Malcolm Bull, Sarah Chalfant, Christopher Clark, Jonathan Galassi, Ian Kershaw, Andrew Kidd, Barry Langford, Cecilia Mackay, Adam Phillips, Sigrid Ruschmeier, Norman Stone, Carole Tonkinson and Andrew Wylie. At work I would particularly like to thank for their help and kindness Alice Dawson, Helen Fraser, Stefan McGrath and Stuart Proffitt. Penny and David Edgar, Jim and Sandy Jones, Steph and Nico Poirier and Christopher and Lizzie Winder are supportive and lovely relatives – I apologize to everyone for misused family anecdotes. In Germany I feel I really ought to acknowledge a tremendous number of patient small-town hoteliers and bratwurst salesmen. Barnaby, Felix and Martha have become strikingly older while I have been spending my spare time wandering along the Rhine or typing this stuff up. Their cheerful welcomes and out-looks on life have made writing the book possible. Christine Jones managed to be both supportive and ironic: everybody else has the option of tossing this book to one side, but she had to spend *years* listening to me droning on about the colonization of the Uckermark or the changing values of the court at Schwarzburg-Rudolstadt. In the face of this sort of waking nightmare she never broke down, never indulged in unhelpful tirades and never changed the locks. There must be a useful, pertinent and pithy German term to describe just how much I owe to her – but as usual I don't know what it is.

Sequim, Wandsworth Town
2006–9

Index